Lecture Notes in Artificial Intelligence   10349

Subseries of Lecture Notes in Computer Science

More information about this series at http://www.springer.com/series/1244

Yves Demazeau · Paul Davidsson
Javier Bajo · Zita Vale (Eds.)

Advances in Practical Applications of Cyber-Physical Multi-Agent Systems

The PAAMS Collection

15th International Conference, PAAMS 2017
Porto, Portugal, June 21–23, 2017
Proceedings

 Springer

Editors

Yves Demazeau
Centre National de la Rech. Scientifique
Grenoble
France

Paul Davidsson
Malmö University
Malmö
Sweden

Javier Bajo
Universidad Politécnica de Madrid
Madrid
Spain

Zita Vale
Polytechnic Institute of Porto
Porto
Portugal

ISSN 0302-9743   ISSN 1611-3349   (electronic)
Lecture Notes in Artificial Intelligence
ISBN 978-3-319-59929-8   ISBN 978-3-319-59930-4   (eBook)
DOI 10.1007/978-3-319-59930-4

Library of Congress Control Number: 2017943015

LNCS Sublibrary: SL7 – Artificial Intelligence

Printed on acid-free paper

This Springer imprint is published by Springer Nature
The registered company is Springer International Publishing AG
The registered company address is: Gewerbestrasse 11, 6330 Cham, Switzerland

Preface

Research on agents and multi-agent systems has matured during the past decade and many effective applications of this technology are now deployed. An international forum to present and discuss the latest scientific developments and their effective applications, to assess the impact of the approach, and to facilitate technology transfer became a necessity and was created a few years ago.

PAAMS, the International Conference on Practical Applications of Agents and Multi-Agent Systems, is the international yearly event in which to present, to discuss, and to disseminate the latest developments and the most important outcomes related to real-world applications. It provides a unique opportunity to bring multi-disciplinary experts, academics, and practitioners together so as to exchange their experience in the development and deployment of agents and multi-agent systems.

This volume presents the papers that were accepted for the 2017 edition of PAAMS. These articles report on the application and validation of agent-based models, methods, and technologies in a number of key application areas, including: daily life and real world, energy and networks, humans and trust, markets and bids, models and tools, negotiation and conversation, and scalability and resources. Each paper submitted to PAAMS went through a stringent peer review by three members of the Program Committee composed of 112 internationally renowned researchers from 26 countries. From the 63 submissions received, 11 were selected for full presentation at the conference; another 11 papers were accepted as short presentations. In addition, a demonstration track featuring innovative and emergent applications of agent and multi-agent systems and technologies in real-world domains was organized. In all, 18 demonstrations were shown, and this volume contains a description of each of them.

We would like to thank all the contributing authors, the members of the Program Committee, the sponsors (IEEE SMC Spain, IBM, AEPIA, AFIA, APPIA, Universidad Politécnica de Madrid, Polytechnic Institute of Porto, and CNRS), and the Organizing Committee for their hard and highly valuable work. Their work contributed to the success of the PAAMS 2017 event. Thanks for your help – PAAMS 2017 would not exist without your contribution.

May 2017

Yves Demazeau
Paul Davidsson
Javier Bajo
Zita Vale

Organization

General Co-chairs

Yves Demazeau	Centre National de la Recherche Scientifique, France
Paul Davidsson	Malmö University, Sweden
Javier Bajo	Polytechnic University of Madrid, Spain
Zita Vale	Polytechnic Institute of Porto, Portugal

Advisory Board

Keith Decker	University of Delaware, USA
Frank Dignum	Utrecht University, The Netherlands
Toru Ishida	University of Kyoto, Japan
Takayuki Ito	Nagoya Institute of Technology, Japan
Jörg P. Müller	Technische Universität Clausthal, Germany
Juan Pavón	Universidad Complutense de Madrid, Spain
Michal Pechoucek	Czech Technical University in Prague, Czech Republic
Franco Zambonelli	University of Modena and Reggio Emilia, Italy

Program Committee

Carole Adam	University of Grenoble, France
Emmanuel Adam	University of Valenciennes, France
Frederic Amblard	University of Toulouse, France
Francesco Amigoni	Politecnico di Milano, Italy
Bo An	Nanyang Technological University, Singapore
Luis Antunes	University of Lisbon, Portugal
Quan Bai	Auckland University of Technology, New Zealand
Javier Bajo	Universidad Politécnica de Madrid, Spain
Joao Balsa	University of Lisbon, Portugal
Cristina Baroglio	University of Turin, Italy
Nick Bassiliades	University of Thessaloniki, Greece
Jeremy Baxter	QinetQ, UK
Michael Berger	DocuWare AG, Germany
Rafael Bordini	Pontifical University of Rio Grande do Sul, Brazil
Vicente Botti	Polytechnic University of Valencia, Spain
Lars Braubach	Universität Hamburg, Germany
Javier Carbó	University Carlos III of Madrid, Spain
Luis Castillo	University of Caldas, Colombia
Sofia Ceppi	University of Edinburgh, UK
Pierre Chevaillier	University of Brest, France
Helder Coelho	University of Lisbon, Portugal

Juan Manuel Corchado	University of Salamanca, Spain
Rafael Corchuelo	University of Seville, Spain
Luis Correia	University of Lisbon, Portugal
Andres Diaz Pace	University of Tandil, Argentina
Frank Dignum	University of Utrecht, The Netherlands
Julie Dugdale	University of Grenoble, France
Johannes Fähndrich	Technical University of Berlin, Germany
Klaus Fischer	DFKI, Germany
Katsuhide Fujita	Tokyo University of Agriculture and Technology, Japan
Naoki Fukuta	Shizuoka University, Japan
Daniela Godoy	University of Tandil, Argentina
Jorge J. Gómez-Sanz	University Complutense de Madrid, Spain
Charles Gouin-Vallerand	Télé-Université du Québec, Canada
Olivier Gutknecht	Apple Inc., USA
James Harland	RMIT Melbourne, Australia
Salima Hassas	University of Lyon, France
David Hennes	DFKI, Germany
Vincent Hilaire	University of Belfort-Montbeliard, France
Benjamin Hirsch	EBTIC/Khalifa University, UAE
Martin Hofmann	Lockheed Martin, USA
Tom Holvoet	Catholic University of Leuven, Belgium
Jomi Hubner	Universidad Federale de Santa Catarina, Brazil
Takayuki Ito	Nagoya Institute of Technology, Japan
Yichuan Jiang	Southeast University of Nanjing, China
Xiolong Jin	Chinese Academy of Science, China
Vicente Julian	Polytechnic University of Valencia, Spain
Achilles Kameas	University of Patras, Greece
Ryo Kanamori	Nagoya University, Japan
Takahiro Kawamura	Toshiba, Japan
Franziska Kluegl	University of Örebro, Sweden
Matthias Klusch	DFKI, Germany
Martin Kollingbaum	University of Aberdeen, UK
Jaroslaw Kozlak	University of Science and Technology in Krakow, Poland
Robin Lamarche-Perrin	University of Paris 6, France
Paulo Leitao	Polytechnic Institute of Bragança, Portugal
Henrique Lopes Cardoso	University of Porto, Portugal
Miguel Angel Lopez-Carmona	University of Alcala, Spain
Rene Mandiau	University of Valenciennes, France
KinJun Mao	National University of Defense Technology, China
Leandro Marcolino	University of Southern California, USA
Ivan Marsa-Maestre	University of Alcala, Spain
Philippe Mathieu	University of Lille, France
Eric Matson	Purdue University, USA
José M. Molina	University Carlos III of Madrid, Spain

Mirko Morandini	University of Trento, Italy
Bernard Moulin	Laval University, Canada
Jean-Pierre Muller	CIRAD, France
Joerg Mueller	Clausthal University of Technology, Germany
Kai Nagel	Technical University of Berlin, Germany
Ribert Neches	ISI, IARPA, USA
Itsuki Noda	Advanced Institute of Science and Technology, Japan
Michael North	University of Chicago, USA
Paolo Novais	University of Minho, Portugal
Ingrid Nunes	Universidad Federal de Rio Grande do Sul, Brazil
Akihiko Ohsuga	University of Electro-Communications, Japan
Andrea Omicini	University of Bologna, Italy
Mehmet Orgun	Macquarie University, Australia
Sascha Ossowski	University of Rey Juan Carlos, Spain
Julian Padget	University of Bath, UK
Juan Pavon	Complutense University de Madrid, Spain
Terry Payne	University of Liverpool, UK
Pascal Perez	University of Wollongong, Australia
Sébastien Picault	University of Lille, France
David Pynadath	University of Southern California, USA
Luis Paulo Reis	University of Porto, Portugal
Alessandro Ricci	University of Bologna, Italy
Deborah Richards	Macquarie University, Australia
Ana Paula Rocha	University of Porto, Portugal
Juan Rodriguez Aguilar	Artificial Intelligence Research Institute, Spain
Sebastian Rodriguez	Universidad Tecnologica Nacional, Argentina
Nicolas Sabouret	University of Paris 11, France
Erol Sahin	Middle East Technical University, Turkey
Silvia Schiaffino	University of Tandil, Argentina
Shun Shiramatsu	Nagoya Institute of Technology, Japan
Jaime Sichman	University of Sao Paulo, Brazil
Elizabeth Sklar	City University of New York, USA
Petr Skobelev	Smart Solutions, Russia
Sonia Suárez	University of La Coruna, Spain
Toshiharu Sugawara	Waseda University, Japan
Patrick Taillandier	UMR IDEES, MTG, France
Viviane Torres da Silva	Universidad Federal Fluminense, Brazil
Paolo Torroni	University of Bologna, Italy
Ali Emre Turgut	Middle East Technical University, Turkey
Domenico Ursino	University of Reggio Calabria, Italy
Laszlo Varga	Computer and Automation Research Institute, Hungary
Wamberto Vasconselos	University of Aberdeen, UK
Laurent Vercouter	University of Rouen, France
Wayne Wobcke	University of New South Wales, Australia
Gaku Yamamoto	IBM, Japan

Organizing Committee

Brigida Teixeira	Polytechnic Institute of Porto, Portugal
Filipe Sousa	Polytechnic Institute of Porto, Portugal
Francisco Silva	Polytechnic Institute of Porto, Portugal
João Soares	Polytechnic Institute of Porto, Portugal
Luís Conceição	Polytechnic Institute of Porto, Portugal
Luís Gomes	Polytechnic Institute of Porto, Portugal
Sérgio Ramos	Polytechnic Institute of Porto, Portugal

PAAMS 2017 Sponsors

Contents

Demo Papers

Invited Speaker

Context-Aware Decision Support in Socio-Cyberphysical Systems: From Smart Space-Based Applications to Human-Computer Cloud Services

Alexander Smirnov[✉], Alexey Kashevnik, Andrew Ponomarev, and Nikolay Shilov

SPIIRAS, 39, 14th Line, St. Petersburg, Russian Federation
{smir,alexey,ponomarev,nick}@iias.spb.su

Abstract. Context-aware decision support is required in situations taking place in dynamic rapidly changing and often unpredictable distributed environments. Such situations can be characterized by highly decentralized up-to-date data sets arriving from various resources located in socio-cyberphysical systems. Systems of this class tightly integrate heterogeneous resources of the physical world and IT (cyber) world together with social networking concepts. The paper addresses context-aware decision support in agent-based environments for smart space-based systems and human-computer cloud services. The application of the proposed decision support methodology is demonstrated on an e-tourism domain, particularly, via a connected car-based e-tourism system.

Keywords: Context-aware decision support · Agent · Service · Smart space · Human-computer cloud

1 Introduction

Modern applications are often based on CyberPhysical Systems (CPS) using the Internet of Things (IoT) paradigm. The European research cluster on the Internet of Things defines it as "a dynamic global network infrastructure with self-configuring capabilities based on standard and interoperable communication protocols where physical and virtual things have identities, physical attributes, and virtual personalities, use intelligent interfaces, and are seamlessly integrated into the information network" [1]. Now IoT is growing fast into a large industry and has a total potential economic impact of $3.9 to $11.1 trillion a year by 2025 [2]. Several specific platforms have been developed that support IoT devices' communication (e.g., OpenIoT [3], AWS IoT [4]). The major innovations driven by advances in the mobility and cloud computing increase the number and variety of networked connections, as well as the opportunities for people and machines to derive unpredictable value from these connections.

CPS in general integrate physical systems (physical production equipment, vehicles, devices, etc.) and IT components (e.g., enterprise resource planning, manufacturing execution systems or other information systems) in real-time. Socio-CPS (SCPS) take

© Springer International Publishing AG 2017
Y. Demazeau et al. (Eds.): PAAMS 2017, LNAI 10349, pp. 3–15, 2017.
DOI: 10.1007/978-3-319-59930-4_1

into account the integration of human actors (e.g., organizational roles and stakeholders) at individual and social network level for value creation and digital transformation.

SCPSs go one step further the ideas of the current progress in SPSs, socio-technical systems and cyber-social systems to support computing for human experience. They tightly integrate physical, cyber, and social worlds based on real time interactions between these worlds. Such systems rely on communication, computation and control infrastructures commonly consisting of several levels for the three worlds with various resources like sensors, actuators, computational resources, services, humans, etc. Since the resources of SCPSs are numerous, mobile with a changeable composition SCPSs are expected to be context-aware. The context is defined as any information that can be used to characterize the situation of an entity, where an entity is a person, place, or object that is considered relevant to the interaction between a user and an application, including the user and applications themselves [5].

SCPSs belong to the class of variable systems with dynamic structures; the application of the agent technology can be efficient at addressing the issue. The smart spaces paradigm assumes the participating agents (autonomous information processing units) to acquire and apply knowledge to service construction [6–8]. Services are constructed by agents interacting on shared information in information hub that supports indirect information-driven interactions. Each agent produces its share of information and makes it available to others via the hub. Similarly the agent consumes information of its own interest from the hub. To support interoperability between these agents and resources the ontologies are applied to knowledge representation and manipulation within the smart space. In these activities the M3 architecture for smart spaces was developed, where M3 stands for Multidevice, Multivendor, and Multidomain [9].

Adaptability of the IT infrastructure of the organization is met by the cloud computing paradigm defined by NIST as «a model for enabling ubiquitous, convenient, on-demand network access to a shared pool of configurable computing resources (e.g., networks, servers, storage, applications, and services) that can be rapidly provisioned and released with minimal management effort or service provider interaction» [10]. The expected advantages of using cloud computing are the reduction of expenses – both on hardware and on skilled IT personnel, the ability to achieve greater flexibility without the capital cost of investment in extra equipment which might not be needed.

Cloud computing paradigm can become a unifying technological basis for integration of different kinds of services and resources: hardware-, software-, and human-based. Though usually clouds are formed of hardware and software resources, there exists a deep analogy between cloud and crowd computing resulting in emergence of "social computers" paradigm and human-computer cloud (HCC) [11]. Alike virtual computers in the cloud, individuals or groups of people from a huge crowd "pool" can be dynamically allocated to perform a specific task (assignment) and then released.

Nowadays tourism is viewed as one of the largest and fastest growing economic sector in the world. The United Nation World Tourism Organization confirms this fact and shows that international tourist arrivals doubled in the last two decades [12]. The aspects of context-aware decision support are demonstrated through e-tourism area.

This paper investigates a context-aware decision support in SCPSs based on smart space-based applications and HCC services. Section 2 presents the major aspects of the context-aware decision support illustrated via an e-tourism application. Section 3 introduces the developed HCC approach to decision making illustrated via an enhanced e-tourism decision support system. The major results are summarized in the conclusion.

2 Context-Aware Decision Support

Decision support in dynamic environments has to take into account a continuously changing situation. In the present research resources of the environment provide information of any changes to the decision support systems (DSSs).

2.1 Smart Space-Based Decision Support Methodology

In the research the context model serves to represent the knowledge about a decision situation (settings, in which decisions occur, or particular problems to be solved). Context is suggested being modeled at two levels: abstract and operational. These levels are represented by abstract and operational contexts respectively [13].

Abstract context is an ontology-based model integrating information and knowledge relevant to the current decision situation. The DSS's user (the decision maker) in his/her request to DSS indicates the type of the current situation or smart sensors provide this type to the system. The relevant information and knowledge are extracted from the application ontology. The abstract context specifies domain knowledge describing the current situation and problems to be solved in this situation. The abstract context reduces the amount of knowledge represented in the application ontology to the knowledge relevant to the decision situation. In the application ontology this knowledge is related to the resources via the alignment, therefore the abstract context allows the set of resources to be reduced to the resources needed to instantiate knowledge specified in the abstract context. The reduced set is referred to as contextual resources.

Operational context is an instantiation of the domain constituent of the abstract context with data provided by the contextual resources. This context reflects any changes in environmental information, so it is a near real-time picture of the current situation.

To enable capturing, monitoring, and analysis of the implemented decisions and their effects the abstract and operational contexts with references to the respective decisions are retained in an archive. In a result, DSS is provided with some reusable models of decision situations. These models, for instance, are used to reveal user preferences based on the analysis of the operational contexts in conjunction with the implemented decisions.

Usage of these context management techniques in a Smart-M3 application allows to formalize current situation in smart space at two layers and take it into account during application functioning. Abstract context level suits well for sharing and reuse, since, on the one hand, this level does not concentrate on any specific properties, and on the other hand, knowledge of this level is not a universal abstraction seldom taken into account when the case considers practical knowledge sharing and reuse. The agent's ontology describes the model of the agent and includes all requirements and possibilities that can be implemented. This ontology is also used to identify tasks for particular agents, and their joint execution would lead to solving the original (current) problem. Abstract context describes the task that can be executed by an agent. The model is formed automatically (or reused) applying ontology slicing and merging techniques [14]. The purpose is to collect and integrate knowledge relevant to the current problem (situation) into the context. Operational context provides description of the task with parameters and values at the moment. Operational context is the information that the agent publishes in smart space according to abstract context (Fig. 1). At that, a concrete description of the current situation is formed, and the current problem is augmented with additional data.

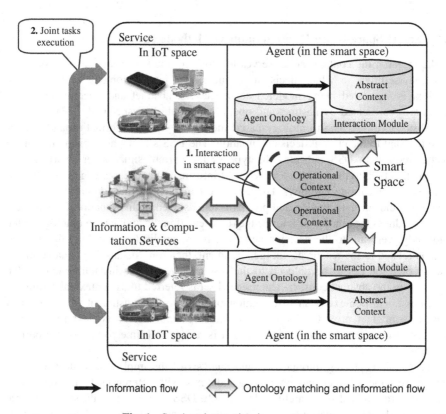

Fig. 1. Services interaction in smart space

2.2 TAIS as Mobile Smart Space-Based Application

The proposed decision support methodology was implemented in the "TAIS – Mobile Tourist Guide" system developed under the EU program for cross-border e-tourism framework in Oulu Region and the Republic of Karelia (Development of Cross-Border e-Tourism Framework for the Program Region – Smart e-Tourism (European Community – Karelia ENPI CBC 2007-2013 Program, 2012-2014 – project KA322)).

TAIS is a mobile application for guiding tourist activities through the mobile clients that are developed for Android devices (smartphones or tablets). The system determines the current tourist location and provides context-aware recommendations about attractions around (e.g., museums, monuments) and their textual and photo descriptions. The user browses attractions and makes decisions about attendance. The personal preferences and the current situation in the region are taken into account. The application also exploits external Internet services for the source of actual information about attractions based on tourists' ratings. The intelligent mobile tourist guide consists of several services united by the smart space technology for providing the tourist with information according to personal preferences [15, 16].

The main application screen is shown in Fig. 2 (left). The tourist can view images extracted from accessible internet sources, clickable map with his/her location, context situation (e.g., weather), and the best attractions around ranked by the recommendation service. The tourist can also see detailed information about the chosen attraction (Fig. 2, right), browse attraction reaching path that is proposed by the system route to an attraction, and/or estimate it.

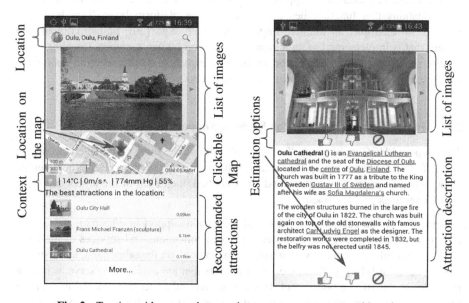

Fig. 2. Tourist guide screenshots: main screen, context menu with actions

3 Human-Computer Cloud Approach to Decision Support

The idea of HCC lies in the usage of human and computer units to create a content, process it, and provide decision support [17]. It applies the distinctive features of cloud computing (namely, resource virtualization, abstraction, and elasticity) to the construction of information processing systems containing hardware, software, and humans [11, 18].

The cloud-managed human resource environments are aiming at managing member's skills and competencies in a standardized flexible way (e.g., [11, 18]) regarding human as a specific resource that can be allocated from a pool for executing some tasks.

The proposed decision support methodology based on HCC is presented in Fig. 3. In accordance with the methodology humans implement two roles: end user (often is a decision maker) or contributor – a computing resource that can be used in manual problem solving. Contributors can join HCC and define the resources they can provide, time and load restrictions, types of tasks they can execute. A contributor may also define the expected compensation for his/her efforts. There are multiple possible schemes of incentivization [19]. Three of them are the most appropriate: monetary reward, artificial reward measured in some cloud-based "contribution points", allowing, in their turn, to use resources of the cloud in the future, and voluntary participation. Resources can also be presented by program services that provide autonomous task execution. Each resource is described by a competency profile defined in terms of application ontology. This profile is used for resource search at the stage of task execution. The profile can be filled out by a developer of the service or contributor/end user and/or autonomously by gathering information from social media.

Each task is executed by appropriate resource of HCC. According to NIST recommendations this function lies on services at the platform layer. This layer can provide, for example, an Iterative-Improvement (see, e.g., [20]) human computation pattern that is implemented as an allocation of several human members (meeting some requirements) and a task redirection to them in sequence. Task execution results are composed into a joint problem solution and returned to the end user.

3.1   Human-Computer Cloud for Decision Support in e-Tourism

The proposed HCC architecture (Fig. 4) deals with all the three cloud layers according to NIST [10]: infrastructure, platform, and software. In this section, firstly, the potential actors who can interact with the cloud are identified, then each of the layers and some of their services are described.

Actors. Two main categories of actors of a decision support in e-tourism are tourists and contributors. Tourists are end users of most applications and services of the HCC environment (like trip itinerary planning). Contributors, on the other hand, are (usually, but not necessarily) local citizens or other tourists that are available to serve as human resources in the HCC environment. Besides, several other actors involved in decision making or system maintenance are identified (see [17] for a detailed description).

Infrastructure layer: Infrastructure layer unifies different types of capabilities: traditional computing and storage capabilities, sensing capabilities and human expertise capabilities. It should also be noted, that in this mixed infrastructure layer resources do not have to be limited to e-tourism. It can be a multi-purpose HCC, where human resources are described in detail to allow the usage in main e-tourism scenarios. Using multi-purpose cloud also has the benefit of resources consolidation that might be crucial in the systems including resources as unique and limited as humans. To make this layer universal the human resource-related components of cloud infrastructure

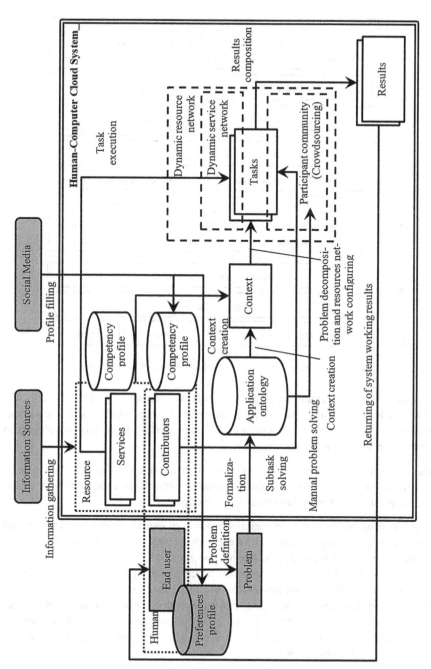

Fig. 3. Decision support methodology based on human-computer cloud

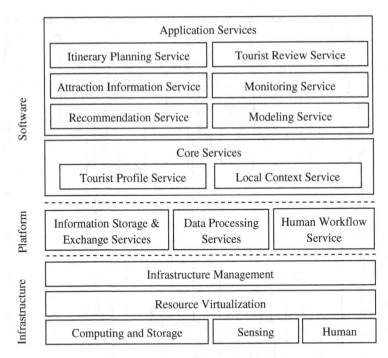

Fig. 4. Human-computer cloud architecture for e-Tourism

management service leverages an extensible skills' vocabulary (e.g., the key skills that are relevant to tourism domain are [17]: multiple language skills, local knowledge, knowledge of the already visited destinations) that is used by application developers to specify requirements for human resources.

Platform layer. This layer consists of a set of multi-purpose services that can be leveraged for building e-tourism applications (among others) that use human expertise. The services of this layer include three main groups:

- scalable information storage and exchange services including database services and various services, implementing different architectural approaches to information exchange (message passing, blackboards, etc.);
- data processing services, which receive, process, and aggregate data from information sources allowing applications to use these data in a flexible way;
- human workflow service providing convenient abstractions for arranging workflows, including human efforts, resource allocation transparent for developers of applications based on human input, and providing human computation patterns (e.g., Iterative-Improvement [20]).

Software layer. This layer includes services that are required for performing auxiliary decision support functions. These services can be divided into two groups: core services, that implement some general operations, and specific services, exposed to end users.

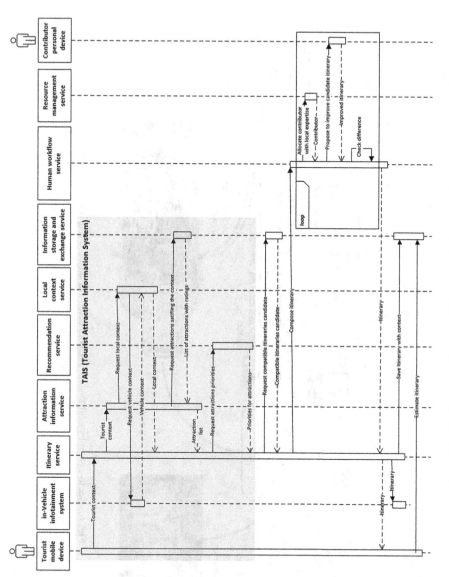

Fig. 5. Sequence diagram of itinerary creation scenario

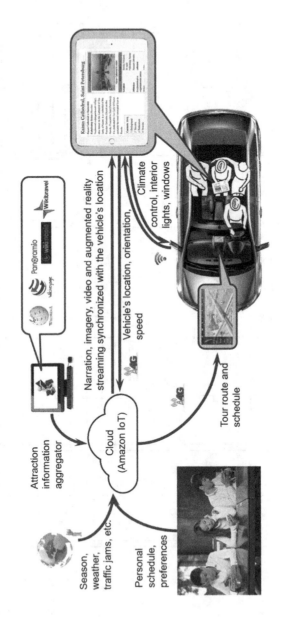

Fig. 6. Socio-cyberphysical system for connected car-based e-tourism: case study

Core services include the profile management service representing a centralized storage of user's history and preferences, and the local context service. A user can define what information of his/her profile can be accessed by other services in different queries (personalized or anonymized). Local context service provides various information about current situation in the selected area.

Application services include attraction information and recommendation services, itinerary planning, local transport information, etc.

3.2 Application Scenario

Creating an itinerary is a typical problem to be solved either by the tourist or by a travel agency. In this case study, based on the schedule analysis (e.g., hotel check-out before 11AM and flight at 08PM) the system proposes a tour that would fit the schedule and end up at the airport. The tour accounts for the person's preferences (preset and revealed via collaborative filtering techniques) and the current situation at the location (season, weather, traffic jams, etc.) based on the earlier developed mobile tourist guide TAIS.

Unlike the original TAIS the itinerary service is built using database service and human workflow service provided by the HCC platform (Fig. 5, grayed part). The database service is used to store the accepted (and probably high quality) itineraries composed for different users in the past, and the human workflow service is used to define an Iterative-Improvement scheme for itineraries being composed. Besides, the itinerary planning service uses some of the core application services, e.g., local context service (providing current and predicted information about weather, traffic situation, etc.). All this information is formalized in accordance with the application ontology.

Initially the itinerary service enriches the incoming request with local context, supplied by local context service, then looks up in the database for the past accepted itineraries for users with similar preferences and in similar contexts, and finally via human workflow service allocates several contributors (both among past tourists and local citizens) to review and possibly improve candidate itineraries. It also incorporates the proactivity engine that allows for making recommendations on tour change in case of the current situation changes.

The tour route is transferred to the driver (to the car's navigation system via Ford AppLink), and the tour guide – to the tourist. The system also provides for basic communication between the driver and the tourist and generates some tour recommendations that the user can accept or decline. The car location and speed are transferred to the car context service to synchronize the vehicle's location and speed with tour's narration, imagery and video. The complete scheme of the application is shown in Fig. 6.

4 Conclusion

The paper proposes the HCC-based approach and methodology for context-aware decision support in SCPSs. The approach is based on the combined usage of agent and services for information exchange and processing through a smart space. Hybrid cloud architecture and unified resource management enable to automatically use crowd resources (crowdsource the problem), when the problem description and pre-requisites for the problem allow. The architecture includes three layers: (i) decision support services layer (corresponding to the SaaS layer of cloud systems) also including workflow management service; (ii) platform layer providing general services for human-workflow management, quality control, etc., and (iii) resource access layer (IaaS), providing for resource management operations. The smart spaces paradigm provides together with the agent technology the efficient and scalable grounds for development of intelligent service-oriented systems as smart spaces-based applications.

Acknowledgements. The HCC for DSS research is supported by the Russian Science Foundation (project # 16-11-10253).

References

1. IERC - European Research Cluster on the Internet of Things, About IoT (2014). http://www.internet-of-things-research.eu/about_iot.htm
2. Manyika, J., Chui, M., Bisson, P., Woetzel, J., Dobbs, R., Bughin, J., Aharon, D.: Unlocking the potential of the Internet of Things. McKinsey Global Institute Report, June 2015
3. Soldatos, J., et al.: OpenIoT: open source internet-of-things in the cloud. In: Podnar Žarko, I., Pripužić, K., Serrano, M. (eds.) Interoperability and Open-Source Solutions for the Internet of Things. LNCS, vol. 9001, pp. 13–25. Springer, Cham (2015). doi:10.1007/978-3-319-16546-2_3
4. Amazon Web Services, AWS IoT (2017). https://aws.amazon.com/ru/iot/
5. Dey, A.K., Salber, D., Abowd, G.D.: A conceptual framework and a toolkit for supporting the rapid prototyping of context-aware applications. In: Moran, T.P., Dourish, P. (eds.) Context-Aware Computing, A Special Triple Issue of Human-Computer Interaction, vol. 16. Lawrence-Erlbaum (2001). http://www.cc.gatech.edu/fce/ctk¬/pubs/-HCIJ16.pdf
6. Cook, D.J., Das, S.K.: How smart are our environments? An updated look at the state of the art. Pervasive and Mobile Computing 3(2), 53–73 (2007). Elsevier
7. Gilman, E., Davidyuk, O., Su, X., Riekki, J.: Towards interactive smart spaces. J. Ambient Intell. Smart Environ. 5(1), 5–22 (2013). IOS Press
8. Chen, J., Abedinb, F., Chaob, K., Godwinb, N., Lic, Y., Tsai, C.: A hybrid model for cloud providers and consumers to agree on QoS of cloud services. Future Gener. Comput. Syst. 50, 38–48 (2015)
9. Korzun, D.G., Kashevnik, A.M., Balandin, S.I., Smirnov, A.V.: The smart-M3 platform: experience of smart space application development for internet of things. In: Balandin, S., Andreev, S., Koucheryavy, Y. (eds.) ruSMART 2015. LNCS, vol. 9247, pp. 56–67. Springer, Cham (2015). doi:10.1007/978-3-319-23126-6_6
10. Mell, P., Grance, T.: The NIST definition of cloud computing. Recommendations of the National Institute of Standards and Technology, NIST Special Publication, 800-145 (2015)
11. Dustdar, S., Bhattacharya, K.: The social compute unit. IEEE Internet Comput. 15(3), 64–69 (2011)
12. UNWTO: Tourism highlights (2016). http://www.e-unwto.org/doi/pdf/10.18111/978928 4418145
13. Smirnov, A., Levashova, T., Shilov, N.: Patterns for context-based knowledge fusion in decision support. Inf. Fusion 21, 114–129 (2015)

14. Smirnov, A., Pashkin, M., Chilov, N., Levashova, T.: Constraint-driven methodology for context-based decision support. J. Decis. Syst. **14**(3), 279–301 (2005)
15. Smirnov, A., Kashevnik, A., Ponomarev, A.: Context-based infomobility system for cultural heritage recommendation: tourist Assistant—TAIS. Pers. Ubiquitous Comput. **21**, 1–15 (2016). Springer
16. Kashevnik, A., Ponomarev, A., Smirnov, A.: A multimodel context-aware tourism recommendation service: approach and architecture. J. Comput. Syst. Sci. Int. **56**(2), 245–258 (2017). Pleiades Publishing
17. Smirnov, A., Ponomarev, A., Levashova, T., Teslya, N.: Human-computer cloud for decision support in tourism: approach and architecture. In: Balandin, S., Tyutina, T. (eds.) Proceedings of the FRUCT'19, pp. 226–235 (2016)
18. Sengupta, B., Jain, A., Bhattacharya, K., Truong, H.-L., Dustar, S.: Collective problem solving using social compute units. Int. J. Coop. Inf. Syst. **22**, 1–21 (2013)
19. Scekic, O., Truong, H.-L., Dustdar, S.: Incentives and rewarding in social computing. ACM Commun. **56**, 72 (2013)
20. Little, G., Chilton, L.B., Goldman, M., Miller, R.C.: Exploring iterative and parallel human computation processes. In: Proceedings of the ACM SIGKDD Workshop on Human Computation – HCOMP 2010, p. 68. ACM Press (2010)

Regular Papers

Concept of a Multi-agent Based Decentralized Production System for the Automotive Industry

Christian Blesing, Dennis Luensch, Jonas Stenzel[(✉)], and Benjamin Korth

Fraunhofer Institute for Material Flow and Logistics, 44227 Dortmund, Germany
{christian.blesing,jonas.stenzel}@iml.fraunhofer.de

Abstract. To face the challenges of today's market requirements, a huge effort is made to plan continuous flow manufacturing systems used today. Simultaneously disturbances during the production have decisive negative effects on the effectiveness. To mitigate this problem, current research programs try to use flexible production systems with a high degree of self-organization. In this paper a novel concept for a flexible decentralized production system is described which combines the planning method of a precedence graph and a multi-agent-system that forms a modular control system. Furthermore first results are presented that have been achieved by a pilot demonstrator and simulation experiments.

Keywords: Cyber-physical systems · AGV routing · Path planning · Task assignment · Production planning · Decentralized production systems · Agent ontology · Industry 4.0 · Intra-logistic simulation

1 Introduction

Nowadays, companies are faced with the increasing need to operate effectively and efficiently. Within automotive industry, mass-market vehicles are commonly produced with a continuous flow manufacturing system that consists of a combination of highly efficient production and assembly lines. Therefore, the automotive industry planning processes needs a high effort to keep assembly lines fully utilized. This is because of the high complexity in the product structure with a high diversity in product variants and the huge number of parts that must be delivered just in time or even just in sequence at the right place at the assembly line. Through the high degree of dependencies in the assembly line the effects of disturbances are critical [4]. Delays in part supply or assembly steps directly influence other orders as uncompleted steps or missing parts can lead to a higher amount of rework. *Yu et al.* [13] present a reconfigurable manufacturing execution system (RMES) to face this problem. Within this paper, a novel concept how to replace the assembly line by a flexible production system based on workstations which is controlled by an autonomous acting planning and transport system is described. Each workstation can have multiple capabilities to execute assembly steps and therefore can provide redundancy. Through the loosely coupling of the assembly stations alternative sequences in the process of assembly

© Springer International Publishing AG 2017
Y. Demazeau et al. (Eds.): PAAMS 2017, LNAI 10349, pp. 19–30, 2017.
DOI: 10.1007/978-3-319-59930-4_2

steps become also feasible. With the new obtained advantages, delays in a single step do not lead to delays for other orders and may be compensated by other stations. Audi, a German automobile manufacturer, has announced that they are working on modular assembly strategies using a similar concept [7]. The project SMART FACE focused on the development of a simulation and a proto-type demonstrator using this approach. Therefore, as a partial result, this paper describes the use of an agent based production planning and control system to move car bodies and parts along a flexible assembly process.

Fig. 1. The vision of SMART FACE: decentrally and autonomously acting units (e.g., assembly stations and automated guided vehicles) are responsible for transporting and producing goods on a self-organizing shop floor. Human workers are still an important part since they exhibit larger flexibility than most of their technical counterparts.

2   Algorithmic Background

Initially, an overview of some promising task assignment and route planning algorithms for **A**utomated **G**uided **V**ehicle (*AGV*) and mobile robot systems within intralogistics is given as these are essential to create highly automated and flexible production systems.

2.1   Overview of Dynamic Task Assignment Algorithms

In order to maximize the throughput of manufacturing systems, warehouses and outbound logistics, the use of AGVs for transporting goods has increased steadily since the 1950s. The main objective to achieve this goal is to find an optimal solution regarding the assignment of transportation tasks to the AGVs. One approach to solve this problem is to optimize both, the loading point-AGV assignment and the scheduling of tasks to different AGVs. *Giglio* therefore sep-arates both tasks and formulates each problem as an optimization problem [5].

Another approach which is described by *Branisso et al.* is the definition of an optimality criterion by defining a fuzzy inference system in which the transport agents that represent the different AGVs, decide which transport order they accept next (cf. [3]). In general, optimality criteria have to match the constraints of the production planning system (e.g., the latest possible finishing time) and they have to be known by the other software modules).

Schwarz et al. [11] presented a decentralized approach based on a multi agent system (*MAS*) for handling transport orders with AGV's in a beverage bottling line. Hence their approach focuses primarily on procurement, routing and conflict resolution. Contracts are assigned through FIPA auctions, with a main focus on the order calculation. AGVs appear as bidders, stations as vendors within the auctions. Bids were made based on the occupancy and position of a vehicle. Within an evaluation the decentralized approach was tested against a central procedure. It turned out that the decentralized approach leads to advantages with regard to a higher utilization of the vehicles as well as a shorter throughput time of the orders.

In this paper, the task assignment problem is solved by applying auctions similar to *Branisso et al.* and *Schwarz et al.* and by defining three decision points (for production order-, partial order- and transport order assignment respectively) whereas each decision point has its own fuzzy sets. The algorithm is further described in Sect. 6.

2.2   Overview of Dynamic Route Planning Algorithms

Path planning and navigation for a fleet of mobile robots or AGVs is a challenge that has been addressed by lots of researchers. The following sections focuses some popular path planning approaches. One approach to the coordination of multi-robot path planning is prioritized planning, where robots plan their trajectories sequentially one after another. *Čáp et al.* adopted variants of classical prioritized planning algorithm to decentralized ones [12]. They proved that the decentralized implementation is guaranteed to provide a solution under the same conditions as its centralized counterpart. In addition, their revised prioritized path planning approaches tend to find path planning solutions for scenarios with a high number of robots where classical prioritized planning approaches or reactive collision-avoidance algorithms like ORCA [2] fail.

Another decentralized path-planning approach, the "Cooperative Dynamic algorithm" (*CoDy*), is described in [9]. It is based on a broadcast exchange of messages between the participants which is used for a dynamic and coordinated path planning of each vehicle. Dynamic conflicts between the robots are solved by the heuristic adjustment of priority values. The advantages of this algorithm are that it can cope with the coordination of large robot teams and that it is able to avoid and solve dead-lock situations.

Our routing approach for the AGV-based production system is based on an implementation of a context aware route planner from *ter Mors* that uses time slots for calculating conflict free route plans with respect to the existing route plans of other vehicles [8]. For a basic concept description of this algorithm please refer to Sect. 5. The advantages of this approach are that it directly computes the expected arrival time and path dynamics of the vehicles which then are used for the task assignment algorithms.

3   System Overview

This section gives an overview of the decentralized production system. At first, the order structure and secondly the concept of the *MAS* that is used to control the production system are described. In the automobile production, so called precedence graphs are used to schedule the assembling steps during the whole production process. This graphs further describes the predecessor-successor relationships between the specific steps. Therefore a certain step can only be executed if all its successor processes where completed before. In the project SMART FACE a simplified precedence graph consisting of ten assembling steps was used (see Fig. 2). Hereinafter, assembling steps are also referred as *partial orders*. Within this project, the shown assembling steps can be considered as workstation capabilities. Therefore each workstation is able to carry out a certain number of steps for e.g. *headlights*, *rims* and *seats*. It is possible to distribute the capabilities redundantly over the workstations. This ensures reliability and increases the throughput.

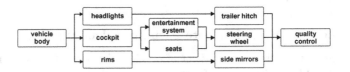

Fig. 2. Precedence graph: the predecessor-successor relationships between the production steps are shown.

3.1   Agent Interaction Concept

In this section, an overview about the system structure and the realized agents is given. All agents are implemented by using the **J**ava **A**gent **D**evelopment Framework (*JADE*). JADE comes along with several interaction protocols, which all correspond to the FIPA standard [1]. All of our agent interactions are based on these protocols. At runtime the agents can be distributed over several independent computers. For better cooperation and coordination between the agent, a layer based approach, which is also presented by *Yu et al.* [13], is chosen. The developed MAS can be divided into three hierarchical layers (see Fig. 3). The top layer is called *Production Planning* and deals with order management and the subordinated planning processes. Furthermore this layer contains a decision point that is part of the **P**roduction **O**rder **M**anagement Agent (POM-Agent). It is used to decide which production order from the order portal will be loaded into the system next. The second layer is called *Production and Warehousing*. This level contains agents that deal with the physical production process in combination with the component supply and delivery management. Furthermore this layer contains two other decision points. One is located in the **P**roduction **O**rder Agent (PO-Agent) and deals with the decision which partial order from the precedence graph is manufactured next. The other decision point is located at the warehouse agent and is responsible for the transport order assignment. The lowest hierarchical layer is called *Material flow*. Basically this layer is responsible for planning, managing and executing the material flow between the warehouse and the workstations. The major element of this layer is the routing agent.

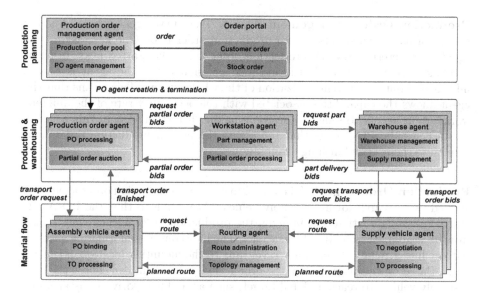

Fig. 3. Schematic system overview: three hierarchical layers with their corresponding tasks and the included agents are shown. Additionally the agent communication within (horizontal) and between the hierarchical layers (vertical) is mapped.

The upcoming conversations during the production process can basically be divided into two interaction protocol specifications. The implemented auctions correspond to the FIPA Contract-Net (CNET) specification. All other conversations are conform to the *FIPA request* or *request when* protocol specifications.

4   Agent Model

The following section describes the applied agent model, the individual agents, their tasks and behaviors. Agents are divided into two agent representations, a physical and a logical agent representation. Additionally the agents can be grouped into two different agents classes which follows the definitions of *Russell and Norvig* [10]. The vehicle, warehouse and POM agent corresponds to the *Simple reflex agents*, whereas all other agents corresponds to the *Model-based reflex agents*. All subsequently described agents refer to Fig. 3.

4.1   Logical Agents

A logical agent represents a software component, which reacts to its environmental influences. Based on the perceived influences the agent acts autonomously within its own behaviors and tries to reach its predefined goals. Subsequently the POM-Agent, PO-Agent, warehouse agent and routing agent will be presented.

Production Order Management Agent. The POM-Agent is able to access the set of particular orders from a production order pool. One key task of this agent is to determine which production order has to be started next. In order to make this decision inside the included decision point, the agent is always informed about the current utilization of the whole system. This means that the agent knows the capabilities associated with the occupancy rate of the different workstation agents. Beside the decision-making a further task of this agent is to start specific PO-Agents that represents the chosen production orders and terminate them after finishing assembly.

Production Order Agent. The initial task after a production order agent was started, is to search for an assembly vehicle. According to this, the PO-Agent starts a binding auction. For binding, the production order agent requests bids from all available assembly vehicle agents. The bids contains information such as: battery life, driving distance and travel time to the mounting location of the car body. Based on this information, the production order agent can choose the best assembly vehicle to reach a global target, such as: reducing driving distances or travel times. The main task of a production order agent is to complete all partial orders of a given precedence graph (see Fig. 2). Therefore, all open and feasible partial orders will be selected and then auctioned to the workstations. After receiving the bids for all auctioned partial orders, an evaluation of them will be proceeded within the decision point of this agent. Within the evaluation process, the best bid for a partial order will be evaluated to reach a global assigned target. Global goals are e.g., maximum utilization for special workstations, uniform utilization of all workstations or shortest throughput times of the production orders.

Warehouse Agent. The responsibilities of the warehouse agent includes the management of part supplies, assignment of supply vehicles and management of stock. For stock management the warehouse agent implements an interface to an external warehouse management system, which persists bin and part movements. For the delivery of goods, transport orders are auctioned to supply vehicles (see Sec. 4.2). Based on the bids of the supply vehicles, the selection of an optimal vehicle can be carried out in a local decision point (shortest route for the supply vehicle, earliest arrival time, etc.).

Routing Agent. The major task of this agent is to compute routes that are requested by both supply and assembly vehicle agents. The incoming route requests are processed and answered in a serial way. Therefore this agent offers a routing service which is based on the centralized routing algorithm described in more detail in Sect. 5. Beside the route calculation another key task is the route administration, whereby previous planned routes are saved and retrievable for new route calculations. The basis of the route calculation is a topology which is managed by the routing agent.

4.2   Physical Agents

A physical agent extends a logical agent by a technical component or a connection to an external control unit. Following the vehicle agents and the workstation agent will be introduced. The physical agents can be executed directly on the specific hardware (e.g. a vehicle controller) or on a dedicated PC. In the latter case, communication is realized via WiFi connection.

Vehicle Agent. A vehicle agent is a physical agent which is directly connected to a real robot, in our case a Cellular Transport Vehicle (CTV) [6]. A CTV is capable of changing its location, carry bins, provide status information for e.g. position and battery information and receive external transport orders. All these functions are bundled in a basic vehicle agent. The basic vehicle agent also contains behaviors to translate calculated routes from a routing agent into driving commands, receive travel destinations from other agents and provide vehicle information to other agents. In our experimental setup two variants of the basic vehicle agent exists, whereby every derived agent supplemented additional behaviors to fulfill the roles of a supply or assembly vehicle.

In our scenario a supply vehicle delivers ordered parts from a highbay warehouse to distributed workstations on the shop floor. Therefor the basic vehicle agent was extended by a behavior to process transport orders. To obtain orders, a supply vehicle sends bids on auctioned transport orders from the warehouse agent. For this purpose, the vehicle agent has an additional behavior to conduct contract negotiations. Auction for orders are given in the form of a direct inquiry of a supply vehicle agent and a request to submit a bid. The bid of a supply vehicle includes information such as: driving distance, travel time, battery life and workload.

An assembly vehicle is used to transport a car body between the workstations on the shop floor. For this purpose a car body is permanently assigned to an assembly vehicle during the entire assembly process, from mounting the car body till completion. Hence, a binding between an assembly vehicle and a production order exist during the overall assembly. After binding the assembly vehicle can directly be instructed by the production order agent, for e.g. sending a transport order request to a workstation. In case of finishing the assembly of the car, the binding will be canceled and the assembly vehicle agent starts bidding on new binding auctions.

Workstation Agent. The workstation agent can be represented by two different physical types of workstations. On the one hand, there are workstations where a robot carries out the assembly of the components. On the other hand, there are workstations where a human worker takes over the assembly (see Fig. 1). To involve workers, an interaction with the system is given via a mobile device, e.g. a tablet, where open tasks are displayed and interaction opportunities are given. An important task of a workstation agent is to manage its own local inventory system. Each station may have buffers for parts whose filling level is monitored by the specific workstation agent. If the filling level falls below a defined level, a re-order is automatically triggered. To carry out partial orders a workstation agent must be able to create bids for these orders which are auctioned by a PO-Agent. In case that the required component is not available locally it will be ordered via the warehouse agent. All the necessary information like availability or travel time are collected and returned to the specific workstation agent.

5   Routing Algorithm

We consider a set V of vehicles, where each vehicle has to find the shortest route from a start to a destination location, without colliding with any of the other agents, or ending up in a deadlock situation. For this purpose a graph routing algorithm, based on the **Context Aware Route Planning** *(CARP)* approach of *ter Mors* [8] was implemented. The calculated routes can be defined as $\pi_n = ([r_1, \tau_1], \ldots, [r_n, \tau_n]), \tau_i = [t_i, t'_i)$ where r_n is a node of the resource graph and τ_n is a time window that indicates that resource r_n is available from time t_i to t'_i. The basic idea of CARP can be defined as follows. Within routing, individual agents plan their routes successively one after the other. If an agent n plans its route, the already planned $(n-1)$ routes are included in the current calculation. Every node of the resource graph has its own time windows that defines when the node is visitable. For planning conflict-free routes, overlapping time windows between the individual nodes of a route are required, in a way that $\tau \cap \tau' \neq \emptyset$. A calculation of the needed time windows takes place on the basis of real time values of the deployed vehicles. These values can be used to estimate the vehicle positions at a given time point. Based on this information the time windows of each node in the graph can be created. The algorithm also offers the possibility to integrate current events, such as delays, into the planning of future routes through a delay propagation approach [8].

6   Decision Making

To make decisions based on different input variables various concepts such as genetic algorithms, fuzzy logic or neuronal networks can be applied. A disadvantage of genetic algorithms and neuronal networks is the high complexity. Decisions are made in a black box and the process of decision-making is not comprehensible. The big advantage by using fuzzy logic is that the solution process can be converted to human understandable operations. *Branisso et al.* evaluates different techniques to increase the performance of an AGV fleet in a warehouse. The best results were obtained by applying fuzzy logic to the decision process [3]. By applying fuzzy logic it is possible to extensively influence the decision making process by changing the fuzzy rules and membership functions which changes the behavior of the whole shop floor. Each of our decision points has corresponding fuzzy input and output sets and specific optimization goals. Subsequently the decision point of the warehouse agent, which is used for the assignment of transport orders, is examined in more detail. For the included auction in that decision point the FIPA CNET protocol was applied. In [3] it is pointed out that CNET produces a larger task throughput as the First Come First Serve approach. All of the following input values are part of a bid that was sent from a supply vehicle agent to the warehouse agent during a transport order auction. Three physical input values are used at this decision point. More precisely, these are the travel distance between the source and destination location, the travel time and the battery charging state of the vehicle. Based on this three input values, the corresponding fuzzy sets (U_n, μ_n) were formed where U_n is a particular set and $\mu_n : U_n \rightarrow [0,1]$ one of the associated membership functions for set U_n. In this particular case the defined output set determines a fitness value for each of the CTV's which has submitted a bid. Subsequently, the warehouse agent notifies the winner CTV (Fig. 4).

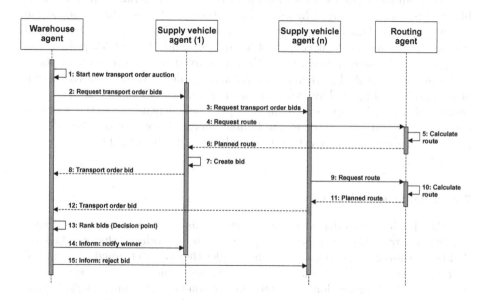

Fig. 4. Sequence diagram of a transport order auction: the participating agents as well as the communication process between them are shown.

7   Evaluation

The evaluation of the concept of the decentralized production system architecture is done by two different approaches. First, a multi-agent system was developed based on the agent model (cf. Sect. 4) that controls the a real-world testbed, called SMART FACE shop floor demonstrator. While running this demonstrator, the behavior of the vehicles can be observed by a visitor. For example, the operability of the decentralized production system can be examined and the lead times of a real-world implementation can be analyzed. The second evaluation step was to create a simulation model that depict a larger order amount that utilized all work stations for a longer period. In the first version of the simulation only the transportation of car bodies and the assembly steps were taken into account. The objectives of the experiments were to determine the makespan, station utilization and the waiting times of the assembly vehicles in dependence of the number of available assembly vehicles.

7.1 Live System

In order to show that the developed agent model is applicable to a real-world scenario, the SMART FACE shop floor demonstrator has been created at Fraunhofer IML. This testbed consists of 4 workstations (3 are human-operated and one is an automated workstation operated by an industrial robot), 4 assembly vehicles and 6 supply vehicles and a highbay warehouse that is accessible by the supply vehicles. The system is capable of producing more than 5000 variants of car models that consist of a car body and different 3D-printed car components. These components are then assembled to the car body at the 4 workstations sequentially whereas the assembly order is defined by the precedence graph (cf. Fig. 2). This cyber-physical production system has shown to be capable of producing up to 6 car models per hour, depending on the speed of the human operators working at the human operated workstations. See following URL for shop floor demonstrator video: https://download.iml.fraunhofer.de/paams17/.

7.2 Simulation Model

For the simulation model an event driven simulation was created. The basic concept was to model the process for products to be produced that can be subdivided in subprocesses and rules in which order they can go through. To execute a process, resources like workstations or assembly vehicles can be requested at resource pools. Workstations are stationary resources with different skills that are needed in processes. Assembly vehicles are mobile resources that can move car bodies. The topology of the shop floor is modeled by discrete locations for workstations and a distance matrix. In addition, every workstation can have a buffer place for assembly vehicles with a adjustable size. With the building blocks described above a simulation model was builded as a reproduction of the live system. This model enables to carry out experiments with larger quantity of orders and with a flexible amount of assembly vehicles in shorter times.

7.3 Simulation Results

In first simulation runs, the simulation results show that the production processes are always executed in a valid order regarding the precedence graph. Because the selection algorithm for the next process to execute takes the distances to possible execution locations into account, the number of necessary transports was reduced. In addition to the proof of concept of the decentralized control system, some experiments to balance the assembly system were carried out. For example in a series of experiments the number of assembly vehicles was considered. Figure 5 shows a summary of these experiments. On the x-Axis, the number of assembly vehicles in an experiment is shown. For each experiment, the blue line shows the average station utilization while the orange bars represent the sum waiting time for the assembly vehicles. The green bar shows the total make span of all orders. In the experiment with four assembly vehicles, the utilization of the workstations is very low (about 60%) while the makespan is high (green bar). As the red bar shows, the assembly vehicles have a low waiting time when they are approaching a workstation. If more vehicles are in use, the station utilization increase fast to over 90% while the makespan decreases. But if the number of vehicles is increased further, the waiting times of them increases disproportionately to the decrease of the makespan time.

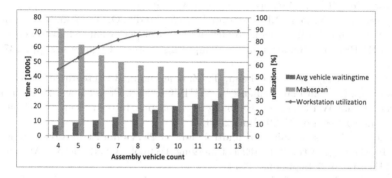

Fig. 5. Simulation results: The station utilization and the relative change of makespan and waiting time at simulations with different numbers of assembly vehicles are shown. (Color figure online)

8   Conclusion and Outlook

Within this paper a new decentralized, agent-based concept for production planning and control has been introduced. The system architecture is defined by an agent model which contains the elements of a modern production system (namely an ERP system, a Warehouse Management System and a routing and task assignment software for AGVs). A first evaluation within a simplified simulation model and results from a testbed with a simplified production process and real assembly vehicles have been proven to be successful. In the future, the time window principle of the routing algorithm might be used to extend it with respect to the integration and prediction of human behavior within intralogistics environments. Additionally, the temporal influence of the human-operated system parts on the decision making and on makespan and waiting times of the vehicles within the live system will be investigated. Another future task is to extend the simulation model. Especially the part supply is a very important part for the assembly that must be integrated.

Acknowledgment. This work was supported by the German Federal Ministry for Economic Affairs and Energy (BMWi) under the "AUTONOMIK fuer Industrie 4.0" research program within the project SMART FACE (Grant no. 01MA13007). The project consortium consists of industrial companies and research institutions, namely Logata Digital Solutions, F/L/S Fuzzy Logik Systeme, Lanfer Automation, Continental AG, SICK AG, Volkswagen AG, TU Dortmund University, and Fraunhofer IML.

References

1. Bellifemine, F.L., Caire, G., Greenwood, D.: Developing Multi-Agent Systems with JADE (Wiley Series in Agent Technology). Wiley, New York (2007)
2. van den Berg, J., Lin, M., Manocha, D.: Reciprocal velocity obstacles for real-time multi-agent navigation. In: IEEE International Conference on Robotics and Automation, ICRA 2008, pp. 1928–1935, May 2008
3. Branisso, L.B., Kato, E.R.R., Pedrino, E.C., Morandin, O., Tsunaki, R.H.: A multi-agent system using fuzzy logic to increase agv fleet performance in warehouses. In: 2013 III Brazilian Symposium on Computing Systems Engineering, pp. 137–142 (2013)
4. Frey, D., Woelk, P.O., Stockheim, T., Zimmermann, R.: Integrated multi-agent-based supply chain management. In: WET ICE 2003. Proceedings. Twelfth IEEE International Workshops on Enabling Technologies: Infrastructure for Collaborative Enterprises, pp. 24–29, June 2003
5. Giglio, D.: Task scheduling for multiple forklift AGVs in distribution warehouses. In: Proceedings of the 2014 IEEE Emerging Technology and Factory Automation (ETFA), pp. 1–6, September 2014
6. Kamagaew, A., Stenzel, J., Nettstraeter, A., ten Hompel, M.: Concept of cellular transport systems in facility logistics. In: 2011 5th International Conference on Automation, Robotics and Applications (ICARA), pp. 40–45, December 2011
7. Koebler, J.: Paula on tour (2017). https://audi-illustrated.com/en/audi-encounter-01-2017/paula-on-tour
8. ter Mors, A.: Conflict-free route planning in dynamic environments. In: International Conference on Intelligent Robots and Systems 2011, pp. 2166–2171 (2011)
9. Regele, R., Levi, P.: Cooperative multi-robot path planning by heuristic priority adjustment. In: 2006 IEEE/RSJ International Conference on Intelligent Robots and Systems, pp. 5954–5959, October 2006
10. Russell, S., Norvig, P.: Artificial Intelligence: A Modern Approach, Global Edition. Always Learning. Pearson Education, Limited, Harlow (2003)
11. Schwarz, C., Schachmanow, J., Sauer, J., Overmeyer, L., Ullmann, G.: Self guided vehicle systems. Logistics J. **2013**(12) (2013)
12. Čáp, M., Novák, P., Kleiner, A., Seleck, M.: Prioritized planning algorithms for trajectory coordination of multiple mobile robots. IEEE Trans. Autom. Sci. Eng. **12**(3), 835–849 (2015)
13. Yu, M., Zhang, W., Klemm, P.: Multi-agent based reconfigurable manufacturing execution system. In: 2007 IEEE International Conference on Industrial Engineering and Engineering Management, pp. 718–722, December 2007

Addressing the Challenges of Conservative Event Synchronization for the SARL Agent-Programming Language

Glenn Cich[1]([✉]), Stéphane Galland[2], Luk Knapen[1], Ansar-Ul-Haque Yasar[1], Tom Bellemans[1], and Davy Janssens[1]

[1] Transportation Research Institute (IMOB), Hasselt University, Agoralaan, 3590 Diepenbeek, Belgium
glenn.cich@uhasselt.be
[2] LE2I, Univ. Bourgogne Franche-Comté, UTBM, 90010 Belfort, France

Abstract. Synchronization mechanism is a key component of an agent-based simulation model and platform. Conservative and optimistic models were proposed in the domain of distributed and parallel simulations. However, the SARL agent-programming language is not equipped with specific simulation features, including synchronization mechanisms. The goal of this paper is to propose a conservative synchronization model for the SARL language and its run-time platform Janus.

Keywords: Multi-agent simulation · Conservative event synchronization · SARL agent programming language · Janus platform

1 Introduction

In agent-based simulations, the entire simulation task is divided into a set of smaller sub tasks each executed by a different agent. These agents may run in parallel, and communicate with each other by exchanging timestamped events or messages. In this paper, an event refers to an update to the simulation system's state at a specific simulation time instant. Throughout the simulation, events arrive at destination agents, and depending on the delivery ordering system of the simulation, they are processed differently. The two commonly used orderings are (i) event reception order and (ii) event timestamp order (the timestamp is assigned to the event by the emitting agent). With the first type, events are delivered to the destination processes when they arrive at the destination. On the other hand, with the timestamp-order, events are delivered in non-decreasing order of their timestamp, requiring runtime checks and buffering to ensure such ordering.

The key question is how to create a synchronization model, and its implementation, based on the SARL agent-programming language, and assuming that the execution platform is fully distributed. In this paper, the SARL agent-programming language is equipped with an event synchronization model with

© Springer International Publishing AG 2017
Y. Demazeau et al. (Eds.): PAAMS 2017, LNAI 10349, pp. 31–42, 2017.
DOI: 10.1007/978-3-319-59930-4_3

the following characteristics: (i) The model follows a conservative synchronization approach. (ii) The synchronization process is hidden to the agents by using the *capacity* and *skill* concepts. (iii) The agent environment is integrated into the synchronization process.

The remainder of the paper is organized as follows: in Sect. 2, an overview of the current state of the art is given. Section 3 introduces the agent based framework SARL that is used in the model described in this paper. Section 4 describes the method used to synchronize events in SARL. The evaluation of this method is described in Sect. 5. Finally, in Sect. 6, the paper is concluded.

2   Related Work

Parallel Discrete-Event Simulation (PDES) has received increasing interest as simulations become more time consuming and geographically distributed. A PDES consists of Logical Processes (LPs) acting as the simulation entities, which do not share any state variables (similar to agents) [3].

A PDES that exclusively supports interaction by exchanging timestamped messages obeys the local causality constraint if and only if each LP processes events in non-decreasing timestamp order [2]. To satisfy the local causality constraint, different synchronization techniques have been proposed for distributed systems which generally fall into two major classes of synchronization: *conservative or pessimistic*, which strictly avoids causality violations; and *optimistic*, which allows violations and recovers from them.

Conservative synchronization algorithms strictly avoid any occurrence of causality errors. To do so, the LP is blocked from further processing of events until it can make sure that the next event in its local future event list has a timestamp smaller than the arrival time of any event that might be arriving at the LP in the future. The main issue of any conservative parallel simulator is determining if it is safe for a processor to execute the next event. To deal with this issue, several techniques have been proposed which are further classified into four categories: methods with dead-lock avoidance, deadlock detection and recovery, synchronous operation, and conservative time windows.

Optimistic synchronization algorithms do not try to stop the LP's execution to synchronize them. It allows causality errors to occur and to be detected by the arrival of an event with a timestamp that is less than the local time of the receiving LP. Optimistic algorithms recover from the causality error by undoing the effects caused by those events processed speculatively during the previous computation. This recovery operation is known as *rollback*, during which the state of the LP is restored to the one that was saved just prior to the timestamp of the violating event. The main issue of any optimistic parallel simulator is related to the necessary storage space that is needed for recovery, and the positive ratio of the time spent for performing the recovery on the time spent for executing the behavior of the system.

In the past three decades, numerous approaches have been proposed by different researchers in this field. A number of surveys can be found in the literature which summarize both conservative and optimistic techniques [2,3,5,9,10,12].

In multiagent systems, several models of synchronization were proposed. In this domain, agents are assimilated to LPs. Weyns and Holvoet [13] describe a conservative synchronization module in the multiagent system that is based on the composition of the *synchronization$_a$* modules for each agent *a*. The approach of the model is to let synchronization be the natural consequence of situatedness of agents and not be part of the agents decision mechanism. This is reflected in the fact that the composition of a set of synchronized agents only depends on the actual perception of the agents. Such synchronization is based on the exchange of a structured set of synchronization messages.

Braubach et al. [1] propose a centralized service that has the role to manage the time evolution, and to notify the agent when the time is evolving. In this model, each agent notifies the time management service when it has finished its task for a given time period. This model is one of the most simple pessimistic synchronization algorithms. Its major drawback is related to the introduction of the centralized service that makes it harder and less efficient to distribute the agents over a computer network.

Xu et al. [15] propose an asynchronous conservative synchronization strategy for parallel agent-based traffic simulations. The authors propose to replace the global synchronization barrier in the multiagent system by a local synchronization strategy that enables agents to communicate individually and providing each of the agents with a heuristic for increasing the time-window look ahead in order to predict the next safe events.

3   SARL: An Agent-Oriented Programming Language

SARL[1] is a general-purpose agent-oriented programming language [11]. Such language should thus provide a reduced set of key concepts that focuses solely on the principles considered as essential to implement a multi-agent system. In this paper, four elements of the metamodel of SARL are used: Agent, Space, Capacity and Skill. These four concepts are explained below.

- **Agent:** An *Agent* is an autonomous entity having a set of skills to realize the capacities it exhibits. An agent has a set of built-in capacities considered essential to provide the commonly accepted competences of agents, such as autonomy, reactivity, proactivity and social capacities. The various behaviors of an agent communicate using an event-driven approach.
- **Space:** A *Space* is the abstraction to define an interaction space between agents or between agents and their environment, which may be the real world or a simulated environment. The simulated environment subsystem could be modeled with a multiagent system by itself. In the SARL toolkit, a concrete default space, which propagates events, called EventSpace is proposed.

---

[1] http://www.sarl.io.

- **Capacity:** *A Capacity is the specification of a collection of functions* that support the agent's capabilities, which are represented by the Capacity concept. This specification makes no assumptions about its implementation. It could be used to specify what an agent can do, i.e. what a behavior requires for its execution.
- **Skill:** A *Skill* is a possible implementation of a capacity fulfilling all the constraints of this specification.

The Janus platform[2] was redesigned and reimplemented in order to serve as the software execution environment of the SARL programs. Janus is designed in order to be a fully distributed platform over threads and a computer network. The execution unit in Janus is the event handler: the part of the SARL agent that is executed when a specific event is received. Each of these units are executed in parallel to the other units, even in the same agent.

The design of the Janus platform may cause issues for creating agent-based simulation applications. Indeed, several notions of time must be considered: user time (the real time, machine time) and simulated time. According to Lamport [7], simulated time is a logical clock that induces a partial ordering of events; it has been refined in distributed context as logical virtual time by Jefferson [6]. The Janus platform does not make any assumption on the ordering of the events that are exchanged by the agents. As a consequence it is impossible to use the Janus platform for agent-based simulation involving a time concept without providing the platform with a specific synchronization mechanism. A model of such a mechanism is described in Sect. 4. Agents timestamp the event notifications they emit using their current perception of simulated time (the logical clock). They perceive each other behavior as a sequence of events ordered by the logical clock. Agents can only emit events that comply to the Lamport partial order for logical time induced by the causality rule. In case agent A_0 uses information about agent A_1 notified by an event E_0 timestamped by $t(E_0)$, it can no longer notify any event E_1 that precedes E_0 in the partial order. This requires agents to synchronize their perception of the common logical clock.

Additionally, agent-based systems often include an *agent environment*, which is the software layer between the external world and the agents. This environment contains objects and resources, a.k.a. artifacts, that are not agents, but could be used by them. All the actions on the artifacts must be also synchronized in order to preserve the integrity of the agent environment state.

4   Event Synchronization Model for SARL

In this section, an event synchronization model for the SARL programming language and its Janus execution environment is presented.

A *time period* is delimited by two discrete moments in (real or simulated) time. Each *moment in time* can be thought to bear a label which is the *timestamp*. In the remaining part of the paper the terms *timestamp* and time

---

[2] http://www.janusproject.io.

period will be used interchangeably. Hence, the term *timestamp* is also used to identify the time period starting at the *moment in time* it is associated with.

According to the SARL metamodel, interaction among the simulation agents on one hand, and between the simulation agents and the agent environment on the other hand is supported by events. Each event e in the set $\mathbb{E}$ of events that are not already fired in the simulation agents is defined by a time stamped t_e and a content c_e. The timestamp t_e is the simulation time for which the event is fired. It is always greater or equal to the current simulation time t: $\forall e \in \mathbb{E}, e = \langle t_e, c_e \rangle \implies t_e \geq t$.

4.1 General Architecture

The proposed event synchronization model is designed by considering the following three major assumptions and constraints (in bold face).

The **synchronization process is hidden to the agents** by using the capacity and skill concepts. Indeed, the synchronization process is related to the simulation and not to the simulation agent architectures and models. For example, the simulation agent models should be the same if they are instantiated during simulation or deployed on embedded computers. In order to enforce this characteristic, we propose to provide skills that are implementing the standard interaction agent capability, which is provided by the SARL metamodel, with the proposed synchronization mechanisms. This approach enables a clear distinction between the application-dependent models in the agents, and the simulator-dependent modules. It increases the level of abstraction that the framework will provide to application developers.

The **agent environment is part of the simulated system**. The agent environment as a key component of the system must be considered in the event synchronization model. In this work, we assume that the agent environment is modeled with a complex hierarchy of agents, as proposed by Galland and Gaud [4]. The root agent in this hierarchy represents the entire environment for the application logic layer (even if the environment is distributed over multiple environmental agents). In the context of this paper, and for simplicity reasons, we make use of two kinds of agents: (i) an *environment agent*, and (ii) a *simulation agent*, which represents the application logic's agent.

The **event synchronization model follows a conservative synchronization approach**. As explained in Sect. 2, two major approaches of synchronization can be considered: conservative and optimistic. In order to select the best approach, we have considered the two types of interaction between the simulation agents and the environment: (i) the simulation agents perceive the state of the environment; and (ii) the simulation agent acts in order to change the state of the environment. First, consider the data representing the perception of an agent at simulation time t: this needs to be extracted from the same state of the environment for all agents in order to ensure the consistency of the agents' behaviors for time t. Second, the simulation agents are supposed to act in the environment simultaneously and autonomously. Solving the joint actions of the agents requires to avoid them to directly change the environment's state.

Agents are sending desires of actions, named *influences*, that are gathered and used by the agent environment in order to compute its next state. This approach is known as the influence-reaction model [8]. Because the agent environment may be modeled by means of a hierarchy of agents, according to Galland and Gaud [4], the influence-reaction model may be locally applied if each subagent inside the environment is supporting a specific spatial zone. The influence-reaction model implies the introduction of at least one rendez-vous point during the simulation process: the agent environment is waiting for all the simulation agents to provide their influences. Besides the types of interaction, one can take into account the possible drawbacks of an optimistic approach. The optimistic approach will need a lot of space in order to store the different states of the simulation. This indicates as well that this approach will be application dependent because the used data structures are application specific which might induce burden to the designer/programmer. The type of applications we have in mind need a strict synchronization between a lot of agents. The possibility of rollbacks will be very high and hence very time consuming. The bottle neck we introduce with our conservative mechanism will probably cause less time loss in these cases. These considerations lead us to select a conservative approach in designing our event synchronization model.

Synchronization-Unaware Simulation Agent Architecture. The general architecture for the simulation agents can be described by Algorithm 1.1. The simulation agents are able to react to `PerceptionEvent` events, which are fired by the agent environment to notify the simulation agent that its perception has changed. When the simulation agent has executed its reaction behavior, it sends its list of desired actions to the agent environment by calling the `influence` function. This function is provided by the `EnvironmentInteractionCapacity` capacity (Algorithm 1.1), which represents the capacity of an agent to interact with its environment. The `EnvironmentInteractionCapacity` implementation will pack the influences into an occurrence of the `AgentIsReadyEvent` event, and send the latter to the agent environment. The simulation agent is also able to react to events that were fired by other simulation agents.

```
   agent SimulationAgent {
2     uses EnvironmentInteractionCapacity
      on PerceptionEvent {
4        /* React on the perception receiving from the environment */
         [...]
6        /* Send AgentIsReadyEvent to the environment */
         influence ([...])
8     }
      on Event {
10       /* React on events from simulation agents */
         [...]
12    }
   }
14 capacity EnvironmentInteractionCapacity {
      def influence(desiredActions : Object*)
16 }
```

Algorithm 1.1. General algorithm for the simulation agents and definition of the `EnvironmentInteractionCapacity` capacity.

All the agents in the SARL specification are provided with built-in capacities for which the execution platform provides the implementation. The first built-in capacity that is relevant to our synchronization model is `Time`. It provides the functions for accessing the value of the current simulation time t. The second built-in capacity is `Behaviors`. It provides the `asEventListener` function, which replies the entry point for all events that are received by the agent. This capacity also provides the `wake` function to emit events inside the context of the agent itself. Specific implementation of these two capacities will be provided in Sect. 4.2 in order to integrate our synchronization model in a way that is transparent to the simulation agent.

Synchronization-Unaware Environment Architecture. The general architecture for the simulation agents can be described by Algorithm 1.2. In this paper, we consider that the agent environment can be modelled using a dedicated (holonic) agent according to the model proposed by Galland and Gaud [4], in which the proposed agent represents the agent environment and is managing time evolution.

```
     agent AgentEnvironment {
2      uses TimeManager
       var expectedNumberOfInfluences : Integer
4      var influences : List
       on StartSimulationStep {
6          sendPerceptionsToAgents
       }
8      on AgentIsReadyEvent {
           influences += occurrence
10         if (influences.size == expectedNumberOfInfluences) {
               appliesInfluencesToEnvironmentState
12             readyForTimeEvolution
           }
14     }
     }
```

Algorithm 1.2. General algorithm for the agent environment.

The agent environment is waiting for the `StartSimulationStep` event that is fired by the platform's time manager[3]. When the event is received, the agent environment computes the agents' perception from the environment's state and sends `PerceptionEvent` events to the simulation agents. The implementation of the `sendPerceptionsToAgents` is application specific; it is not detailed in this paper. When receiving the `PerceptionEvent` occurrence, each simulation agent updates its knowledge with the timestamp of the event.

After sending the perception to the simulation agents, the agent environment is waiting for the agents' influences, according to the influence-reaction model [8]. When all the expected influences are received, the agent environment updates its state, and notifies the time manager that the simulation time t can evolve. Indeed, inside a simulation process including an environment as a whole entity, the simulation agent at time t can evolve according to the state of the

---

[3] The time manager is a platform module or another agent that is storing and managing the time t over the simulation.

environment [8,14]. Basically, time evolution might be modeled by $t' := t + \Delta t$, where t is the current simulation time, Δt is a constant time evolution amount, and t' is the new simulation time.

Additionally, we have considered to dynamically determine the time increment using $t' := \min\{t_e | \forall e \in \mathbb{E}, t_e > t\}$. This approach is still vulnerable to deadlocks of simulation agents when they enter a deadlock or unexpectedly crash. In this case, the agent environment will wait infinitely for their response and hence the simulation will end in a deadlock as well. However this issue can be solved by using the machine time in order to detect a deadlock. The environment agent could keep track of the expected execution time per agent. When an agent exceeds this time, the environment agent could assume there is something wrong; the environment agent can proceed and ask the agent in deadlock to leave the simulation. In case a simulation agent wants to leave the simulation (deliberately stop, or crash) the environment agent is aware of that by listening the specific events fired by the execution platform and can update its list of agents to monitor.

4.2 Conservative Event Synchronization Mechanism

The event buffering is needed to ensure a pessimistic approach. The main idea is that simulation agents can send events to each other, but the events are not directly fired to the appropriate simulation agent. Hence, if a simulation agent decides to send an event to another simulation agent, this event is saved somewhere within the agent. This is done for every event that is sent for a given time period.

In the SARL specification, events may be received by an agent from another agent or from itself. In the first case, the Behaviors built-in capacity provides the agent's event listener that could be used for receiving the events. For supporting the second case, the Behaviors capacity provides the wake function for firing an event inside the context of the agent. For every simulation agent, the events that are received from other agents, or from itself are intercepted by a specific skill implementation of the Behaviors capacity. The intercepted events are kept in a bucket until a specific event of type TimeStepEvent that is representing a time step in the simulation is received. The PerceptionEvent event described in the previous section is a subtype of TimeStepEvent. Consequently, when a simulation agent receives its perception from the agent environment, all the buffered events for the current simulation time are fired in the agent context as well as the PerceptionEvent whose occurrence advances the agent's time to the next timestamp. Algorithm 1.3 provides a SARL implementation of the specific skill. The internal class InternalBuffer is defined to represent the event buffer (defined as a multiple-value map).

If the received event e is not of type TimeStepEvent, e is buffered. Each event is mapped to a time interval with the *filter* function $(t_e \mapsto [t_i, t_{i+1}[)$ where $t_e \in [t_i, t_{i+1}[$ is the event timestamp and t_i and t_{i+1} are consecutive values of discrete time in the simulation. Hence for a given time t, the agent has to process a list of events $\{e | e \in \mathbb{E}, \textit{filter}(t) = \textit{filter}(t_e)\}$. If the event e is not explicitly timestamped, then the default timestamp is assumed to be equal to the time of the next simulation step (computed by the nextTimeStep function in Algorithm 1.3).

In a simulation agent, if the received event e is of type TimeStepEvent, the current simulation *time* is updated with the timestamp of e. Due to our conservative synchronization approach, this timestamp is equal to the global time simulation. Additionally, the buffered events are consumed and fired into the current simulation agent by using the default event listener (provided by the execution platform). Finally, the SynchronizationAwareSkill implements the two functions of the Behaviors capacity that correspond to the two methods for receiving events: the asEventListener and wake functions.

```
     skill SynchronizationAwareSkill implements Behaviors , Time {
2       val defaultSkill : Behaviors
        val eventBuffer : EventListener
4       var time : Integer
        new (platformSkill : Behaviors) {
6         defaultSkill = platformSkill; eventBuffer = new InternalBuffer
        }
8       def asEventListener : EventListener { return eventBuffer }
        def wake(e : Event) { eventBuffer.receiveEvent(e) }
10      def getTime : Integer { return time }
        def nextTimeStep : Integer { return time + 1 }
12      class InternalBuffer implements EventListener {
          val buffer : Map<Integer , Collection<Event>> = new MultiMap
14        def receiveEvent(e : Event) {
            if (e instanceof TimeStepEvent) {
16            time = e.timestamp
              var events = buffer.remove(time)
18            for (be : events) {
                defaultSkill.asEventListener.receiveEvent(be)
20            }
              defaultSkill.asEventListener.receiveEvent(e)
22          } else {
              var timestamp = if (e instanceof TimestampedEvent) e.
     timestamp
24                                    else nextTimeStep
              if (timestamp > time) {
26              buffer.put(timestamp , e)
              }
28          }
          }
30      }
      }
```

Algorithm 1.3. Skill implementation of behaviors and time capacities.

The second built-in capacity that must be overridden to enable event synchronization is the Time capacity. This capacity provides the getTime function that is returning the current simulation time. In Algorithm 1.3, we define the local attribute time, which is the local simulation time from the agent point of view. According to our conservative approach, this local time is updated with the global simulation time that is the timestamp of a received TimeStepEvent occurrence.

In order to use the previously defined SynchronizationAwareSkill skill, it must be given to the simulation agent as the skill to be used when the functions of Behaviors and Time are invoked. In order to ensure that the synchronization process is hidden to the agents, we cannot change the definition of the simulation agents. Algorithm 1.4 describes this discarded approach, which is based on the explicit creation of an instance of the `SynchronizationAwareSkill` skill, with the `Behaviors` skill from the platform as argument. This skill instance is mapped to the two capacities `Behaviors` and `Time`. From this point the agent is automatically synchronized with the rest of the system.

```
  agent SimulationAgent {
2   on Initialize {
      var syncSkill = new SynchronizationAwareSkill(getSkill(Behaviors))
4     setSkill(syncSkill, Behaviors, Time)
    }
6   [...]
  }
```

Algorithm 1.4. Bad practice: explicit set of the synchronization skill in the simulation agents.

We consider that a better approach is to install the `Synchronization AwareSkill` skill when a another simulation-based skill is installed into the agent. We have defined the `EnvironmentInteractionCapacity` capacity in Sect. 4.1. The corresponding skill may be defined in order to install the synchronization skill when it is installed, as illustrated by Algorithm 1.5.

```
  skill SimulationEnvironmentInteractionSkill implements
      EnvironmentInteractionCapacity {
2   def install {
      var syncSkill = new SynchronizationAwareSkill(getSkill(Behaviors))
4     setSkill(syncSkill, Behaviors, Time)
    }
6   [...]
  }
```

Algorithm 1.5. Good practice: installing the synchronization skill from another simulation skill.

5 Performance

In order to be able to measure the performance without being biased by application related calculations, we created a very simple ping-pong application.

In the time period starting at T_0, every agent has 20 % probability to emit a *ping* message to X other agents where $X \sim Uniform(1 : 100)$. The message needs to be delivered in the time period $T_d \sim Uniform(T_1 : T_e)$ where T_e denotes the end of simulated time. The measured time is illustrated in Fig. 1, where T_0 and T_1 denote the start and the end of the interval; T_a denotes the end of the reception of the events sent by the environment to the simulation agents; T_b the end of "application level payload work" done by the agents, and finally T_c the end of delivering the `AgentIsReadyEvent` to the environment. For every time period, the amount of emitted messages is computed together with the total amount of time needed to execute this time period. Experiments are realized for 200 agents on a Linux Ubuntu 14.04LTS laptop with 8 GB memory and a Intel Core i5-4210M CPU 2.60 GHz × 4. The number of time periods that are simulated is 2 500.

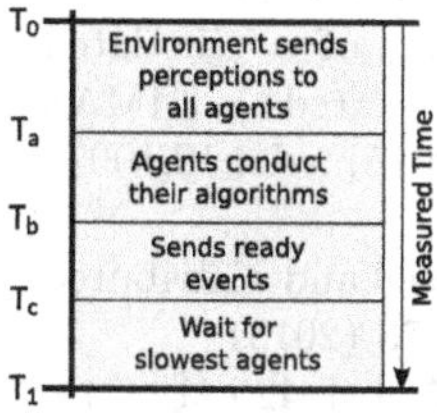

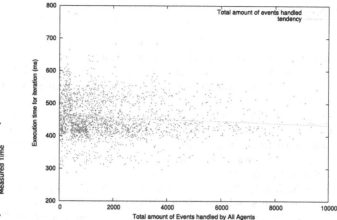

Fig. 1. An overview of the time measurement in our experiments.

Fig. 2. Graph that represents the total amount of events handled in a specific iteration (x-axis) against the total execution time for that iteration in ms (y-axis) for the case of 200 agents and 2 500 iterations.

Experimental results are illustrated in the graph represented in Fig. 2. In our experiments, all the agents have the same actions to do. Consequently, they have approximately the same execution time. It is clear to see that the execution time follows a constant tendency, and hence seems to be independent of the number of processed events over the full range of observations. The execution time for a single period between two consecutive increments of simulated time includes: perception of the environment, application specific *payload* work and end-of-period notification. The duration required for the payload work in the experiment is negligible. The large variance of the execution time masks the expected dependency on the number of events.

6 Conclusion and Perspectives

A proof of concept is given for the support of the event synchronization using the SARL language and its Janus execution platform, without changing neither the specification of SARL nor the code of the Janus platform. Similar to Weyns and Holvoet [13], we plan refining our model by including regional synchronization. Another perspective is to provide an optimistic synchronization model. From a technological point-of-view, our synchronization mechanism will be included into the Janus execution platform.

Acknowledgments. The research reported was partially funded by the IWT 135026 Smart-PT: Smart Adaptive Public Transport (ERA-NET Transport III Flagship Call 2013 "Future Traveling").

References

1. Braubach, L., Pokahr, A., Lamersdorf, W., Krempels, K.-H., Woelk, P.-O.: A generic simulation service for distributed multi-agent systems. In: In From Agent Theory to Agent Implementation (AT2AI 2004), pp. 576–581 (2004)
2. Fujimoto, R.: Parallel discrete event simulation. Commun. ACM **33**(10), 30–53 (1990)
3. Fujimoto, R.: Parallel and Distributed Simulation Systems. Wiley, New York (2000)
4. Galland, S., Gaud, N.: Organizational and holonic modelling of a simulated and synthetic spatial environment. In: Weyns, D., Michel, F. (eds.) E4MAS 2014. LNCS, vol. 9068, pp. 147–169. Springer, Cham (2015). doi:10.1007/978-3-319-23850-0_10
5. Jafer, S., Lui, Q., Wainer, G.: Synchronization methods in parallel and distributed discrete-event simulation. Simul. Model. Pract. Theory **30**, 54–73 (2013)
6. Jefferson, D.: Virtual time. ACM Trans. Program Lang Syst. **7**, 404–425 (1985)
7. Lamport, L.: TI clocks, and the ordering of events in a distributed system. Commun. ACM **21**, 558–565 (1978)
8. Michel, F.: The IRM4S model: the influence/reaction principle for multiagent based simulation. In: Sixth International Joint Conference on Autonomous Agents and Multiagent Systems (AAMAS07). ACM, Honolulu, Hawaii, USA (2007)
9. Perumalla, K.: Parallel and distributed simulation: traditional techniques and recent advances. In: Proceedings of the 2006 Winter Simulation Conference, Monterey, CA, pp. 84–95 (2006)
10. Perumalla, K., Fujimoto, R.: Virtual time synchronization over unreliable network transport. In: Proceedings of the 15th International Workshop on Parallel and Distributed Simulation, Lake Arrowhead, CA, pp. 129–136 (2001)
11. Rodriguez, S., Gaud, N., Galland, S.: SARL: a general-purpose agent-oriented programming language. In: 2014 IEEE/WIC/ACM International Joint Conferences on Web Intelligence (WI) and Intelligent Agent Technologies (IAT), vol. 3, pp. 103–110, August 2014
12. Tropper, C.: Parallel discrete-event simulation applications. J. Parallel Distrib. Comput. **62**(2), 327–335 (2002)
13. Weyns, D., Holvoet, T.: Model for situated multi-agent systems with regional synchronization. In: Concurrent Engineering. Agents and Multi-agent Systems, Madeira, Portugal, pp. 177–188 (2003)
14. Weyns, D., Omicini, A., Odell, J.: Environment as a first-class abstraction in multi-agent systems. Auton. Agent. Multi-Agent Syst. **14**(1), 5–30 (2007)
15. Xu, Y., Cai, W., Aydt, H., Lees, M., Zehe, D.: An asynchronous synchronization strategy for parallel large-scale agent-based traffic simulations. In: SIGSIM-PADS 2015, London, United Kingdom, June 2015

Agent-Based Integration of Complex and Heterogeneous Distributed Energy Resources in Virtual Power Plants

Anders Clausen[1]([✉]), Aisha Umair[1], Yves Demazeau[2],
and Bo Nørregaard Jørgensen[1]

[1] University of Southern Denmark, Odense, Denmark
{ancla,bnj}@mmmi.sdu.dk
[2] University of Grenoble Alpes, CNRS, LIG, 38000 Grenoble, France
yves.demazeau@imag.fr

Abstract. A Virtual Power Plant aggregates several Distributed Energy Resources in order to expose them as a single, controllable entity. This enables smaller Distributed Energy Resources to take part in Demand Response programs which traditionally only targeted larger consumers. To date, models for Virtual Power Plants have considered Distributed Energy Resources as simple, atomic entities. However, often Distributed Energy Resources constitute complex and heterogeneous entities with a mix of multiple, controllable loads, generators and electrical storage units which must be coordinated locally. This paper proposes an agent-based method for integration of complex, heterogeneous Distributed Energy Resources into Virtual Power Plants. The approach models Distributed Energy Resources and Virtual Power Plants as agents with multi-objective, multi-issue reasoning. This enables modeling of VPPs constituting complex and heterogeneous Distributed Energy Resources with multiple, local objectives and decision points. The properties of the approach are illustrated using different Virtual Power Plant scenarios, which include Distributed Energy Resources of various types and complexities.

Keywords: Demand response · Load balancing · Load management · Multi-agent systems · Distributed Energy Resources · Virtual Power Plant

1 Introduction

Distributed Energy Resources (DER) encompass generators, electricity storage and flexible loads or consumers [13]. The penetration of DER in the electricity grid is increasing as a result of several factors, including deployment of renewable energy generators, and small "home-sized" generators in the form of photovoltaic rooftop panels and local storage units such as the Tesla Powerwall. When this is combined with the fact that the pervasiveness of home automation systems is increasing, this implies that what was traditionally considered a passive

© Springer International Publishing AG 2017
Y. Demazeau et al. (Eds.): PAAMS 2017, LNAI 10349, pp. 43–55, 2017.
DOI: 10.1007/978-3-319-59930-4_4

demand side, becomes a potentially valuable active asset in a grid management context. Grid management has traditionally considered large, centralized generation capacity. This is reflected in electricity markets, which lacks support for smaller resources to be integrated. To this end, the concept of a virtual power plant (VPP) aggregates several DER, in order to expose them as a single, controllable entity [12]. This means that smaller DER are able to overcome entrance thresholds of existing markets, and offer their services through a VPP. In a VPP context, the autonomous nature of such resources must be preserved. Furthermore, DER are inherently heterogeneous constituting either generators, electrical storage or flexible loads or a combination of these. Existing approaches for VPP can generally be classified as either a centralized or a decentralized. Centralized VPPs assume control over assets on the DER side, and control these in response to external events. Examples include [9,10], who suggest an algorithm for integration of DER using an Integer Linear Program (ILP), [8] who proposes the "PowerHub" concept, a centralized VPP which been deployed into a real-life market context and [6,7] who propose a bidding strategy for VPPs to enable participation in the energy and spinning reserves market. However, common for the centralized approach is that it generally violates the autonomy of the DER. Decentralized VPPs on the other hand are designed to preserve the autonomy of DER. Here the VPP entity negotiates with DER in order to influence their operation schedule in a way, which ensures that external events are considered. In [11] the authors propose an algorithm for self-organizing, dynamic VPPs, where the current market situation is used to form VPPs which best suits the contemporary conditions. PowerMatcher presented in [3–5] is another example of a decentralized VPP, where an agent-based approach is taken to integrate "behind the meter" devices into electricity markets. However, although recognizing DER as autonomous and heterogeneous, these approaches fail to recognize DER as complex entities with several local decision points (e.g. actuators in the form of generators, controllable loads and electric storage units) and objectives. The authors of [2] propose a method for integrating complex, manageable loads into a VPP. They do however not consider generators or storage units in their DER portfolio.

This paper proposes a MAS-based approach for integrating complex, heterogeneous and autonomous DER in VPPs. The approach extends the model presented in [2] by including formal descriptions of an agent model as well as models for DER constituting generators, storage units and manageable loads which reflects the complexity faced in real-life scenarios. We illustrate the properties of the model in several experiments with VPP scenarios of varying types and complexity.

In Sect. 2 the proposed model is presented and formalized. Section 3 then applies the model to a VPP design. Section 4 presents the experiments conducted based on the design, along with their results and Sect. 5 concludes the paper.

2   Agent Model

We model DER and VPP entities as agents in a MAS. Agents have multi-objective, multi-issue reasoning decision making capabilities. This is enabled by mapping decision points, constitution points of actuation in the agent's domain into *issues*. Objectives in the agent domain are mapped into *concerns* which form an agent-specific utility space for the agents' issues. Concerns will map suggestions for issue values into a resulting domain state and compare this towards a concern-specific preferred domain state referred to as a *preference*. Agents employ a genetic algorithm (GA) to explore the solution space for a valid solution. Initially, a population of random candidate solution proposals for values of issues in the agent domain are generated. Each concern in the agent will evaluate each candidate solution proposal by calculating a cost for the proposal. The GA applies elitism based on the Pareto criteria to create a population of solution proposals which marks a new generation. This population is used to generate a new population of candidate solution proposals and this process continues until the epoch ends, where a solution is chosen from the final population.

2.1   Issue Model

An issue is associated with a name and specifies the format of the values which the issue can take on. In general, an issue generates values on a vector-form, which means that the issue value specification includes a dimension of the value vector, s^{size}, the minimum and maximum values that the issue may take on, s^{min} and s^{max}, as well as a step size, s^{step}, which defines valid values within the boundaries defined by s^{min} and s^{max}. The issue model is formally defined in Eqs. 1, 2 and 3.

$$\left(s^{min}, s^{max}\right) \in \mathbb{R}, s^{min} < s^{max} \tag{1}$$

$$s^{step} = \frac{s^{max} - s^{min}}{w}, w \in \mathbb{N}_{>0} \tag{2}$$

$$\boldsymbol{s} = [s_1, ..., s_{s^{size}}]$$
$$\text{where} \tag{3}$$
$$s \in \left\{x | x \leq s^{max}, x = s^{min} + j \cdot s^{step}, j \in \mathbb{N}\right\}$$

As an example consider a thermostat: A thermostat can take on integer values in a given range, e.g. 15 °C to 40 °C. If we assume, that we want to find a setpoint schedule across 24 hours in 1 hour resolution for this thermostat, we can define it as an issue with $s^{min} = 15$, $s^{max} = 40$, $s^{step} = 1$ and $s^{size} = 24$. The implementation of our issue model then ensures that values generated by the issue will always be vectors with 24 elements, where each element is an integer-value in the interval $[15, 40]$.

2.2 Concern Model

A concern extracts values for issues in which it has an interest, from each solution proposal. The concern transforms these issue values into a domain state vector, which is comparable to the concern's preference. As this perception is specific to the concern, the transformation of issue values into a domain state vector is concern specific as well. The concern then performs an evaluation by calculating the Euclidean distance between the preference and the domain state vector. The concern may either choose to evaluate based on absolute distance between the preference and the domain state vector, or use "at least" or "at most" operators to determine, if a distance between two elements in the vectors should contribute to the cost calculated in the evaluation. To extend the example from before, a concern could have an interest in the temperature of a room. If the temperature of a room depends on the heating contribution from a radiator and the airflow of a ventilation system, the concern has an interest in issues which maps to the thermostat of the radiator and the setpoint of the ventilation system (or the opening of its valve). The concern will extract issue values from solution proposals which maps to the respective ventilation system and thermostat issues, calculate the effects on the room temperature, and compare the result with the concern's preference for room temperatures.

2.3 Inter-agent Negotiation

An agent uses concerns to engage in communication with other agents. The concept is reflected in Fig. 1. Agents assign values from the message bus as preferences of concerns, in order to make decisions which take into account the decisions of other agents. An agent may choose to publish its decisions or subsets of these in order to make these available to other agents. Finally, agents may control decision points in physical domains but this is an optional property, as agents can represent virtual entities. An agent prioritizes concerns in order to control the influence that other agents exert on its decision making. *Mission critical concerns* reflect concerns, which must be fulfilled to satisfy local requirements in the agent's domain. *Negotiation critical concerns* are concerns which are configured to obtain preferences based on the decision making of other agents. Finally, *non-mission critical concerns* are used to represent desirable or nice-to-have features. An example here could be a concern who strives to operate the domain energy efficiently. Agents will select solutions which first minimize cost for mission critical concerns, then the negotiation critical concerns and finally the non-mission critical concerns.

3 VPP Model

The purpose of the VPP in our model is to expose an electricity profile which adheres to incoming demand response (DR) [2] events. The VPP will create electricity profiles for each DER which considers their local properties while

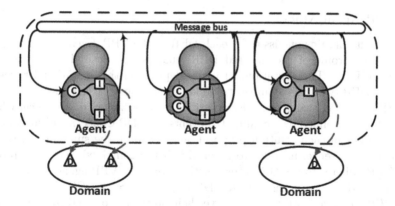

Fig. 1. Illustration of inter-agent negotiation. Triangles marked with a D reflect domain decision points, circles marked with a C reflect objectives and squares marked with an I reflect issues

addressing the DR event. The VPP model contains two types of agents: VPP agents and DER agents. A VPP constitutes a single VPP agent which engages in bilateral negotiation with DER agents, representing DER in the VPP. The VPP agent obtains knowledge of the forecasted electricity profile of the DER agents before they engage in the negotiation as shown in Fig. 2. Here, the VPP agent reacts to a DR event by calculating proposals for DER agents. The VPP agent propagates the proposals to the DER agents, who respond with counter proposals. Negotiation continues until either an agreement is reached (where the proposals of the VPP agent is equal to the counter proposals of the DER agents), a fixed number of negotiation cycles has been reached or a time limit is reached. The protocol is synchronous which means that the VPP agent will generate solution proposals to DER agents, who will generate and send counter proposals in response to this.

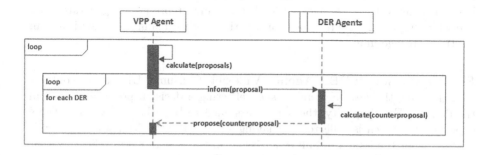

Fig. 2. Interaction between VPP- and DER agents.

3.1 VPP Agent Model

A VPP agent contains one issue for each DER in the VPP. Each issue describes an electricity profile of a connected DER; that is, the desired future domain state of the DER. The definitions of issues depend on the operational range of connected DER, which is assumed to be known to the VPP-agent.

A VPP-agent contains one mission-critical concern, the *DR Concern*, which has a preference defined by incoming DR events. The DR Concern will summarize all issue values in each solution proposal, and compare the summarized vector towards its preference, in order to determine if the combined electricity profile of the VPP adheres to the DR event. Furthermore, the VPP agent contains two negotiation critical concerns for each DER agent: A *Sum-DER concern* and a *Time-DER concern*. Both concerns have their preference defined by the counter proposal of the DER agent they represent. The Time-DER concern compares the values of the counter proposal towards the values of its corresponding issue in solution proposals. It will calculate a cost as the absolute Euclidean distance between the two. The Sum-DER Concern looks at the distance between the sum of allocations in the counter proposal and the sum of its corresponding issue values in solution proposals. The configuration with two concerns for each DER is necessary for supporting load shifting, where the VPP wants to reallocate electricity from a time slot. If only the Time-DER concern is present in the VPP, a situation can arise, where a solution which takes one unit of allocation from one DER, and allocates it to another DER is selected over one, which shifts allocation for a single DER. To overcome this, the Sum-DER Concern will add a cost, if the combined allocation does not match the counter proposal of the DER it represents. Hence, if a unit of allocation is removed or added to a DER, this concern will return a cost higher than 0. In this way, load shifting of one DER is preferred over combination of load shedding/valley filling across two DER.

3.2 DER Agent Models

In this paper we present three DER agent models: One which represents a flexible consumer with a manageable load, one which represents a generator and one which represents a prosumer constituting both a manageable load and an electrical storage unit.

Flexible Consumer DER Agent. A Flexible Consumer DER agent contains a single issue, the *Load Schedule issue*, reflecting a decision point for a load in the domain. For simplicity, the load is assumed to be either on or off in these experiments, which is reflected by having $s^{min} = 0$, $s^{max} = 1$ and $s^{step} = 1$. s^{size} is 24 for the issue (and all other issues in the experiments) reflecting that an electricity profile is calculated for the next 24 h. The Flexible Consumer DER agent also contains three concerns: A *Production concern*, a *VPP concern* and a *Minimize Consumption* concern. The Production concern strives to achieve some production target in the domain, and is configured as being mission-critical. The production is assumed to be depending on the output of the load. Hence, the

Production concern has an interest in the operation of the load to achieve a production goal within a given time frame (in this experiment assumed to be 24 h). This means that the preference of the Production concern only holds a single element which specifies the production target. The Production concern has a model which specifies the contribution of the load towards the production target over the course of 24 h, which means that time of allocation plays a role. Hence, the Production concern is not interested in the time of allocation of electricity. Instead, it is interested in reaching a production goal, which yields the intrinsic flexibility of the DER. This means that electricity can be allocated to any slot, as long as the combined contribution of the electricity profile (i.e. the output of the load) is sufficient to reach the production target. The Minimize Consumption concern attempts to minimize the amount of electricity consumed in the domain. It does so by having a preference with a single element of value 0, which represent the sum of electricity that the Minimize Consumption concern would like to reach. Naturally, this conflicts with the Production concern (assuming the Production concern has a production target > 0). Hence, in order to guarantee that the production target is reached in the domain, the Minimize Consumption concern is prioritized as non-mission critical. By default this means that a Flexible Consumer DER agent will reach its production target with the most energy efficient schedule. The VPP concern maps the connected VPP-agent into the decision logic of the Flexible Consumer DER agent with a preference containing the current suggestion of the VPP for an electricity profile for the DER. The VPP concern will attempt to minimize distance between this suggestion and the value for the Load Schedule issue.

Generator DER Agent. A Generator DER agent is configured with two concerns, a *Generator concern* and a *VPP concern*, as well as a single issue, the *Generator issue*. The Generator issue represents the only decision point of the generator domain used here - namely the operation of the generator. Generator Issue values constitute suggestions for operation levels of the generator. This issue is defined by $s^{min} = -2$, $s^{max} = 0$ and $s^{step} = 1$ which gives it three operating levels (-2, -1 and 0 respectively). s^{size} is again 24. Note that the value-range of the issue is negative. This reflects a negative contribution to an electricity profile, where positive values indicate consumption.

The Generator concern is responsible for local operation of the generator and - as a result - it is modeled as a mission-critical concern. The Generator concern has a preference, which reflects a desired operation schedule of the generator. Thus, here the preference maps directly to the values of the Generator issue. The Generator concern will evaluate suggestions for Generator issue values as an absolute distance between the suggestion and the preference. The preference of the Generator concern used in the experiment is shown in Fig. 3a. The last concern in the Generator DER agent, the VPP concern, has a configuration which resembles that of the VPP concern in the Flexible Consumer DER agent.

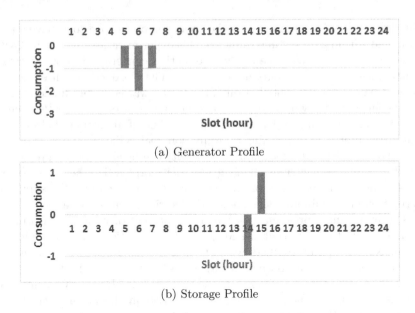

(a) Generator Profile

(b) Storage Profile

Fig. 3. Preferences for the Generator- and Storage concerns.

Prosumer DER Agent. A Prosumer DER agent is similar to the Flexible Consumer DER-agent but with an additional issue, the *Storage issue*, which represents the charge/discharge schedule of the storage unit. This issue is defined with $s^{min} = -1$, $s^{max} = 1$ and $s^{step} = 1$, which gives the storage unit 3 operating levels at -1, 0 and 1 respectively. Here negative values means that the unit discharges and positive values means that the unit charges. s^{size} is 24 as in the other cases. This means that the Prosumer DER agent has an operating range from -1 (when discharging the storage unit and not consuming) to 2 (when charging and consuming simultaneously), and the issue definition in the VPP agent for Prosumer DER agents must reflect this. Furthermore, the preferences of the Sum-DER concern and Time-DER concern representing the Prosumer DER Agent in the VPP-agent's decision logic, must be defined as the sum of issue values for the Load Schedule issue and the Storage issue proposed by the Prosumer DER Agent. A Prosumer DER agent also contains an additional concern, the *Storage concern*, which is similar to the Production concern except that it addresses the Storage issue (and not the Load Schedule issue), and has a preference which resembles a desired storage operating profile. This profile shown in Fig. 3b where positive values reflect charge and negative values reflect discharge of the storage unit.

4 Experiments

To illustrate the properties of the proposed VPP model, two sets of experiments have been conducted. For all experiments, the goal is to determine an electricity profile for each DER, which conforms to an external request for a combined electricity profile of the VPP. The external requests for a combined electricity profile in the VPP simulate different DR actions. The DR actions include "load shedding" which is a reduction in the electricity consumption without any compensation at another time, "load shifting" where consumption is moved from one slot to another, and valley filling which is an increase in consumption in one slot without shedding consumption in another slot [1]. Assuming we have a baseline electricity profile across 24 h for the VPP, which corresponds to the electricity consumption of the VPP with no external influence, DR may be performed by requesting an alteration of the baseline electricity profile. The baseline electricity profile for the VPP varies across the two sets of experiments, as the baseline electricity profile of each DER depends on the type of DER agent used.

4.1   VPP with Generator DER and Flexible Consumer DER

This set of experiments was conducted with 1 Generator DER agent and 3 Flexible Consumer DER agents. To simulate heterogeneous consumer domains, contribution ascribed to load operation is varied across the agents. Four experiments were conducted: A baseline experiment, an experiment with load shedding, an experiment with valley filling and an experiment with load shifting. The baseline experiment serves to show the combined electricity profile of the VPP when no DR event is pending. From Fig. 4a we see the demand of each DER as well as the allocation proposed by the VPP. Each color represent a DER, with the lighter colored bars being allocations and the darker colored bars being electricity profiles of the DER. Numbers 1 to 3 cover the Flexible Load DER agents and 4 maps to the Generator DER agent. For brevity, we will refer to these as DER 1 to 4 in the following. The red dotted line is used throughout the experiments to have a reference towards the baseline, when the electricity profiles are altered. As can be seen from the Fig. 4a, allocation in this case matches electricity profiles of the DER, as would be expected. In the load shedding experiment, a DR event has been received which forces the VPP to reduce consumption in slot 10. As can be seen from Fig. 4b, the VPP agent proposes a reduced allocation for DER 1. But as DER 1 is not compensated with additional allocation in a different time slot, this leads to a conflict, where allocation and demand is not equal, as would be expected. How to deal with this conflict depends on the type of VPP. In a commercial VPP, the demand of DER 1 is likely to be honored, thereby accepting a probable loss of electricity market revenue, whereas in a technical VPP, the allocation represents an absolute limit on allocation, hence forcing DER 1 to alter its consumption. It should be noted however, that general methods for handling these conflicts are outside the scope of this paper. In the valley filling experiment of Fig. 4c, the VPP receives a DR event which mandates an increase of consumption in slot 6. As the Flexible Consumer DER agents are unable to consume more than a single unit of electricity in these experiments, DER 4 is allocated less generation from the VPP-agent. However, as DER 4 must adhere to its mission critical concern, which follows a fixed generation schedule, this leads to a conflict, as expected. Again the handling of these conflicts depends

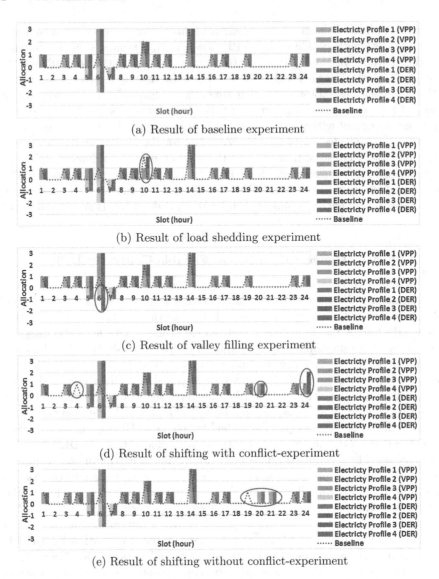

(a) Result of baseline experiment

(b) Result of load shedding experiment

(c) Result of valley filling experiment

(d) Result of shifting with conflict-experiment

(e) Result of shifting without conflict-experiment

Fig. 4. Results of 1st set of experiments (Color figure online)

on the type of VPP being operated. In the load shifting experiments, the VPP receives a DR event in which a move of consumption between slots is requested. As DER 1 through 3 do not value electricity equal across the slots, and as they initially operate at their most energy efficient electricity profiles, one of two things can happen: (1) The VPP receives a DR event which does not allow it to compensate a DER sufficiently, i.e. only offers increase in consumption in one slot in response to a reduction in another slot. Here, a conflict arises, as the

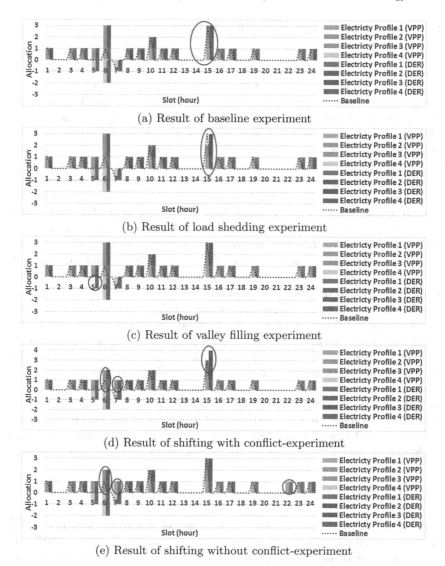

(a) Result of baseline experiment

(b) Result of load shedding experiment

(c) Result of valley filling experiment

(d) Result of shifting with conflict-experiment

(e) Result of shifting without conflict-experiment

Fig. 5. Results of 2nd set of experiments (Color figure online)

DER agent is unable to reach its production goal. This situation is reflected in Fig. 4d where the DER 2 is allocated one unit of electricity less in hour slot 4, and compensated with a single unit of electricity in slot 20. However, as can be seen, DER 2 also demands additional electricity in slot 24. (2) The VPP receives a DR event which **does** allow it to compensate a DER sufficiently. As can be seen in Fig. 4e DER 1 is allocated one unit of electricity less in slot 19 and compensated by one unit of electricity more in slots 20 and 21. Here, allocation and demand is equal, which means that no conflict is present.

4.2   Complex, Heterogeneous Virtual Power Plant

In this set of experiments all Flexible Consumer DER agents were replaced with Prosumer DER agents to increase the complexity of the VPP. This will show how more complex scenarios are handled by the model as well as show causality between the obtained results and an increasingly complex configuration of the MAS. Again 4 experiments were conducted to reflect a baseline scenario, a load shedding scenario, a valley filling scenario and a load shifting scenario. As in the experiments before, a baseline experiment has been conducted to establish a reference baseline. From Fig. 5a, we see that the introduction of Prosumer DER agents which discharges in slot 14 and charges in slot 15 has led to a situation where all consumption of slot 14 has been moved to slot 15. This of course reflects that each of the Prosumer DER agents have the same charge/discharge profile for their electricity storage unit. The results of the load shedding experiment in Fig. 5b resemble that of the previous load shedding-experiment shown in Fig. 4b. However, here the shedding is done in slot 15, which leads to a conflict with DER 2. The results of the valley filling-experiment in Fig. 5c shows an outcome which resemble that of the previous valley filling-experiment, although this time in slot 5. In the load shifting experiment, the VPP receives a request to shift load from slot 6. In Fig. 5d, that DER 3 is allocated less electricity in slot 6, and compensated with allocation in slot 7. However, as this is insufficient to fulfill its production goal, DER 3 requests an additional unit of allocation in slot 15, leading to a conflict as expected. As can be seen, the electrical storage units in the Prosumer DER agents makes it possible for each of these DER to request more than a single unit of electricity in a single slot. When sufficient compensation is provided, we again see from Fig. 5e that load shifting does not lead to a conflict. In this case, DER 1 is allocated less electricity in slot 6 and compensated with a single unit of electricity in slots 7 and 22, leading to a conflict free situation.

5   Conclusion

The paper extends the approach of [2] with a model and design for the creation of VPPs with complex, heterogeneous DER. The model describes VPP and DER as agents with decision logic based on concerns and issues. Agents may engage in multiple, bilateral negotiations with other agents, by representing these in their decision logic as concerns. In this way, a VPP agent may engage in bilateral negotiations with DER agents, in order to find appropriate allocations for electricity across the VPP. Two sets of experiments have been conducted in order to illustrate the properties of the model, namely one with one VPP agent, a Generator DER-agent and 3 Flexible Consumer DER agents and one with one VPP agent, a Generator DER agent and 3 Prosumer DER agents. It was shown that the VPP will allocate electricity based on incoming DR events, i.e. load shedding, valley filling and load shifting events, which will adhere to the demands of the DER-agents to the best degree possible in case of conflicts.

References

1. Clausen, A., Ghatikar, G., Jørgensen, B.N.: Load management of data centers as regulation capacity in Denmark. In: 2014 International Green Computing Conference (IGCC), pp. 1–10. IEEE (2014)
2. Clausen, A., Umair, A., Ma, Z., Jørgensen, B.N.: Demand response integration through agent-based coordination of consumers in virtual power plants. In: Baldoni, M., Chopra, A.K., Son, T.C., Hirayama, K., Torroni, P. (eds.) PRIMA 2016. LNCS, vol. 9862, pp. 313–322. Springer, Cham (2016). doi:10.1007/978-3-319-44832-9_19
3. Hommelberg, M., Warmer, C., Kamphuis, I., Kok, J., Schaeffer, G.: Distributed control concepts using multi-agent technology and automatic markets: An indispensable feature of smart power grids. In: 2007 Power Engineering Society General Meeting, pp. 1–7. IEEE (2007)
4. Kok, J.K., Warmer, C.J., Kamphuis, I.: PowerMatcher: Multiagent control in the electricity infrastructure. In: Proceedings of the Fourth International Joint Conference on Autonomous Agents And Multiagent Systems, pp. 75–82. ACM (2005)
5. Kok, K., Derzsi, Z., Hommelberg, M., Warmer, C., Kamphuis, R., Akkermans, H.: Agent-based electricity balancing with distributed energy resources, a multiperspective case study. In: Proceedings of the 41st Annual Hawaii International Conference on System Sciences, p. 173. IEEE (2008)
6. Mashhour, E., Moghaddas-Tafreshi, S.M.: Bidding strategy of virtual power plant for participating in energy and spinning reserve markets-part i: Problem formulation. IEEE Trans. Power Syst. **26**(2), 949–956 (2011)
7. Mashhour, E., Moghaddas-Tafreshi, S.M.: Bidding strategy of virtual power plant for participating in energy and spinning reserve markets-part ii: Numerical analysis. IEEE Trans. Power Syst. **26**(2), 957–964 (2011)
8. Meibom, P., Hilger, K.B., Madsen, H., Vinther, D.: Energy comes together in denmark: The key to a future fossil-free danish power system. IEEE Power Energ. Mag. **11**(5), 46–55 (2013)
9. Molderink, A., Bakker, V., Bosman, M.G., Hurink, J.L., Smit, G.J.: Domestic energy management methodology for optimizing efficiency in smart grids. In: 2009 IEEE Bucharest PowerTech, pp. 1–7. IEEE (2009)
10. Molderink, A., Bakker, V., Bosman, M.G., Hurink, J.L., Smit, G.J.: Management and control of domestic smart grid technology. IEEE Trans. Smart Grid **1**(2), 109–119 (2010)
11. Niesse, A., Beer, S., Bremer, J., Hinrichs, C., Lunsdorf, O., Sonnenschein, M.: Conjoint dynamic aggregation and scheduling methods for dynamic virtual power plants. In: 2014 Federated Conference on Computer Science and Information Systems (FedCSIS), pp. 1505–1514. IEEE (2014)
12. Pudjianto, D., Ramsay, C., Strbac, G.: Virtual power plant and system integration of distributed energy resources. IET Renew. Power Gener. **1**(1), 10–16 (2007)
13. Pudjianto, D., Ramsay, C., Strbac, G.: Microgrids and virtual power plants: Concepts to support the integration of distributed energy resources. Proc. Inst. Mech. Eng. Part A: J. Power Energy **222**(7), 731–741 (2008)

Interactions Among Information Sources in Weather Scenarios: The Role of the Subjective Impulsivity

Rino Falcone and Alessandro Sapienza[(⊠)]

ISTC-CNR, Rome, Italy
alessandro.sapienza@istc.cnr.it

Abstract. The topic of critical hydrogeological phenomena, due to flooding, has a particular relevance given the risk that it implies. In this paper we simulated complex weather scenarios in which are relevant forecasts coming from different sources. Our idea is that agents can build their own evaluations on the future weather events integrating these different information sources also considering how much trustworthy the single source is with respect to each individual agent. These agents learn the trustworthiness of the sources in a training phase. Agents are differentiated on the basis of their own ability to make direct weather forecasts, on their possibility to receive bad or good forecasts from an authority and on the possibility of being influenced by the neighbors' behaviors. Quite often in the real scenarios some irrational behaviors rise up, whereby individuals tend to impulsively follow the crowd, regardless of its reliability. To model that, we introduced an impulsivity factor that measures how much agents are influenced by the neighbors' behavior, a sort of "crowd effect". The results of these simulations show that, thanks to a proper trust evaluation of their sources made through the training phase, the different kinds of agents are able to better identify the future events.

Keywords: Trust · Social simulation · Hydrogeological risk

1 Introduction

The role of the impulsivity in human behaviors has relevant effects in the final evaluations and decisions of both individuals and groups. Although we are working in the huge domain of social influence [4, 8, 7], we consider here impulsivity as an attitude of making a decision just basing this decision on a partial set of evidence, also in those cases in which more evidence is easily reachable and acquirable. Sometimes this kind of behavior can produce consequences that were not taken in consideration at the moment of the decision [16]. Impulsivity is a multifactorial concept [5], however we are interested in identifying the role that it can play in a specific set of scenarios. In particular, in this paper we simulated complex weather scenarios in which there are relevant forecasts coming from different sources. Our basic idea is that agents can build their own evaluations on the future weather events integrating these different information sources also considering how trustworthy the single source is with respect to each individual agent. These agents learn the trustworthiness of the sources in a training phase. Agents are differentiated (i) on the basis of their own ability to make direct weather forecasts, (ii) on their possibility to receive bad or good forecasts from an authority, and (iii) on the

© Springer International Publishing AG 2017
Y. Demazeau et al. (Eds.): PAAMS 2017, LNAI 10349, pp. 56–69, 2017.
DOI: 10.1007/978-3-319-59930-4_5

possibility of being influenced by the neighbors' behaviors. Given this picture, our simulations inquired several interactions among different kinds of agents testing different weather scenarios with different levels of impulsivity. We also considered the role that both expertise and information play on the impulsivity factor. The results show that, thanks to a proper trust evaluation of their sources made through the training phase, the different kinds of agents are able to better identify the future events. Some particular and interesting results regard the fact that impulsivity can be considered, in specific situations, as a rational and optimizing factor, in some way contradicting the nature of the concept itself. In fact, as in some human cases, it is possible that we learned specific behaviors just basing on one information source that is enough for the more efficient behavior although we could access to other different and trustworthy sources. In that case we consider as impulsive a behavior that is in fact fully effective.

2   The Trust Model

According to the literature [1, 2, 10, 11, 17], trust is a promising way to deal with information source. In particular in this work we are going to use the computational model of [13], which is in turn based on the cognitive model of trust of Castelfranchi and Falcone [3]. It exploits the Bayesian theory, one of the most used approaches in trust evaluation [9, 12, 18]. Here information is represented as a probability distribution function (PDF).

In this model each information source S is represented by a trust degree called *TrustOnSource* [6], with $0 \leq TrustOnSource \leq 1$, plus a bayesian probability distribution PDF (Probability Distribution Function) that represents the information reported by S. The *TrustOnSource* parameter is used to smooth the information referred by S: the more I trust the source, the more I consider the PDF; the less I trust it, the more the PDF is flattened. Once an agent gets the contribution from all its sources, it aggregates the information to produce the global evidence (GPDF), estimating the probability that each event is going to happen.

2.1   Feedback on Trust

We want to let agents adapt to the context in which they move. This means that, starting from a neutral trust level (that does not imply trust or distrust) agents will try to understand how much to rely on each single information source (*TrustOnSource*), using direct experience for trust evaluations [14, 15]. To do that, they need a way to perform feedback on trust. We propose to use weighted mean. Given the two parameters α and β[1], the new trust value is computed as:

---

[1] The values of α and β have an impact on the trust evaluations. With high values of α/β, agents will need more time to get a precise evaluation, but a low value (below 1) will lead to an unstable evaluation, as it would depend too much on the last performance. We do not investigate these two parameters in this work, using respectively the values 0.9 and 0.1. In order to have good evaluations, we let agents make a lot of experience with their information sources.

$$newTrustOnSource = \alpha * TrustOnSource + \beta * performanceEvaluation$$

$$\alpha + \beta = 1$$

TrustOnSource is the previous trust degree and *performanceEvaluation* is the objective evaluation of the source performance. This last value is obtained comparing what the source said with what actually happened. Considering the PDF reported by the source (that will be split into five parts as we have 5 possible events), we will have that the estimated probability of the event that actually occurred is completely taken into account and the estimated probability of the events immediately near to it is taken into account for just 1/3. We in fact suppose that even if the evaluation is not right, it is not, however, entirely wrong. The rest of the PDF is not considered. Let's suppose that there was the most critical event, which is event 5. A first source reported a 100% probability of event 5, a second one a 50% probability of event 5 and a 50% of event 4 and a third one asserts 100% of event 3. Their performance evaluation will be: Source1 = 100%; Source2 = 66.67% (50% + (50/3)%); Source3: 0%. Figure 1 shows the corresponding PDFs.

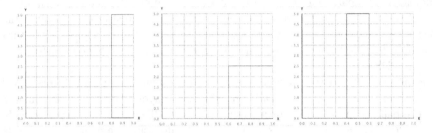

Fig. 1. (a) A source reporting a 100% probability of event 5. (b) a source reporting a 50% probability of event 5 and 50% probability of event 4. (c) a source reporting a 100% probability of event 3.

3   The Platform

Exploiting NetLogo [19], we created a very flexible platform, taking into account a lot of parameters to model a variety of situations. Given a population distributed over a wide area, some weather phenomena happen in the world with a variable level of criticality. The world is made by 32 × 32 patches, which wraps both horizontally and vertically where agents are distributed in a random way and is populated by a number of cognitive agents (citizens) that have to evaluate which will be the future weather event on the basis of the information sources they have and of the trustworthiness they attribute to these different sources. We provided the framework with five possible events, going from 1 to 5, with increasing level of criticality: level 1 stands for no events, there is no risk at all for the citizens; level 5 means that there will be a tremendous event due to a very high level of rain, with possible risks for the agents sake. The other values represent intermediate events with increasing criticality. In addition to citizens, there is another agent called authority. Its aim is to inform promptly the citizens about the weather phenomena. The problem is that, for their nature, weather forecasts improve their precision nearing to the event. Consequently, while the time passes the authority is able to produce a better forecast, but it will not be able to inform all the citizens, as there will be less time to spread information.

3.1 Information Sources

To make a decision, citizens consult a set of information sources, reporting to it some evidence about the incoming meteorological phenomenon. We considered the presence of three kinds of information sources for citizens:

1. Their *personal judgment,* based on the direct observation of the phenomena. Although this is a direct and always true (at least in that moment) source. In general, a common citizen is not always unable to understand the situation, maybe because it is not able, it does not possess any instrument or it is just not in the condition to properly evaluate a weather event. So we have introduced two kinds of agents: the expert ones and the inexpert ones.
2. *Notification from authority:* the authority distributes into the world weather forecast, trying to prepare citizens to what is going to happen. While the time pass, it is able to produce a better forecast, but it will not be able to inform everyone. In this sense we have two kinds of agents: the well-informed ones and the ill-informed ones.
3. *Others' behavior:* agents are in some way influenced by community logics, tending to partially or totally emulate their neighbors' behavior (other agents in the radius of 3 NetLogo patches). The probability of each event is directly proportional to the number of neighbors making each kind of decision. This source can have a positive influence if the neighbors behave correctly, otherwise it represents a drawback.

None of these sources is perfect. In any situation there is always the possibility that a source reports wrong information.

3.2 Agents' Description

At the beginning, all the citizens have the same neutral trust value 0.5 for all their information sources. This value represents a situation in which citizens are not sure if to trust or not a given source (1 represents complete trust and 0 complete distrust). There are two main differences between citizens. The first one relies on how much they are able to see and to read the phenomena. In fact, in the real world not all the agents have the same abilities. In order to shape this, we associated to the citizens' evaluations different values of standard deviation related to the meteorological events, dividing them in two sets.

1. Class 1: good evaluators; they have good capabilities to read and understand what is going to happen. They will be quit always able to detect correctly the event (90% of times; standard deviation of 0.3), and then we expect them to highly trust their own opinion.

2. Class 2: bad evaluators; they are not so able to understand what is going on (20% of times, that is the same performance of a random output; standard deviation of 100). For better understanding which will be the future weather event they have to consult other information sources.

The second difference is due to how easily they are reached by the authority. The idea is that the authority reaches everyone, but while the time passes it produces new updated information. There will be agents able to get update information, but not all of them will be able to do it. To model this fact, we defined two agent classes: (1) Class A: the have the newest information produced by the authority; the information they receive has a 90% probability to be correct; (2) Class B: they are only able to get the first prevision of the authority; the information they receive has a 30% probability to be correct.

3.3 The Authority

The authority's aim is to inform citizens about what is going to happen. The best case is the one in which it to produce a correct forecast and it has the time to spread this information through all the population. However this is as desirable as unreal. The truth is that weather forecast's precision increases while the event is approaching. In the real world the authority does not stop making prediction and spreading it. As already said, in the simulations we modeled this dividing the population into two classes. Agents belonging to the class B will just receive the old information. This is produced with a standard deviation of 1.5, which means that this forecast will be correct in 30% of times. Then the authority will spread updated information. Being closer to the incoming event, this forecast has a higher probability to be correct. It is produced with a standard deviation of 0.3, so that it sill be correct in 90% of times. As a choice, in the simulation it is more convenient to use as a source the authority rather than personal evaluations, except for experts that are as good as a reliable authority.

3.4 Citizens' Impulsivity

Sometimes impulsivity overcomes logic and rationality. This is more evident in case of critical situations, but it is still plausible in the other cases. Maybe the authority reports a *light* event, but the neighbors are escaping. In this case it is easy to be influenced by the crowd decision, to make a decision solely based on the social effect, letting "irrationality" emerge. Let us explain better this concept of "irrationality": in fact we consider that an agent follow an "irrational" behavior when it makes a decision considering just one of its own information sources although it has also other available sources to consult. In this work we consider just the social source as subjected to the impulsivity conditioning.

Impulsivity is surely a subjective factor so our citizens are endowed with an **impulsivity threshold**, which measures how much they are prone to a less informed choice due to the crowd effect. This threshold is in turn affected by the other two sources, the authority and the experience, as they add rationality in the decisional process. The threshold goes from 0 to 1, and given a value of this threshold, being well informed or an expert gives a plus 0.2 to it (it an agents is both informed and expert, it is a plus 0.4). Therefore it is important for individual to be informed, so that they are less sensible to a sort of irrational choice and they are able to produce decisions based on more evidence. In our experiments we consider a common impulsivity threshold (Ith_{Com}) that is the same for all the agents and two additional factors (Add_{Inf} and Add_{Exp}) due to the potential information and the expertise each agent has that determine the individual impulsivity threshold (Ith_{Agent}). In practice, given an agent A, we can say that:

$$Ith_A = Ith_{Com} + Add_{Inf} + Add_{Exp}$$

The threshold is compared with the PDF reported by the social source. If there is one event that has a probability to happen (according to this source) greater than the impulsivity threshold, then the agents act impulsively.

3.5 Platform Inputs

The first thing that can be customized is the **number of citizens** and their distribution between the **performance categories** and the **reachability categories**. Then, one can set the value of the two parameters α **and** β, used for updating the sources' trust evaluation. It is possible to change the **authority reliability** concerning each of the reachability categories. One can also set the **events' probability** that is the frequency with which each event will happen. Concerning the training phase, it is possible to change its **duration**. Finally, it is possible to set the **impulsivity threshold** and how much it will be modified by each rational source.

3.6 Workflow

Each simulation is divided into two steps. The first one is called "**training phase**" and has the aim of letting agents make experience with their information sources, so that they can determine how reliable each source is. At the beginning of this phase, the citizens start collecting information, in order to understand which event is going to happen.

The authority gives forecast reporting its estimated level of criticality. As already explained, it produces two different forecasts. All the citizens will receive the first one, but it is less precise as it is not close enough to the event. The second one is much more precise, but being close to the event it is not possible for the authority to inform all the citizens. In any case, being just forecasts, it is not sure that they are really going to happen. They will have a probability linked to the precision of the authority (depending on its standard deviation). Then citizens evaluate the situation on their own and also exploit others' evaluations (by the effect of their decisions). Remember that the social source is the result of the process aggregating the agents' decisions in the neighborhood: if a neighbor has not decided, it is not considered. If according to the social source there is one event that has a probability to happen greater than the impulsivity threshold, then they act impulsively: they will not consider the other sources. If this does not happen, then they consider all the information they can access and they aggregate each single contribution according to the corresponding trust value. Finally they estimate the possibility that each event happens and select the choice that minimizes the risk.

While citizens collect information they are considered as "thinking", meaning that they have not decided yet. When they reach the decisional phase, the citizens have to decide. This information is then available for the others (neighborhood), which can in turn exploit it for their decisions. At the end of the event, citizens evaluate the performance of the source they used and adjust the corresponding trust values. This phase is repeated for 100 times (then there will be 100 events) so that agents can make enough experience to judge their sources.

After that, there is the **"testing phase"**. Here we want to understand how agents perform, once they know how much reliable their source are. In this phase, we will compute the accuracy of their decision (1 if correct, 0 if wrong).

4   Simulations

We investigated two main scenarios. In the first one we tested the effect of impulsivity on a population with different abilities to interpret the events and with different possibility to be informed by the authority. In this case impulsivity affects everyone, as even the more expert or informed can be misled by their neighbors' decisions. In the second simulation we introduce a decisional order between agents. The best informed will be the first to decide, followed by the most able to understand the events. In this second ideal world impulsivity has a much smaller influence on decision. In addition, as the most rational agents (which also possess more evidence about the events) will decide before the worst informed and able agents, there will be a positive effect on the performance of all the agents.

In order to understand and analyze each simulation, we are going to use two metrics. The first one is **agents' performance**. Concerning a single event, the performance of an agent is considered correct (and assumes value 1) if it correctly identified the event or wrong (and assumes value 0) if it made a mistake with the events. The second dimension is the **trust on the information sources**. Section 2.1 explains how agents produce their trust evaluations, based on the source performance. They possess a trust value for each of their three sources.

We introduced these metrics for individual agents. Actually in the results they will be presented aggregating the values of a category of agents and mediating them for the number of times that the experiment is repeated (500 times). In particular, in order to provide a better analysis of the results, we are not going to simply consider the category of agents indicated in Sect. 3.2 but their combinations: 1A = well informed and expert agents; 2A = well informed and not expert agents; 1B = less informed and expert agents; 2B = less informed and not expert agents.

4.1 First Simulation

Here there is no decisional order, so that each citizen can influence and be influenced by everyone. In the scenarios we investigated, the percentage of well informed citizens and the percentage of expert citizens is the same, as we are mainly interested in increasing/decreasing the quantity of good information and expertise that the population possesses. Of course, as the assignment of citizens to categories is random, it is possible an overlap between these categories: a well informed citizen can also be an expert.

Simulation settings: *number of agents* = 200; α *and* β = respectively 0.9 and 0.1; *authority reliability* = we used a standard deviation of 1.5 to produce the first forecast reported by the authority (it is correct about 90% of time) and 0.3 for the second one (its forecasts are correct about 30% of time); *percentage of well informed citizens and percentage of expert citizens* = {10-10, 20-20, 30-30, 45-45, 60-60, 75-75}; *events' probability* (from the lightest to the most critical one) {35%, 30%, 20%, 10%, 5%}; *training phase duration* = 100 events; *impulsivity threshold* = we experimented the four cases {0.3, 0.5, 0.7, 0.9}

For sake of simplicity, as the percentage of well informed citizens and of expert citizens is the same in each experiment, we will use this value to identify the specific case. For instance, the "case 10-10" is the one with 10% of well informed citizens and of expert citizens.

It is worth noting that when the impulsivity threshold (Ith_{Com}) is 0.9 then well informed or expert agents are not impulsive for sure (given that for those agents Ith_{Agent} saturates the max value 1). When the impulsivity threshold (Ith_{Com}) is 0.7, it is necessary to be both informed and expert to not be impulsive in any case. In the other cases agents could act impulsively, according to the modality explained in Sect. 3.4. This is clearly visible with an impulsivity threshold of 0.7, especially in Fig. 2 but also in Fig. 3: there is a big difference between 1A agents' performance and the others. In practice, in the given composition of agents showed in Figs. 2 and 3, impulsive agents are penalized. Let us explain in detail. Figure 2 shows the case 10-10 (10% of well informed citizens and 10% of expert citizens). Here the majority of the citizens, approximately the 81%, belongs to the category 2B (not well informed and not expert) represented in violet. They are so many that their evaluation of the events influences negatively their neighbors through the social source, especially when there is a low value of common impulsivity threshold. Increasing the percentage of informed/expert citizens this effect tends to disappear, as showed by Figs. 3 and 4. From Figs. 2, 3 and 4 it clearly results that the performance of 1A, 1B and 2A agents increases when we increase the value of the impulsivity threshold (agents are less impulsive). In fact increasing this component, these agents will not be influenced by the crowd effect and they will be able to decide on the basis of all their sources.

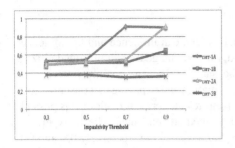
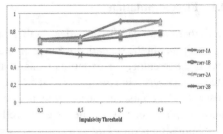

Fig. 2. Agents' correctness in the case 10-10   **Fig. 3.** Agents' correctness in the case 30-30

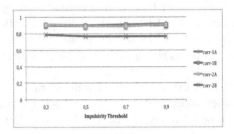

Fig. 4. Agents' correctness in the case 75-75

Differently form the others, if we focus on the 2B category (both bad evaluators and misinformed) we notice an interesting effect: in all the cases, increasing the impulsivity threshold the performance of 2B citizens decreases. This is due to the fact that, being less impulsive will have more weight on their own information and their own expertise in their final evaluations. But not being well informed or experts, there is a higher probability that they will be wrong.

4.2   Second Simulation

In this scenario we suppose that there is a decisional order, so that who is well informed (independently on its expertise) will be the first to decide; then the experts decide; finally the remaining agents decide, the ones with the lowest reliable information. Doing so there is a double effect: who has good information is not negatively influenced by who does not have it; who does not have good information is mainly much more influenced by who has it. The settings are exactly the same of the previous experiment. Let's start analyzing agents' performance.

Looking at Fig. 5, it is clear that the impulsivity has no negative effect on agents that are well informed or expert. This does not imply that they are not impulsive. Let's consider well informed agents: the first to decide will be just influenced by the authority. The others could be impulsive, following the social source. But the social source is just influenced by what the authority reports. In conclusion, the impulsivity factor has no influence in this scenario.

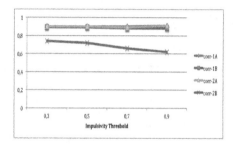 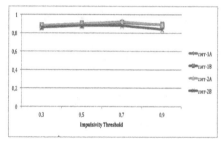

Fig. 5. Agents' correctness in the case 10-10 with decisional order.

Fig. 6. Agents' correctness in the case 30-30 with decisional order

The impulsivity is still relevant for expert agents, which will be strongly influenced by the well informed ones (but their performance would be high in any case), and it is clearly fundamental for 2B agents (which are both bad evaluators and misinformed): in this case, much more than the agents 1B, impulsivity seems to help them. The proof is given by the fact that their performance decreases while their impulsivity threshold increases.

Obviously, increasing the quantity of information in the world, agents' performance improves and the 2B's curve tends to be equal to the others (Figs. 6 and 7).

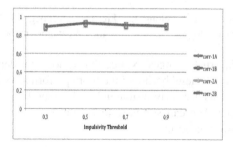

Fig. 7. Agents' correctness in the case 75-75 with decisional order

4.3   Trust Analysis

Talking about trust, analyzing the four categories 1A, 1B, 2A and 2B the components of self trust and authority trust do not change. They in fact assume a fixed value in all the cases, not being influenced by the impulsivity threshold or by the quantity of information in the world (just by its quality). Figures 8, 9, 10 and 11 show these values respectively to the categories 1A, 1B, 2A and 2B. Not even the decisional order influences them, so that they are the same in both the experiments.

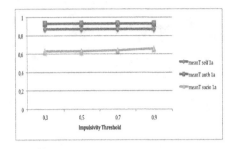

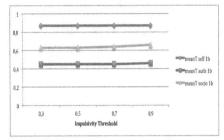

Fig. 8. Trust degrees of the agents belonging to the 1A category in the case 30-30.

Fig. 9. Trust degrees of the agents belonging to the 1B category in the case 30-30

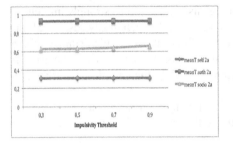

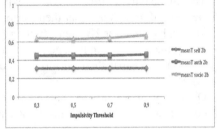

Fig. 10. Trust degrees of the agents belonging to the 2A category in the case 30-30

Fig. 11. Trust degrees of the agents belonging to the 2B category in the case 30-30

Of course the social trust changes. Notice that it does not depend on the agent's nature; it just depends on its neighborhood: the more performative they are, the higher the social trust will be. This is clearly visible in Fig. 12, reporting the social trust levels without decisional order. We can see how the social trust increases increasing the percentage of expert/informed citizens.

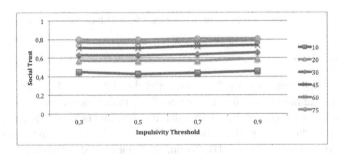

Fig. 12. Social trust of all the agents in the six cases

With the decisional order, there is a big difference for the social source: each category of agents will be differently influenced by the other categories. For instance, well informed agents (1A and 2A) are the first to decide, so that they will be influenced just by agents of the same kind. Then 1B agents decide, exploiting the decision of agents belonging to their category, but also those of well informed agents. 2B agents decide last, on the basis of everyone else's choices. Within this picture we clearly expect to have different trust levels for the different categories.

The trust values of 1A (Fig. 13) and 2A (Fig. 15) agents are almost the same[2]. Even if they have the best performance, their social trust is very low. This is reasonable as quite often they will be the first to decide: in those cases, as none of their neighbors decided yet, their social source is flat, reporting no evidence. Not being able to exploit this source, agents lower the trust in it. Then 1B agents decide, basing its decision on 1A and 2A agents. Their social trust levels (Fig. 14) are higher than those of these last. The higher trust values are the ones of 2B (Fig. 16) agents. In fact, given that all the other agents decided and their decisions were strongly influenced by well informed agents (and then indirectly by the authority), 2B agents are able to exploit a lot of correct decisions.

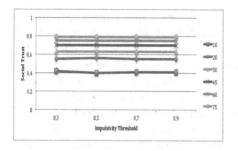

Fig. 13. Social trust of 1A agents in the six cases, with decisional order

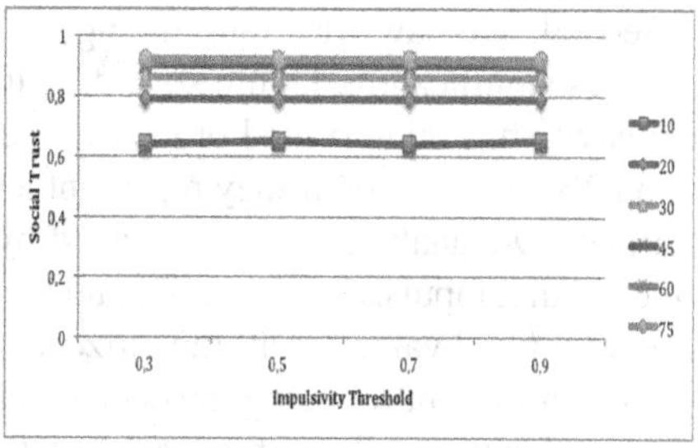

Fig. 14. Social trust of 1B agents in the six cases, with decisional order

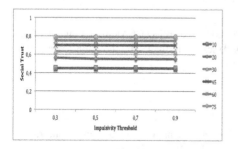

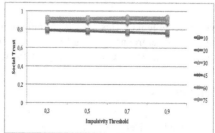

Fig. 15. Social trust of 2A agents in the six cases, with decisional order

Fig. 16. Social trust of 2B agents in the six cases, with decisional order

---

[2] Actually there is a little difference: in the case 10-10 the social trust level is a little bit higher in the 2A case. The reason of this difference is the extremely low percentage of 1A agents in this scenario, so that it is quite unlikely that a 1A agent influences another 1A agent, but there is a higher possibility that it influences a 2A agent.

5 Conclusions

In this work we analyzed the effect of subjective impulsivity inside critical weather scenarios. We proposed some simulations in which a population of citizens (modeled through cognitive agents) has to face weather scenarios and needs to exploit its information sources to understand what is going to happen.

In these situation agents can act "rationally" (basing their choice in the global evidence they possess) or impulsively, just emulating their neighbors due to a sort of "crowd effect".

First of all, we saw that impulsivity has a strongly negative impact on informed or expert agents, while on the contrary it is useful for the remaining 2B agents. In particular, it is not good to have a high percentage of 2B agents, as they have a negative impact also on the agents belonging to the other categories. This is a quite predictable effect, even if it is interesting appreciate the various levels of impulsivity that determine the different impacts.

Second, we saw that introducing the decisional order the agents' performance improves significantly. Doing so in fact it is possible to avoid the negative effect that impulsivity has on informed or expert agents and to increase the positive effect that it has on 2B agents, even if they represent a substantial percentage of the population.

Finally we analyzed the role played by social trust. In the first simulation, given a value for the impulsivity threshold and a percentage of informed and expert citizens, it assumes a fixed value for all the citizens, as it is independent by the agent's category. On the contrary, introducing the decisional order the social trust changes depending on the agents' category. In particular the first to decide will have the lowest trust value and it increases until the last to decide, 2B agents, just thanks to the decisional order. In this way, the agents that would be hindered by the social source use it less, while the agents that need it to decide correctly exploit it more.

Acknowledgments. This work is partially supported by the project CLARA—CLoud plAtform and smart underground imaging for natural Risk Assessment, funded by the Italian Ministry of Education, University and Research (MIUR-PON).

References

1. Amgoud, L., Demolombe, R.: An argumentation-based approach for reasoning about trust in information sources. J. Argumentation Comput. **5**(2), 191–215 (2014)
2. Barber, K.S., Kim, J.: Belief revision process based on trust: agents evaluating reputation of information sources. In: Falcone, R., Singh, M., Tan, Y.-H. (eds.) Trust in Cyber-societies. LNCS, vol. 2246, pp. 73–82. Springer, Heidelberg (2001). doi:10.1007/3-540-45547-7_5
3. Castelfranchi, C., Falcone, R.: Trust Theory: A Socio-Cognitive and Computational Model. Wiley, Hoboken (2010)
4. Cialdini, R.B.: Influence: Science and Practice, 4th edn. Allyn & Bacon, Boston (2001). ISBN 0-321-01147-3
5. Evenden, J.L.: Varieties of impulsivity. Psychopharmacol. **146**(4), 348–361 (1999). doi: 10.1007/PL00005481

6. Falcone, R., Sapienza, A., Castelfranchi, C.: The relevance of categories for trusting information sources. ACM Trans. Internet Technol. (TOIT) **15**(4), 13 (2015)

7. Genter, K., Stone, P.: Adding influencing agents to a flock. In: Proceedings of the 2016 International Conference on Autonomous Agents & Multiagent Systems, pp. 615–623. International Foundation for Autonomous Agents and Multiagent Systems, May 2016

8. Latané, B.: The psychology of social impact. Am. Psychol. **36**, 343–356 (1981)

9. Melaye, D., Demazeau, Y.: Bayesian dynamic trust model. In: Pěchouček, M., Petta, P., Varga, L.Z. (eds.) CEEMAS 2005. LNCS, vol. 3690, pp. 480–489. Springer, Heidelberg (2005). doi:10.1007/11559221_48

10. Melo, V.S., Panisson, A.R., Bordini, R.H.: Trust on beliefs: source, time and expertise. In: Proceedings of the 18th International Workshop on Trust in Agent Societies co-located with the 15th International Conference on Autonomous Agents and Multiagent Systems (AAMAS 2016), Singapore, May 10, vol. 1578, paper 6. Ceur Workshop Proceedings (2016)

11. Parsons, S., Sklar, E., Singh, M.P., Levitt, K.N., Rowe, J.: An argumentation-based approach to handling trust in distributed decision making. In: AAAI Spring Symposium: Trust and Autonomous Systems, March 2013

12. Quercia, D., Hailes, S., Capra, L.: B-trust: bayesian trust framework for pervasive computing. In: Stølen, K., Winsborough, W.H., Martinelli, F., Massacci, F. (eds.) iTrust 2006. LNCS, vol. 3986, pp. 298–312. Springer, Heidelberg (2006). doi:10.1007/11755593_22

13. Sapienza, A., Falcone, R.: A bayesian computational model for trust on information sources. In: Proceedings of the Conferenze WOA 2016, vol. 1664, pp. 50–55. Ceur workshop proceedings, Catania (2016)

14. Schmidt, S., Steele, R., Dillon, T.S., Chang, E.: Fuzzy trust evaluation and credibility development in multi-agent systems. Appl. Soft Comput. **7**(2), 492—505 (2007)

15. Theodorakopoulos, G., Baras, J.S.: On trust models and trust evaluation metrics for ad hoc networks. IEEE J. Sel. Areas Commun. **24**(2), 318–328 (2006)

16. VandenBos, G.R.: APA Dictionary of Psychology. APA, Washington, DC (2007)

17. Villata, S., Boella, G., Gabbay, D.M., Torre, L.: Arguing about the trustworthiness of the information sources. In: Liu, W. (ed.) ECSQARU 2011. LNCS, vol. 6717, pp. 74–85. Springer, Heidelberg (2011). doi:10.1007/978-3-642-22152-1_7

18. Wang, Y., Vassileva, J.: Bayesian network-based trust model. In: IEEE/WIC International Conference on Web Intelligence, WI 2003 Proceedings, pp. 372–378). IEEE, October 2003

19. Wilensky, U.: NetLogo, Center for Connected Learning and Computer-Based Modeling, Northwestern University, Evanston, IL (1999). http://ccl.northwestern.edu/netlogo/

TRIoT: A Proposal for Deploying Teleo-Reactive Nodes for IoT Systems

Diego Fernández[✉], Pedro Sánchez[✉], Bárbara Álvarez,
Juan Antonio López, and Andrés Iborra

División de Sistemas e Ingeniería Electrónica (DSIE), Universidad Politécnica de Cartagena,
Plaza del Hospital n° 1, 30202 Cartagena, Spain
{diego.fernandez,pedro.sanchez,balvarez,jantonio.lopez,
andres.iborra}@upct.es

Abstract. In this paper we present a multi-agent architecture for IoT systems based on the Teleo-Reactive paradigm. Our final goal is to prove that the Teleo-Reactive (TR) paradigm is suitable for IoT systems, allowing them the ability of being responsive to changes in the state of the environment while being directed to achieve their final tasks and conferring the network the robustness and reliability that IoT systems demand. A hierarchical architecture in which Coordination Nodes, Local Coordination Nodes and Local Nodes running Erlang and TR code, communicating among themselves and asking for services to the Cloud is described and the hardware, software and communications protocols used are specified. For validating this approach, a case-study for precision farming is being developed. A GUI will allow non-technical users to simply specify the TR rules of their IoT systems, fueling the development of IoT.

Keywords: Internet of Things · Teleo-Reactive programming · Precision farming

1 Introduction

The Internet of Things (IoT) is a growing paradigm that is gaining more and more adepts every day. Although the concept had been discussed before, the term Internet of Things became popular in 1999 when Kevin Ashton, a British technology pioneer, used it to describe a system in which objects in the physical world could be connected to the Internet by the use of sensors [1]. Nowadays, the extent of the concept is much wider and there is no single universally accepted definition for the term yet. In order to promote their particular view of the IoT, different actors (e.g. business alliances, stakeholders, research and standardization bodies) have given many different definitions according to their interests and backgrounds. Atzori et al. states in [2] that the difference in the definitions given are due to the issue being approached either from an "Internet oriented", "Things oriented" or "Semantic oriented" perspective and the authors establish that actually, the Internet of Things paradigm is the result of the convergence of these three main visions. Some of the technologies on which the IoT relies are Wireless Sensor Networks, RFID, Cloud, Edge and Fog Computing and Big Data Analytics [3].

© Springer International Publishing AG 2017
Y. Demazeau et al. (Eds.): PAAMS 2017, LNAI 10349, pp. 70–81, 2017.
DOI: 10.1007/978-3-319-59930-4_6

Thanks to the price reduction of computation, sensors and actuators that allow to harvest information from the physical world and respond to it; and to the networking capabilities and the power that the Internet can provide to embedded devices, IoT is now achievable. Ideally, IoT would allow any device to be connected to the Internet anytime, anywhere, with anything and anybody and by using any path or network and any service. A mesh of devices producing information and building a worldwide network of real physical objects is in this way created. Some of the applications of IoT are in the fields of transportation and logistics, healthcare or smart environments. According to Cisco [4], the number of IoT devices by 2020 will surpass 50 billion. However, in order to achieve these numbers, a series of challenges must still be faced concerning security, privacy, standardization or reliability among others.

One of the issues when developing IoT systems is the specification of the system's behavior. Most of the approaches are based on programming language, so only experts are able to specify and evolve the behavior of the deployed system. We think that the IoT landscape could benefit from the application of the Teleo-Reactive (TR) paradigm, and thus, a proposal for deploying TR nodes in IoT systems is given. The TR paradigm was first introduced in 1994 by Professor Nils Nilsson at Stanford University [5] and plenty of work has been developed since then [6, 7]. TR programs are conceived as a set of rules that lead a system to its final goal (hence Teleo) by constantly sensing the environment and responding to changes (hence Reactive) by triggering actions that assure that the system always gets closer to such final goal. The main advantage of TR programs is their ability to robustly react to changes in the environment owing to the continuous computation of sensing values. Thus, the TR paradigm suits in a natural way the always sensing - changing - reacting nature of IoT systems and its application would confer these often unreliable networks of devices the robustness required to achieve their goals and self-repair. To our knowledge, this is an innovative first proposal for the use of the TR approach for IoT systems and it is made due to our previous positive experiences in this field [8, 9].

Throughout this first Section, a brief introduction to the IoT and the TR paradigm has been given. The remainder of this paper is organized as follows. Section 2 presents the topology of the hierarchical multi-agent network that will be deployed and the characteristics and contents of the three different kinds of nodes that will be employed. This is followed in Sect. 3 by the proposal of a smart agriculture study case in which the hardware, software and communication protocols chosen to carry out the study are specified and all the principles and architectural decisions made in Sect. 2 are tested. In Sect. 4 we enumerate the benefits of this approach and in Sect. 5 we summarize the most relevant related works. Finally, we conclude this paper in Sect. 6 by summing up the main points of the approach, open issues that require further research and future work.

2 Overview of the Architecture and Nodes Implementation

IoT has experienced massive research in the recent years and multiple open-source and commercial platforms and middleware have appeared to try to give either vertical or horizontal solutions to different domains [10–13]. However, to our knowledge, the use of the TR approach for IoT systems is an innovative solution never tried before that addresses the development of these systems from a goal oriented agent perspective, different to anything found in the current literature. It is our opinion that the TR paradigm can highly simplify the specification, implementation and deployment of IoT systems; allowing end-users with a basic programming background to set the behavior of their systems by using a simple approach and philosophy (e.g. similar to the one used by Gamesalad for games creation [14]). Involving end-users as auxiliary developers will rapidly make IoT systems transform and evolve as it already happened with Web 2.0 [15], which is our main aim.

Razzaque et al. establishes in [13] functional, non-functional and architectural requirements that a middleware for IoT should comply with. It is our goal to make our framework able to satisfy as many of these requirements as possible, especially: programming abstraction, interoperability, context-awareness, autonomy, adaptive, scalability, availability, reliability, real-time, privacy and security. As a result of this, a hierarchical multi-agent architecture (named TRIoT) is considered in order to deploy the TR nodes network (see Fig. 1).

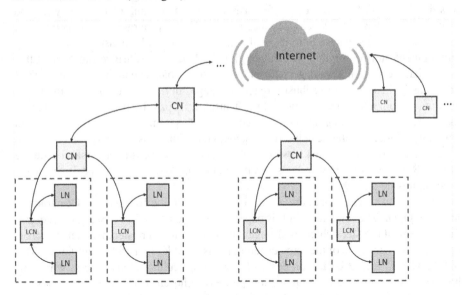

Fig. 1. TR hierarchical architecture for IoT.

The information can either flow downwards from the Cloud to the nodes when services are requested or upwards from the nodes to the Cloud when data requires to be stored or analyzed. The hierarchical architecture leaves the door open for the use of modern techniques such as data aggregation and edge computing that would reduce the network overload and increase the overall reliability. The network is composed of three different kinds of nodes, each of them with their own capabilities and place in the hierarchy: Local Nodes at the bottom, Local Coordination Nodes in the middle and Coordination Nodes at the top of the hierarchy.

- Local Nodes (LNs): These physical nodes are the most basic ones and their main function is to sense the environment and to react accordingly to it. They could also exchange messages with other nodes or ask for web services although it is not their main purpose. They are directly subordinated to the Local Coordination Nodes.
- Local Coordination Nodes (LCNs): Located in the middle of the hierarchy, the main purpose of these physical nodes is to coordinate the different LN networks and to act as a broker with external agents or services. Although it is not a must, sensing and actuating capabilities are a possibility too.
- Coordination Nodes (CNs): These top hierarchy nodes have no sensing or actuating capabilities and they just coordinate the different LCN networks, serve as brokers with external agents and services and connect to the Cloud. Some of these nodes could be virtual using cloud computing facilities instead of physical, depending on the needs of the application.

A star topology has been chosen for the communication between the LNs and the LCNs. This topology has the advantages of simplicity and low latency and power consumption with the only disadvantage of the LNs having to be located inside the range of the LCN. Figure 2 presents the configuration of each of the nodes previously mentioned.

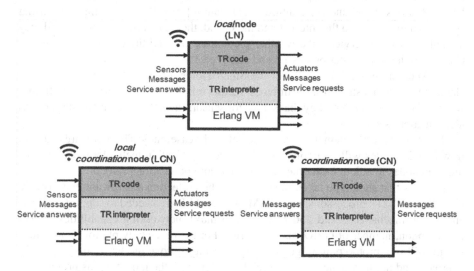

Fig. 2. LN, LCN and CN implementation.

All the nodes will contain two main elements: a lightweight Erlang Virtual Machine [16] and a TR interpreter running the TR code implemented. This code will be split in two parts, the main code that is in charge of the basic behavior of the node; and a meta-level for coping with system evolution. The meta-level will have the ability to modify the main code whenever the situation requires it, changing in this way the behavior of the overall system and making the network dynamic and responsive to events, and consequently more robust and reliable. Since Erlang was designed to support fault tolerant, distributed, soft-real-time and non-stop applications, it seems the appropriate language for this kind of IoT implementation; although the need of a virtual machine could be an impediment in the case of the most resource constrained embedded devices. To specify the behavior of the nodes, a simple visual editor will be designed to set the TR rules given a group of sensors, actuators, and available services; allowing the non-technical users to easily set their own TR IoT systems.

3   A Case-Study for Validating the Approach

A case-study for validating the whole approach is currently being developed in the field of precision farming (also known as smart agriculture) due to our knowledge in this domain [17, 18]. Precision farming is one of the multiple fields in which IoT finds application. Precision farming involves the use of communication technologies for the automated monitoring of crops, as well as related environmental, soil, fertilization and irrigation conditions. By the 24/7 monitoring and data collection of crops and environment it is possible to take actions to improve farm profitability, quality of the products, save water, reduce the use of fertilizers, fight climate change and be ready to meet the increasing population's food demand (food production must increase a 60% by 2050 in order to feed the 9 billion people that will populate the Earth by then, according to the United Nations' Food and Agriculture Organization [19]). By connecting the sensing and actuating devices to the Internet and the Cloud, their capabilities increase and they are able to ask for services like weather predictions or send the data collected to the Cloud in order to be better processed and analyzed.

As Makonin et al. did in [20] for the Smart Home, domain concept maps can be elaborated, as a first step, to show different factors relevant to our smart farming framework and to define the ontology that serves for sensors, actuators and available services identification (see Fig. 3).

There are three key elements to select to define the case study: The hardware platform in which the nodes will be implemented, the communication technology used by the different nodes to talk to each other and the IoT communication protocol.

Features that should be taken into account when selecting a hardware platform are the following [21]: processor speed, RAM (at least 4 kB are needed to support standard encryption mechanisms and 256 MB to run Linux), networking capabilities, power consumption, number of GPIO, size and price. For the case-study platform, and since we are still in a prototyping stage and we just want to prove the feasibility of the TR approach and not to produce a commercial product, only the most famous prototyping boards have been assessed. Finally, the Raspberry Pi 2 Model B [22] was the platform chosen to implement the nodes due to three reasons: high capabilities, the possibility of having a Linux based Operative System and the already existence of an Erlang Virtual Machine. These benefits come with a disadvantage too: "high" price. In the future it will be needed to migrate to a cheaper and more constrained customized platform in order to make the development more scalable.

In respect of the communication technology, in agriculture applications variables change slowly, so bandwidth is not an impediment. Power consumption is needed to be as low as possible to increase battery duration and when it comes to range, thanks to the

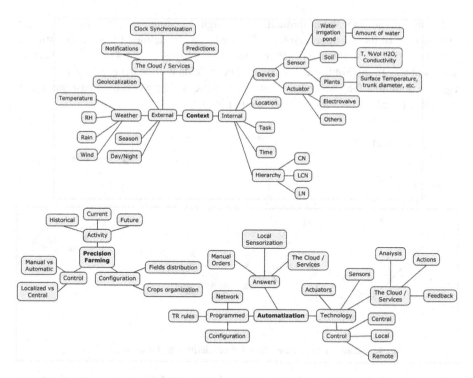

Fig. 3. Concept maps of different factors relevant for the smart farming framework.

hierarchical topology of our network, high ones are not required. So our focus of attention was low range and low power consumption technologies and among them Zigbee [23] was the one chosen. Zigbee allows low-cost wireless and interoperable device communications. It is built over IEEE 802.15.4 standard, can work in the 2.4 GHz band and uses AES128 encryption. It is suitable for applications with low data rate (~250 kBps), low range (max. 500 m outdoors), and on-body sensors like ours.

To select the IoT communication protocol for our application, an assessment of the most popular IoT protocols was made and MQTT-S [24] was the one chosen. MQTT [24] is a lightweight, mature and reliable protocol created by IBM and optimized for resource and power constrained devices. It is ideal for telemetry applications in which big networks of small devices have to be monitored from the Cloud. It takes data from many different points and sends it to one for analysis. It works in real-time over TCP and uses a publish/subscription mechanism with interesting features such as three different quality of service levels or last will statement messages. Its main disadvantages are that if the broker fails, most of the system fails; and that TCP was not designed for embedded devices so it can affect their battery. MQTT-S was created to solve these issues. MQTT-S works over UDP and supports all MQTT features while considering wireless network constraints such as high link failures, low bandwidth and short message payload. The MQTT protocol has been used for example for Facebook's famous messaging app and for Flood Net and Smart Lab projects of University of Southampton.

Taking into account the aforementioned design decisions, a case-study to validate the suitability of the TR approach for IoT systems can be defined for a Smart Farming application. Our hierarchical TR network will be deployed in two 4 ha fields, which is the typical size in the South-East of Spain. These fields will be irrigated by a common irrigation pond that they will have to share and there will be a common base station or farm office for coordination too, as shown in Fig. 4.

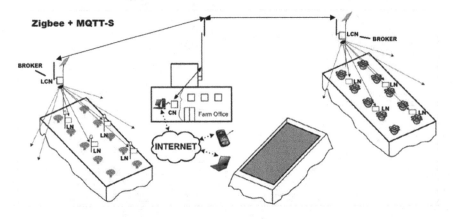

Fig. 4. Smart farming case-study for validating the TR approach [25].

In each field, the LNs will be placed together with a LCN in a star topology and MQTT-S over Zigbee will be used for the communications. The CN will be at the base station. LNs will use batteries while LCNs and CN will be connected to the network, so their power consumption is not an issue. The LNs will sense (every 30 min approx.) the environment (temperature, wind, soil moisture) and health of the crops and react to their measures (open and closing valves, sending notifications, etc.) or to the orders of the LCN (clock synchronization, resets, events, etc.). The LCN will act as a broker between the LNs and the CN, mainly managing the flow of information, taking decisions and giving orders. The CN in the base station will manage the network, allowing to upload or download data from the Internet (web services, weather predictions, cloud data computation, etc.) or a data base and coordinating the LCNs (e.g. by giving priority to one field when both of them need irrigation, i.e., resource sharing). The final goal of this system is to produce the best products in the minimum amount of time required and in a cost-effective way. LNs, LCNs and CN will have their own final goal: to reach stability. By reaching stability the global goal of the system will be accomplished too. Stability has been defined, in the case of the LNs, as: having battery to work, having executed any order received, having sensed the environment and sent packages, and being connected to the LCN. In the case of the LCNs means: having executed any order received, having received packets from the LN and delivered them to the CN or having analyzed them and taken a decision, and being connected. Finally, in the case of the CN, stability means: being connected, having uploaded the data received to the Cloud and having attended and made a decision about all petitions received, even if it means asking for forecast predictions to The Internet in order to share a resource (e.g. the irrigation pond when both fields need to be irrigated). In a simplified way, the kind of TR rules that each node could handle is given in Table 1.

Table 1. TR rules for LNs, LCNs and CN

LN	
Condition	**Action**
Stability	→ Sleep
<15% Battery	→ Notification to user
Order received	→ Execute
10 readings	→ Send data to LCN
DevicesWork&30min	→ Sense environment
LCN Connection Opened	→ Check devices work
True	→ Ask for LCN connection

LCN		CN	
Condition	**Action**	**Condition**	**Action**
Stability	→ Nil	Stability	→ Nil
CN order received	→ Execute	Rain B % > Rain A %	→ Irrigate Field B, then Field A
Field sector needs fertilizer	→ Send fertilizing order	Rain A % > Rain B %	→ Irrigate Field A, then Field B
Field sector needs water	→ Send irrigation order	Both fields need water	→ Check forecast
LN packet received	→ Collect&Analyze &Deliver packets	Field B needs water	→ Irrigate field B
		Field A needs water	→ Irrigate field A
LN Connection not established after 30 min	→ Notification to user	Packets received	→ Send data to Database
CN connection opened	→ Wait for LN connection	LCN Connection not established after 30 min	→ Send notification to user
True	→ Ask for CN connection	Connection opened	→ Wait for packets/petitions
		True	→ Wait for LNC connection

Table 1 shows how by using the TR approach, each node tasks and dependencies can be easily specified making the system react to events and always evolve to its final goal, even if at some point the conditions of the environment change. According to the semantic of a TR program, starting from the top of the list all the conditions are continually evaluated and once that one condition is satisfied, its action is executed. The LN will ask for the connection with the LCN, take measures every 30 min and execute any order it receives. When there are no more tasks left, it will go to sleep for thirty minutes and wake up again to take more measures. If at any point any of the conditions is not achieved, the process will not restart from the beginning but from the not achievable condition. Something similar happens to the LCN and CN. The set of rules that defines their behavior and leads them to stability is established, and whenever any of the rules is not accomplished, the system falls back and tries to recover and reach stability again.

4   Benefits of the Approach

By using the innovative goal oriented agent architecture described, systems that other-wise would need hundreds of states in a statechart approach or really complex program-ming by using formal languages, can be easily specified. This is how the TR approach and TRIoT can make a difference. Thanks to the combination of the TR paradigm and IoT ecosystem, a highly robust, fully-functional, fault-tolerant and hence, reliable network of monitoring and actuating devices empowered by the Internet can be deployed. The TR programming will allow the network to be dynamic and reconfigure in case of some of the nodes disconnection or failure and will make sure that the overall system always moves forward to achieve its final goal. The system will be able to sense the environment in a continuous way and intelligently respond to changes whenever they take place. This approach would be especially advisable in the case of distributed systems with high reliability and soft real-time requirements. In addition, the specifica-tion of IoT systems in the form of a set of TR rules is easier to understand for end-users, encouraging the development of the IoT. The major limitation of TR programs compared to ordinary programs is the involvement of higher computation. Computing time is trade for ease of programming. Nevertheless, we believe that the advantages of the approach clearly outweigh the disadvantages.

5   Related Work

As it has already been established throughout this paper, IoT is one of the most promising technologies of our times and research on the topic has recently multiplied, mainly focusing on communication protocols, network architecture and other limitations [26, 27]. Open and proprietary platforms or middleware have emerged to try to give either vertical or horizontal solutions to different domains [10–13] but, to our knowledge, there is no previous attempt of using the TR approach for IoT systems, which makes our solution pioneer and innovative. Therefore, this section provides a review of the litera-ture on other approaches to specify IoT systems.

Choe et al. presents in [28] a visual environment called SAVE to model IoT systems with dynamic and static properties by making use of a process algebra called δ-Calculus and a first order logic called GTS-Logic. Thramboulidis et al. in [29] extends UML to consider the properties of IoT systems, and Cubo et al. [30, 31] use UML sequence diagrams to indicate the interactions between agents and finite state machines for the behavior of each node. Jayaraman et al. [32] introduces a semantically enhanced digital agriculture use case Phenonet based on the OpenIoT platform and in [33] describes SmartFarmNet, an IoT platform that allows visualization, analysis and scalable sensor acquisition in smart farming applications. IBM makes use of the well-known Node-RED [34] for "wiring" the IoT and Spanoudakis et al. use Ambient Intelligence [35]. At the same time, IoT systems can be specified by the use of statecharts but, in complex systems, this approach has the drawback of huge unmanageable number of states. Despite of the benefit of using statecharts compared with state diagrams, TR programs provide a much more concise way to specify the behavior of a system and all the possible ways are implicitly modelled as part of the specification. In a statechart, all the transitions to deal with every possible alternative in the execution have to be explicitly considered. Ambient Intelligence or general purpose domain–specific programming languages (Java, Python, etc.) have the drawback of being too formal and complex specifications, unsuitable for inexperienced developers.

It is our opinion that the TR approach is a way to easily simplify the specification, implementation and deployment of IoT systems. People with basic programming background will be encouraged to set the behavior of their own IoT systems by using a simple GUI similar to ECA rules, fueling therefore the IoT development.

6 Conclusion and Future Work

Throughout this paper, TRIoT, a new approach for combining the IoT and TR paradigm taking advantage of their synergy in a feasible and useful way, has been proposed and a case-study for validating the approach in the field of smart agriculture has been described. Though the case-study still has to be deployed in real life and its results and performance should be analyzed in detail, it cannot be denied that at first sight, the TR paradigm looks rather promising and its application for IoT systems seems a natural approach, especially when dealing with non distributed and highly unreliable networks. The work should focus on validating the suitability of the TR specification for implementing IoT systems.

One of the open issues that still have to be addressed is, as said before, the deployment of TR nodes in real life scenarios and the assessment of their performance. Other open issues include: assessing nodes' power consumption, Minimum Event Separation Time assessment or developing a web interface to allow anybody to simply deploy his own TR IoT network. Future work will include, apart from giving solution to these issues, the extension of the architecture to other fields different from agriculture and the application of fuzzy logic for decision making, among others.

Acknowledgements. This work has been partially supported by the Spanish Government's cDrone Project (ref. TIN2013-45920-R). This paper is the result of the research carried out under the Research Program for Groups of Scientific Excellence of the Seneca Foundation (Agency for Science and Technology of the Region of Murcia, ref. 19895/GERM/15).

References

1. Mulani, T., Pingle, S.: Internet of Things. Int. Res. J. Multidisciplinary Stud. SPPP's 2(Special Issue 1) (2016)
2. Atzori, L., Iera, A., Morabito, G.: The Internet of Things: a survey. Comput. Netw. **54**, 2787–2805 (2010)
3. Gubbi, J., Buyya, R., Marusic, S., Palaniswami, M.: Internet of Things (IoT): a vision, architectural elements, and future directions. Future Gener. Comput. Syst. **29**, 1645–1660 (2013)
4. Tillman, K.: How Many Internet Connections are in the World? Right. Now. Cisco Blogs, 29 July 2013. http://blogs.cisco.com/news/cisco-connections-counter

5. Nilsson, N.: Teleo-Reactive programs for agent control. J. Artif. Intell. Res. **1**, 139–158 (1994)
6. Nilsson, N.: TR Programs. http://teleoreactiveprograms.net. Accessed Jan 2017
7. Morales, J.L., Sánchez, P., Alonso, D.: A systematic literature review of the teleo-reactive paradigm. Artif. Intell. Rev. **42**(4), 945–964 (2014)
8. Sánchez, P., Álvarez, B., Morales, J.M., Alonso, D., Iborra, A.: An approach to modeling and developing teleo-reactive systems considering timing constraints. J. Syst. Softw. **117**, 317–333 (2016)
9. Morales, J.M., Navarro, E., Sánchez, P., Alonso, D.: A family of experiments to evaluate the understandability of TRiStar and i* for modeling teleo-reactive systems. J. Syst. Softw. **114**, 82–100 (2016)
10. Mineraud, J., Mazheli, O., Su, X., Tarkoma, S.: A gap analysis of Internet-of-Things platforms. Comput. Commun. **89–90**, 5–16 (2016)
11. Pflanzner, T., Kertesz, A.: A survey of IoT cloud providers. In: 2016 Proceedings of the 39th International Convention on Information and Communication Technology, Electronics and Microelectronics (MIPRO) (2016)
12. Botta, A., de Donato, W., Persico, V., Pescapé, A.: Integration of cloud computing and Internet of Things: a survey. Future Gener. Comput. Syst. **56**, 684–700 (2016)
13. Abdur Razzaque, M., Milojevic-Jevric, M., Palade, A., Clarke, S.: Middleware for internet of things: a survey. IEEE Internet Things J. **3**(1), 70–95 (2016)
14. Gamesalad website. http://gamesalad.com/. Last Accessed Jan 2017
15. Yu, H., Shen, Z., Leung, C.: From Internet of Things to internet of agents. In: IEEE International Conference on Green Computing and Communications and IEEE Internet of Things and IEEE Cyber, Physical and Social Computing (2013)
16. Erlang official website. https://www.erlang.org/. Last Accessed Jan 2017
17. López Riquelme, J.A., Soto, F., Suardíaz, J., Sánchez, P., Iborra, A., Vera, J.A.: Wireless sensor networks for precision horticulture in Southern Spain. Comput. Electron. Agric. **68**(1), 25–35 (2009)
18. Martínez, R., Pastor, J.A., Álvarez, B., Iborra, A.: A testbed to evaluate the FIWARE-based IoT platform in the domain of precision agriculture. Sensors **16**(11), 1979 (2016)
19. Food and Agriculture Organization of the United Nations. http://www.fao.org/home/en/. Last Accessed Jan 2017
20. Makonin, S., Bartram, L., Popowich, F.: A smarter smart home: case studies of ambient intelligence. IEEE Pervasive Comput. **12**(1), 58–66 (2013)
21. McEwen, A., Cassimally, H.: Designing the Internet of Things. Wiley, Chichester (2014)
22. Raspberry 2 model B features. https://www.raspberrypi.org/products/raspberry-pi-2-model-b/. Last Accessed Jan 2017
23. Zigbee Alliance. http://www.zigbee.org/. Last Accessed Jan 2017
24. MQTT.org. http://mqtt.org/. Last Accessed Jan 2017
25. López Riquelme, J.A.: Contribución a las redes de sensores inalámbricas. Estudio e implementación de soluciones hardware para agricultura de precisión. Doctoral thesis, Universidad Politécnica de Cartagena (2011)
26. Angulo-Lopez, P., Jimenez-Perez, G.: Collaborative agents framework for the Internet of Things. Ambient Intell. Smart Environ. **13**, 191–199 (2012)
27. do Nacimento, N.M., de Lucena, C.J.P.: FIoT: an agent-based framework for self-adaptive and self-organizing applications based on the Internet of Things. Inf. Sci. **378**, 161–176 (2017)
28. Choe, Y., Lee, S., Lee, M.: SAVE: an environment for visual specification and verification of IoT. In: IEEE 20th International Enterprise Distributed Object Computing Workshop (EDOCW) (2016)

29. Thramboulidis, K., Christoulakis, F.: UML4IoT - A UML-based approach to exploit IoT in cyber-physical manufacturing systems. Comput. Ind. **82**, 259–272 (2016)
30. Cubo, J., Brogi, A., Pimentel, E.: Behaviour-aware compositions of things. In: IEEE International Conference on Green Computing and Communications (2012)
31. Cubo, J., Brogi, A., Pimentel, E.: A cloud-based Internet of Things platform for ambient assisted living. Sensors **14**, 14070–14105 (2014)
32. Jayaraman, P.P., Palmer, D., Zaslavsky, A., Georgakopoulos, D.: Do-it-yourself digital agriculture applications with semantically enhanced IoT platform. In: IEEE Proceedings of the Tenth International Conference on Intelligent Sensors, Sensor Networks and Information Processing (ISSNIP), Singapore (2015)
33. Jayaraman, P.P., Yavari, A., Georgakopoulos, D., Morshed, A., Zaslavsky, A.: Internet of Things platform for smart farming: experiences and lessons learnt. Sensors **16**(11), 1884 (2016)
34. IBM Node-RED. https://nodered.org/. Last Accessed Jan 2017
35. Spanoudakis, N., Moraitis, P.: Engineering ambient intelligence systems using agent technology. IEEE Intell. Syst. Mag. **30**(3), 60–67 (2015)

Practical Reasoning About Complex Activities

Esteban Guerrero[⊠] and Helena Lindgren

Computing Science Department, Umeå University, Umeå, Sweden
{esteban.guerrero,helena.lindgren}@umu.se

Abstract. In this paper, we present an argument-based mechanism to generate hypotheses about belief-desire-intentions on dynamic and complex activities of a software agent. We propose to use a composed structure called *activity* as unit for agent deliberation analysis, maintaining actions, goals and observations of the world always situated into a context. Activity transformation produces changes in the knowledge base activity structure as well in the agent's mental states. For example, in car driving as a changing activity, experienced and novice drivers have a different mental attitudes defining distinct deliberation processes with the same observations of the world. Using a framework for understanding activities in social sciences, we endow a software agent with the ability of deliberate, drawing conclusion about current and past events dealing with activity transformations. An argument-based deliberation is proposed which progressively reason about activity segments in a bottom-up manner. Activities are captured as extended logic programs and hypotheses are built using an answer-set programming approach. We present algorithms and an early-stage implementation of our argument-based deliberation process.

Keywords: Practical reasoning · Agents · Complex activity · Argumentation · Deliberation · Tool

1 Introduction

In social sciences, an *activity*[1] in general is understood as a purposeful interaction of the subject with the world [15]. This activity-theoretical concept [20] has been used to frame human behavior around the conscious pursue of goals to fulfill human needs. Key element of this theory is the concept of activity as a complex, dynamic and hierarchical structure. Among other approaches from social sciences, activity theory (AT) has been typically used for describing and explaining past events, for instance investigating activity dynamics considering current situations.

On the other hand, in artificial intelligence, *practical reasoning* investigates about what it is best for a particular agent to do in a particular situation [3]. Roughly, it explores the pursuing of goals by rational agents through two processes: *deliberation* deciding which of a set of options an agent should pursue;

---

[1] Not only human activity but activity of any subject.

© Springer International Publishing AG 2017
Y. Demazeau et al. (Eds.): PAAMS 2017, LNAI 10349, pp. 82–94, 2017.
DOI: 10.1007/978-3-319-59930-4_7

and *means-end reasoning*, solving the question how to achieve the selected goal. In other words, this models endow agents with abilities to plan ahead.

This work addresses the research question: how a software agent can look ahead for the next goal to execute when current and past events are considered? This problem is solved in two phases: (1) framing the evaluation of current and past events under an *activity analysis*, using AT to structure the agent knowledge, and argumentation theory[2] to deliberate about it; and (2) planning ahead using consistent hypothesized intentions which follow a well-known approach in practical reasoning, the *Belief, Desire* and *Intention* (BDI) model [8,25].

In our approach, deliberation is performed using a bottom-up method, drawing conclusions progressively using results from previous computation, *i.e.,* explanations in the *operative level* about atomic no-purposeful elements of an activity are generated; then explanations in the *objective level* about purposeful goals and conditions that need to be hold (from operative level) are build; then, explanations in the *intentional level* conclusions about an explicit conscious action to perform a goal under certain circumstances (from operative and objective level) are generated. In summary, the following technical contributions are presented: (1) a notion of practical reasoning about complex agent activities; (2) a progressive bottom-up deliberation based on answer-set programming and argumentation theory; (3) algorithms for practical reasoning; and (4) an open source tool for argument-based deliberation on complex activities.

The paper is organized as follows. In Sect. 2 we introduce basic notions about what a dynamic and complex activity is along with the syntax language that we use in the paper. In Sect. 3 we present our main contributions, where the deliberation process is formalized and exemplified. We implemented a first step on practical reasoning on activities developing a Java-based tool described in Sect. 4; in this section we also introduce algorithms that were implemented on the tool. In Sect. 5 we discuss about our approach regarding close related work. We highlight our main contributions in Sect. 6.

2 Preliminaries

2.1 Dynamic Activities

Activity theory defines an *activity* as a hierarchical structure composed by *actions*, which are, in turn, composed of *operations*. These three levels correspond, respectively, to *motives*, *goals*, and *conditions*, as indicated by arrows in Fig. 1. According to AT, actions are directed to goals; goals are conscious, *i.e.,* a human agent is aware of goals to attain. Actions, in their turn, can also be decomposed into lower-level units of activity called *operations*. Operations are routine processes providing an adjustment of an action to the ongoing situation, they are oriented toward the *conditions* under which the agent is trying to attain a goal. In this paper, an activity can be defined by the tuple $\mathcal{A} = \langle Go, Ac, Op, Co \rangle$ where $Go = \{g_1, \ldots, g_i\}$ is the set of $i > 0$ goals of the activity; $Ac = \{ac_1, \ldots, ac_j\}$ is

---

[2] A general perspective about argumentation theory is presented in [4].

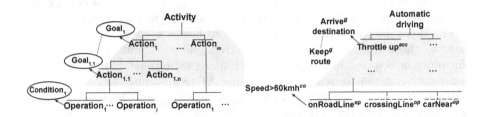

Fig. 1. The hierarchical structure of activity in activity theory. Adapted from [15]

the set of $j > 0$ actions associated with the set Go; $Op = \{op_1, \ldots, op_k\}$ is the set of $k > 0$ operations; and $Co = \{co_1, \ldots, co_l\}$ is the set of $l > 0$ conditions related to operations.

2.2   Underlying Logical Language

In the hierarchical structure of an activity mentioned above, the agent current state depends on external information to the agent's knowledge base. This information can be incomplete or uncertain. In order to capture and deals with this information during the deliberation process we use logic programs with negations as failure (NAF).

We use a propositional logic with a syntax language constituted by propositional symbols: $p_0, p_1, \ldots$; connectives: $\wedge, \leftarrow, \neg,$ *not*, $\top$; and auxiliary symbols: $(,)$, in which $\wedge, \leftarrow$ are 2-place connectives, $\neg$, *not* are 1-place connectives and $\top$ is a 0-place connective. Propositional symbol $\top$ and symbols of the form $\neg p_i (i \geqslant 0)$ stand for indecomposable propositions which we call *atoms*, or *atomic propositions*. Atoms of the form $\neg a$ are called *extended atoms* in the literature. An *extended normal clause*, C, is denoted: $a \leftarrow b_1, \ldots, b_j,$ *not* $b_{j+1}, \ldots,$ *not* b_{j+n} where $j + n \geqslant 0$, a is an atom and each $b_i (1 \leqslant i \leqslant j + n)$ is an atom. When $j + n = 0$ the clause is an abbreviation of $a \leftarrow \top$ such that $\top$ always evaluates true. An *extended normal program* P is a finite set of extended normal clauses. By $\mathcal{L}_P$, we denote the set of atoms which appear in a program P. ELP use both strong negation $\neg$ and *not*, representing common-sense knowledge through logic programs. On programs with NAF, the consequence operator: $\leftarrow$ is not monotonic, which means that the evaluation result, may change as more information is added to the program. Two major semantics for ELP have been defined: (1) answer set semantics [11], an extension of *Stable model semantics*, and (2) the Well-Founded Semantics (WFS) [27]. Let $ASP(S)$ be a function returning a *semantic evaluation*[3] of a set $S \subseteq P$ in which any of

---

[3] Semantic in terms of a semantic system [23]. A semantic system relates a set F of logical formulae to a set M of formal models, each representing a conceivable state of the world in enough detail to determine when a given formula represents a true assertion in that state of the world.

these two ELP semantics is used. In consequence, the range of this function is: $ASP(S) = \langle T, F \rangle$. Roughly speaking, $ASP()$ will return true (T) or false (T) for a given set S. ASP function will be use to make a consistency checking of rules sets, dealing with possible inconsistencies of the agent's activity *e.g.*, detecting "loops" such as $S = \{a \leftarrow not\ b,\ b \leftarrow not\ a\}$.

In order to exemplify our approach, we introduce an example about how an activity can be captured using this underlying formalism:

Example 1. A rational agent is deployed in a self-driving vehicle[4]. In this context, *driving* is an activity for the agent. This example is reduced to exemplify rational deliberation only. This activity consists of different actions, goals, operations and conditions which are indicated by superscripts $^{acc}, ^g, ^{op}$ and ^{co} respectively as follows:

$$P := \left\{ \begin{array}{c} \neg legalSpeed^g \leftarrow speed > 60kmh^{co} \wedge limitSign^{op} \wedge idle^{acc} \\ avoidCollision^g \leftarrow carNear^{op} \wedge carDist < 10m^{co} \wedge steeringLeft^{acc} \\ arriveDestination^g \leftarrow keepRoute^g \wedge throttleUp^{acc} \\ keepRoute^g \leftarrow onRoadLine^{op} \wedge not\ carNear^{op} \wedge speed > 60kmh^{co} \\ \dots \\ verifySocialNet^g \leftarrow touchScreen^{op} \wedge internetAvailab^{co} \\ \dots \\ inMove^{op} \leftarrow onRoadLine^{op} \wedge speed > 0kmh^{co} \\ carNear^{op} \leftarrow not\ carDistant^{op} \\ safeSpeed^{op} \leftarrow not\ limitSign^{op} \\ onRoadLine^{op} \leftarrow not\ crossingLine^{op} \\ crossingLine^{op} \leftarrow not\ onRoadLine^{op} \\ throttleDown^{acc} \leftarrow not\ throttleUp^{acc} \\ throttleUp^{acc} \leftarrow not\ throttleDown^{acc} \\ \dots \end{array} \right\}$$

$$G := \{legalSpeed^g, \neg legalSpeed^g, avoidCollision^g, keepRoute^g\}$$

$$Ac := \left\{ \begin{array}{c} brakeDown^{acc}, idle^{acc}, steeringLeft^{acc}, \\ throttleDown^{acc}, throttleUp^{acc} \end{array} \right\}$$

$$Op := \left\{ \begin{array}{c} limitSign^{op}, carNear^{op}, onRoadLine^{op}, \\ crossingLine^{op}, safeSpeed^{op}, carDistant^{op}, carNear^{op} \end{array} \right\}$$

$$Co := \left\{ \begin{array}{c} morning^{co}, evening^{co}, \\ speed > 60kmh^{co}, carDist < 10m^{co} \end{array} \right\}$$

In P, an intuitive reading of a clause *e.g.*: $keepRoute^g \leftarrow onRoadLine^{op} \wedge not\ carNear^{op}$, indicates that given that there is not evidence about a car nearby and the vehicle is in the road line, then the vehicle keeps its route.

Relevance is a property that some logic programming semantics satisfies, including WFS. The *relevant rules* of a program P *w.r.t.* a literal L contains all rules, that could ever contribute to L's derivation. Roughly speaking, the truth-value of an atom, *w.r.t.* any semantics, only depends on the *subprograms* formed from the *relevant clauses* with respect to that specific atom [7].

Definition 1. *Let P be an extended logic program capturing an activity $\mathcal{A}$ and let $x \in \mathcal{L}_P$ be an action or operation in $\mathcal{A}$.* rel_rules(P, x) *is a function which returns the set of clauses containing $a \in$* dependencies_of(x) *in their heads.*

---

[4] Some actions and operations are based on a self-driving vehicle example in [22].

Example 2. Following Example 1, we can obtain related rules from a given action, *e.g.*, $steeringLeft^{acc}$ as follows: $\mathsf{rel\_rules}(P, steeringLeft^{acc}) = \{avoidCollision^g \leftarrow carNear^{op} \wedge carDist < 10m^{co} \wedge steeringLeft^{acc}\}$

3 Deliberation on Activities

Deliberation is performed on related information about an activity *w.r.t.* a particular atom, *e.g.* an operation or an action. Our bottom-up approach for deliberation starts with an analysis in the operative level of the activity as follows.

3.1 Deliberation in the Operative Level

According to AT, an activity analysis in the operative level implies the examination of processes that become a routine [15]. For a rational agent, the importance of building operative level hypotheses lies in dealing with uncertainty of the external world observations, handling inconsistencies of its internal knowledge base and reasoning about *belief* routines. Hypotheses at this level can be built as follows:

Definition 2 (Operative hypothesis). *Let $\mathcal{A} = \langle Go, Ac, Op, Co \rangle$ be an agent activity. Let $S \subseteq P$ be a subset of an extended logic program; let $op \in Op$ be an operation and let $R = \mathsf{rel\_rules}(S, op)$ be the set of clauses related to op. An operative level hypothesis is a tuple $H_{op} = \langle R, op \rangle$ if the following conditions hold:*

1. *$ASP(R) = \langle T, F \rangle$ such that $op \in T$.*
2. *R is minimal w.r.t. the set inclusion, satisfying condition 1.*
3. *$\nexists\, op \in \mathcal{L}_P$ such that $\{op, \neg op\} \subseteq T$ and $ASP(R) = \langle T, F \rangle$.*

where $Op, Co \subseteq R$.

An operative hypothesis as is presented in Definition 2, defines a consistent knowledge structure allowing to an agent ascertain about a reliable belief about the world. Moreover, the first step in Definition 2 can be seen as a consistency checking process for dealing with uncertain information of the current belief.

Example 3. Let us continue with Example 1. Using P the following is an operative hypothesis that an agent can build from its driving activity:

$$H_{op_1} = \langle \underbrace{inMove^{op} \leftarrow onRoadLine^{op} \wedge ...; onRoadLine^{op} \leftarrow not\ crossLine^{op}\}}_{S},$$

$$\underbrace{inMove^{op}}_{op} \rangle$$

H_{op_1} says that there is consistent and well-supported evidence that the vehicle is in movement $inMove^{op5}$.

---

[5] Please, note that in atom: $speed > 0kmh^{co}$ the symbol $>$ does not belong to the underlying language, it is a semantic interpretation of a world observation.

Operations in AT are well-defined routines [18], *e.g.* in driving, as an agent's activity, the continuous verification to keep the vehicle on the road line can be considered as an operation, a routine. In this context, a sub-routine example can be collect information about distance between the road line and the vehicle wheel location. Sub-routines can be also captured using the concept of sub-operative hypotheses as follows:

Definition 3. *Let* $H_{op_A} = \langle R_A, op_A \rangle$, $H_{op_B} = \langle R_B, op_B \rangle$ *be two operative hypotheses.* H_{op_A} *is a sub-operative hypotheses of* H_{op_B} *if and only if* $R_A \subset R_B$.

In Example 3, a sub-operative hypothesis can also be built from the *atomic* rule: $onRoadLine^{op} \leftarrow not\ crossLine^{op}$, *e.g.*:

$$H_{sub_{op_1}} = \langle \underbrace{\{onRoadLine^{op} \leftarrow not\ crossLine^{op}\}}_{S}, \underbrace{onRoadLine^{op}}_{op} \rangle$$

Conflicts Among Operative Hypotheses. At some point in the deliberation, an agent can build a number of operative hypotheses about its beliefs, these can be conflicting each other invalidating or supporting other. This process has been used in argumentation theory for endowing non-monotonic reasoning to agents.

Definition 4 (Attack relationship between hypotheses). *Let* $H_A = \langle R_A, op_A \rangle$, $H_B = \langle R_B, op_B \rangle$ *be two operative level hypotheses such that* $ASP(R_A) = \langle T_A, F_A \rangle$ *and* $ASP(R_B) = \langle T_B, F_B \rangle$; *with* $R_A, R_B \subseteq R$ *i.e., hypotheses with related information. We can say that* H_A *attacks* H_B *if one of the following conditions holds: (1)* $op_A \in T_A$ *and* $\neg op_A \in T_B$; *and (2)* $op_A \in T_A$ *and* $op_A \in F_B$. *Att*$(\mathcal{H})$ *denotes the set of attack relationships among hypotheses belonging to a total set of possible built hypotheses* $\mathcal{H}$.

In argumentation theory literature, Dung in [9] introduced patterns of selection for arguments, the so called *argumentation semantics* which are formal methods to identify conflict outcomes for sets of arguments. The sets of arguments suggested by an argumentation semantics are called *extensions* which can be regarded as conflict-free and consistent explanations. In our approach, using an argumentation semantics to a set of hypotheses (at any level), for instance in the operative level: $SEM(Att(\mathcal{H}_{op}), \mathcal{H}_{op})$ the function SEM returns "the best" explanations for the current situation, where $\mathcal{H}_{op}$ denotes the set of all operative hypotheses that can be built from P. We can denote $SEM(AF_{op}) = \{Ext_1, \ldots, Ext_m\}$ as the set of m extensions generated by an argumentation semantics *w.r.t.* an *argumentation framework* formed by operational level hypotheses $AF_{op} = \langle \mathcal{H}_{op}, Att_{op} \rangle$. Sets of justified conclusions from the argumentation process can be defined as follows:

Definition 5 (Justified conclusions). *Let* P *be an extended logic program capturing an activity; let* $AF_{op} = \langle \mathcal{H}_{op}, Att_{op} \rangle$ *be the resulting argumentation framework from* P *and* SEM *be an argumentation semantics. If* $SEM(AF_{op}) = \{Ext_1, \ldots, Ext_m\}, (m \geqslant 1)$, *then:* Concs$(E_i) = \{$Conc$(H) \mid H \in E_i\}$ $(1 \leqslant i \leqslant m)$ *and* Output $= \bigcap_{i=1\ldots n}$ Concs(E_i).

In the remainder of this paper, we use subscripts with this functions to define the deliberation context, *e.g.*, Output_{op} indicates an output set of a deliberation process in the operative level of an activity.

Proposition 1. Concs *from operative hypotheses are candidate beliefs for an agent.*

Proposition 2. Output *in the operational level suggests an unambiguous belief for an agent.*

3.2   Deliberation in the Objective Level

Objective hypotheses captures the notion of consistent agent desires, describing necessary conditions to achieve a goal as objective. In this sense, an objective hypothesis is composed by operative level hypotheses directed to a goal, more formally:

Definition 6 (Objective hypothesis). *Let* $\mathcal{A} = \langle Go, Ac, Op, Co \rangle$ *be an agent activity. Let* $S \subseteq P$ *be a subset of an extended logic program; let* $g \in Go$ *be a goal and let* $R = \mathsf{rel\_rules}(S, g)$ *be the set of clauses related to* g. *Let* Output_{op} *be the output of the deliberation process in the operative level*[6]. *An objective hypothesis is a tuple* $H_{ob} = \langle R', g \rangle$ *if the following conditions hold:*

1. $ASP(R) = \langle T, F \rangle$ *such that* $g \in T$.
2. R *is minimal w.r.t. the set inclusion, satisfying condition 1.*
3. $R' = R \cup \mathsf{Output}_{op}$.
4. $\nexists\, g \in \mathcal{L}_P$ *such that* $\{g, \neg g\} \subseteq T$ *and* $ASP(R) = \langle T, F \rangle$.

where $Op, Co, Go \subseteq R$. Output_{op} *is a set of unambiguous beliefs in the operational level.* $\mathcal{H}_{ob}$ *will denote the set of all the objective hypotheses that can be built from* P.

In Definition 6, R is extended with a set of unambiguous belief from the operative level: Output_{op} *i.e.*, a number of facts from the operative level are added to the subset of clauses related to a given goal. This bottom-up building approach has two advantages: (1) restricts the search space for building objective desires; and (2) limits the generation of agent's desires by constraining the output of the deliberation process to sets of unambiguous beliefs using Output_{op}.

Example 4. Let us continue with Example 1. Let us assume the following output from the deliberative process in the operative level: $\mathsf{Output}_{op} = \{onRoadLine^{op}\}$ (see Example 3), an operative hypothesis can be built:

---

[6] Assuming that $AF_{op} = \langle \mathcal{H}_{op}, Att_{op} \rangle$ is the resulting argumentation framework obtained from R and $SEM(AF_{op}) = \{Ext_1, \ldots, Ext_m\}, (m \geqslant 1)$ is the set of extensions suggested by an argumentation semantics SEM.

$$H_{ob_1} = \langle \, \{keepRoute^g \leftarrow onRoadLine^{op} \wedge not\ carNear^{op} \wedge \dots;$$
$$\underbrace{onRoadLine^{op} \leftarrow not\ crossLine^{op}; \underbrace{onRoadLine^{op} \leftarrow \top}_{Output_{op}}\}, \underbrace{keepRoute^g}_{g}}_{R'} \rangle$$

Where $\leftarrow \top$ is a clause that always evaluates true, so called *fact*.

In the hierarchical structure of AT, goals can be composed by other goals inducing the notion of a sub structure of an objective hypothesis, as follows:

Definition 7. *Let* $H_{ob_C} = \langle R_C, ob_C \rangle$, $H_{ob_D} = \langle R_D, ob_D \rangle$ *be two objective hypotheses.* H_{ob_C} *is a sub-objective hypotheses of* H_{ob_D} *if and only if* $R_C \subset R_D$.

Similarly to operative hypotheses, among objective hypotheses attack relationships may exist. Moreover, *inter-level* attacks, *i.e.*, hypotheses from a level attacking other hypotheses in different level, can also occur due to the bottom-up deliberation process that is performed using AT approach.

Proposition 3. *Output in the objective level suggests unambiguous desires for an agent.*

Proposition 4. *Agent desires can be composed by operative and objective hypotheses, i.e. desires can be formed by other desires or consistent beliefs.*

3.3   Deliberation in the Intentional Level

A third type of hypotheses allowing to an agent deliberate about how to reach a goal by executing an action under certain circumstances is proposed.

Definition 8 (Intentional hypothesis). *Let* $\mathcal{A} = \langle Go, Ac, Op, Co \rangle$ *be an agent activity. Let* $S \subseteq P$ *be a subset of an extended logic program; let* $g \in Go$ *and* $acc \in Ac$ *be a goal and an action; let* $R' = \mathsf{rel\_rules}(S, acc)$ *be the set of clauses related to* acc. *Let* $Output_{obj}$ *be the output of a deliberation process in the objective level[7]. An intentional hypothesis is a tuple* $H_{in} = \langle R'', g, acc \rangle$ *if the following conditions hold:*

1. $ASP(R'') = \langle T, F \rangle$ *such that* $g \in T$.
2. R'' *is minimal w.r.t. the set inclusion satisfying 1.*
3. $R'' = R' \cup Output_{obj}$.
4. $\nexists\ g, acc \in \mathcal{L}_P$ *such that* $\{g, \neg g\} \subseteq T$, $\{acc, \neg acc\} \subseteq T$ *and* $ASP(R'') = \langle T, F \rangle$.

where $Op, Co, Acc, Go \subseteq R'$. $Output_{obj}$ *is a set of unambiguous desires in the objective level.* $\mathcal{H}_{in}$ *will denote the set of all the intentional hypotheses that can be built from* P.

---

[7] Similarly Definition 6, assuming that $AF_{obj} = \langle \mathcal{H}_{obj}, Att_{obj} \rangle$ is the resulting argumentation framework obtained from R' and $SEM(AF_{obj}) = \{Ext_1, \dots, Ext_m\}$, $(m \geqslant 1)$ is the set of extensions suggested by an argumentation semantics SEM.

Similarly to the deliberation process in operative and objective levels, Definition 8 establishes a bottom-up process using previous deliberations but including information *how* to achieve the given goal.

Example 5. Example 1 continuation. Following the bottom-up approach, desires and beliefs from previous deliberative process are added to the related rules of action $throttleUp^{acc}$. Using Definition 8 an intentional hypothesis can be built:

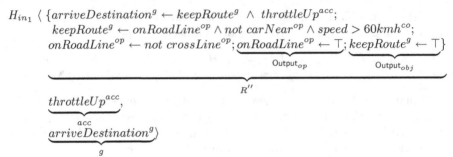

The intentional hypothesis H_{in_1} has an action $throttleUp^{acc}$ that when is executed under certain operations-conditions, hypothetically the agent will achieve the goal $arriveDestination^g$.

An argument-based deliberation in the intentional level of an activity, can suggest sets of consistent intentions in an agent. $Output_{in}$ can be defined as a set of conclusive hypotheses supporting means (actions) to reach goals. As a result of this hierarchical structure and similarly in the objective and operative levels, *sub-intentional hypotheses* can be also defined (we omit these formal definition).

Proposition 5. $Output_{in}$ *suggests unambiguous intentions for an agent.* $Concs_{in}$ *are candidates for agent intentions.*

4   A Tool for Argument-Based Deliberation on Complex Activities

In this section, we briefly describe the tool[8] for lack of space. The first module in Fig. 2 evaluates the inference feasibility of an atom considering if an atom belongs to the head of a rule or not. We obviate present this algorithm for a lack of space and simplicity of the process.

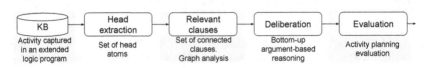

Fig. 2. Deliberation tool modules and implementation notes.

---

[8] Sources and manual instructions of the tool can be download in: https://github.com/esteban-g/recursive_deliberation.

Relevant clauses search is one of the key components in our approach. For a lack of space we cannot present this algorithm. Nevertheless we implement this in our tool using a graph library for detect connected components treating the logic program as a graph. *Deliberation* module takes a mapping between heads and their relevant rules and generates hypotheses first in the operative level, considering only atoms that are in the heads of rules which belong to operational level rules. Then, a semantic argumentation is applied using an external tool, a modification of the WizArg tool [12]. The output set is stored and the algorithm for selecting heads is again applied to obtain new facts which are added to the subprograms. This process is repeated for the objective and intentional layers of the activity. Based on the notion of a *semantic-based construction of arguments* [13] we developed a similar tool using DLV [19]. In Algorithm 1 line 5, MIN() is a function returning the minimal set *w.r.t.* the evaluated answer-set. Let us note that in the same line, ASP() function can be implemented using well-founded or stable semantics. In our implementation, we use the well-founded semantics evaluation provided by DLV (option -WF).

Algorithm 1. Deliberation at operational level

---

    input : $map(atom, \text{rel\_rules}(P, atom))$
    output: $Output_{op}$
1   Let R, Hyp_{op} and out be empty sets
2   Let ASP () be an answer-set evaluation of a rule set
3   Let OUTPUT () be a function following Definition 5
4   Let SEM () be an argumentation semantics evaluation of hypotheses set
5   Let MIN () be a function selecting the minimal set
6   **foreach** $atom \in map(atom, \text{rel\_rules}(P, atom))$ **do**
7       $R = \text{MIN}\,(\text{ASP}\,(\text{rel\_rules}(P, atom)))$
8   **if** $R \neq \{\varnothing\}$ **then**
9         $Hyp_{op} = Hyp_{op} \cup \langle R, atom \rangle$
10   **end**
11   **end**
12   $out = \text{OUTPUT}\,(\text{SEM}\,(Hyp_{op}))$
13   Returns out

---

5 Discussion

In this paper, the research question: how a software agent can look ahead for the next goal to execute when current and past events are considered? is addressed. For this purpose, we propose a bottom-up process for building consistent hypotheses allowing to an agent deliberate about what action (or set of actions) take to accomplish a goal (or set of goals). Current and past events are considered here no as temporal occurrences, *i.e.* considering the time when actions are performed (*e.g.* temporal reasoning), but as the "classical" notion of *fluents* [21]. Argument-based hypotheses are built to characterize mental states of the agent framed on a particular activity. Knowledge representation structure of the agent is based on an activity theory perspective, which allows us to clearly define the role of goals and actions *w.r.t.* an activity. In different approaches of practical reasoning using a Belief-Desire-Intention model, some agent's goals have analogous interpretation than desires[9]. In our approach, a well-known theory for activity analysis defines an interpretation of actions, goals, operations and conditions. Belief, desires and intentions of the agent are built upon an activity. In this sense, our approach is close to the Kautz *plan recognition* [16,17], where a hypothetical reasoning method is proposed in which an agent tries to find some set of actions whose execution would entail some goal.

There are key points to highlight why we consider this framework a valuable resource to be considered in practical reasoning: (1) *granularity of actions and goals*, in a number of approaches in computer science, actions are considered atomic processes directed to another atomic structure, the goal (see [14,28] reviewing agent theories). In different approaches of activity recognition, deviations in what is considered a "normal" activity have been amply investigated (see [26] as survey). In our approach, granularity in acts is the key for our bottom-up agent deliberation. (2) *Activity as a hierarchical dynamic structure.* Essential in our approach is activity dynamics. Roughly speaking, in most of computer science approaches the notion of an activity is statically defined. While this makes it relatively easy to design laboratory experiments, real-world human activities are far more complex and practical agent's activities became compound rather than atomic. Activity theory establishes a valuable approach for explaining real-world activity dynamics, *e.g.*, activities changing in time.

The closest approaches of our bottom-up deliberation are formal models for reasoning about desires, generating desires and plans for achieving them, based on argumentation theory in [1,2,24]. In those approaches, authors propose three frameworks for reasoning about belief, desire and intentions. There are considerable differences between Amgoud *et al.* and our approach: (1) in [24] an agent has different and independent knowledge bases for beliefs, *desire-generation* rules, and plans; we propose one knowledge base capturing an activity in a logic program. Nevertheless, our approach can deal with multiple concurrent programs given the well known properties of extended-logic programs and ASP semantics (see [6,7]); (2) in [1] the argument-based structure of actions and desires can lead to inconsistencies of the form: $\{desire \leftarrow desire\}$[10]; (3) an action in [1] is a tuple $\langle desire, Plan \rangle$ (original notation is different); in our approach *action* is an established notion in social sciences of a higher level act; (2) in [1,24], deliberation process is linked to the semantic meaning of atoms; we proposed our bottom-up approach considering an activity as a reference background framework where beliefs can change not only under more evidence or information (Definition 2) but also by a process called *automatization* in AT literature, where actions transform in operations[11]. A key advantage of our approach is the ability of maintain a *reasoning focus*, *e.g.*, in program P of Example 1 a clause about checking information about social activities: $verifySocialNet^g \leftarrow touchScreen^{op} \wedge internetAvailab^{co}$ does not affect the inference about driving, the so-called *conflict propagation* [10] or *contamination* [5].

---

[9] *e.g.* the so called, "potential desires" and "potential initial goals" in [1,2].

[10] In [1] Definition 4 it is state that "Note that each desire is a sub-desire of itself".

[11] In this paper we do not address automatization, this particular topic is being currently explored by the authors.

6   Conclusions

We present a formalization about an argument-based deliberation method for building explanations about current and past agent's events. Knowledge of the agent is represented using an activity-theoretical framework captured in an extended logic program. A bottom-up progressive approach for building structured beliefs, desires and intentions is formalized and implemented. We present algorithms used for developing our deliberation tool which we released as opensource. This is a first step in the integration of an activity-theoretical approach for knowledge representation of software agents. In our future work we want to investigate the process of change in complex software agent's activities similarly as is analyzed in social sciences. In this manner, an agent can re-orient plans when actions become operations, *e.g.*, when a software agent learns an activity by imitation or using human support, then such activity changes.

References

1. Amgoud, L.: A formal framework for handling conflicting desires. In: Nielsen, T.D., Zhang, N.L. (eds.) ECSQARU 2003. LNCS, vol. 2711, pp. 552–563. Springer, Heidelberg (2003). doi:10.1007/978-3-540-45062-7_45

2. Amgoud, L., Kaci, S.: On the generation of bipolar goals in argumentation-based negotiation. In: Rahwan, I., Moraïtis, P., Reed, C. (eds.) ArgMAS 2004. LNCS, vol. 3366, pp. 192–207. Springer, Heidelberg (2005). doi:10.1007/978-3-540-32261-0_13

3. Atkinson, K., Bench-Capon, T.: Practical reasoning as presumptive argumentation using action based alternating transition systems. Artif. Intell. **171**(10), 855–874 (2007)

4. Bench-Capon, T., Dunne, P., Bench-Capon, T., Dunne, P.E.: Argumentation in artificial intelligence. Artif. Intell. **171**(10), 619–641 (2007)

5. Caminada, M.W.A., Carnielli, W.A., Dunne, P.E.: Semi-stable semantics. J. Log. Comput. **22**(5), 1207–1254 (2012). http://dx.doi.org/10.1093/logcom/exr033

6. Dix, J.: A classification theory of semantics of normal logic programs: I. Strong properties. Fundam. Inform. **22**(3), 227–255 (1995)

7. Dix, J.: A classification theory of semantics of normal logic programs: Ii. Weak properties. Fundam. Inform. **22**(3), 257–288 (1995)

8. Doyle, J.: Rationality and its roles in reasoning. Comput. Intell. **8**(2), 376–409 (1992)

9. Dung, P.M.: On the acceptability of arguments and its fundamental role in nonmonotonic reasoning, logic programming and n-person games. Artif. Intell. **77**(2), 321–357 (1995)

10. Dung, P.M., Thang, P.M.: Closure and consistency in logic-associated argumentation. J. Artif. Intell. Res. **49**, 79–109 (2014)

11. Gelfond, M., Lifschitz, V.: Classical negation in logic programs and disjunctive databases. New Gener. Comput. **9**(3–4), 365–385 (1991)

12. Gómez-Sebastià, I., Nieves, J.C.: Wizarg: visual argumentation framework solving wizard. In: Artificial Intelligence Research and Development Conference, pp. 249–258. IOS Press, Amsterdam (2010)

13. Guerrero, E., Nieves, J.C., Lindgren, H.: Semantic-based construction of arguments: an answer set programming approach. Int. J. Approximate Reasoning **64**, 54–74 (2015)

14. Jennings, N.R., Sycara, K., Wooldridge, M.: A roadmap of agent research and development. Auton. Agent. Multi-Agent Syst. **1**(1), 7–38 (1998)
15. Kaptelinin, V., Nardi, B.A.: Acting with Technology: Activity Theory and Interaction Design. Acting with Technology. MIT Press, Cambridge (2006)
16. Kautz, H.A.: A formal theory of plan recognition and its implementation. In: Allen, J.F., Kautz, H.A., Pelavin, R.N., Tenenberg, J.D. (eds.) Reasoning About Plans, Chap. 2, pp. 69–125. Morgan Kaufmann, San Francisco (1991)
17. Kautz, H.A., Allen, J.F.: Generalized plan recognition. In: Proceedings of the 5th National Conference on Artificial Intelligence, 11–15 August 1986, Philadelphia, PA, Volume 1: Science, pp. 32–37 (1986)
18. Kuutti, K.: Activity theory as a potential framework for human-computer interaction research. In: Context and Consciousness: Activity Theory and Human-Computer Interaction, pp. 17–44 (1996)
19. Leone, N., Pfeifer, G., Faber, W., Eiter, T., Gottlob, G., Perri, S., Scarcello, F.: The DLV system for knowledge representation and reasoning. ACM Trans. Comput. Logic (TOCL) **7**(3), 499–562 (2006)
20. Leontyev, A.N.: Activity and consciousness. Personality, Moscow (1974)
21. McCarthy, J., Hayes, P.: Some philosophical problems from the standpoint of artificial intelligence. Stanford University USA (1968)
22. Naranjo, J.E., Sotelo, M.A., Gonzalez, C., Garcia, R., De Pedro, T.: Using fuzzy logic in automated vehicle control. IEEE Intell. Syst. **22**(1), 36–45 (2007)
23. O'Donnell, M.J.: Introduction: logic and logic programming languages. In: Logic Programming, Chap. 1, vol. 5. Oxford University Press (1998)
24. Rahwan, I., Amgoud, L.: An argumentation based approach for practical reasoning. In: Proceedings of the Fifth International Joint Conference on Autonomous Agents and Multiagent Systems, pp. 347–354. ACM (2006)
25. Rao, A.S., Georgeff, M.P.: Modeling rational agents within a bdi-architecture. KR **91**, 473–484 (1991)
26. Turaga, P., Chellappa, R., Subrahmanian, V.S., Udrea, O.: Machine recognition of human activities: a survey. IEEE Trans. Circ. Syst. Video Technol. **18**(11), 1473–1488 (2008)
27. Van Gelder, A., Ross, K.A., Schlipf, J.S.: The well-founded semantics for general logic programs. J. ACM **38**(3), 619–649 (1991)
28. Wooldridge, M., Jennings, N.R.: Agent theories, architectures, and languages: a survey. In: Wooldridge, M.J., Jennings, N.R. (eds.) ATAL 1994. LNCS, vol. 890, pp. 1–39. Springer, Heidelberg (1995). doi:10.1007/3-540-58855-8_1

Integrating Decentralized Coordination and Reactivity in MAS for Repair-Task Allocations

Hisashi Hayashi$^{(\boxtimes)}$

System Engineering Laboratory, Corporate Research and Development Center,
Toshiba Corporation, 1 Komukai-Toshiba-cho, Saiwai-ku, Kawasaki 212-8582, Japan
hisashi3.hayashi@toshiba.co.jp

Abstract. Task allocation is an important research area for multi-agent systems (MASs). In a large system of systems, multiple MASs are connected through the network, and decentralized coordination among MASs is vital. In general, it takes time to coordinate task allocations. However, when a task has to be done within a short time, it is necessary to start the task execution immediately. In this paper, we present a new task-allocation algorithm that reconciles decentralized coordination and reactivity. We consider scenarios where multiple causes of future agent failures are created simultaneously and consecutively, and if they are not removed by repair actions within limited times, some agents become out of order with high probability. In this paper, we show that the combination of decentralized coordination and reactivity significantly increases (more than doubles) the average numbers of successful repairs when the time available for decision-making and repairing is short.

Keywords: Multi-agent systems · Coordination and reactivity · Decentralized task allocation · Emergency repair

1 Introduction

Task allocation is an important research area for multi-agent systems (MASs). In order to allocate tasks to agents, agents need to communicate and cooperate with one another through the network. In general, it takes time to allocate tasks to agents because of various delays such as communication, computation process, action preparation, planning, or human confirmation. However, in the case of an emergency, there is insufficient time for task allocation. In this paper, we present two new algorithms for task allocation that handle delay times. In particular, one of the algorithms reconciles decentralized coordination among agents and reactivity by local agents, which is our main contribution.

We consider large MASs where multiple unit MASs are connected through the network. We also consider the scenarios where multiple disaster events happen simultaneously and consecutively, which trigger many causes of future agent failures. If a cause of a future agent failure is not repaired within a limited

© Springer International Publishing AG 2017
Y. Demazeau et al. (Eds.): PAAMS 2017, LNAI 10349, pp. 95–106, 2017.
DOI: 10.1007/978-3-319-59930-4_8

time, an agent will stop functioning with high probability. Some agents in unit MASs can execute repair actions. Therefore, the problem we consider is that of allocating repair tasks to unit MASs within limited times in order to prevent agent failures.

As discussed in [5,11,14], task-allocation algorithms are roughly divided into two kinds of algorithms: centralized algorithms and decentralized algorithms. In centralized algorithms, only one manager agent collects information from its child agents, computes the combination of tasks and agents, and allocates the tasks to its child agents. On the other hand, in decentralized algorithms, multiple manager agents communicate with one another to allocate tasks to other manager agents or to themselves. Many existing task-allocation algorithms are centralized algorithms. However, decentralized task-allocation algorithms are robust because the total MAS continue to function as a whole even when some managers breakdown. Auction algorithms such as the contract net protocol [15] are often used for dynamic task allocation [1,2,4,6,8,10] and it is not difficult to use them in a decentralized manner. Therefore, we modify and extend decentralized task-allocation algorithms that use the contract net protocol so that the new algorithm can allocate multiple emergency repair tasks that need to be completed within a limited time.

The rest of this paper is organized as follows. In Sect. 2, we discuss related work. In Sect. 3, we explain the MAS architecture and the problem. In Sect. 4, we define two new decentralized algorithms for repair-task allocations. In Sect. 5, we explain the simulation settings in detail. In Sect. 6, we show and analyze the simulation results. In Sect. 7, we conclude this paper.

2   Related Work

In this section, we discuss related work. In typical approaches for task allocations, meta-heuristics are used for optimizing combination of tasks and agents considering various constraints. In [9,17], multiple meta-heuristics for task allocation are compared. In [17], it is shown that a variant of tabu search is better than the other algorithms including variants of GA and ACO in terms of computation times and optimality. In [9], it is shown that a variant of PSO produces slightly better results in terms of optimality when the computation time is limited, and the other algorithms including variants of GA and fast greedy algorithms are nearly as good as PSO. However, in general, the algorithms of meta-heuristics are time-consuming and they are based on the centralized MAS architecture. Even if we use fast greedy algorithms, it is still impossible to avoid the delay times of the other computation, network delay, or human confirmation. On the other hand, we need to dynamically allocate tasks within very short times based on a decentralized MAS architecture. Therefore, to enhance reactivity, we try to avoid human confirmation and coordination among agents when the time for decision-making is short.

In [11,13], variants of max-sum algorithms for distributed constraint optimization (DCOP) are used for task allocation problems. Compared with other algorithms of DCOP that utilize connectivity graphs of agents, max-sum is robust against agent failures. However, many messages are repeatedly sent between agents in DCOP, which causes delays of communication and computation.

There is some research on task allocation that is robust for agent failures. In [14], the probabilities of future agent failures are considered when allocating tasks to agents. However, the algorithm does not consider repairing. In [7], backup agents are used in the case of an emergency. However, the cost of backup agents is high when additional hardware is needed. Similarly, in [12], robust agent teams are created by preparing more agents than needed, considering future agent failure.

Our repair-task-allocation problem is closely related to the task-allocation problems of combat ships [2,3], weapon-target assignment [4,9,17], and disaster relief [1,13,16] where tasks with hard deadlines such as threat removal and civilian rescue are allocated to teams.

3   MAS Architecture and Problem Description

We consider a MAS for repair-task allocations that is composed of multiple **unit MAS**s, each of which includes **sensing agents**, **action-execution agents**, and a **manager agent**: sensing agents detect causes of future agent failures, action-execution agents fix causes of future agent failures using limited resources, and manager agents communicate with one another to allocate repair tasks to action-execution agents. In this section, we define unit MASs and the agents that belong to unit MASs. We define the functions of unit MASs as agents because each function is often deployed on different hardware and becomes out of order independently.

As shown in Fig. 1, a unit MAS is a MAS comprising 0 or more sensing agents, 0 or more action-execution agents, and 1 manager agent. When a sensing agent senses a cause of a future agent failure, it reports the information to the manager agent in the same unit MAS. When receiving the information of a cause of a future agent failure, the manager agent allocates the repair task to an action-execution agent that belongs to the same unit MAS or allocates the repair task to the manager agent of another unit MAS if there are multiple unit MASs and their manager agents are connected by the network.

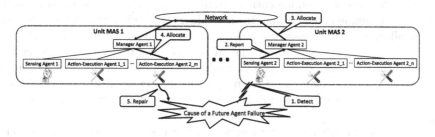

Fig. 1. MAS Architecture for repair-task allocations

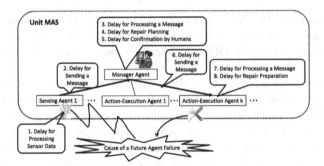

Fig. 2. Delay times

When allocated a repair task, the action-execution agent will execute a repair action consuming one resource. Execution of a repair action will succeed or fail according to the predefined probability. Unless a cause of a future agent failure is removed by a repair action, one of the agents will stop functioning according to the predefined probability.

Because we need to tackle time-critical problems, we consider delay times as illustrated in Fig. 2: time for a sensing agent to process sensor data to detect a cause of a future agent failure, time for an agent to send a message, time for an agent to receive and process a message, time for a manager agent to plan for repair, time for the human operator of a manager agent to confirm the repair plan, and time for an action-execution agent to prepare for repairing.

4   Algorithms

In this section, we introduce two new decentralized algorithms for repair-task allocations that are based on the contract net protocol [15]. These algorithms are equipped with replanning capabilities. Replanning is triggered when an action-execution agent fails to execute a repair action, which is very effective as shown in our previous study [8]. Replanning is also triggered when a manager agent with no available resource receives a repair-task allocation due to delay times.

We modify the contract net protocol so that we can handle multiple causes of future agent failures that are detected nearly simultaneously when repairing is delayed because of communication, computation process, action preparation, planning, or human confirmation. In these algorithms, when a manager agent M tries to allocate a repair-task R to a manager agent of another unit MAS, M tries to allocate R to a manager agent that M has not allocated a task for a certain period of time because even when multiple new causes of future action failures are found at nearly the same time, only a few agents are likely to be selected for repair-task allocations during the delay times, which triggers unnecessary replanning.

The second algorithm is an extension of the first algorithm. In the second algorithm, we combine decentralized coordination and reactivity. This is the main contribution of this paper. The idea is that in the case of an emergency, the manager agent that has the information of a cause of a future agent failure allocates the task to itself without communicating with the other manager agents and avoids confirmation by the human operator, which saves much time and enhances reactivity. We expect this new algorithm to become more effective when the time available for decision-making and repairing is short.

Algorithm 1 (Decentralized Coordination). *The sensing agents, the manager agent and the action-execution agents in each unit MAS work as follows if they are alive:*

- *Algorithm of Sensing Agents*
  1. *When a sensing agent detects a new cause of a future agent failure, it reports the information to the manager agent in the same unit MAS if the manager agent is alive.*
- *Algorithm of Manager Agents*
  1. *When the manager agent M of a unit MAS U receives the information of a new cause of a future agent failure C from a sensing agent of U, M asks each alive manager agent M2, if it exists, whether the unit MAS U2 of M2 can be in charge of the repair task R of C and how quickly an action-execution agent of U2 can start the repair action of R.*
  2. *If there exists a unit MAS that can be in charge of the repair task R of C, then the manager agent M performs the following procedure:*
     - **If there exists a unit MAS that can be in charge of the repair task R of C and has not been in charge of any repair task for a certain period[1] of time, then from those manager agents, M selects the manager agent M3 of the unit MAS U3 such that an action-execution agent of U3 can start the repair action of R the quickest and allocates R to M3.**
     - *Otherwise, M selects[2] the manager agent M4 of the unit MAS U4 such that an action-execution agent of U4 can start the repair action of R the quickest and allocates R to M4.*
  3. *When the manager agent M5 receives the allocation of a repair task R, M5 performs the following procedure:*
     - *If there exists an action-execution agent E5 in the same unit MAS such that E5 is alive, the number of resources of E5 is more than 0 and E5 is not reserved for another cause of a future agent failure, then M5 performs the following procedure:*
       - *(a) The manager agent M5 selects and reserves the action-execution agent E5 for R.*
       - *(b) The manager agent M5 calculates the plan P for R.*
       - *(c) The human operator of M5 confirms the plan P for R.*

---

[1] We set the period of time to be 1 min in our experiments.

[2] M4 has been in charge of a repair task for a certain period of time in this case.

(d) *When it becomes possible for the reserved action-execution agent E5 to start executing the repair action A for the reserved repair task R, if E5 is alive, the manager agent M5 orders E5 to execute A and erases the reservation information.*

(e) *When the manager agent M5 receives the result of action execution of A for the repair task R from the action-execution agent E5 in the same unit MAS, if the result is a failure, M5 asks each alive manager agent and reallocates R to one of the manager agents in the same way.*

- **Otherwise[3], M5 asks each alive manager agent and reallocates R to one of the manager agents in the same way.**

- *Algorithm of Action-Execution Agents*
  1. *When receiving an execution order of the repair action A, from the manager agent M in the same unit MAS, the action-execution agent E executes A, decrements 1 resource whether the result of A is a success or a failure, and reports the result to M.*

Algorithm 2 (Decentralized Coordination + Reactivity). *The sensing agents, the manager agent and the action-execution agents in each unit MAS work as follows if they are alive:*

- *Algorithm of Sensing Agents*
  - *Same as the algorithm of sensing agents in Algorithm 1*
- *Algorithm of Manager Agents*
  1. *When the manager agent M of a unit MAS U receives the information of a new cause of a future agent failure C from a sensing agent of U, M performs the following procedure:*
     - **If there is time[4] to communicate with other manager agents to allocate the repair task R of C before an agent fails owing to C,** *then the manager agent M allocates R to one of the manager agents in the same way as step 1 and step 2 of the algorithm of manager agents in Algorithm 1.*
     - **Otherwise[5], M allocates the repair task R to itself.**
  2. *When a manager agent M5 receives the allocation of a repair task R, M5 tries to do the repair task R in the same way as step 3 of the algorithm of manager agents in Algorithm 1 except that step 3c is modified as follows:*
     - *The human operator of M5 confirms plan P for R* **if[6] the repair action A of R can be completed before an agent fails after the human confirmation.**
- *Algorithm of Action-Execution Agents*
  - *Same as the algorithm of action-execution agents in Algorithm 1*

---

[3] In this case, M5 has received repair-task allocations beyond its currently available resources because multiple manager agents in different unit MASs tried to allocate a task to M5 at nearly the same time during the delay times.

[4] The threshold is calculated based on Table 5 in our experiments.

[5] In this case, M does not have the time to communicate with other manager agents.

[6] This step is skipped when there is insufficient time for human confirmation. The threshold is calculated based on Table 5 in our experiments.

5 Simulation Settings

In this section, we explain the details of simulation settings to compare and evaluate the two new algorithms defined in the previous section. In the following, we set typical values of unit MASs, considering our target applications.

5.1 The Number of Agents and Resources in Unit MASs

As shown in Table 1, we use 5 kinds of unit MASs: UMAS 1, . . . , and UMAS 5, which are typical unit MASs of our target application. The numbers of UMAS 1, . . . , and UMAS 5 are 1, 2, 2, 4, and 8, respectively. The total number of these unit MASs is 17 ($=1 + 2 + 2 + 4 + 8$). Each unit MAS has exactly one manager agent and one sensing agent. Because high-performance unit MASs are costly in general, considering the balance, we use a smaller number of high-performance unit MASs and a larger number of low-performance unit MASs. We introduce the performance of each unit MAS in the next subsection.

The numbers of action-execution agents in UMAS 1, . . . , and UMAS 5 are 0, 0, 4, 2, and 1, respectively. The total number of action-execution agents is 24 ($=2 * 4 + 4 * 2 + 8 * 1$). An action-execution agent cannot execute more than one repair action in parallel but multiple action-execution agents can execute repair actions at the same time. The numbers of initial resources that each action-execution agent in UMAS 3, . . . , and UMAS 5 has are 6, 4, and 8, respectively. The total number of initial resources is 144 ($=2 * 4 * 6 + 4 * 2 * 4 + 8 * 1 * 8$).

UMAS 1 and UMAS 2 do not have action-execution agents, which means that the causes of agent failures found by the sensing agent of UMAS 1 or UMAS 2 need to be repaired by the action execution agents of UMAS 3, . . . , or UMAS 6.

Table 1. The number of unit MASs, Agents, and Resources

Type of unit MAS	# of Unit MASs	# of Manager agents	# of Sensing agents	# of Action-execution agents	# of Resources of each action-execution agent
UMAS 1	1	1	1	0	-
UMAS 2	2	1	1	0	-
UMAS 3	2	1	1	4	6
UMAS 4	4	1	1	2	4
UMAS 5	8	1	1	1	8

5.2 Performances of Sensing Agents and Action-Execution Agents

Table 2 shows the times for sensing agents to start detecting causes of future agent failures before the expected times of agent breakdown. The probability of detecting causes of future agent failures is 90%. The sooner the sensing agent detects a cause of a future agent failure, the higher the performance is, which means that performance of the sensing agent in UMAS 1 is the best.

Table 3 shows the times for action-execution agents to start repairing and removing causes of future agent failures before the expected time of agent breakdown. The sooner the action-execution agent can start repairing, the higher the performance is, which means that performance of the action-execution agent in UMAS 3 is the best. The success probability of repairing is 80%.

Table 4 shows the times for action-execution agents to repair and remove causes of future agent failures when they start repairing x seconds before the expected time of agent's breakdown. We assume a situation where a cause of agent failure approaches the target agent at constant speed and the action-execution agent sends the resource for a repair to the cause of future agent failure at constant speed. Among the three causes of future agent failures, cause 3 approaches the target agent at the fastest speed.

Table 2. Probability and time to start detecting a cause before an agent failure

Type of unit MAS	Cause type of future agent failure		
	Cause 1	Cause 2	Cause 3
UMAS 1	90%, 43.2 s	90%, 120.0 s	90%, 42.4 s
UMAS 2	90%, 43.2 s	90%, 60.0 s	90%, 21.2 s
UMAS 3	90%, 43.2 s	90%, 24.0 s	90%, 8.5 s
UMAS 4	90%, 43.2 s	90%, 14.4 s	90%, 5.1 s
UMAS 5	90%, 18 s	90%, 6 s	90%, 2.1 s

Table 3. Success probability and time to start repairing before an agent failure

Type of unit MAS	Cause type of future agent failure		
	Cause 1	Cause 2	Cause 3
UMAS 3	80%, 36.0 s	80%, 12.0 s	80%, 4.2 s
UMAS 4	80%, 18.0 s	80%, 6.0 s	80%, 2.1 s
UMAS 5	80%, 10.8 s	80%, 3.6 s	80%, 1.3 s

Table 4. Repair time when starting the repair x seconds before an agent failure

Type of unit MAS	Cause type of future agent failure		
	Cause 1	Cause 2	Cause 3
UMAS 3	x/2.5 s	x/4.5 s	x/9.5 s
UMAS 4	x/2.5 s	x/4.5 s	x/9.5 s
UMAS 5	x/2.5 s	x/4.5 s	x/9.5 s

5.3   Delay Times

In our simulation scenarios, we take various delay times into consideration because they affect the simulation results when the time is limited. Table 5 shows

Table 5. Delay times

Time for processing sensor data	Time for sending a message	Time for processing a message	Time for repair planning	Time for human confirmation	Time for repair preparation
1 s	1 s	1 s	5 s	0, 10, 12, 13, 14, 15, 20, 30 s	5 s

the delay times. When a sensing agent detects a cause of future agent failure, it takes 1 s for processing sensor data. When an agent sends a message to another agent, it takes 1 s. When an agent receives and processes a message, it takes 1 s. When a manager agent calculates a plan for a repair task, it takes 5 s. When a human operator of a manager agent confirms a plan for a repair task, it takes 0, 10, 12, 13, 14, 15, 20, or 30 s. (We change the times for human conformation to see how the length of each delay affects the simulation results.) When an action-execution agent prepares for the execution of a repair action, it takes 5 s.

5.4   Occurrence Patterns of Disasters and Agent Failures

Table 6 summarizes the occurrence patterns of disaster events and causes of future agent failures. In our simulation scenarios, when a disaster event occurs, a cause of a future agent failure is created every second. The total number of causes of future agent failures created by a disaster event is 10. Disaster events repeatedly happen up to 10 times, and the interval between disaster events is 1 h. Note that the total number of causes of future agent failures created by 10 disaster events is 100 (=10 * 10) whereas the total number of initial resources is 144. It seems that the resources are sufficient for repairing. However, when an action-execution agent or its manager agent fails, its resource becomes unavailable. When a cause of a future agent failure is not removed, an agent becomes out of order with the probability of 90%. The proportions of cause 1, cause 2, and cause 3 are 60%, 30%, and 10%, respectively. The times from occurrence of cause 1, cause 2, and cause 3 to agent failures are 1800, 600, and 212 s, respectively.

Table 6. Occurrence patterns of disasters and causes of future agent failures

# of Disaster events	Occurrence interval of disaster events	# of Causes of future agent failures created by a disaster event	Occurrence interval of causes of future agent failures	Prob. of agent failures when not repaired	Proportions of causes of future agent failures and times from occurrence of a cause to an agent failure
1, 2, 3, 4, 5, 6, 7, 8, 9, 10	1 h	10	1 s	90%	Cause 1: 60%, 1800 s Cause 2: 30%, 600 s Cause 3: 10%, 212 s

6   Simulation Results

This section shows the simulation results. We conducted simulations 1000 times using different random seeds for each algorithm and for each simulation setting.

Figure 3 shows the simulation results after 10 disaster events when changing the times for human confirmation in the x-axis. Recall that 100 causes of agent

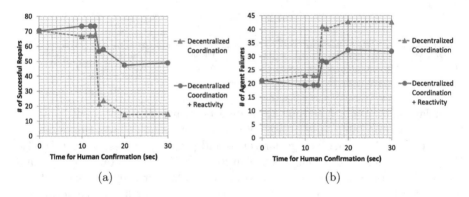

Fig. 3. Simulation results when changing the times for human confirmation

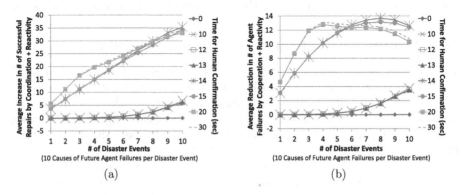

Fig. 4. Simulation results when changing # of disaster events

failures are created by 10 disaster events. In the graph of Fig. 3(a), the average number of successful repairs is shown in the y-axis. In the graph of Fig. 3(b), the average number of agent failures is shown in the y-axis.

In the two graphs of Fig. 3, we can see that Algorithm 2 (Decentralized Coordination + Reactivity) always produces better results than Algorithm 1 (Decentralized Coordination). The differences of these two algorithms are slight when the times for human confirmation are between 0 and 13 s. Algorithm 2 suddenly produces better results than Algorithm 1 when the time for human confirmation changes from 13 s to 14 s. The simulation results do not change much afterwards. This means that reactivity is very effective when the delay times are long compared with the remaining times before the agents become out of order. In other words, reactivity becomes very effective when there is insufficient time for coordination among unit MASs and for human confirmation.

Figure 4 shows the simulation results when changing the number of disaster events in the x-axis for different times for human confirmation. In the graph of Fig. 4(a), the average increase in the number of successful repairs by combining decentralized coordination with reactivity is shown in the y-axis. In the graph of Fig. 4(b), the average reduction in the number of agent failures by combining decentralized coordination with reactivity is shown in the y-axis.

We can confirm that reactivity is very effective when the delay times are long even for different numbers of disasters. When the times for human confirmation are between 14 and 30 s, the average increase in the number of successful repairs linearly increases as the number of disaster events increases in the graph of Fig. 4(a). However, the average reduction in the number of agent failures does not increase beyond 14 in the graph of Fig. 4(b). This is because the number of agent failures increases as the number of disaster events increases, and repairing a cause of an agent failure does not reduce the number of agent failures when the agent is already out of order.

7   Conclusions

In this paper, we presented two new algorithms (Algorithms 1 and 2) for decentralized repair-task allocation. These two algorithms were developed by modifying the contract net protocol so that we can dynamically handle multiple causes of future agent failures even when repairing is delayed because of communication, computation process, action preparation, planning, or human confirmation.

Although we improved decentralized repair-task allocation algorithms considering delay times, this was insufficient when a repair task has to be completed within a short time. In this case, we do not have time for coordination among agents and human confirmation. Therefore, in Algorithm 2, we combined decentralized coordination and reactivity, which is the main contribution of this paper. The idea of this algorithm is to skip coordination among agents and human confirmation when there is insufficient time.

We compared Algorithm 2 (Decentralized Coordination + Reactivity) with Algorithm 1 (Decentralized Coordination) by means of simulation. In our severe simulation scenarios of disasters, causes of future agent failures are created simultaneously and consecutively. We conducted simulation 1000 times for each simulation setting and for each algorithm using different random seeds. We evaluated the simulation results by the average number of successful repairs and the average number of agent failures. As a result, we found the following in our simulation scenarios:

- Algorithm 2 (Decentralized Coordination + Reactivity) always produces better results than Algorithm 1 (Decentralized Coordination).
- Algorithm 2 (Decentralized Coordination + Reactivity) is effective when the delay times are long compared with the remaining times before the agents become out of order.
- There is a clear borderline of delay times such that the combination of decentralized coordination and reactivity becomes very effective.

Although these results are confirmed in a limited number of simulation scenarios, we anticipate that these results hold in general. In future work, we intend to evaluate the algorithms in more detail in our target application using many different scenarios and parameters.

References

1. Ahmed, A., Patel, A., Brown, T., Ham, M., Jang, M.-W., Agha, G.: Task assignment for a physical agent team via a dynamic forward/reverse auction mechanism. In: International Conference on Integration of Knowledge Intensive Multi-Agent Systems, pp. 311–317 (2005)
2. Beaumont, P., Chaib-draa, B.: Multiagent coordination techniques for complex environments the case of a fleet of combat ships. IEEE Trans. Syst. Man Cybern. Part C **37**(3), 373–385 (2007)
3. Brown, C., Lane, D.: Anti-air warfare co-ordination - an algorithmic approach. In: International Command and Control Research and Technology Symposium (2000)
4. Chen, J., Yang, J., Ye, G.: Auction algorithm approaches for dynamic weapon target assignment problem. In: International Conference on Computer Science and Network Technology, pp. 402–405 (2015)
5. Choi, H.-L., Brunet, L., How, J.P.: Consensus-based decentralized auctions for robust task allocation. IEEE Trans. Rob. **25**(4), 912–926 (2009)
6. Gerkey, B.P., Mataric̀, M.J.: Sold!: auction methods for multirobot coordination. IEEE Trans. Robot. Autom. **18**(5), 758–768 (2002)
7. Guessoum, Z., Briot, J.P., Faci, N., Marin, O.: Toward reliable multi-agent systems: an adaptive replication mechanism. Multiagent Grid Syst. **6**(1), 1–24 (2010)
8. Hayashi, H.: Comparing repair-task-allocation strategies in MAS. In: International Conference on Agents and Artificial Intelligence, vol. 1, pp. 17–27 (2017)
9. Johansson, F., Falkman, G.: Real-time allocation of firing units to hostile targets. J. Adv. Inf. Fusion **6**(2), 187–199 (2011)
10. Lagoudakis, M.G., Markakis, E., Kempe, D., Keskinocak, P., Kleywegt, A., Koenig, S., Tovey, C., Meyerson, A., Jain, S.: Auction-based multi-robot routing. In: International Conference on Robotics: Science and Systems, pp. 343–350 (2005)
11. Macarthur, K.S., Stranders, R., Ramchurn, S.D., Jennings, N.R.: A distributed anytime algorithm for dynamic task allocation in multi-agent systems. In: AAAI Conference on Artificial Intelligence, pp. 701–706 (2011)
12. Okimoto, T., Schwind, N., Clement, M., Riberio, T., Inoue, K., Marquis, P.: How to form a task-oriented robust team. In: International Conference on Autonomous Agents and Multiagent Systems, pp. 395–403 (2015)
13. Ramchurn, S.D., Farinelli, A., Macarthur, K.S., Jennings, N.R.: Decentralized coordination in RoboCup rescue. Comput. J. **53**(9), 1447–1461 (2010)
14. Rahimzadeh, F., Khanli, L.M., Mahan, F.: High reliable and efficient task allocation in networked multi-agent systems. Auton. Agent Multi-agent Syst. **29**(6), 1023–1040 (2015)
15. Smith, R.G.: The contract net protocol: high-level communication and control in a distributed problem solver. IEEE Trans. Comput. **C−29**(12), 1104–1113 (1980)
16. Suárez, S., Quintero, C., de la Rosa, J.L.: Improving tasks allocation and coordination in a rescue scenario. In: European Control Conference, pp. 1498–1503 (2007)
17. Xin, B., Chen, J., Zhang, J., Dou, L., Peng, Z.: Efficient decision making for dynamic weapon-target assignment by virtual permutation and tabu search heuristics. IEEE Trans. Syst. Man Cybern. Part C **40**(6), 649–662 (2010)

Coordination of Mobile Mules via Facility Location Strategies

Danny Hermelin, Michael Segal, and Harel Yedidsion[✉]

Ben-Gurion University of the Negev, Beer-sheva, Israel
{hermelin,segal,yedidsio}@bgu.ac.il

Abstract. In this paper, we study the problem of wireless sensor network (WSN) maintenance using mobile entities called *mules*. The mules are deployed in the area of the WSN in such a way that would minimize the time it takes them to reach a failed sensor and fix it. The mules must constantly optimize their collective deployment to account for occupied mules. The objective is to define the optimal deployment and task allocation strategy for the mules, so that the sensors' downtime and the mules' traveling distance are minimized. Our solutions are inspired by research in the field of computational geometry and the design of our algorithms is based on state of the art approximation algorithms for the classical problem of facility location. Our empirical results demonstrate how cooperation enhances the team's performance, and indicate that a combination of k-Median based deployment with closest-available task allocation provides the best results in terms of minimizing the sensors' downtime but is inefficient in terms of the mules' travel distance. A k-Centroid based deployment produces good results in both criteria.

1 Introduction

Wireless Sensor Networks (WSN) have recently become a prevalent technology used in a wide range of environmental monitoring applications such as temperature, pollution and wildlife monitoring. Typically a WSN is composed of a large number of sensor nodes (n) coupled with short range radio transceivers. The sensors transfer their sensed data to a central hub via multi-hop communication. A communication tree is formed based on physical proximity and must be maintained through technical failures such as battery drainage or memory overload. The root of such a tree is usually a special node having significant power and communication abilities (for example, it is able to send an alert message to the control center which is far away from the actual sensors' location). In case some sensor in the communication tree fails, it not only stops monitoring its environment but, it might also disconnect the communication from other parts of the network.

We study the use of mobile agents called *mules* which have the ability to reach failed nodes, fix them and temporarily replace their role in the task of data collection and transfer. The mules are used to maintain and improve the networks resiliency and reliability.

© Springer International Publishing AG 2017
Y. Demazeau et al. (Eds.): PAAMS 2017, LNAI 10349, pp. 107–119, 2017.
DOI: 10.1007/978-3-319-59930-4_9

We aim to optimize the mules' deployment and to design the cooperation protocol between them as to minimize the duration of failures and the mules' travel distance. The decision on which exact objective function to measure involves some conflicting considerations.

By limiting the maximal downtime that any sensor may experience we can make sure that there is no loss of data for longer than a certain period of time. This guarantee is important for WSNs where data is sensed or transmitted periodically. On the other hand, minimizing the average downtime minimizes data loss in WSNs where sensors constantly sense and transmit data.

As for the mules' movement, since the mules are battery operated, it is important to limit the maximal movement by any mule to prevent its total battery depletion. Nonetheless, minimizing the mules' average travel distance would extend the total lifetime of the team as a whole and would enable them to fix more failures. As a consequence, we try to minimize both objectives (i.e., downtime and movement) under the two criteria (i.e., average and max) while focusing on minimizing the average downtime.

We propose algorithms that differ in their positioning methods and their suggested level of cooperation between mules. The contribution of our work lies in the novel use of known facility location approximation algorithms for solving the mule team problem.

Definition 1. *The k-Center problem is defined as follows: given a set of n points S and an integer k, find a set S' of k points for which the largest Euclidean distance of any point in S to its closest point in S' is minimum.*

Definition 2. *The k-Median problem is defined as follows: given set of n points S and an integer k, find a set S' of k points for which the sum of Euclidean distances of any point in S to its closest point in S' is minimum.*

Definition 3. *The centroid of a set of points S is the arithmetic mean of their coordinates.*

Definition 4. *A Voronoi diagram is a partitioning of a plane into regions based on distance to a given set of points S. For each point in S there is a corresponding region consisting of all points in the plane closer to that point than to any other point in S. These regions are called Voronoi cells.*

1.1 Related Work

Coordinating a team of mobile agents to perform tasks in a dynamic environment is a fundamental problem in AI that has received much attention from researchers [9,29,32]. Some of the popular methods that have been used to tackle this problem include: game theory [11,30], machine learning [17,33], multi-agent path planning and scheduling [8], distributed constraint optimization [6,35], economic market based approaches and auctions [15,21], virtual potential fields [25] and probabilistic swarm behavior [16].

We aim to further contribute to the study of multi-agent coordination by investigating the integration of known facility location techniques into the design of the algorithms which are meant to solve the mule team problem.

The term MULE (Mobile Ubiquitous LAN Extensions) was coined in [28] to refer to mobile agents capable of short-range wireless communication that can exchange data with a nearby sensor.[1] In the field of WSN, mobile elements have been proposed to improve maintenance, data collection, connectivity and energy efficiency [7]. Crowcroft et al. [5] define the (α, β)-Mule problem, where α is the number of simultaneous node failures and β is the number of traveling mules. Unlike our work where the topology of the network is given, their aim is to define the topology of the network in order to minimize the mules' tours. In [18], Levin et al. study the tradeoff between the mules' traveling distance and the amount of information uncertainty caused by not visiting a subset of nodes by the mules. The authors of [27] utilize autonomous mobile base stations (MBSs) to automatically construct new routes to recover disconnected infrastructure, while in [1] mobile backbone nodes (MBNs) are controlled in order to maintain network connectivity while minimizing the number of MBNs that are actually deployed. In [31], the k-Traveling Salesman Problem (TSP) approach is used to plan the data collection routes of k mules. TSP with neighborhood was applied for the same purpose in [14].

The k-Server problem proposed by [19] and researched by many others is closely related to our problem. However, the major difference is that the objective of the k-Server problem is to minimize the total traveling distance of the servers while in our problem this is a secondary objective. Our main interest is finding an optimal deployment scheme for the mules as to minimize the downtime of failed sensors. Another similar strand of work relates to the ambulance redeployment problem [20,34]. The difference from our model is that the set of deployment bases is predefined and finite while in our case agents can be placed anywhere in the environment.

The static version of a single iteration of our problem relates to the k-Center and k-Median problems (see Definitions 1 and 2 respectively). Since both of these problems are NP-Hard, we integrate into our algorithms known greedy heuristics for these problems that guarantee some approximation ratio of the optimal solution. These solutions run in polynomial time and thus are suited for practical applications that require quick responses. Specifically, Gonzalez [10] proposed the Farthest-First (FF) algorithm that provides a 2-approximation for the k-Center problem in $O(n)$ time. In [4] it is shown that the reverse greedy algorithm (RGreedy) guarantees at most an approximation ratio of $O(\log n)$ in $O(n^2 \log n)$ time for the k-Median problem.

1.2   Problem Definition

Formally, the mule team problem is defined as follows: V is the set of n wireless sensor nodes embedded in the Euclidean plane. Let M be a set of m mobile agents

---

[1] We use the term mules and agents interchangeably.

(mules) that can travel anywhere in the plane and fix sensors that experience technical failures. The sensors are subject to a set of failures F. Each failure occurs at a certain node, at a certain time and has a predefined failure duration F_d, which is the time it takes to fix a node from the moment a mule has reached it. The term *downtime* of a node v, denoted v_d, refers to the time from when v failed until a mule reaches it. Mule m's travel distance is denoted m_t The mules are immediately aware of any failure and can communicate with each other. Once a mule is engaged in fixing a failed node v, experiencing failure f, it is unable to attend to any other tasks for the time it takes to travel to v plus f's specified fail duration, f_d. It is assumed that the time to fix a failure is greater than the average time between consecutive failures and much greater than the average time it takes a mule to move to a failure.

The **goal** is to find a continuous deployment strategy and a cooperation method for the mules, which minimize two opposing objectives. The primary objective is to minimize the nodes' downtime and the secondary objective is to minimize the mules' traveling distance. These objectives are measured according to two criteria, namely average and max, while our focus is on the average criterion, we also monitor the max criterion. There exists a trade-off between these two objectives since minimizing downtime requires the mules to redeploy after every failure thus increasing their travel distance. The **challenge** is to design an algorithm that would produce the best results on both objectives and according to both criteria.

The first objective is to minimize the nodes' average downtime and is formalized as: $\min(\sum_{v \in V} v_d / |V|)$. The second objective is to minimize the mules' average travel distance: $\min(\sum_{m \in M} m_t / |M|)$. The same objectives under the max criterion are: minimizing the nodes' maximal downtime, $\min(\max_{v \in V} v_d)$, and minimizing the mules' maximal traveling distance, $\min(\max_{m \in M} m_t)$.

2   Algorithms

2.1   Facility Location Strategies

The facility location problem is a well studied problem in computer science and operations research [26]. It has many variations which primarily deal with optimally placing k facilities to service n given cities. Two classical variants of this problem which are closely related to our problem are the k-Center and k-Median problems, both proven NP-hard problems [12,13]. Consequently, there is a significant body of work that deals with approximation algorithms for these problems.

An optimal solution to the k-Center problem minimizes the maximal distance of any city to its closest facility and thus, any algorithm that provides a good solution for this problem can be useful in the design of an algorithm that would minimize the mules' maximal movement and the sensors' maximal downtime in the mule team problem.

The FF algorithm proposed in [10] provides a 2-approximation for the k-Center problem in $O(n)$ time. The algorithm greedily selects k points in the following way. The first point is selected arbitrarily and each successive point is chosen out of the n nodes as far as possible from the set of previously selected points.

An optimal solution to the k-Median problem minimizes the sum of distances of all the cities from their closest facility and thus, any algorithm that provides a good solution for this problem can be useful in the design of an algorithm that would minimize the mules' average movement and the sensors' average downtime in the mule team problem.

The Reverse Greedy algorithm (RGreedy) proposed in [4] to solve the k-Median problem, works as follows: it starts by placing facilities on all nodes. At each step, it removes a facility to minimize the total distance to the remaining facilities. It stops when k facilities remain. It runs in $O(n^2 \log n)$ time.

Finally, in [22] it was proven that a centroid of a set of points P provides a 2-approximation for the 1-median of P. Table 1 summarizes these findings.

It should be mentioned that there are additional approaches to deal with variants of k-Center and k-Median problems. So-called ε-nets [24] and Linear Programming relaxation [3] are just few examples. However, these approaches do not allow distributed implementation which is essential to make our solutions feasible for real life deployments.

Table 1. Summary of facility location approximation algorithms

Name	Reference	Performance bounds
FF	Gonzalez [10]	2-Apx. for k-Center
RGreedy	Chrobak et al. [4]	$\log n$-Apx. for k-Median
Centroid	Milyeykovski et al. [22]	2-Apx. for 1-Median

2.2 Proposed Algorithms

The proposed algorithms differ in their approach to four main traits, i.e., the mules' initial deployment, task allocation, continuous redeployment and cooperation methods. Each trait can be implemented in several ways.

1. The mules' initial deployment:
   - Grid - The mules are uniformly distributed in the area of the nodes.
   - Farthest-First - The mules are deployed according to the FF algorithm which approximates the k-Center problem.
   - Reverse-Greedy - The mules are deployed according to the RGreedy algorithm which approximates the k-Median problem.
   - Centroid-Adjustment - Each of the above methods can be combined with an additional repositioning stage of centroid adjustment where each mule moves to the centroid position of its closest nodes i.e., the nodes within its Voronoi cell. This process is performed iteratively until convergence.
2. The mules' cooperation method:
   - No cooperation - Each mule is in charge of the nodes in its Voronoi cell according to the initial deployment. This allocation is static and does not change as the mules move.
   - Cooperation - Here there is no strict node-to-mule allocation and every mule can fix any node even if it lies in another mule's Voronoi cell.

3. The mules' task allocation strategy (Only applicable for cooperative algorithms):
   - Closest - Send the closest mule to each failure thus minimizing average travel distance.
   - Closest-Available - Send the closest available mule thus minimizing downtime.
   - Closest-Least Traveled - Send the closest mule whose total travel distance after tending to the current failure is the lowest, thus minimizing the maximal travel distance.
4. The mules' redeployment:
   - No redeployment - This case has two options, either the mule that moves simply stays in its new position to minimize travel distance or it returns to its initial position to return to a deployments that was calculated to offer good reaction times and minimize downtime.
   - Farthest-First - The available mules are redeployed according to the FF algorithm and the occupied mules are disregarded. After recalculating the new positions, the closest mule is sent to every new location as to minimize their traveling distance during redeployment.
   - Reverse-Greedy - The mules are redeployed according to the RGreedy algorithm yet only $(k - b)$ medians are calculated out of $(n - b)$ node locations where b is the number of busy, occupied mules. Occupied mules and nodes that are being fixed are disregarded in the RGreedy calculation. After recalculating the new positions, the closest mule is sent to every new location as to minimize their traveling distance during redeployment.
   - Centroid-Adjustment - Unoccupied mules perform centroid adjustment by moving to the centroid position of their closest nodes while disregarding occupied mules.

The redeployment stage poses another interesting problem of mule's reassignment, i.e. which mule to assign to which location as to minimize the total traveling distance of mules. This problem is similar to the Minimum Weight Bipartite Matching Problem which can be solved optimally in $O(n^3)$ time, where n is the number of assignments, using the Hungarian Algorithm, [23]. We implemented this algorithm to determine the assignments of mules to new locations of the redeployment.

The different combinations of traits produce a large number of possible algorithms. Although we tested many algorithms in a wide variety of settings we limit our analysis to the few algorithms that yielded the best results and in addition, provide clear insights on the performance of the facility location techniques. Here are the proposed algorithms:

- **Basic Grid Algorithm** - This algorithm is designed to be a baseline algorithm to which we will compare the others. In our preliminary testing it provided the best results out of the algorithms that do not perform any redeployment. It uses uniform grid placement for the initial mules' deployment. The closest-available mule is assigned to a failure. No redeployment is performed.

- **No Cooperation Algorithm** - This algorithm is designed to compare the performance of the non-cooperative approach to the cooperative one. It uses uniform grid placement for the initial mules' deployment. Each mule is assigned the nodes in its Voronoi cell. This assignment is constant and there is no cooperation. This means that if a failure occurs in a Voronoi cell of an occupied mule, none of its neighbors would help out even if they are available. No redeployment is performed.
- **k-Center Algorithm** - This algorithm uses FF for the initial mules' deployment and for their redeployment. Mules cooperate and the closest-available allocation is used.
- **k-Median Algorithm** - This algorithm uses RGreedy for the initial mules' deployment and for their redeployment. Mules cooperate and the closest-available allocation is used.
- **k-Centroid Algorithm** - The initial deployment is done using FF but is immediately followed by a procedure called centroid-adjustment, where each mule moves to the centroid of the nodes in its Voronoi cell. Centroid-adjustment is also used to redeploy the mules after every movement. Here too, the closest-available mule is sent to any failure.
- **Local Search Algorithm** - While approximation algorithms can provide certain theoretical guarantees, there is no guarantee that they perform as good as local search methods in practice. For this reason we also implemented a local search algorithm, based on the scheme proposed in [2], to evaluate the overall performance of our proposed algorithms which are based on approximation algorithms.

  One of the difficulties in applying local search is the fact that the number of steps to reach a local optimum could be exponential. Since we are dealing with low polynomial time solutions, it would not be fair to compare between both approaches. We deal with this issue by using a limited time frame for search and an anytime mechanism for maintaining the best achieved state during the search process. The mules' deployment strives to achieve the k-Median criterion. The search process is performed in a distributed concurrent manner. At each iteration, every agent moves to a nearby position that minimizes the sum of distances from it to the nodes closest to it. The number of iterations is limited to a constant, the number of nodes n, or until convergence thus maintaining $O(n)$ runtime. Here too, the closest-available mule is sent to any failure.

3   Experimental Evaluation

In order to compare the performance of the different algorithms, we developed a dedicated software simulator, representing a WSN with failures and a team of mobile mules. The area of the simulated problem is an X over Y plane. Any number of nodes (N), and mules (M) can be positioned in the area. Within the total duration of the experiment (E_t), we can randomly induce any number of failures (F) on the nodes either in uniform or in non-uniform distribution.

The nodes which fail are randomly chosen from N and the start time of each failure is randomly chosen from $(0, E_t)$. For each experimental setting we test several values of failure durations (F_d), which is the time it takes to fix a failure from the time a mule has reached it.

In each experiment the specific values for N, M, E_t, F, F_d are chosen differently to demonstrate the algorithms' behavior in different scenarios. We ran several tests to find a combination of parameters that gives a good separation in the algorithms' performance and that adhere to natural assumptions of such a practical system such as $N > M$. Each reported result represents an average of 50 random experiments. In each experiment the initial node locations, failure location and start times are randomly selected. We used the same set of random seeds so that each algorithm is presented with the same 50 randomly generated problems. To analyze the statistical significance of the results, we performed T-Tests to validate the difference between the algorithms' performances. We state verbally in the text whether the differences between the results are statistically significant (i.e. p-value < 0.05) or not. For sake of readability, we refrain from adding error bars to the figures.

In the following subsections we analyze specific representative cases.

3.1   Comparing Cooperative vs. Non-Cooperative Algorithms

In this subsection we analyze the differences between the performance of non-cooperative algorithms where the node-to-mule assignment is static, and cooperative algorithms where any mule can attend to any failure even if it is not the closest mule to this failure. To this end we use the No-Cooperation algorithm to represent non cooperative behavior. It uses grid initial deployment and static task allocation, the mules do not return to their initial position as this strategy proved better than returning to the initial position on both objectives.

The experimental setting included problems with 10 mules and 100 nodes that were randomly deployed in a $X = 100$ over $Y = 100$ area. 100 failures were generated with $F_d = 0, 100, ..., 1000$ and $E_t = 10000$. Failure distribution is uniform i.e., each sensor has the same probability of failing.

Figures 1 and 2 present a comparison of the average downtime per failure between cooperative and non-cooperative algorithms. It is evident that as failure durations increase, the non-cooperative algorithm's performance worsens. The k-Median algorithm performs significantly better than all other algorithms.

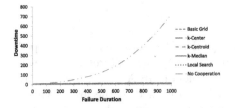

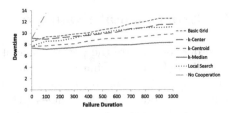

Fig. 1. Comparing cooperative vs. non-cooperative algorithms.

Fig. 2. A closer look.

3.2   Comparison of Cooperative Algorithms

This subsection presents a comparison between the three facility location inspired algorithms (i.e., k-Center, k-Median, k-Centroid) and, following the conclusions derived in the previous subsection, we do not compare them to a non cooperative algorithm but instead to the best performing cooperative algorithm that does not use any redeployment i.e., the Basic Grid algorithm, and to the Local Search algorithm.

The experimental setting uses the following parameter values: 10 mules, 100 nodes, $X = 100$ over $Y = 100$ area, 10 failures with $F_d = 0, 1000, ..., 10000$ and $E_t = 10000$. Failure distribution is uniform.

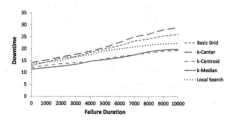

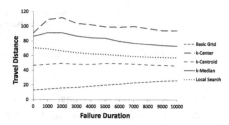

Fig. 3. Average downtime per failure as a factor of increasing failure durations.

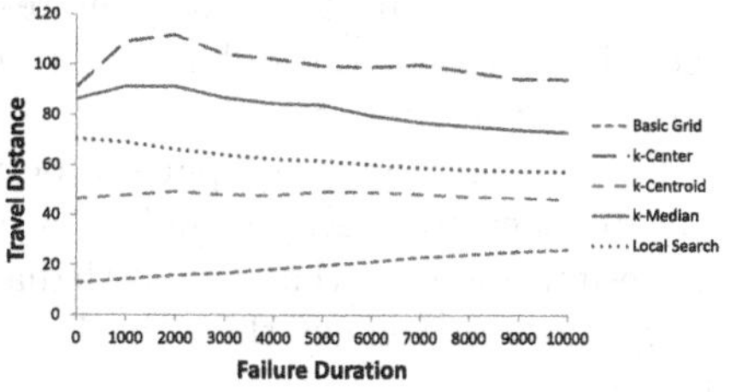

Fig. 4. Average distance per mule as a factor of increasing failure durations.

The results depicted in Fig. 3 demonstrate the advantage of the k-Median and the k-Centroid algorithms in terms of average downtime. The difference in the results of the k-Median algorithm to the Local Search algorithm and to the Basic Grid algorithm is statistically significant within 5%. The k-Center algorithm performs worse than the Basic Grid algorithm.

Figure 4 presents a comparison between the algorithms in terms of the average distance traveled per mule. The results indicate that the k-Median and k-Center algorithms cause significantly more movement than the other algorithms. This is due to the fact that after every movement of a mule to a failure, a new deployment is calculated according to the occupied mules. As a result, all the

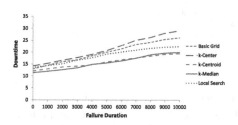

Fig. 5. Maximal downtime per failure as a factor of increasing failure durations.

Fig. 6. Maximal traveled distance of all the mules as a factor of increasing failure durations.

available mules move with every failure as opposed to the Basic Grid algorithm where only one mule moves. The centroid-adjustment phase and local search create less movement since they only fine-tune the positions of the mules and in most cases only the mules that are very close to the one that moved are effected. In our experiments, usually after one or two rounds no mules move and only the nearest neighbors are effected. The reason that we see almost 10 times more movement in redeploying algorithms compared with the Basic Grid algorithm is due to the fact that there are 10 mules in this experiment. Another interesting phenomena is that as failure durations increase, the average movement in k-Median and k-Center decreases since there are less un-occupied mules to reposition.

Figure 5 presents a comparison of algorithms in terms of the maximal downtime experienced by any node. The results show an advantage of the k-Centroid algorithms though the differences from it to the k-Median algorithm are not statistically significant within 5%.

Figure 6 presents a comparison between the algorithms in terms of the maximal distance traveled per mule. As in the average traveled distance, here too the results indicate that the k-Median and k-Center algorithms cause significantly more movement than the Basic Grid, Local Search and the k-Centroid algorithms.

3.3 Non Uniform Failure Distribution

In this case the failures were not generated randomly with equal probability of any node failing. Instead, once a node fails, the probability of failures in its vicinity is increased.

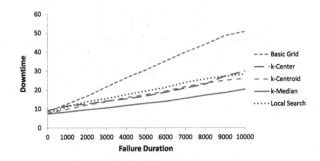

Fig. 7. Average downtime with non-uniform failure distribution.

Figure 7 presents a comparison between the algorithms in terms of the average downtime per failure. It is interesting to see that unlike the uniform failure scenario, here the k-Center algorithm performs very good and significantly better than the Basic Grid algorithm. Here too the k-Median algorithm produces the best results, significantly better than the k-Centroid algorithm.

4   Conclusion

In this paper we proposed the use of facility location approximation algorithms for the coordination of a team of mobile agents charged with maintaining a WSN. Specifically, we designed three algorithms based on approximation algorithms for the k-Center and k-Median problems and compared them to two baseline algorithms. The first, Basic Grid, is the best performing algorithm which does not use any redeployment techniques. The second, Local Search, enables to compare the algorithms to a heuristic local search approach. Our empirical results indicate that:

- Redeployment using the k-Median heuristic (RGreedy) paired with a task allocation strategy that sends the closest-available mule to any failure, provides the best results in terms of minimizing the nodes' downtime.
- Algorithms that perform redeployment using either FF or RGreedy are less efficient in terms of mobility than using centroid adjustment or not redeploying at all.
- The k-Center algorithm performs poorly when failures are uniformly distributed but produces good results in non-uniform failure distribution in terms of downtime.
- Cooperative strategies that enable mules to tend to failed nodes outside of their Voronoi cells are more effective than non-cooperative ones and this advantage becomes more apparent with larger failure durations.
- Allocation of the closest-available mule to a failure is more effective than allocating the closest mule in terms of minimizing downtime and performs only slightly worse in terms of mobility. This advantage become apparent with larger failure durations.

A key contribution of this paper is the introduction and experimental assessment of facility location approximation algorithms into the well studied AI problem of multi-agent coordination. Future work will extend the model to handle different node weights that represent the node's importance in data collection and communication, and non-deterministic failure fix durations.

Acknowledgments. The research was been supported by the following sources: Israel Science Foundation grant No. 1055/14 and grant No. 317/15, IBM Corporation, the Israeli Ministry of Economy and Industry, and the Helmsley Charitable Trust through the Agricultural, Biological and Cognitive Robotics Initiative of Ben-Gurion University of the Negev.

References

1. Anand, S., Zusseman, G., Modiano, E.: Construction and maintenance of wireless mobile backbone networks. IEEE/ACM Trans. Netw. **17**(1), 239–252 (2009)
2. Arya, V., Garg, N., Khandekar, R., Meyerson, A., Munagala, K., Pandit, V.: Local search heuristics for k-median and facility location problems. SIAM J. Comput. **33**(3), 544–562 (2004)

3. Charikar, M., Guha, S., Tardos, É., Shmoys, D.B.: A constant-factor approximation algorithm for the k-median problem. J. Comput. Syst. Sci. **65**(1), 129–149 (2002)
4. Chrobak, M., Kenyon, C., Young, N.E.: The reverse greedy algorithm for the metric k-median problem. In: Computing and Combinatorics Conference, pp. 654–660 (2005)
5. Crowcroft, J., Levin, L., Segal, M.: Using data mules for sensor network data recovery. Ad Hoc Netw. **40**, 26–36 (2016)
6. Farinelli, A., Rogers, A., Jennings, N.: Agent-based decentralised coordination for sensor networks using the max-sum algorithm. J. Auton. Agents Multi-Agent Syst. **28**(3), 337–380 (2013)
7. Francesco, M.D., Das, S.K., Giuseppe, A.: Data collection in wireless sensor networks with mobile elements: A survey. ACM Trans. Sens. Netw. (TOSN) **8**(1), 7–38 (2011)
8. Genter, K., Stone, P.: Placing influencing agents in a flock. In: AAAI (2015)
9. Gerkey, B., Matari, M.J.: A formal analysis, taxonomy of task allocation in multi-robot systems. Int. J. Robot. Res. **23**(9), 939–954 (2004)
10. Gonzalez, T.F.: Clustering to minimize the maximum intercluster distance. Theoret. Comput. Sci. **38**, 293–306 (1985)
11. Jiang, A., Procaccia, A., Qian, Y., Shah, N., Tambe, M.: Defender (mis) coordination in security games. In: AAAI (2013)
12. Kariv, O., Hakimi, S.: An algorithmic approach to network location problems. I: The p-centers. SIAM J. Appl. Math. **37**(3), 513–538 (1979)
13. Kariv, O., Hakimi, S.: An algorithmic approach to network location problems. II: The p-medians. SIAM J. Appl. Math. **37**(3), 539–560 (1979)
14. Kim, D., Abay, B., Uma, R., Wu, W., Wang, W., Tokuta, A.: Minimizing data collection latency in wireless sensor network with multiple mobile elements. In: INFOCOM (2012)
15. Koenig, S., Keskinocak, P., Tovey, C.A.: Progress on agent coordination with cooperative auctions. In: AAAI 2010, pp. 1713–1717 (2010)
16. Konur, S., Dixon, C., Fisher, M.: Analysing robot swarm behaviour via probabilistic model checking. Robot. Auton. Syst. **60**(2), 199–213 (2012)
17. Krause, A., Singh, A., Guestrin, C.: Near-optimal sensor placements in gaussian processes: Theory, efficient algorithms and empirical studies. J. Mach. Learn. Res. **9**, 235–284 (2008)
18. Levin, L., Efrat, A., Segal, M.: Collecting data in ad-hoc networks with reduced uncertainty. Ad Hoc Netw. **17**, 71–81 (2014)
19. Manasse, M.S., McGeoch, L.A., Sleator, D.D.: Competitive algorithms for server problems. J. Algorithms **11**(2), 208–230 (1990)
20. Maxwell, M.S., Restrepo, M., Henderson, S.G., Topaloglu, H.: Approximate dynamic programming for ambulance redeployment. INFORMS J. Comput. **22**(2), 266–281 (2010)
21. McIntire, M., Nunes, E., Gini, M.: Iterated multi-robot auctions for precedence-constrained task scheduling. In: AAMAS (2016)
22. Milyeykovski, V., Segal, M., Katz, V.: central nodes for efficient data collection in wireless sensor networks. Comput. Netw. **91**, 425–437 (2015)
23. Munkres, J.: Algorithms for the assignment and transportation problems. J. Soc. Ind. Appl. Math. **5**(1), 32–38 (1957)
24. Mustafa, N.H., Ray, S.: Improved results on geometric hitting set problems. Discrete Comput. Geom. **44**(4), 883–895 (2010)

25. Poduri, S., Sukhatme, G.S.: Constrained coverage for mobile sensor networks. In: Proceedings of the IEEE International Conference on Robotics and Automation, pp. 165–171 (2004)
26. ReVelle, C., Eiselt, H.: Location analysis: A synthesis and survey. Eur. J. Oper. Res. **165**(1), 1–19 (2005)
27. Rui, T., Li, H., Miura, R.: Dynamic recovery of wireless multi-hop infrastructure with the autonomous mobile base station. IEEE Access **4**, 627–638 (2016)
28. Shah, R.C., Roy, S., Jain, S., Brunette, W.: Data mules: Modeling and analysis of a three-tier architecture for sparse sensor networks. Ad Hoc Netw. **1**(2), 215–233 (2003)
29. Stone, P., Kaminka, G.A., Kraus, S., Rosenschein, J.S., et al.: Ad Hoc autonomous agent teams: Collaboration without pre-coordination. In: AAAI (2010)
30. Tambe, M.: Security and Game Theory: Algorithms, Deployed Systems, Lessons Learned. Cambridge University Press, New York (2011)
31. Tedas, O., Isler, V., Lim, J.H., Terzis, A.: Using mobile robots to harvest data from sensor fields. IEEE Wirel. Commun. **16**(1), 22 (2009)
32. Urra, O., Ilarri, S., Mena, E., Delot, T.: Using hitchhiker mobile agents for environment monitoring. In: Demazeau, Y., Pavón, J., Corchado, J.M., Bajo, J. (eds.) 7th International Conference on Practical Applications of Agents and Multi-Agent Systems (PAAMS 2009). AISC, vol. 55, pp. 557–566. Springer, Heidelberg (2009)
33. Wang, Y., de Silva, C.: A machine-learning approach to multi-robot coordination. Eng. Appl. Artif. Intell. **21**(3), 470–484 (2008)
34. Yue, Y., Marla, L., Krishnan, R.: An efficient simulation-based approach to ambulance fleet allocation and dynamic redeployment. In: AAAI (2012)
35. Zivan, R., Yedidsion, H., Okamoto, S., Glinton, R., Sycara, K.P.: Distributed constraint optimization for teams of mobile sensing agents. J. Auton. Agents Multi-Agent Syst. **29**, 495–536 (2015)

OPC UA Based ERP Agents: Enabling Scalable Communication Solutions in Heterogeneous Automation Environments

Max Hoffmann[(✉)], Tobias Meisen, and Sabina Jeschke

Institute of Information Management in Mechanical Engineering,
RWTH Aachen University, Dennewartstr. 27, 52068 Aachen, Germany
{max.hoffmann,tobias.meisen,sabina.jeschke}@ima.rwth-aachen.de
http://www.ima.rwth-aachen.de/en/home.html

Abstract. This work contributes to a technology stack that pursues the goal of integrating intelligent entities in a production environment by means of communication technologies based on scalable interfaces supporting semantic modeling. The proposed architecture is realized based on a model-driven interconnection of multi-agent systems with OPC Unified Architecture. The integration of these technologies enables a usage of intelligent mechanisms within modern production sites while ensuring semantic integrity during all communication processes and compliance to essential security standards. The goal of this work is to enable a autonomous, reactive production by means of intelligent communication in autonomous systems. By making use of a model-based representation of intelligent software agents, an integration of cyber-physical systems with products and production units in manufacturing systems can be realized. The integrability of these multi-agent systems with high-level applications in terms of generic vertical interoperability is shown by means of seamless information exchange with an ERP system.

Keywords: Interoperability · Vertical integration · OPC UA · Semantic interface standards · Multi-agent systems · Enterprise resource planning

1 Introduction

One major topic of current research on modern production is dedicated to an intelligent utilization of resources [8]. With regard to industrial production, on the one hand these resources are characterized by the availability of manufacturing entities such as machines or engineering plants and on the other hand by means of human resources. The machine-related components of production plants are nowadays characterized by a high degree of automation, while the human-related tasks are moving from manual activities towards decision making. However, current developments show that autonomous decision making and intelligent behavior of manufacturing units can be also achieved by smart embedded autonomous systems working together in a cooperative manner [2].

© Springer International Publishing AG 2017
Y. Demazeau et al. (Eds.): PAAMS 2017, LNAI 10349, pp. 120–131, 2017.
DOI: 10.1007/978-3-319-59930-4_10

In order to utilize the full potential of human decision making, automated legacy systems and autonomously acting intelligent systems, an efficient cooperation between these different players is required. The goal of this cooperation is to reach a holistic optimization of current and future processes in manufacturing systems by taking into account highly granular data from the lowest level of a production plant (shop floor) and combining them with high-level logic of planning systems, e.g. enterprise resource planning (ERP). The key for incorporating these highly heterogeneous systems is to reach a communication that suits low-level automated systems, intelligent entities as well as high-level systems that interact directly with human beings at the same time [3].

In the ideal scenario, an integration of all systems enabled by scalable communication leads to an omnipresent availability of information from the production. One major goal is to reach an optimal provision of data from the field level with the purpose of serving valuable information to human decision makers. To reach this target, raw data from the manufacturing level has to be preprocessed and appropriately visualized in order to serve as a suitable basis for interpretable information. Another major interest focuses on the utilization of data directly on the shop floor based on computer-aided tools [4]. These smart embedded systems usually focus on methods of artificial intelligence that go beyond simple algorithmic correlations and calculation rules that are already present within current control units and programmable logic controllers (PLC).

Although both of these strategies – integration of information from the shop floor and autonomous processing of this data – play an important role in production, pursuing only one of those will not exploit the potential of optimizing the entire process. Thus, this work is about combining both strategy goals – enabling profound human decisions by means of an interconnection between different systems and utilizing the potential of smart autonomous systems in the field. The interaction and vertical integration is realized through an information modeling approach that allows for scalable machine to machine communication through semantic model definitions for multi-agent systems (MAS) in the field.

The proposed model based representation of agents covers the modeling of agent entities and their communication with other systems of the manufacturing infrastructure. The state-of-the-art section covers basics about the communication in modern production sites and MAS. Section 3 describes a software stack for modeling MAS using a scalable approach. In Sect. 4 the scalability of the approach together with higher systems of the enterprise planning layer is validated by means of an extended ERP agent communication stack and use-case.

2   State of the Art

2.1   Communication in Modern Manufacturing Environments

Optimization strategies in automation systems depend on the availability of up-to-date information that is collected through various devices, such as sensors or other data acquisition tools. However, the collection, aggregation and automated interpretation of the available information poses huge challenges to current information management systems as production data from different sources

122   M. Hoffmann et al.

is usually represented in various forms. Especially with regard to automated systems some distinct characteristics of available information can be pointed out:

- Production data collected in automation systems is naturally characterized by a strong degree of heterogeneity. The information does not only differ due to syntactical variance of data structures, but also in the manner different semantical concepts are used to represent the information.
- Modern production sites are comprised of a vast number of complex systems structured by means of hierarchically organized architectures, thus posing high challenges regarding vertical interoperability throughout these systems.

Hence, an integration of consistent interface technologies that connects all of these complex systems and subsystems with higher levels of the production planning and organization is difficult to achieve (see Fig. 1).

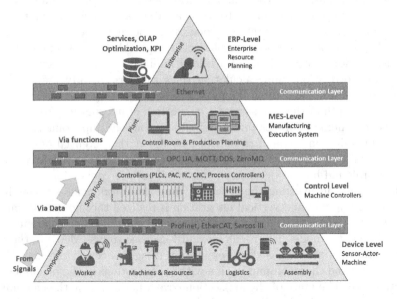

Fig. 1. Communication systems throughout the automation pyramid [1].

Seamless, integrative communication is generally only realizable in horizontal layers of automated processes, i.e. between programmable logic controllers or within closed control loops. Information to higher levels is mostly exchanged only in form of aggregated or condensed information that does not appropriately represent the complexity and granularity of the underlying production data.

In order to enable full availability of precise production data within higher systems for flexible process adaptation, the information from the shop floor has to be appropriately preprocessed and semantically annotated in order to fit the information management requirements on higher systems [11]. A promising communication interface standard that fits these requirements is OPC UA.

2.2 OPC UA – Scalable Interface Standard for Automated Systems

OPC UA has been derived from an initiative of a few major automation companies to a de-facto standard in automated industrial environments [5]. The OPC UA specification does not attempt to define another proprietary communication protocol, but rather introduces a metamodel that defines how information has to be represented in order to be integrable with information from other systems. For this purpose, OPC UA proposes an information modeling stack (Fig. 2) that allows for scalable extension of existing standards in order to fit the needs of each application or device that attempts to communicate through OPC UA.

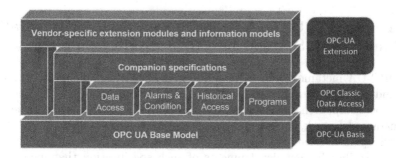

Fig. 2. OPC UA metamodel and information model stack

At the bottom of the information modeling stack the *OPC UA Base Model* is located. On top of the base model, additional models from former versions of the OPC standard preserve legacy system compatibility of OPC UA. The specifications of other organizations expand the standard by additional information models that comply to existing specifications, e.g. such as the IEC 61131-3 standard for PLC programming or AutomationML just to name two. On top of the model stack vendor specific namespaces can be defined., e.g. to facilitate an integration of common programmable logic controllers or similar pervasive device families. This approach pursued by OPC UA enables scalability on top of existing standardizations. The underlying design pattern can be used for a object-oriented modeling of arbitrary components, such as intelligent agents.

2.3 Enabling Cyber-Physical Systems in Production Through MAS

In order to cope with the growing complexity of modern production systems, ideas to facilitate optimization procedures based on intelligent, autonomous systems have been emerged in the last couple of years. In the matter of fact, the extensive increase of technical systems in automation environments brings centralized systems to its limits [10]. A key concept that is able to tackle these arising challenges consists in the introduction of cyber-physical systems (CPS).

The CPS idea is based upon the concept that all physical actions can be linked to a digital representation. Through this approach, it is possible to incorporate physical procedures with a *digital twin* that reflects real world processes with their digital counterpart [9]. An intelligent software agent as applied within multi-agent systems represents such a cyber-physical system. According to the definition of these intelligent entities, software agents provide capabilities to independently interact with their surrounding environment and performing autonomous actions while cooperating with other systems [7].

In accordance to CPS, agents are capable of sensing their direct environment and thus transporting physical actions into a digital context. In order to integrate these agents with other systems of the automation pyramid, this contextual information needs to be integrated with the semantics and information representation of the system architecture as demonstrated in the next section.

3   Agent OPC UA – A Scalable Approach for Integrating Multi-agent Systems into Real Production Sites

The OPC UA metamodel for information modeling is capable of incorporating any kind of object-oriented structure into its model definitions. In the same manner as companion specifications on the third and fourth layer of the OPC UA metamodel stack, an integration of complex concepts such as an object-oriented representation of MAS is also realizable by means of such approach. This section describes further developments of such specification that incorporates the representation and communication flow between agents and with high-level enterprise systems based on previous works of the authors [6].

3.1   Information Modeling for CPS

Similar to other smart embedded devices, intelligent software agents can be interpreted as some sort of cyber-physical system (CPS) as they are located on the interface of the physical process and its digital representation. The modeling of such entities is strongly inspired by the Internet of Things (IoT), which is also characterized by the formation of agile (ad-hoc) networks cooperating in agile infrastructures. Such open, dynamic and autonomous network compounds are only realizable through flexible information transport approaches that do not rely on central management instances, e.g. based on fixed servers, which mediate the communication processes between clients. The goal of the targeted network structures is to enable client as well as server functionalities on each communicating instance as vital part of the production network.

The presented approach aims at reaching such kind of generic interoperability between agents by enabling scalable communication solutions being part of a MAS metamodel. The proposed architecture is presented in the following section.

3.2   Semantic Integration of Intelligent Software Agents

The model representation of software agents based on OPC UA is performed by extending the existing OPC UA metamodel structure by an object-oriented mapping of the agents and their according communication skills (Fig. 3).

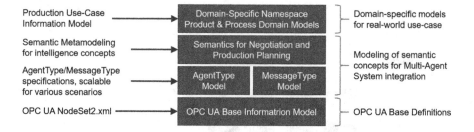

Fig. 3. Metamodel stack of OPC UA based multi-agent systems

On top of the base model, the *AgentType* and *MessageType* object models are located. The *AgentType* specification contains basic properties of an agent, e.g. the *capabilities* of an agent and its interactions facilities in terms of *environmental perception* through sensors and other data acquisition techniques.

The *MessageType* specification is located on the same semantic level as the *AgentType* and defines the inner design of messages that are exchanged between agents. The defined types reflect the different purposes of messages, e.g. for information exchange or for negotiation with other agents. Both metamodel specifications, the *AgentType* and the *MessageType* model, are designed by means of object-oriented modeling paradigms and comply with the basic requirements of OPC UA. This way, the information models are scalable in terms of new agent types or semantic enrichment of the message payload. Figure 4 shows the most important parts of the information model focusing on the *MessageType*.

The *BaseObjectType* is part of the base model and is located on the top representing the entry point for the information model. The *AgentType* as well as the *MessageType* are modeled as direct subtypes of the *BaseObjectType* inheriting the basic properties of an OPC UA *node*. The *MessageType* is further detailed by deriving subtypes of messages such as the *GetOfferMessageType* that represents the negotiation capabilities of an agent in terms of pursuing production steps or the *SetOrderMessageType* for representing concrete production assignments. The process-related type definitions are structured by means of a *domain-specific namespace*. Unlike the *information model namespace*, domain-specific extensions of the OPC UA metamodel focus on the requirements of a certain application domain, e.g. an engineering domain or a special type of process.

As shown in terms of the *MessageType* example, the utilization of the OPC UA metamodel offers a high variety and in-depth modeling capabilities for any kind of objects, entities or even domain ontologies. That being said, the ultimate goal of the OPC UA based representation of multi-agent system becomes clear: The described form of representing software agents in a digital way enables an integration of the agents' capabilities with other services by means continuous semantics and context information.

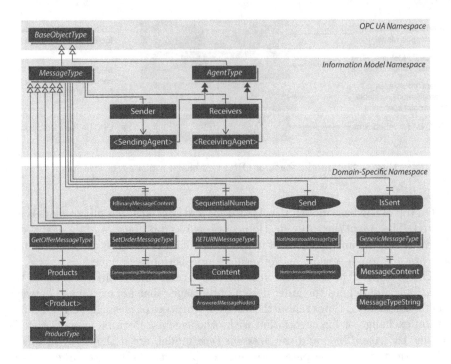

Fig. 4. Detailed *MessageType* specification of the OPC UA agent metamodel

With regard to the manufacturing related context that is in the focus of this work, some specific capabilities of software agents can be pointed out, which can all be represented in accordance to the described modeling concepts:

- The basic functionality of an agent is to sense its direct environment. With regard to a production scenario, this includes the capability to observe the state of surrounding agents, e.g. whether they are occupied, free, etc.
- Another crucial feature of an agent is the capability to receive messages from other entities. The advantage of the presented approach is that a form of generic interoperability can be guaranteed as long as the messages exchanged comply with the metamodel definition of the OPC UA agent model.
- In the same manner as receiving messages, the agents modeled in terms of the presented framework are also capable of placing messages to every OPC UA *node*, e.g. to communicate with other agents or to propagate information to high-level systems of the production planning and organization.
- Furthermore, an agent is capable of processing the content of messages, e.g. to perform actions based on the gained knowledge. The metamodel definition of the message objects ensures that each message is interpretable by the agents and can be processed in accordance to the underlying context, i.e. the specific application domain the agents comply to.
- The capability to process information from the surrounding environment enables agents to take autonomous decisions and accordingly negotiate with other entities. In terms of a manufacturing scenario, this can either be the

negotiation with regard to a production step or the execution of actions such as performing a transport or the conduction of a manufacturing step.

In order to utilize the described capabilities not only in the context of a dedicated subsystem on the shop floor, but also in terms of interactions with other systems of the automation pyramid, the software agents need to be capable of communicating with these higher system. The OPC UA metamodel already provides the basic enablers for this purpose. However, in order to communicate with higher instances, e.g. enterprise resource planning systems, an interface is required that does not only deliver a suitable protocol, but does also provide an understanding of the context information of the agents' application domain.

The purpose of the next section is to describe the design of an interface agent that interconnects agents from MAS in the shop floor to high level ERP systems.

4   OPC UA Based ERP Agents

Traditionally, interface technologies on the shop floor, e.g. enabled by service buses or similar technologies, enable a horizontal integration of the components by providing syntactical and semantic concepts for an information exchange. These concepts are usually focused on proprietary, fixed protocols and communication channels. Even though, these systems provide a functional cooperation of the entities in the field, the information exchange capabilities with higher systems is very often limited to a single interface as seen in Fig. 5.

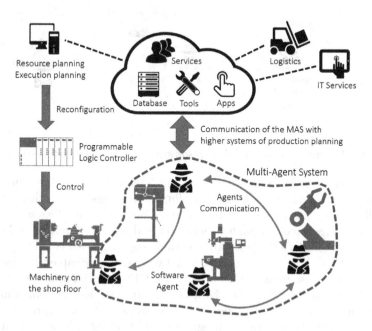

Fig. 5. Interface of tightly coupled MAS with higher systems

The software agents in the field represent certain machines and their capabilities that are shared by means of communicating with each other. However, their connectivity to high-level systems, e.g. Manufacturing Execution System (MES) is depending on a single interface that serves as a fixed gateway between a tightly coupled MAS and all high-level systems. Thus, the information that is changed throughout this interface is generally aggregated and represented in a highly condensed form. Profoundly granular information that could be of major importance during the execution planning, is usually not exchanged.

4.1   ERP System Connectivity Through OPC UA Based Messages

The architecture that results from the semantic information modeling approach that was carried out in terms of this work is depicted in Fig. 6.

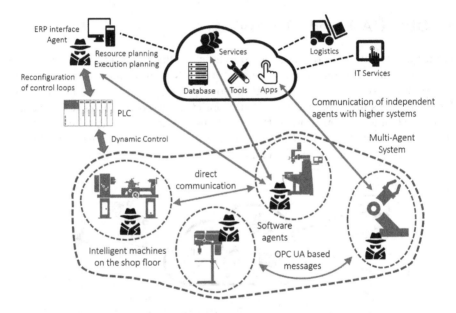

Fig. 6. Generic interoperability of software agents with higher systems

Compared to the MAS architecture in Fig. 5 the resulting architecture shown in Fig. 6 is characterized by higher flexibility. The agents remain their identity, thus still representing manufacturing machines for enabling intelligent utilization of production resources through negotiation and similar cognitive techniques. However, in contrast to the prior architectural approach, rich communication is not limited to an information exchange between agents. Enabled by the usage of a generic message representation based on OPC UA, information exchange can be realized either within the MAS, but also beyond, e.g. by communicating directly with MES or ERP systems. The advantage of this approach is that the actual manufacturing control programs can be adjusted in-process in terms of self-optimization, e.g. for compensating intolerances from earlier production steps through later actions in similar manufacturing sequences.

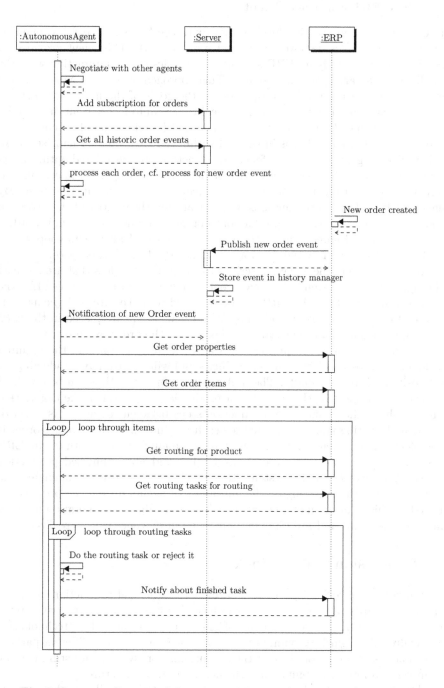

Fig. 7. Sequence diagram of the autonomous agent's process order method

4.2 The ERP Interface Agent

In order to incorporate high-level systems with the MAS in a seamless manner, an interface agent is deployed on the edge of the ERP. This agent provides all services of the underlying ERP system and enables direct interaction with the intelligent software agents in the field. This approach enables an agile planning and execution of the production process as the goals of the manufacturing can be dynamically adjusted with regard to real-time requirements from the ongoing processes. On the other hands, the agents on the shop floor can also benefit from the process knowledge that is integrated within the ERP domain namespace. In this way, the agents are able to focus on the actual process-related optimization strategies without having to deal with structural knowledge, i.e. managing different orders of products or the precise sequence of several production steps. By encapsulating these basic functions from the agents, the entities of the MAS can cooperate based on common production programs and accordingly finish orders more efficiently. Figure 7 shows the logical sequence of an agents cooperating with the ERP system by means of a common OPC UA address space.

In the first step, the agent subscribes to the product orders that are received through the ERP system. If a new agent is logging into an existing MAS the historic order events in the ERP will be returned to make sure that the agent is aware of the current production state. When new orders are placed in the ERP system, the agent is automatically notified about the order by an event.

Based on the order properties, each agent is able to compare the required production steps with their own capabilities and will accordingly decide about a proposition of its availability. The routing of the products that can be obtained for each order specifies the sequence of production steps. When the negotiation process about the execution of production steps between the agents is finished, the manufacturing steps are looped for each product until the product order is completed. Each agent that takes part in the manufacturing notifies the ERP system about the current state of production and about finished production steps. That way the ERP system stays in charge in terms of managing the process flow without infringing the autonomy of agents during the production. Based on this clear distinction of responsibilities a valuable cooperation between managing systems and solutions for embedded intelligence can be realized.

5 Conclusion and Outlook

The high level of technology present in modern industrial production opens up various new applications, many of them based on the usage of data driven technologies. However, there is still a lack of generic integration of these technologies, especially with regard to communication processes between the different parts of a technical system. Most state-of-the-art automation systems are still far away from vertical interoperability through their system architecture.

The current work offers an approach to meet these challenges by presenting an architectural approach that combines two completely different types of technology – communication interface standardization and artificial intelligence.

An incorporation of multi-agent systems and OPC Unified Architecture bears the potential to use adaptive behavior embedded into small devices on the field of a production more effectively by combining the knowledge and capabilities of agents with information from the enterprise layers such as ERP or other high-level systems. Especially the combination with resource planning systems as shown in this work brings decisive advantages in terms of agile planning, reconfiguration and flexible execution scenarios for customized production processes.

The stated solutions are already embedded and evaluated in terms of an Industry 4.0 demonstration test bed presented at the Hannover Fair 2016 in Germany. Future work in the field will focus on the embedding and combination of more sophisticated learning strategies of the agents, which include machine learning solutions, e.g. with regard to predictive maintenance scenarios in combination with an efficient resource planning and product life cycle evaluation.

Acknowledgment. The authors would like to thank the Cluster of Excellence on "Production Technology for High-Wage Countries" at the RWTH Aachen University for the support during the development process of the presented framework.

References

1. Munz, H.: Requirements for time sensitive networks in manufacturing. Why right now? Becuase Industry 4.0 needs it! IEEE 802.1 TSN Standard Meeting (2015). Accessed 22 May 2015
2. Barbosa, J., Leitão, P., Adam, E., Trentesaux, D.: Dynamic self-organization in holonic multi-agent manufacturing systems: The ADACOR evolution. Comput. Ind. **66**, 99–111 (2015)
3. Colombo, A.W., Karnouskos, S.: Towards the factory of the future: a service-oriented cross-layer infrastructure. In: ICT Shaping the World, pp. 65–81. ETSI world class standards, Wiley, Chichester (2009)
4. Feng, S., Stouffer, K., Jurrens, K.: Manufacturing planning and predictive process model integration using software agents. Adv. Eng. Inf. **19**(2), 135–142 (2005)
5. Hannelius, T., Salmenpera, M., Kuikka, S.: Roadmap to adopting OPC UA. In: 6th IEEE International Conference on Industrial Informatics, pp. 756–761 (2008)
6. Hoffmann, M., Thomas, P., Schütz, D., Vogel-Heuser, B., Meisen, T., Jeschke, S.: Semantic integration of multi-agent systems using an OPC UA information modeling approach. In: 14th International Conference on Industrial Informatics (INDIN), Poitiers, France (2016)
7. Jennings, N.R.: On agent-based software engineering. AI **117**(2), 277–296 (2000)
8. Kagermann, H., Wahlster, W., Helbig, J.: Securing the future of German manufacturing industry: recommendations for implementing the strategic initiative INDUSTRIE 4.0 (2013)
9. Lee, J., Lapira, E., Bagheri, B., Kao, H.A.: Recent advances and trends in predictive manufacturing systems in big data environment. Manuf. Lett. **1**(1), 38–41 (2013)
10. Leitão, P., Karnouskos, S., Ribeiro, L., Lee, J., Strasser, T., Colombo, A.W.: Smart agents in industrial cyber-physical systems. Proc. IEEE **104**(5), 1086–1101 (2016)
11. Sauter, T.: The three generations of field-level networks-evolution and compatibility issues. IEEE Trans. Ind. Electron. **57**(11), 3585–3595 (2010)

Agent-Based Modelling for Security Risk Assessment

Stef Janssen[✉] and Alexei Sharpanskykh

Delft University of Technology, Kluyverweg 1, 2629 HS Delft, The Netherlands
{S.A.M.Janssen,O.A.Sharpanskykh}@tudelft.nl

Abstract. Security Risk Assessment is commonly performed by using traditional methods based on linear probabilistic tools and informal expert judgements. These methods lack the capability to take the inherent dynamic and intelligent nature of attackers into account. To partially address the limitations, researchers applied game theory to study security risks. However, these methods still rely on traditional methods to determine essential model parameters, such as payoff values. To overcome the limitations of traditional methods, we propose an approach which combines agent-based modelling with Monte Carlo simulations. Agent-based models allow more realistic representation of essential aspects and processes of socio-technical systems at cognitive, social and organisational levels. Such models can be used to estimate risks and parameters related to them. An application of the approach is illustrated by a case study of an airport security checkpoint.

1 Introduction

Security Risk Management is a field in which one aims to identify, calculate and mitigate security risks of a system by utilizing a finite set of resources. An important step within Security Risk Management is Security Risk Assessment, in which one aims to qualitatively or (semi-)quantitatively define security risks. A commonly used method to do this is the Threat, Vulnerability & Consequence (TVC) methodology [18], of which an adaptation is outlined in Fig. 1.

In this method, *Threat Identification* forms the first step, where a set of security scenarios is identified. Then, for each identified security scenario, *Consequence Assessment* is performed, where one aims to quantify losses in case the identified security scenario were to happen. *Threat Likelihood Assessment* is then used to estimate the probability that the security scenario will happen in some time period. *Vulnerability Assessment* is performed to determine the probability that all defense measures in the security scenario fail, and thus, the attackers are successful. *Risk* then forms the product of each of these three aforementioned factors. In Security Risk Management these risks values are then used to setup proper defense measures.

In general, each of the steps is quantified using analytic tools at the disposal of a security expert. This can for instance be linear probabilistic tools like Event trees [5], historical data, intelligence data and the experience of security experts

© Springer International Publishing AG 2017
Y. Demazeau et al. (Eds.): PAAMS 2017, LNAI 10349, pp. 132–143, 2017.
DOI: 10.1007/978-3-319-59930-4_11

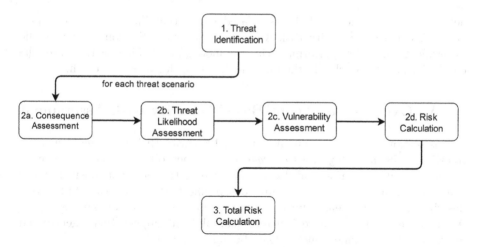

Fig. 1. The Threat, Vulnerability & Consequence (TVC) methodology.

[9,18]. It is often observed that these methods do not properly take the inherent dynamic and intelligent nature of an adversary into account [4,11].

To partially overcome this problem, researchers applied game theoretic methods that model a security scenario s_i as a security game [3,13]. In such a security game, a defender agent and an attacker agent are modelled as the respective row and column players of this game. Columns represent the options an attacker has to attack a target, while rows represent the available actions the defender has to defend the target. Based on the chosen strategies of the attacker and defender a pay-off is determined.

While security games allow for the modelling of intelligent and dynamic adversaries, they still require the definition of pay-off values. These pay-off values still have to be defined by relying on the above discussed methods to quantify *Vulnerability* and *Consequence*.

We therefore propose an Agent-based modelling and simulation method, which forms a promising alternative method for *Vulnerability* and *Consequence* assessment. It is capable of more realistic modelling of the underlying socio-technical processes, often problematic for the above mentioned methods. It can include rich cognitive, social and organisational models and explicit representation of the environment. As these models form a closer representation of the underlying socio-technical system, this can lead to improved estimates of security risks. It further reduces dependency on security experts and leads to more consistent quantitative results. Further, results of this method can be used as input for both the TVC methodology and game-theoretic method described above.

This paper sets a first step towards the development of this approach. We provide an illustrative case study in the area of an airport security checkpoint, and show the results of some basic experiments.

This paper is structured as follows. Section 2 provides an overview of the Agent-based Security Risk Assessment approach. Then, Sect. 3 discusses the

details of a case study and the associated model that illustrate the workings
of the Agent-based Security Risk Assessment approach. Section 4 discusses the
experiments that were performed with the model, and finally, Sect. 5 states the
conclusions of this work and the possible directions for future research.

2   An Overview of Agent-Based Security Risk Assessment

In this section, we describe our Agent-based Security Risk Assessment method
to estimate *Vulnerability* and *Consequence*. The method focuses on outcomes of
specific security scenarios, and *Threat Likelihood* is therefore not considered. For
generality purposes we do not commit to a specific MAS architecture, but merely
describe the set of agents and environment objects present in the underlying
Agent-based model. A more concrete example that applies this Agent-based
Security Risk Assessment method can be found in Sect. 3.

Agent-based simulation model m_i replicates and elaborates on some security
scenario s_i. It contains the following sets of agents: D_i, A_i and O_i. The set D_i
contains defender agents, the agents that are responsible for the defense in s_i.
A_i is the set of adversary agents, executing the subversive actions in security
scenario s_i. O_i is the set of other agents present in s_i. This can for instance be
a set of pedestrians or airport passengers. The set of environment objects E_i,
then represent the environment objects present in s_i.

Consequence and *Vulnerability* are estimated using a Consequence function
and a Fail function respectively. We define the (real-valued) Consequence function $C(m_i^j)$ determining the *Consequence* value for simulation run j, denoted
m_i^j. This Consequence function incorporates estimates of direct losses and indirect losses. Direct losses for instance include fatalities and physical damages of
an attack are estimated from m_i^j. Indirect losses like decreased number of future
passengers and business disruptions are then based on the estimated direct losses
and historical data. A boolean Fail function $F(m_i^j)$ is defined, determining the
adversaries' success (and therefore the failure of the defense) in m_i^j. The function
is equal to 1 if the defenders failed and 0 otherwise. Monte Carlo simulations
are performed to estimate *Consequence* and *Vulnerability* values. This is done by
performing N simulations and calculating the following estimates of *Consequence*
and *Vulnerability* in s_i respectively.

$$\hat{C}(m_i) = \frac{\sum_{j=1}^{N} C(m_i^j)}{N}$$

$$\hat{F}(m_i) = \frac{\sum_{j=1}^{N} F(m_i^j)}{N}$$

This approach can easily be extended to multiple security scenarios of a
system by replacing the set of adversary agents with a new set that executes
different actions. The next section will describe a case study to illustrate the
workings of this approach.

3   Illustrative Case Study

To illustrate the workings of the agent-based approach for Security Risk Assessment, a case study in the area of airport security is elaborated. In this case study, a terrorist aims to bring an improvised explosive device (IED) past a security checkpoint of an airport in his/her carry on luggage. Employees of the security checkpoint aim to find illegal items of passengers, while being under constant (time) pressure influencing their performance.

An agent-based modelling framework is defined and outlined in Fig. 2. In this framework, Human Agents and an Environment are distinguished. These elements will be discussed in the following subsections.

3.1   Human Agent

A human agent is the representation of a human in the airport environment. Human agents can interact with their environment, other (human) agents and have a (set of) goal(s) that they want to complete. Based on the works of Blumberg [1], Hoogendoorn [8] and Reynolds [14] we distinguish three levels of abstraction in a human agent: the Motivation Layer, the Task Layer and the Motor Layer. The Motivation Layer is responsible for high-level goal planning, (processing of) communication with other agents and the selection of activities. It further is responsible for setting and reaching high level goals. The Task Layer is responsible for the execution of specific activities and navigation. Then, the Motor Layer is responsible for low level interactions with the environment. It is responsible for sensing the environment and determines and executes the next move accordingly.

Three different types of human agents are distinguished: defending agents, passengers and attacker agents.

Defending Agents. Defending Agents in this model work at the security checkpoint to detect illegal items from passengers. They form the boundary between the secure and public areas of the airport. Four types of checkpoint employees exists, each having a different task within checkpoint operations: WTMD officer, Bag Checker officer, X-Ray officer and Directions officer.

The X-Ray officer is discussed in detail, while other employees are modelled in a similar fashion. The X-Ray officer has one activity, the *detect illegal items activity*, which is always active. In this activity, the X-Ray officer observes the output of the X-Ray machine he/she controls. An observation of an X-Ray machine is interpreted by the X-Ray officer to determine if the bag under consideration contains an illegal item. If an illegal item was detected, it is communicated to the Bag Checker officer, who then manually checks the bag. Three relevant parameters are distinguished: T_{base} representing the mean processing time of an observation, FN_{base} representing the false negative probability (i.e. the bags that *did* contain an illegal item, but were not observed by the X-Ray officer) and FP_{base} representing the false positive probability (i.e. the bags that *did not* contain an illegal item, but were identified as such).

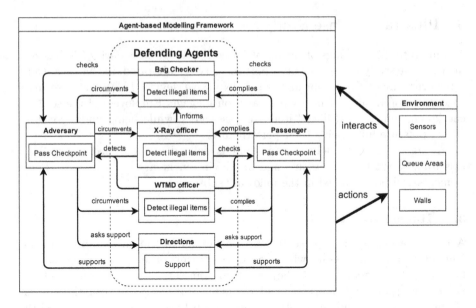

Fig. 2. Overview of the Agent-based Modelling Framework, containing attackers, defenders and passengers. The body of each agent shows a single activity that he/she can execute, represented in the Task Layer of the model. The two other layers are not visualized in this figure.

To incorporate varying performances of checkpoint employees under demanding circumstances, the Function State Model [2] is used. The Function State Model is used to determine the experienced pressure ($EP \in [0, 1]$) and performance quality ($PQ \in [0.4, 1.6]$) of an agent, based on factors like personality profile, cognitive abilities and external task demands ($TL \in [150, 500]$).

Task level is defined as a combination of two factors: queue length and bag complexity. These factors were shown to be influential on the performance of X-Ray officers in literature [6,16]. Specifically, it is defined as follows:

$$TL(t) = C_{bag} \times TL_{bag}(t) + (1 - C_{bag}) \times TL_{queue}(t)$$
$$TL_{bag}(t) = Norm(BC(t))$$
$$TL_{queue}(t) = Norm(QL(t))$$

where $TL_{bag}(t)$ and $TL_{queue}(t)$ represent the task demand with respect to the baggage and queue at time t respectively. C_{bag} is a weighing parameter ($\in [0, 1]$) and $BC(t)$ is the bag complexity at time t. $QL(t)$ is the queue length at time t and finally, $Norm(x)$ represents a (unity-based) normalizing function. $BC(t)$ is equal to 0 when the X-Ray officer has no bag under consideration.

We relate the performance quality to the base values for both false negative probability and false positive probability of illegal item detection, as shown below.

$$FN_{x-ray}(t) = FN_{base} \times Norm(PQ(t))$$
$$FP_{x-ray}(t) = FP_{base} \times Norm(PQ(t))$$

Where $FN_{x-ray}(t)$ and $FP_{x-ray}(t)$ represent the current false negative and false positive probability of illegal item detection respectively, and $Norm(x)$ is a normalizing function.

Previous work showed that experienced pressure influences processing time positively, while bag complexity influences the processing negatively [6]. This is modelled as follows.

$$T_{x-ray}(t) = T_{base} \times I(t)$$
$$I(t) = C_{EP} \times Norm(EP(t)) + (1 - C_{EP}) \times Norm(TL(t))$$

where $T_{x-ray}(t)$ is the current mean processing time, C_{EP} is a weighing parameter ($\in [0,1]$) and $I(t)$ is the current influence factor. The influence factor is a combination of two contributing factors $EP(t)$ and $TL(t)$. A linear relationship is assumed here, while other types of relationships are possible too.

Passenger and Attacker Agent. The Passenger aims to pass the security checkpoint of the airport. It contains a *pass checkpoint activity*, which enables the passenger to move past the checkpoint. The checkpoint activity consists of three sub-activities: baggage drop-off, WTMD passage and baggage collection. Baggage drop-off and baggage collection are parametrized by T_{drop} and $T_{collect}$ respectively. These parameters determine the mean processing time of the associated sub-activities. Passengers are randomly generated in a designated area with interarrival time $T_{arrival}$.

The Motor Layer of Passengers is defined using the Social Force Model [7], which defines movement in terms of interacting particles.

The attacker agent is a special type of passenger, that carries an IED in his/her carry on luggage. He/she shows standard passenger behavior, but aims to pass the security checkpoint without being detected.

3.2   Environment

The Environment of the model consist of sensors and physical objects. Sensors are devices that enable agents to sense using a mechanic object. We distinguish two types of sensors: X-ray machines and Walk Through Metal Detectors (WTMD). X-ray machines produce an observation based on the bag under consideration, which is then interpreted by the X-ray officer. WTMDs also produce an observation based on the passenger under consideration. This observation is then interpreted by the WTMD officer.

Two important physical objects exist: *walls* and *queue separators*. Queue separators specify boundaries of queuing areas, which allow for measurements of the number of people in the queue ($QL(t)$) and average queuing time ($QT(t)$).

4   Experiment and Results

In this section, the implementation of the above described simulation model is discussed. Two experiments performed with this simulation model are discussed and the corresponding results are shown.

4.1   Implementation and Setup

For the implementation, we created an open-source microscopic agent-based simulator specifically built for Agent-based Security Risk Assessment[1]. The simulator is entirely Java-based and can therefore easily be used across different platforms. It allows for simple visualization and is modularly structured. It contains a collection of airport specific structures, like checkpoint functionality and basic passenger behavior. A visualization of the simulator is shown in Fig. 3.

The following is specified in our experiments. Defending agents, $D = \{d_{x-ray}^1, d_{x-ray}^2, d_{bag}^1, d_{bag}^2, d_{wtmd}, d_{directions}\}$, consists of two X-Ray officers, two Bag Checker officers, a WTMD officer and a Directions officer. The set of attackers is defined to be $A = \{a_{IED}\}$, a single attacker agent carrying an IED. $O = \{o_1, ..., o_q\}$ is a set of q passengers, randomly generated over time. The environment, $E = \{e_{wall}, e_{queue}, e_{wtmd}, e_{x-ray}^1, e_{x-ray}^2\}$ is specified, which consists out of walls, a single queuing area, a Walk Through Metal Detector and two X-ray machines. A visualization of the experimental setup is shown in Fig. 3. Finally, the Fail function is defined as follows.

$$F(m_i^j) = \begin{cases} 1 & a_{IED} \text{ passed the checkpoint undetected.} \\ 0 & \text{otherwise.} \end{cases}$$

We do not define the Consequence function $C(m_i^j)$ as this is outside the scope of this experiment. Further, two types of personality profiles based on the work of Bosse et al. [2] are specified, denoted as *Type I* and *Type II*. *Type I* has the capability to cope well with high stress levels, while *Type II* does not cope with stress well. For simpler comparison, we adapt personality *Type I* such that it has the same *optimal experienced pressure* level as *Type II*. Some important parameters were set using values provided in literature and are shown in Table 1. If relevant data is unavailable in literature, experts can be consulted to estimate a range for each parameter. Here, we show results of two experiments that were performed with this model. In one experiment we study the influence of interarrival time $T_{arrival}$ on estimated vulnerability, while in the other experiment we study the influence of bag complexity BC_μ on estimated vulnerability.

4.2   Interarrival Time Experiment

We set C_{bag} to be 0, meaning that the task level $TL(t)$ of an X-Ray officer is only influenced by the queue length $QL(t)$. C_{EP} is set to 0.5, meaning that

---

[1] The simulator can be found at: https://github.com/StefJanssen/SeRiMa-ABM.

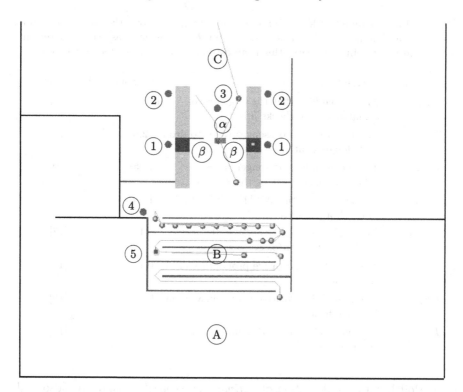

Fig. 3. A visualization of the experimental setup in the simulation tool. The following agents are shown in this figure. 1: X-Ray officers d_{x-ray}, 2: Bag Checker officers d_{bag}, 3: WTMD officer d_{wtmd}, 4: Directions officer $d_{directions}$, 5: attacker agent a_{IED}. All unlabelled agents are passengers o_i. The area in which A is located represents the agent-generation area, area B represents the queuing area and area C is the secure area. Passengers o_i and the attacker agent a_{IED} are generated in area A and go to area C. Walk Through Metal Detector e_{wtmd} is indicated by α and the X-Ray machines are indicated by β.

experienced pressure $EP(t)$ and $TL(t)$ equally influence the processing time of the X-Ray officer. We generate a_{IED} after 20 min of simulation time, while we vary the interarrival time $T_{arrival}$. We perform $N = 10000$ simulation runs and for each run record both the queue length $QL(t)$ at the time that the attacker passes the checkpoint and if the defenders failed to detect the attacker ($F(m_i^j)$).

Results of the experiment are shown in Fig. 4. This figure shows $\hat{F}(m_i)$, the estimated *Vulnerability* and the average queue length $QL(t)$ at the time that the attacker passes the checkpoint for each of the interarrival times $T_{arrival}$.

The results show that both personality types perform best with an interarrival time of 17.5 s, corresponding to a queue length $QL(t)$ of around 20 passengers. The corresponding *Vulnerability* is 0.116 for Type I and 0.126 for personality type II. This can be explained from the definition of the Functional

Table 1. Basic parameters for the experimental setup. It shows the parameter name, description and standard value. It also refers to the work which was used to determine the standard value. In some cases this is an estimate based on related parameters.

Parameter	Description	Standard value	Source
P_{bag}	The probability that the bag checker agent randomly checks a bag	0.1	[10]
T_{drop}	The mean time a passenger takes to drop its belongings at the x-ray system	12.5 s	[10]
$T_{collect}$	The mean time a passenger takes to collect its belongings at the x-ray system	12.5 s	[10]
T_{wtmd}	The mean time the WTMD officer takes to check a passenger	10.0 s	[17]
P_{wtmd}	The probability that the WTMD officer randomly checks a passenger	0.1	[17]
FN_{base}	The base False Negative probability of an X-Ray officer	0.1	[15]
FP_{base}	The base False Positive probability of an X-Ray officer	0.2	[15]
T_{base}	The mean time an X-Ray officer takes to check a bag	6.0 s	[12]

State Model, with the definition of *optimal experienced pressure*. We also find, as expected, that X-Ray officers with personality *Type I* generally produce a lower *Vulnerability*, implying a higher performance quality $PQ(t)$ at the moment attacker agent a_{IED} passes.

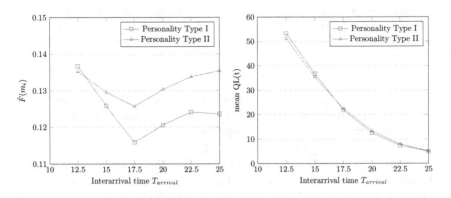

Fig. 4. The left plot shows the estimated *Vulnerability* $\hat{F}(m_i)$ of the system for varying interarrival times $T_{arrival}$, calculated using the defined Fail function. The right plot shows the mean queue length $QL(t)$ at the time a_{IED} was processed.

4.3   Bag Complexity Experiment

In this experiment we investigate the influence of bag complexity on the performance of the defense agents. We use the same two personality profiles as used in the previous experiment. We set C_{bag} to be 0.75, meaning that the task level $TL(t)$ of an X-Ray officer is influenced by the queue length $QL(t)$ for 25% and the bag complexity $BC(t)$ for 75%. C_{EP} is set to 0.5, meaning equally influence importance for $EP(t)$ and $TL(t)$ processing time. We set the interarrival time $T_{arrival}$ to be 15 s and generate a_{IED} after 20 min of simulation time. We vary the bag complexity of each agent by drawing a number from a normal distribution with mean BC_{μ} and standard deviation BC_{σ}. We perform $N = 10000$ simulation runs and for each run record the performance quality $PQ(t)$ of the responsible d_{x-ray}^{k} at the time that a_{IED} passes the checkpoint and the outcome of Fail function $F(m_i^j)$.

Results of the experiment are shown in Fig. 5. The figure shows $\hat{F}(m_i)$, the estimated *Vulnerability* and the mean performance quality $PQ(t)$ at the time that the attacker passes the checkpoint for each of the bag complexities BC_{μ}.

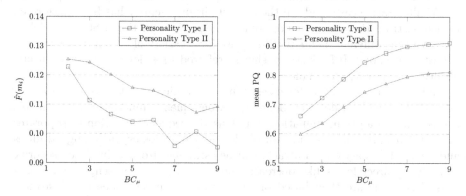

Fig. 5. The left plot shows the estimated *Vulnerability* $\hat{F}(m_i)$ of the system for different mean bag complexities BC_{μ}, calculated using the defined Fail function. The right plot shows the mean performance quality $PQ(t)$ of the responsible d_{X-ray}^{k} at the time the attacker agent was processed.

The graphs show that the estimated *Vulnerability* decreases while bag complexity increases. While this sounds counter intuitive, it can be understood from the specification of the Functional State Model. In the FSM a so-called *recovery effort* is defined, allowing an agent to decrease exhaustion in the absence of (large) tasks. Task demand with respect to the baggage $TL_{bag}(t)$ is defined to be 0 in the absence of baggage. This allows for timely decrease of exhaustion and therefore, high performance quality in case a new bag arrives. Higher task demand can, in the short term, result in higher performance qualities due to a direct link between the task level and *current contribution*. This is reflected in the increasing performance quality $PQ(t)$ and the resulting estimated *Vulnerabilities*.

5   Conclusions and Discussion

This paper introduced a novel Security Risk Assessment approach which is based on Agent-based modelling and simulation. It uses Monte Carlo simulations to estimate both *Vulnerability* and *Consequence*, which are important parameters in Security Risk Assessment. It defines an Agent-based model with both defender agents and attacker agents. An attacker agent aims to execute subversive actions within some security scenario identified by security experts, while defender agents are modelled to perform their security tasks.

This approach enables modelling of essential aspects and processes of sociotechnical systems at cognitive, social and organisational levels. This is problematic for traditional and game theory based approaches. *Vulnerability* and *Consequence* produced by this method can be used to improve both traditional and game theory based Security Risk Assessment methods. Outputs of this method can be used as estimates for each of the payoffs in a game theoretic approach.

An illustrative case study in the area of airport security has been performed to demonstrate the use of this approach. Using the Functional State Model, it is shown that different *Vulnerabilities* arise for a variety of circumstances at the security checkpoint. It for instance shows preferred stress levels for X-ray officers, resulting in higher performance.

In the future, we will perform case studies in which we estimate *Consequence* as well. This will be done by defining a Consequence function that estimates consequence in a given simulation run. This Consequence function incorporates estimates of direct losses and indirect losses. Direct losses, including fatalities and physical damages of an attack, can be estimated from a simulated security scenario. Indirect losses like decreased number of future passengers and business disruptions are then based on the estimated direct losses and historical data. This work will be extended with a theoretical analysis, more elaborate experiments and different underlying models to investigate the theoretical and practical strengths and weaknesses of this approach.

References

1. Blumberg, B.M., Galyean, T.A.: Multi-level direction of autonomous creatures for real-time virtual environments. In: Proceedings of the 22nd Annual Conference on Computer Graphics and Interactive Techniques, pp. 47–54. ACM (1995)
2. Bosse, T., Both, F., Van Lambalgen, R., Treur, J.: An agent model for a human's functional state and performance. In: Proceedings of the 2008 IEEE/WIC/ACM International Conference on Web Intelligence and Intelligent Agent Technology, vol. 2, pp. 302–307. IEEE Computer Society (2008)
3. Brown, M., Sinha, A., Schlenker, A., Tambe, M.: One size does not fit all: a game-theoretic approach for dynamically and effectively screening for threats. In: AAAI Conference on Artificial Intelligence (AAAI) (2016)

4. Cox Jr., L.A.T.: Some limitations of risk = threat vulnerability consequence for risk analysis of terrorist attacks. Risk Anal. **28**(6), 1749–1761 (2008)
5. Ezell, B.C., Bennett, S.P., Von Winterfeldt, D., Sokolowski, J., Collins, A.J.: Probabilistic risk analysis and terrorism risk. Risk Anal. **30**(4), 575–589 (2010)
6. Graves, I., Butavicius, M., MacLeod, V., Heyer, R., Parsons, K., Kuester, N., McCormac, A., Jacques, P., Johnson, R.: The role of the human operator in image-based airport security technologies. In: Jain, L.C., Aidman, E.V., Abeynayake, C. (eds.) Innovations in Defence Support Systems-2. Studies in Computational Intelligence, vol. 338, pp. 147–181. Springer, Heidelberg (2011). doi:10.1007/978-3-642-17764-4_5
7. Helbing, D., Molnar, P.: Social force model for pedestrian dynamics. Phys. Rev. E **51**(5), 4282 (1995)
8. Hoogendoorn, S.P., Bovy, P.H.L.: Pedestrian route-choice and activity scheduling theory and models. Transp. Res. Part B Methodol. **38**(2), 169–190 (2004)
9. ICAO: Aviation security manual (doc 8973 restricted) (2014). http://www.icao.int/Security/SFP/Pages/SecurityManual.aspx. Accessed 27 May 2016
10. Kirschenbaum, A.A.: The cost of airport security: the passenger dilemma. J. Air Transp. Manage. **30**, 39–45 (2013)
11. Laszka, A., Felegyhazi, M., Buttyan, L.: A survey of interdependent information security games. ACM Comput. Surv. (CSUR) **47**(2), 23 (2015)
12. Leone, K., Liu, R.R.: Improving airport security screening checkpoint operations in the us via paced system design. J. Air Transp. Manage. **17**(2), 62–67 (2011)
13. Pita, J., Jain, M., Marecki, J., Ordez, F., Portway, C., Tambe, M., Western, C., Paruchuri, P., Kraus, S.: Deployed armor protection: the application of a game theoretic model for security at the los angeles international airport. In: Proceedings of the 7th International Joint Conference on Autonomous Agents and Multiagent Systems: Industrial Track, pp. 125–132. International Foundation for Autonomous Agents and Multiagent Systems (2008)
14. Reynolds, C.W.: Steering behaviors for autonomous characters. In: Game Developers Conference, vol. 1999, pp. 763–782 (1999)
15. Rusconi, E., Ferri, F., Viding, E., Mitchener-Nissen, T.: Xrindex: a brief screening tool for individual differences in security threat detection in x-ray images. Front. Hum. Neurosci. **9**, 439 (2015)
16. Thomas, L., Schwaninger, A., Heimgartner, N., Hedinger, P., Hofer, F., Ehlert, U., Wirtz, P.H.: Stress-induced cortisol secretion impairs detection performance in x-ray baggage screening for hidden weapons by screening novices. Psychophysiology **51**(9), 912–920 (2014)
17. van Boekhold, J., Faghri, A., Li, M.: Evaluating security screening checkpoints for domestic flights using a general microscopic simulation model. J. Transp. Secur. **7**(1), 45–67 (2014)
18. ASME Washington: All-Hazards Risk and Resilience: Prioritizing Critical Infrastructures using the RAMCAP Plus SM Approach. ASME (2009)

Scheduling Access to Shared Space in Multi-robot Systems

Yara Khaluf[1]([✉]), Christine Markarian[2], Pieter Simoens[1], and Andreagiovanni Reina[3]

[1] Department of Information Technology, Ghent University, Ghent, Belgium
{yara.khaluf,pieter.simoens}@ugent.be
[2] Department of Computer Science, University of Paderborn, Paderborn, Germany
chrissm@mail.uni-paderborn.de
[3] Department of Computer Science, University of Sheffield, Sheffield S1 4DP, UK
a.reina@sheffield.ac.uk

Abstract. Through this study, we introduce the idea of applying scheduling techniques to allocate spatial resources that are shared among multiple robots moving in a static environment and having temporal constraints on the arrival time to destinations. To illustrate this idea, we present an exemplified algorithm that plans and assigns a motion path to each robot. The considered problem is particularly challenging because: (i) the robots share the same environment and thus the planner must take into account overlapping paths which cannot happen at the same time; (ii) there are time deadlines thus the planner must deal with temporal constraints; (iii) new requests arrive without a priori knowledge thus the planner must be able to add new paths online and adjust old plans; (iv) the robot motion is subject to noise thus the planner must be reactive to adapt to online changes. We showcase the functioning of the proposed algorithm through a set of agent-based simulations.

1 Introduction

Consider the example of a hospital where patients are transported to the required location within the hospital (e.g., a medical ward or an operating theater) and this transportation is performed by dedicated robots (e.g., the robots presented in [17]). Each patient may have a different medical situation which determines the urgency of the transportation, thus, a specific temporal deadline. Additionally, in most cases, the arrival of new patients cannot be predicted in advance but the system must deal with online requests. The robots that operate in this transportation system share a given environment, thus share the same limited resources. For instance, a lift or a corridor can be accessed by a limited number of robots at a time. Finally, robots may not have a deterministic arrival time, but their motion may be subject to delays (e.g., due to the avoidance of unexpected obstacles, such as humans, or due to a noisy robot motion). This example presents a very challenging problem which requires the robust online planning of paths for multiple robots with temporal and spatial constraints. In this study,

© Springer International Publishing AG 2017
Y. Demazeau et al. (Eds.): PAAMS 2017, LNAI 10349, pp. 144–156, 2017.
DOI: 10.1007/978-3-319-59930-4_12

we investigate this problem and propose an algorithm that deals with such types of constraints. The proposed algorithm does not provide the complete solution that can be directly applied to this example but it is a significant step forward in such direction which tackles various challenging aspects.

The considered challenges can be ascribed as the core problems investigated in the two research areas of path planning and scheduling (which we review in Sect. 2). The former area studies solutions to plan the sequence of intermediate locations (configurations) that a robot has to visit (implement) for moving from a starting position to a final destination. Almost every mobile robot system has to deal with this aspect and, in fact, this research area has been very active since a few decades and several solutions have been proposed [3,7]. The latter research area, scheduling, studies how to plan the times of access to shared resources. Solutions in this area typically aim at problems of sharing computational power [2], while we are not aware of any work that considered the space as the resource that needs to be scheduled for a shared access under deadline constraints. Our work lays at the interface of these two areas; the main idea is to get inspiration from solutions in scheduling, and employ and adapt them for multi-robot path planning with arrival time deadlines. We illustrate this idea by proposing an exemplified time-space planner which we present in Sect. 3. Additional constraints that make the investigated problem more challenging, while closer to a real world application, are (i) stochasticity in robot motion and (ii) online requests for new paths. The proposed algorithm is reactive and thus able to modify online the planned paths in response to delays in the robot motion. Additionally, the algorithm evaluates online new requests and either rejects or accepts them. The rejection of a request means that there is no possible plan that would allow reaching the destination within the given deadline without cancelling already scheduled paths. In this case, possible solutions are either to cancel already planned paths, or to extend the temporal deadline. The current version of our algorithm does not make decisions of this type. Instead, when a request is accepted, the planner may modify, if necessary, other planned paths which may include the preemption (i.e., the pausing) of a robot that was moving to allow another robot with a higher priority to access to a spatial resource. We perform a set of agent-based simulations to verify the correctness and efficiency of our algorithm in Sect. 4. Finally, we give final remarks on our study in Sect. 5.

2   Related Work

Path planning algorithms can be organised in two macro-categories: deterministic algorithms and stochastic algorithms. Deterministic algorithms are preferred when agents have few degrees of freedom that determine a limited number of possible configurations; here, the algorithm can exploit a tractable solution space and provide provable bounds on the solution quality. Instead, stochastic algorithms are preferred when the solution space to explore is extremely large and stochastic exploration is the only resort to speed up the planning time. In this work, we plan paths over a small graph that allows us to implement a deterministic algorithm. Among the most known deterministic algorithms for planning are Dijkstra's and A^*; and several variants and extensions of these algorithms have been proposed (e.g., D^*, or the jump point search) [3,7]. Path planning in multi-robot systems has been often tackled as an optimization problem focused on finding the shortest collision-free path [1,11,15,16]. Some of these works [1,15] included priorities to give precedence to some robots in case of conflicting access to space. Differently from other works in multi-robot motion planning, our study takes into account a specific temporal deadline for each robot (thus, for each path) and hence the planner has to schedule movements both in space and in time.

Traditionally, real-time **scheduling** algorithms have dealt with deterministic execution times such as the worst case execution time [2]. While, stochastic execution times of tasks have been considered only in a limited number of studies. Some of them modified existing deterministic algorithms to support variable execution times, e.g., [10]. Others have implemented heuristic approaches to schedule tasks with stochastic execution times on multi-processors [9]. All these works, similarly to ours, have in common the use of probability distributions to characterize the stochastic execution time of the tasks. In fact, in our study, tasks are not pieces of code to execute (as in traditional scheduling), but tasks are robot motions which are characterized by stochastic execution times. Accounting for time constraints, such as deadlines, in multi-robot systems has been studied only in a limited number of works, e.g., [5,6].

Other works tackled the problem of **allocating resources in multiagent systems** through various methods such as continuous-time DEC-MDP and DEC-POMDP—decentralised (partially observable) markov decision processes—e.g. [18], or distributed negotiation protocols, e.g. [8], or metaheuristic approaches, e.g., in vehicle routing [13]. Differently from ours, this class of studies aim to minimize the costs of resource allocation and therefore solve an optimization problem. Instead, we assume specific deadlines for each task and the minimization of execution time is not required. Solving a minimization problem adds a level of complexity that is unnecessary for our problem; for example, tasks with very far deadlines can make a relaxed use of resources. This difference led us to tackle the problem in a different way, i.e., through a scheduling algorithm.

Another class of problems that presents strong similarities with our study is **railway scheduling** [4,14] where train journeys with given arrival times are scheduled. As a main difference, our study considers the unpredicted arrival of new tasks which requires to alter the previous schedule and to determine if accepting the new task is possible or not. Additionally, as presented in Sect. 3, we include the notion of link congestion which might allow us to consider the use of resource by entities external to the system under control (e.g. humans).

3   Time-Space Planning Algorithm

The proposed algorithm plans access to a shared space complying with specific deadlines. We model the environment as a graph in which nodes represent locations and links represent connections between locations. We assume that a link between two locations can be used by only one robot at a time (even if the other robots move in the opposite or in the same direction, e.g. a lift in a building). We assume a system composed of N identical robots. A robot may get a task T_i which is characterized by four attributes: the start time $a_{i,0}$, the start location, the destination, and the temporal deadline D_i. This information is not known a priori but becomes available to the planner only when a new task arrives. In our work we deal with stochastic execution times that can be characterized through its probability distribution.

When a new task arrives, the algorithm evaluates whether to accept or reject it through an *acceptance test*[1]. A task passes the acceptance test if (i) a feasible path connecting its start location to its destination is found (space planing) (ii) and if this path can be completed before the deadline expiration and without violating any deadline of previously-scheduled tasks (time planning). Our algorithm is reactive to unexpected delays in the robot motion which requires the adjustments of the generated time-space plan. A robot delay is treated as the arrival of a new task using as start location the location where the unexpected delay is reported and as a start time the time at which the robot arrived at that specific location. The acceptance test evaluation is composed of two phases: space planning and time planning. The goal of this study is to illustrate the utility of including a time planning phase—based on scheduling techniques—to allocate spatial resources in a multi-robot system. To highlight and measure the impact of the time planning phase in a clean way, we want to limit as much as possible the influence of arbitrary design choices in the space planning phase, e.g., possible stochastic components. To this end, in the proposed exemplified algorithm we rely on a complete and deterministic planning solution. This choice allows us to illustrate the advantages (and drawbacks) of the time planning phase through a set of experiments on a small size grid environment. In larger environments, this solution would not be viable and the space planning phase can be replaced by any stochastic planning algorithm [3,7].

Space Planning. In this phase, the algorithm finds and orders all feasible paths between the start location and the destination. These paths are ordered by their weight which is computed combining two measures: (i) the length of the path and (ii) the congestion of the links along the path. The path length is a deterministic measure that is defined as the sum of the lengths of all links in the path. The congestion of a link is a stochastic measure—characterised by a probability distribution—that represents the number of individuals (including robots and other entities: e.g. humans) that cross the link during a time unit. The congestion measure allows the system to operate on more realistic assumptions with which the robots are not isolated from other systems operating in the same environment. The algorithm uses the expected value of the congestion distribution. Since we are dealing with known environments, solid distributions for the links

---

[1] The term "acceptance test" or "schedulability test" is also used in traditional real-time systems to refer to the decision process of accepting or rejecting a task based on the ability of scheduling it under the given time constraints.

congestion can be obtained. These can be time-variant distributions, where the congestion over links varies over time. Our algorithm applies the expected value of the congestion according to the distribution valid during the time of planning. The algorithm combines these two measures (the path length and the path congestion) to compute a weight W_{π_j} for the j-th path π_j and then order the set of paths Π according to their weights. The weight W_{π_j} is computed as:

$$W_{\pi_j} = \alpha l_{\pi_j} + (1 - \alpha)c_{\pi_j}, \tag{1}$$

where l_{π_j} is the length measure and c_{π_j} is the congestion measure of the path π_j and α is a design parameter. The length l_{π_j} is a normalised value in the range $[0, 1]$ computed as $l_{\pi_j} = L_{\pi_j}/Max(L_\pi)$ with $Max(L_\pi)$ the longest path between any two locations in the environment (we do not consider loops). Similarly, the congestion c_{π_j} is normalised in the range $[0, 1]$ as $c_{\pi_j} = C_{\pi_j}/Max(C_\pi)$ with $Max(C_\pi)$ the maximum congestion over all paths in the environment. The computation of all feasible paths may be computationally expensive. We assume a static environment, therefore, the set of paths Π can be computed offline for all pairs of start locations and destinations. On the contrary, the congestion measure may possibly vary over time which requires the online computation of weights W_{π_j} and the online ordering of Π. Additionally, in case a link has a limited capacity (i.e., a limited number of robots can use a link at the same time), the congestion measure must be updated online each time a new path is planned. In this study, however, we assume that a link has a very limited capacity for robots: it can be used by only one robot at a time. This assumption allows us to simplify the algorithm by ordering Π offline and focusing on the scheduling algorithm to allocate one link at a time to each robot.

Time Planning. During this phase, the algorithm assesses the validity of the paths in Π sequentially following the ascending order of their weights. The selection of the parameter α determines the order of the paths. This parameter has no crucial effect on the performance of the algorithm since we consider an offline average of the link congestion and the goal is not to select the shortest path, but a path that respects the task deadline. The time planning phase algorithm is complete, thus, will evaluate all paths before rejecting a task, therefore, the choice of the parameter α may influence only the algorithm speed. A path is considered *valid* if it allows the robot to move between the start location and the destination before the task's deadline is expired and without violating any of the deadlines of already accepted tasks. When a valid path π_j (j is the order of the path in the set Π) is found, the task is accepted and the path π_j is assigned to the task without further checking of the remaining paths in Π.

Each link in the path π_j represents a spatial resource that could be shared among several tasks that may attempt to access it with time intersections. Hence, we need to schedule the time access to these links. We do so through the widely-used EDF (Earliest Deadline First) scheduling algorithm[2]. In traditional

---

[2] EDF is a preemptive optimal scheduling algorithm for dynamic priorities. The tasks' priorities are updated during the execution of the tasks based on the current conditions.

real-time systems, EDF uses the worst-case execution time to check the task's schedulability and to generate feasible schedules. For multi-robot systems, this is not trivial because of two challenges to overcome: First, the execution time of individual links (i.e., the time spent in crossing a link) is stochastic; Second, scheduling the access to a particular link influences the execution times of all further links used by the related tasks due to new preemptions which were not planned before accessing the link. Therefore, we propose the following approach to facilitate scheduling.

The execution time $\rho_i(h)$ of a link h by robot i on task T_i is a stochastic measure that we model using the normal probability distribution. The time is determined by two components: the speed and reliability of the robot resulting in the particular motion time e_i of the robot performing T_i, and the congestion on the link C_h, thus, $\rho_i(h) = e_i + C_h$. The distribution of $\rho_i(h)$ can be approximated by a normal distribution [12] according to the central limit theorem. Hence, $\rho_i(h) \sim \mathcal{N}(\mu, \sigma)$, $\forall i, h$. When links have different congestion, the normal distribution that models the execution time of each links has a different mean and standard deviation, nevertheless, it does not influence the computations of the algorithm. Following the statistical 3-σ rule of the normal distribution, the probability that the execution time of link is smaller than $\mu + 3\sigma$ is 0.99. Hence, considering the planning value $\rho_i(h) = \mu + 3\sigma$ allows the system to operate with the probability of having delays with respect of the planned time on link h minimized to $0.01 = 1 - 0.99$. Using this planning value is similar to planning with the worst-case execution time but considering 99% of the cases.

Evaluating the acceptance of path π_j for task T_i consists in checking if executing all links $h \in \pi_j$ (i.e. moving through them) complies with the deadline D_i and does not violate the deadlines of the already-scheduled tasks. To make this evaluation, the algorithm computes for task T_i its ready-to-run time $\theta_i(h)$ at each link h, which is the time at which the robot on task T_i is ready to move through link h. The expected ready-to-run time $\mathbb{E}(\theta_i(h))$ on link h is computed as:

$$\mathbb{E}(\theta_i(h)) = \mathbb{E}(a_i(h)) + \mathbb{E}(\gamma_i(h)) \tag{2}$$

where $\mathbb{E}(a_i(h))$ is the expected arrival time of robot i at link h and $\mathbb{E}(\gamma_i(h))$ is the expected preemption time of robot i before executing link h. The expected arrival time $\mathbb{E}(a_i(h))$ is computed as the sum of the planned times spent in crossing all the previous links $q \in \{1, \ldots, h-1\}$ plus the times spent in preemption on the previous links:

$$\mathbb{E}(a_i(h)) = a_{i,0} + \sum_{q=1}^{h-1}(\rho_i(q) + \mathbb{E}(\gamma_i(q))) \tag{3}$$

where $a_{i,0}$ is the start time of task T_i and $\rho_i(q)$ is the estimated motion time (e.g., $\rho_i(q) = \mu + 3\sigma$) on link q.

The expected preemption time $\mathbb{E}(\gamma_i(h))$ at link h is calculated as a result of the dynamic priorities assigned by EDF to all the tasks requiring access to this particular link at the same time. These priorities are assigned based on the links' deadlines $D_i(h)$, $h \in \pi_j$. The deadline $D_i(h)$ of link h is computed as a fraction of the total deadline D_i of task T_i:

$$\mathbb{E}(D_i(h)) = \mathbb{E}(a_i(h)) + \frac{l_h}{l_{\pi_j}} \times (D_i - a_{i,0}) \tag{4}$$

where l_h is the length of link h and l_{π_j} is the total length of path π_j. After computing the expected deadline of link h for all tasks that are attempting to access link h with time intersections, EDF assigns them dynamic priorities based on their computed deadlines (i.e., shorter deadline higher priority). After assigning the order in which tasks are allowed to execute link h, it becomes possible to compute the preemption times for the tasks at this link. For task T_i, this is given by:

$$\mathbb{E}(\gamma_i(h)) = \mathbb{E}(RE_s(h)) + \sum_{q=1}^{r} \rho_i(q) \tag{5}$$

where $RE_s(h)$ is the execution time left for task T_s —that was running when task T_i arrived at the link h— to finish executing link h. This execution time is zero when there is no task running over link h when task T_i arrives. Furthermore, r is the number of tasks with a higher priority than T_i. After the algorithm schedules the access to link h and computes the preemption times of all the tasks attempting to access this link, it updates the arrival times of these tasks at all the future links of their planned paths. This update may result in new time intersections which need to be scheduled. While updating the tasks' preemption times, the algorithm checks, at each link, whether there is any violation of the link deadline $D_i(h)$:

$$\mathbb{E}(\theta_i(h)) + \rho_i(h) \leq \mathbb{E}(D_i(h)) \tag{6}$$

If a violation appears on at least one of the links, the corresponding path is rejected. Otherwise, it is accepted and assigned to the robot.

Algorithm Complexity. The computations with the highest complexity are performed by the algorithm during the space planning phase in which the algorithm iterates over all possible paths between any two nodes. Since we are dealing with known static environments, all these computations are done *offline*, with complexity $O(mn^2)$. As mentioned above, we selected a complete (but expensive) space planning algorithm to remove any possible bias coming from the specific implementation and parameterization of a stochastic path planning algorithm. However, in case needed, the space planning phase could use a stochastic algorithm to save time and to generate a smaller set of paths.

Since robots (tasks) arrive online, the computations performed by the algorithm during the time planning phase are made *online*. For a given pair of start-end locations, the algorithm verifies the time constraints of the paths between these two locations. The worst case for the algorithm is when no path among these satisfies the time constraints (i.e., does not meet the corresponding task's deadline without violating previously planned paths). This is when the algorithm rejects the task after going over all these paths and checking Eq. (6), which takes $(m - 1 + n - 1)!/(m - 1)!(n - 1)!$ time.

Task	Start time	Start Location	Destination	Deadline
Task 1	0.1465	3	6	0.34
Task 2	0.47	3	7	12.82
Task 3	0.54	2	7	14.73
Task 4	0.75	2	6	7.2
Task 5	1.09	2	9	10.4

Task	Start time	Start Location	Destination	Deadline
Task 1	0.03	3	6	0.78
Task 2	0.13	1	6	15.36
Task 3	0.58	3	7	25.67
Task 4	1.055	1	8	13.53
Task 5	1.67	2	8	17.34

Task	Start time	Start Location	Destination	Deadline
Task 1	0.29	1	8	10.357
Task 2	1.36	3	8	12.90
Task 3	2.045	1	6	22.9
Task 4	2.745	2	7	38.14
Task 5	2.96	3	8	19.1

Task	Start time	Start Location	Destination	Deadline
Task 1	1	1	9	40
Task 2	1	1	9	30
Task 3	1	1	9	20
Task 4	1	1	9	10

Fig. 1. The environment considered in our scenario and the four configurations used to verify our algorithm. Tasks marked with light-gray are those not accepted by the algorithm.

4   Results

We performed a set of experiments to validate and showcase the correctness of the proposed algorithm, to prove the utility of having a time planning phase, and to estimate the scalability performance for increasing robot density. We evaluate the algorithm performance in two planning strategies: *safe* planning and *risky* planning. With safe planning, the algorithm estimates the robot motion execution time (on a link h) as $\rho_i(h) = \mu + 3\sigma$ and thus the probability of missing the planned execution time is only 0.01. Instead with risky planning, the algorithm computes $\rho_i(h) = \mu + \sigma$ and thus the probability of missing the planned execution time of a link is 0.32. Testing these two strategies allows us to compare the predicted algorithm performances with our simulations' results. For simplicity, we assume that all links have the same length, and hence their execution times are sampled from a normal distribution with the same mean μ and standard deviation σ. The parameter α of Eq. (1) for computing the path weight is set to 0.5.

4.1   Validation Case Studies

We first start with verifying the correctness and efficacy of the proposed time-space planning algorithm for a multi-robot system of $N = 5$ identical robots through a set of agent-based simulation experiments. The environment that we consider in our experiments is depicted in Fig. 1, where robots can move between 9 partially connected locations—a small environment increases the chances of concurrent requests for a same link. In our simulations, we model the arrival of tasks using a homogeneous Poisson process with rate of 3 tasks/second. The tasks are generated with random start locations, destinations, start times, and deadlines. The start location is a node that is selected randomly between the nodes on the left side of the grid of Fig. 1 (i.e., either node 1, 2 or 3), while the destination is selected among nodes on the right plus node 6 (i.e., node 6, 7, 8 or 9). The task deadline D_i is randomly selected through a uniform distribution $\mathcal{U}(a_{i,0}, 3e_M)$ where e_M is the expected execution time of the longest path between the task's start location and its destination. We keep $\mu = 0.7$ in all experiments while we vary σ, with $\sigma = 0.1$ for safe planning and $\sigma = 0.3$ for risky planning.

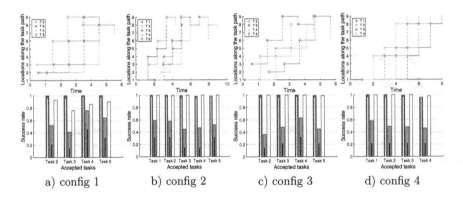

a) config 1   b) config 2   c) config 3   d) config 4

Fig. 2. Results of the agent-based simulations for the four considered task configurations. (upper part) Time-space plans generated by the algorithm (safe planning without re-planning). (lower part) Success rate for 100 simulation runs in three setups. (Color figure online)

We let the algorithm to schedule paths for four task configurations, three of which were randomly generated (config 1, 2 and 3) and one manually chosen (config 4), see the tables in Fig. 1. The plan is generated online while we simulate the task arrival and the robot motion through an agent-based simulator. We execute 100 runs for each configuration and for each planning strategy (i.e., safe and risky). The upper part of Fig. 2 shows the four plans generated by the algorithm (in safe planning with no re-planning). As previously defined, more tasks (i.e., robots) can stay simultaneously on the same node, however, a link can be used by at most a robot at a time. In the plots, solid (horizontal) lines represent a movement on a link departing from that node; the change of node is then visualised as a vertical dashed line of the same color. Preemption (pausing) of a task happens when the horizontal line is missing.

We can see that the algorithm generates plans that do not let two robots access the same link concurrently and produces plans where the accepted tasks meet their deadline. However, we can also see that in some cases (i.e., configs 1 and 3) the algorithm rejects two tasks (which have very short deadlines). Configuration 4 has been manually chosen and represents the case in which all tasks have the same start time, start location and destination while have different deadlines. In this example, we observe the sequential use of the links according to their respective deadlines. The lower part of Fig. 2 shows the success rate of 100 simulation runs, i.e., the proportion of runs in which the robot has reached its destination before its deadline. In each experiment, we simulate the motion of each robot through its planned path, which is generated online as soon as the new task request arrives. The robot motion time on each link is computed by drawing a random number from the probability distribution $\mathcal{N}(\mu, \sigma)$. When the robot motion is slower than planned and the robot misses a link deadline (see Eq. (6)), the algorithm needs to re-plan the task. We execute simulation experiments with three setups: (i) safe planning without re-planning if deadline are missed (red bars of Fig. 2(lower part)), (ii) risky planning without re-planning (green bars), and (iii) risky planning with online re-planning when robot motion has delays (white bars). The first two setups do not allow re-planning, therefore in case a robot does not meet a link deadline, it stops and the task is considered as a failure. These two setups, without re-planning, allow us to match the predicted performances of the algorithm with the agent-based simulation results. In fact, the algorithm that operates in safe planning (i.e., using $\rho_i(h) = \mu + 3\sigma$ to estimate the robot motion execution time) predicts that its plans meets each link deadline more than 99% of the times. Therefore a path that is composed by k links is expected to have a success rate of 0.99^k. The simulation results match the predictions: the red bars of Fig. 2(lower part) are always above the respective white overlaying line which marks the lower bound of success. Similarly, the risky planning algorithm (which uses $\rho_i(h) = \mu + \sigma$) has 0.32 probability to fail on each link and, thus, a path composed of k links will succeed with probability greater than 0.68^k. Although we see a noticeable decrease in the success rate, the green bars of Fig. 2(lower part) are always above the predicted lower bound marks (black overlaying lines). The third set of simulations is performed to highlight the role of online re-planning. In this case, we allow the algorithm to re-plan the paths of the tasks which have missed a deadline on a link. While the algorithm operates with a risky planning strategy, we can appreciate that the system performance noticeably increases (compared to the no re-planning case, green bars).

4.2   Effect of Time Planning

To evaluate the utility of time-scheduling to access shared space, we compared our algorithm with a simple algorithm that assigns to each task its shortest path. Rather than applying time planning, it solves conflicts for accessing shared space resources choosing at random which path to divert (i.e., robots access shared links in arbitrary order). We use $\mu = 0.7$ and $\sigma = 0.3$ in all our experiments and we report results for varying number of task requests up to 40. As above, tasks are generated with random start locations, destinations, start times, and deadlines. For each data point, we generate 10 different sets of tasks and we simulate 30 task executions on each plan. The lines connect the average success rate and the vertical bar indicates the standard deviation of the 300 runs. Figure 3a shows the proportion of completed tasks over the number of requested tasks. For being considered as completed, a task must be first accepted and scheduled by the planner, then the robot must execute the plan and reach the destination before the deadline. Instead, Fig. 3b shows the success rate which is computed as the rate of an accepted task to arrive at destination by its deadline.

The simple algorithm accepts all tasks, however many of them fails (i.e., have a very low rate in reaching destinations by their deadlines). Instead, the time-space planning refrains to accept a task that have a probability to miss its deadline above a certain threshold (which depends on the strategy whether it is risky or safe). For low number of tasks the performance of the three algorithms is comparable, however, when the number of tasks increases, our time-space solution largely outperforms the simple algorithm. Even if this result is expected because the simple algorithm does not have any strategy to deal with

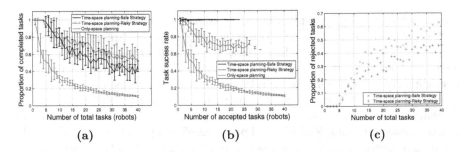

Fig. 3. Comparison between time-space planning (both with safe and risky strategy) and the simple algorithm without time planning phase, in terms of the (a) proportion of completed tasks and (b) task success rate. (c)Proportion of rejected tasks as a function of total number of requested tasks.

deadlines, the result displays the effectiveness and utility of the time planning phase.

4.3 Scalability on Number of Tasks

Figure 3a–c show how, respectively, the proportion of completed tasks, the success rate of a task and the proportion of rejected tasks changes as a function of the number of tasks. The plot of Fig. 3a shows that the risky strategy completes a higher number of tasks in average. This results is due to the fact that the risky planning accepts a larger number of tasks, however presents an higher risk of failure (with a success rate that converges to 0.68, in agreement with the 1-σ rule). Differently, the safe planning accepts fewer tasks but assures a higher success rate (around 0.99 according to the 3-σ rule). Additionally, we can see that while the simple algorithm accepts all tasks, the time-space algorithm does not accept anymore tasks above a certain upper bound, visualised through the interrupted lines (around 25 tasks) in Fig. 3b. This upper bound is determined by both the number of tasks (robot density) and the distance between deadlines.

The idea behind time-space planning algorithms is to make a decision before the beginning of a task's execution about the probability of that task to succeed in meeting its deadline. A task begins only if it has a probability of success higher than a certain value, otherwise the task is rejected before beginning. This rejection mechanism has the goal to inform beforehand the user which may look for alternative solutions rather than missing the deadline halfway through.

5 Conclusions

We present an algorithm to plan paths for multiple robots that move in the same shared static environment. The algorithm plans new paths online as new requests arrive and manages possible conflicts if more robots want to access the same resource (space) at the same moment (time). The novel characteristic of the proposed time-space algorithm is its capability to plan paths that comply with temporal deadlines. Additionally, the algorithm is able to adapt online to unexpected delays in the robot motion which may be caused by internal robot failures/noise or by external factors that could hamper the normal movement. Finally, we show through agent-based simulations that the algorithm is able to generate plans that respect the given deadlines with predictable performance levels. Natural extensions of this study consists in experimenting the algorithm performance in more challenging setups where each link has different congestion and the system is composed of heterogeneous robots, each with different motion speeds and reliability. Further extensions would consider dynamic environments (with time variant topologies), and larger link capacities.

References

1. Bennewitz, M., Burgard, W., Thrun, S.: Finding and optimizing solvable priority schemes for decoupled path planning techniques for teams of mobile robots. Robot. Auton. Syst. **41**(2), 89–99 (2002)
2. Buttazzo, G.: Hard Real-time Computing Systems: Predictable Scheduling Algorithms and Applications, Real-Time Systems Series, vol. 24. Springer, Heidelberg (2011)
3. Choset, H.M.: Principles of Robot Motion: Theory, Algorithms, and Implementation. MIT Press, Cambridge (2005)
4. Dorfman, M., Medanic, J.: Scheduling trains on a railway network using a discrete event model of railway traffic. Transp. Res. B-Methodol. **38**(1), 81–98 (2004)
5. Khaluf, Y., Birattari, M., Rammig, F.: Probabilistic analysis of long-term swarm performance under spatial interferences. In: Dediu, A.-H., Martín-Vide, C., Truthe, B., Vega-Rodríguez, M.A. (eds.) TPNC 2013. LNCS, vol. 8273, pp. 121–132. Springer, Heidelberg (2013). doi:10.1007/978-3-642-45008-2_10
6. Khaluf, Y., Rammig, F.: Task allocation strategy for time-constrained tasks in robot swarms. Adv. Artif. Life (ECAL) **12**, 737–744 (2013)
7. LaValle, S.M.: Planning Algorithms. Cambridge University Press, Cambridge (2006)
8. Mailler, R., Lesser, V., Horling, B.: Cooperative negotiation for soft real-time distributed resource allocation. In: Proceedings of AAMAS 2003, pp. 576–583. ACM (2003)
9. Manolache, S., Eles, P., Peng, Z.: Task mapping and priority assignment for soft real-time applications under deadline miss ratio constraints. ACM Trans. Embed. Comput. Syst. (TECS) **7**(2), 19 (2008)
10. Mills, A., Anderson, J.: A stochastic framework for multiprocessor soft real-time scheduling. In: the 16th IEEE Real-Time and Embedded Technology and Applications Symposium, pp. 311–320. IEEE Press (2010)
11. Quottrup, M.M., Bak, T., Zamanabadi, R.I.: Multi-robot planning: A timed automata approach. In: Proceedings of ICRA 2004, vol. 5, pp. 4417–4422 (2004)
12. Smith, R., Self, M., Cheeseman, P.: Estimating uncertain spatial relationships in robotics. In: Cox, I.J., Wilfong, G.T. (eds.) Autonomous Robot Vehicles, pp. 167–193. Springer, New York (1990)
13. Toklu, N.E., Gambardella, L.M., Montemanni, R.: A multiple ant colony system for a vehicle routing problem with time windows and uncertain travel times. J. Traffic Logistics Eng. **2**(1), 52–58 (2014)

14. Törnquist, J., Persson, J.A.: N-tracked railway traffic re-scheduling during distur-
    bances. Transp. Res. B-Methodol. **41**(3), 342–362 (2007)
15. Van Den Berg, J., Overmars, M.: Prioritized motion planning for multiple robots.
    In: Proceedings of IROS 2005, pp. 430–435. IEEE Press (2005)
16. Wagner, G., Choset, H.: M*: A complete multirobot path planning algorithm with
    performance bounds. In: Proceedings of IROS 2011, pp. 3260–3267 (2011)
17. Wang, C., Savkin, A.V., Clout, R., Nguyen, H.T.: An intelligent robotic hospital
    bed for safe transportation of critical neurosurgery patients along crowded hospital
    corridors. IEEE Trans. Neural Syst. Rehabil. Eng. **23**(5), 744–754 (2015)
18. Yin, Z., Tambe, M.: Continuous time planning for multiagent teams with temporal
    constraints. In: Proceedings of IJCAI 2011, vol. 22, p. 465 (2011)

Multi-Agent System for Distributed Cache Maintenance

Santhilata Kuppili Venkata[1]([✉]), Katarzyna Musial[2], Samhar Mahmoud[1],
and Jeroen Keppens[1]

[1] Department of Informatics, King's College London, London, UK
santhilata.kuppili_venkata@kcl.ac.uk
[2] Faculty of Science and Technology, Bournemouth University, Poole, UK

Abstract. With the growing number of applications that require large
data transfers from distributed databases, there is a great need for
efficient distributed data caching methods. It is essential that data is
cached at the best and optimal locations between users and data stores.
Cache management should consider patterns about data usage and make
dynamic decisions to place data across cache units. In this paper, we have
modelled the distributed data caching mechanism using multi-agent system allowing to test strategies and algorithms for data placement that
later can be incorporated in the real life applications. Subsequently, we
demonstrate the application of this system to study various distributed
coordination strategies for identifying effective data placement and thus
improving overall cache performance. This study is significant for distributed system applications.

Keywords: Distributed cache · Agent based modelling · Coordination
strategies

1 Introduction

Introducing multi-agent systems (MAS) into distributed computing can facilitate
implementation and also provide novel characteristics such as more autonomy
to the application system [22]. MAS allows construction of models to solve problems with variety of frameworks for environment centered analysis, design [3]
and programmable architectures [9]. These architectures enable to create application examples such as distributed situation assessment, distributed coordination etc. to accurately represent and help researchers to develop new insights.
Other examples include, large-scale distributed multi-agent systems in open systems such as E-Commerce [7], E-Health [14] and E-Governance [23]. Very few
systems in distributed caching have implemented the agent-based approach. In
industrial applications, TIBCO[1]. has come up with distributed cache scheme
for distributed object management using MAS. In their work, MAS is used

---

[1] https://docs.tibco.com/pub/businessevents-express/5.2.1/doc/html/
GUID-5CA44A37-01E9-4EE4-9922-8F8E70D50E7B.html.

© Springer International Publishing AG 2017
Y. Demazeau et al. (Eds.): PAAMS 2017, LNAI 10349, pp. 157–169, 2017.
DOI: 10.1007/978-3-319-59930-4_13

to define functions such as partitioning, replication, distribution, failure recovery and event handling. In another work in distributed caching, Dimakopoulos et al. [5] simulate peer-to-peer resource discovery using MAS. Each cache agent is used to store information to enable the distribution of data.

Distributed data caching is used in applications that need to cope with large volumes of data which are distributed all over the world[2]. For users' queries, data may have to be collected from multiple data stores before the reply is sent to the user. When groups of users work on related projects, queries tend to be repeated fully or partially. Repeated queries need same data to be retrieved and processed several times causing repeated data transfers, high bandwidth utilization and thus delayed responses [20]. Setting up several interconnected cache units to store the most repeated data at locations between users and data servers help to reduce response time and save processing resources [18]. Thus distributed caching is an interface between users and data stores.

Distributed caching is a complex system consisting of physical components such as multiple units of data servers, communication networks, middleware cache storage units, cache server (processing resources), and users. Cache management or maintenance is a software component which is considered to be the soul of the entire system. Maintenance typically happens on cache servers. Traditionally, cache storage units are small in size. Hence during the cache maintenance process, the decision has to be made about storing in cache units the most relevant data and removing the obsolete data. This means that we have to identify **'what data'** to store, **'where'** a given data segment should be stored, and for **'how long'**. This is the data placement problem in distributed cache maintenance. Periodically, an analyzer component (please refer to Sect. 2) collects meta-data by performing an assessment of the data freshness and location relevance for each of the data segments stored. Analyzer helps cache maintenance to predict future needs based on the meta-data collected. In order to maximize cache utilization, management must employ approaches to make optimal decisions. Usually cache units are considered to be passive resource units and they are used only for storage purposes. But often global decision makers are hampered with knowledge about association between data units at a particular location. Also, as the overall system grows, global decision making may prove to be a bottle neck. To overcome these issues, we introduce the idea of delegating some responsibility to cache. With the knowledge about local data, caches actively participate in data placement decisions.

Typical applications that use distributed caches have huge number of cache units set worldwide. Coordinating management component, cache units should be able to analyze meta-data characteristics of the data usage and communicate with each other. All these entities are autonomous, intelligent, and contribute their knowledge towards solving data placement problem. We need to model interactions between these entities that cooperate and negotiate to make a collective decision about the best possible location for each data segment. All of these characteristics make agent-based system very well suited as a tool to model dis-

---

[2] www.ivoa.net.

tributed caching and its processes. Therefore, we propose an agent-based design and agent-based simulation for evaluation of the presented ideas.

2   Background

Depending on application requirements, several types of architectures are available to describe the distributed cache system. The architecture we follow is as shown in Fig. 1a. For the sake of clarity, we mention a data unit stored in cache as *'data segment'* and each cache storage unit as *'cache unit'* here after.

Each cache unit in the overall cache system stores data segments. A cache system can be in two states - (i) active state and (ii) maintenance state. Periodically, cache alters between these two states. Usually, maintenance state is much shorter than active state. During the active state, the *query analyzer* receives requests from users and identifies part of the query that can be answered from the cache. It fragments the request and searches for the data needed by each of those fragments in cache units. For any data segment that is not found in a cache, the coordinator sends requests to databases. It then aggregates all segments together and sends is to user [11]. During this period, it collects meta-information about the user query patterns in order to predict future data needs.

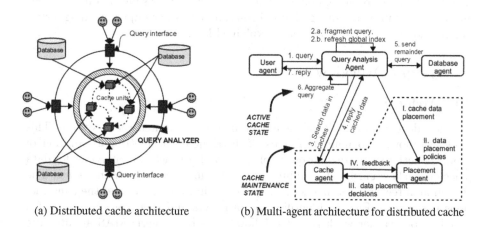

(a) Distributed cache architecture   (b) Multi-agent architecture for distributed cache

Fig. 1. Distributed cache system and multi-agent model

During the maintenance state, cache refreshment and data placement is performed. While coordinator keeps track of the changes in user query patterns globally, each cache unit governs the data segments stored locally. In smaller systems, the query analyzer can keep track of the global index of the data and hence user interests. But, when the system grows, some of the information is delegated to caches. Cache units keep track of the information related to each data segment stored at its own location. Hence, it is important to place each data segment at appropriate cache unit, so the overall performance of the cache system is maximised. Query analyzer and cache units should work together and coordinate their actions to maintain the overall cache system (shown in Fig. 1b).

Typical diagnostics used for decision making in placing data segments are: *frequency* of each data segment queried, *time* when a data segment was used, *location* preference where the data segment was requested, *association* among data segments at a given location, *number of joins* in a query, storage *capacity* of the cache unit, and *workload characteristics* depicting the pattern of query requests.

Many researchers have worked in the area of distributed caching [21]. But since we are concentrated on semantic caching based on materialized views (a hybrid concept) in cooperative environment, we relate our work to this type of caching only. In an environment and goal similar to us, D'Orazio et al. [6] proposed a flexible locality based resolution and dual cache solution, based on semantic caching to improve query evaluation in grid middleware. But, their work does not use active cache participation. This solution may not be scalable due to the heavy cache operations. Lillis et al. [13] developed a cooperative caching scheme for XML documents. This scheme allows sharing cache content among a number of peers. The proactive cache replacement policy is implemented by each peer cache checking its nodes before performing a split whenever a specific node overflows. This work is similar to us but, since caches take decisions independently, they tend to miss global data access patterns. Our solution differs in this aspect. Cache units consult global information and other important diagnostics before taking decisions on eviction (explained later).

3 System Overview

3.1 Architecture

We have developed a multi-agent model for the distributed cache system. This model supports two main functions of distributed cache: (i) participation of agents in active state (regular query process) and (ii) cache maintenance for data placement (shown inside dotted lines of Fig. 1b) in cache maintenance state. The system architecture together with major participating agents and their interactions is shown in Fig. 1b. Identification of agents and their roles are modelled based on our earlier work [10]. We follow a flexible, generic MAS architecture that can use decision making and information gathering techniques. We have applied GAIA agent-oriented software engineering methodology [24] because of its capacity to formally describe agents in distributed systems. The functionality of agents and GAIA role models are presented in Table 1. Interaction diagrams to represent interactions among agents are developed using the standards defined for Agent Unified Modelling Language (AUML) [17].

User agents (UA) are modelled as the software representation of humans that query databases. Query process is instigated when UA sends a query to databases. Query response time is measured as the time elapsed from the query sent from UA to the reply received by a user (Fig. 1b). The main responsibility of a user agent is to monitor the query response time. UA synchronizes its clock with

Table 1. Description of GAIA role model of agents

The User Agent Role Model
Role Schema: User Agent (Software representation of a single or group of users).
Description: Agent is the instigator of query process. It calculates query response time
Protocols and activities: formulateQuery, sendQuery, set_LocalClock, receiveReply, calculate_responseTime
Permissions: prepares a Query, suspends queryState, reads queryStatus, accesses Globalclock
Responsibilities
liveness: USER AGENT =(*formulateQuery.sendQuery*) (*receiveReply.calculateResponseTime*) (*setLocalClock*)
The Query analysis Agent Role Model
Role Schema: Query Analysis Agent
Description: Plays coordinator role. Monitors overall execution during active and maintenance states of cache
Protocols and activities: queryFragmentation, globalIndexUpdate, aggregateResponse, collectMetaQualifiers, prepareDiagnostics, createDataPlacementPlans
Permissions: reads workLoadCharacteristics; updates globalQueryIndex, reads userData, reads acceptQuery, prepares WorkloadAnalysis
Responsibilities
liveness:
QUERYANALYZER =(*startQueryProcess. globalIndexUpdate. aggregateResponse*), (*prepareDiagnostics*); MAINTENANCE-MANAGER = (*createDataPlacementPlans*);
The Cache Agent Role Model
Role Schema: Cooperative Cache Agent.
Description: Plays active role in cache maintenance. Coordinates with QAA,PA and peers to prepare data placement plans.
Protocols and activities: analyzeLocalData,vote, negotiate, generateLocalPlan
Permissions: acceses LocalSiteInformation, reads/writes/modifies LocalPlan
Responsibilities
liveness: CACHEAGENT = (*analyzeLocalData.vote——analyzeLocalData.generateLocalPlan*) INFORMATION-EXCHANGER = (*negotiate*)
The Placement Agent Role Model
Role Schema: Placement Agent.
Description: Supports QAA in creating optimal placement plans based on various strategies; helps cache agents
Protocols and activities: collectVotes, collectPlans,negotiatePlans, collectQualifierData, createPlacement
Permissions: generates *Plan*, distributes *FinalPlan*, gathers *DataAnalysis,localCacheInfo*
Responsibilities
liveness: PLACEMENT-HANDLER = (*collectQualifierData*),(*collectVotes——generatePlans*), (*collectPlans——generatePlans*), (*negotiatePlans——generatePlans*), (*createPlacement*)
The Database Agent Role Model
Role Schema: Resource role
Description: Agent asses data store performance characteristics
Protocols and activities: receiveQuery, lookupData processQuery, synchronizeClock, sendData
Permissions: access DataServer, process Query
Responsibilities
liveness: DATABASE-SERVER = (*receiveQuery. synchronizeClock. lookupData.processQuery.sendData*)

the global clock to measure response time. During the query process, UA can be in one of the three states, *query sent, wait for response* or *query completion*. Also, user agents exhibit querying patterns related to their interests.

Query analysis agent (QAA) assumes coordinator role in the distributed caching. It has combined responsibilities for analysis and management. Hence QAA is a high level abstraction for multiple supporting agents. This agent assumes coordination and monitoring of the whole query-reply process. It interacts with UAs, maintenance agents and cache agents. In the active state, QAA is the single point access to user agents. It then fragments incoming queries, and searches within the cache for the data need by query. QAA divides query into fragments and resolves which part of the query can be answered by cache. It then sends the *remainder query* (part that cannot be answered by cache) to respective databases. After collecting all the data from sources, data is aggregated to formulate a response. QAA maintains the global index of data availability for lookup. QAA also gathers meta characteristics of user query patterns from the workloads during the active state. It sets diagnostics for the use during maintenance state. During the maintenance state, QAA runs prediction algorithms for future needs with the help of diagnostics collected during the active state. With the help of other supporting agents QAA creates optimal data placement plans.

Cache agents (CA) are designed to take active part in cache maintenance. They are cooperative agents. Cache agents handle local data during active phase and prepare meta data to be used during maintenance phase. Meta data include knowledge about query pattern, data requirements and associations among data stored within a cache storage unit. CAs share information and negotiate with other agents while creating plans for ideal data placement. Cache agents are functional elements in deciding the scalability of the system.

Placement agent (PA) is an executor agent in the cache maintenance phase. It revises and recreates data placement plans and supports QAA during the maintenance state. PA interacts with cache agents to get feedback over the local information. PA holds multiple responsibilities. PA helps cache agents in negotiations. It aggregates plans made by cache agents and sends positive or negative feedback.

Database agents (DBA) are resource (passive) agents. They understand database load characteristics of the data usage and periodically submits this information to QAA. Database agents are mainly needed in the evaluation of database performance for various cache algorithms. DBA is responsible for assessing data store performance with respect to cache algorithms and decisions on replication.

Apart from the above main agents, **Negotiator Agent** supports QAA in handling negotiations among CAs. Similarly, a **Planning Agent** is another supporting role for QAA. Planning Agent is responsible for creating a master placement plan (distributed query planner) and distributing sub plans to others. **Communication Agent, Network Agent,** and **Processing Agents** have specific tasks in the overall distributed cache scenario, but they are not discussed in detail due to lack of space.

3.2   Coordination Strategies in Multi-Agent Systems

Many coordination strategies are available, each of them has its advantages and disadvantages and there is no universally best method [12]. We choose the most common strategies used in distributed computing [4] and multi-agent systems.

One of the foremost coordination approaches is the **master/slave** or **client-server** technique [16]. In this technique, the master agent plans and distributes fragments of plans to slaves. Master has the authority to do task and resource allocation. Slaves typically are cooperative in achieving common goals visualized by the master. Master/slave coordination approach is more suitable for centralized market structure. **Voting methods** [1] refer to techniques used to describe decision making processes involving multiple agents. Voting methods are useful in applications related to political science, game theory (for conflict resolution) and pattern recognition. In *weighted voting methods*, each vote carries equal weight while, *ranked* and *confidence voting methods* provide a bias to candidates. In **multi-agent planning** [16], agents build a plan that details all future actions and interactions required to achieve their goals as well as interleave execution with more planning and re-planning to avoid inconsistent and conflicting actions. In multi-agent planning, there is usually a coordinating agent that, on receipt of all partial or local plans from individual agents, analyses them in order to identify potential inconsistencies and conflicting interactions. The coordinating agent then attempts to modify these partial plans and combines them into a multi-agent plan where conflicting interactions are eliminated. **Negotiation protocols** are used in the case where agents have different goals or the use of a resources by agents can prevent another agent to achieve its goal. The protocol followed in the negotiation and decision making process that determines each agent uses its positions and criteria for agreement [2,15]. We also adopt a coordination approach from automatic control systems by obtaining **feedback** [8]. This strategy is similar to the effective negotiation, where agents reason their beliefs and desires [19].

3.3   Interaction Among Agents for Data Placement

This section describes implementation of coordination strategies using the agent model. All strategies are assumed to follow standard rules: (i) all agents abide by the coordination by agreement (COA); as and when priorities and conditions of requirements change, coordinator agent broadcasts them to all participating agents; (ii) all agents accomplish coordination one phase at a time in a joint activity.

In **Master/slave coordination** strategy, query analysis agent (QAA) acts as the master coordinating agent as shown in Fig. 2a. Master aims for equal distribution of data caching at each cache location. With the help of a planning agent, QAA decides the placement of data using first come first placed basis according to cache storage space availability. Thus master follows a greedy strategy and

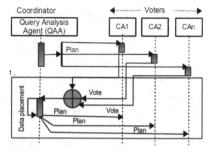

(a) Master/slave strategy among cache agents and query analysis agent

(b) Voting strategy among cache agents and query analysis agent

Fig. 2. Master/slave and voting coordination strategies in the system

ensures to place each data segment at a first available best position. This strategy is the simplest of all and needs minimum number of inter agent-message communications. But, master/slave strategy suffers from improper distribution of data placement and thus longer query response time as there is no feedback from cache units (slaves).

Unlike master/slave, **voting strategy** enables cache agents to vote for the QAA's (coordinator) decisions. This strategy allows local interests of a cache to be expressed through voting as shown in Fig. 2b.

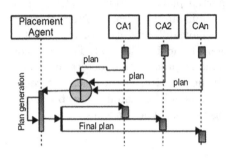

Fig. 3. Multi-agent planning

Cache units can vote based on the local knowledge (bias) such as affinity among all data stored within a cache unit. Polling of votes is done to accept or reject the whole plan. A plan is accepted only when it is accepted by majority of voters. Coordinator first starts with a basic plan. If rejected, improved plans are created by adding another qualifier to the heuristic. Coordinator follows a greedy strategy and ensures to place each data segment at first available best position. In **Multi-agent planning** strategy, cache agents develop plans keeping local benefit in view. Agents make individual plans using different heuristics. Here the Placement Agent (PA) acts as coordinator and resolves conflicts and develops a new global plan. Coordinator resolves contention when more than one cache unit bids to store a specific data segment or placement of new data (shown in Fig. 3). For example, a cache agent with larger data storage capacity may use storage capacity for heuristic where as another agent with high cache hit ratio might consider data frequency. PA must consider common interests to resolve conflicts. Thus placement agent follows a greedy strategy and ensures to place each data segment at a first best position.

In **Negotiation strategy**, cache agents negotiate with each other to maximize cache site utilization as shown in Fig. 4a. In multi-agent planning, participating cache agents generate separate plans and submit them to the coordinator. Negotiation allows peer to peer communication with other cache agents to discuss plans. Negotiations are carried on till they reach to a mutually agreed solution. Each cache agent starts with their own objectives and benefits. This strategy uses all of its diagnostics to calculate the cost of placement to decide the ideal place. Hence many iterations of negotiations are needed before agents converge to a final decision. With a decentralized approach, the cache system may not suffer from bottlenecks with the scaling up of the system. Also, by considering multiple diagnostics, negotiation can predict user preferences well and recommend the most ideal place for each data segment. On the other hand, it suffers from the big inter agent message communication overhead. When negotiations run into infinite number of iterations, the coordinator agent (QAA in this case) may force cache agents to stop from going into infinite interactions.

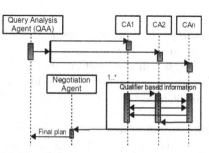

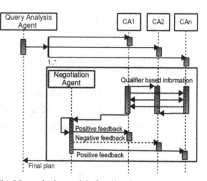

(a) Negotiation among cache agents and query analysis agent in the system

(b) Negotiation with feedback among cache agents and query analysis agent

Fig. 4. Negotiation and feedback coordination strategies in the system

Feedback strategy is an extension of negotiation strategy that aims to reduce inter agent message communication overhead. Feedback strategy employs a negotiation agent to provide feedback after every iteration to cache agents. It calculates the overall cost of data placement and provides feedback (shown in Fig. 4b). When negotiations are not contributing to the improvement of the final results, negotiation agent may provide negative feedback refraining concerned agents from further negotiations. Thus feedback helps to reduce communication overhead and help the negotiations to converge quickly.

4 Evaluation

We have conducted a number of experiments to study various variables using Java based simulator developed for the research project. Due to space constraints studies related to three important metrics are presented. We have used synthetic workloads generated in our tool[3] to evaluate distributed strategies devoid of noise introduced due to communication networks, etc. Each workload is a set of queries with varied repetition distribution of queries. A workload is defined as a tuple: $\mathcal{W} = < \mathcal{N}, s, r, t, n >$; where, $\mathcal{W}$ is the workload, $\mathcal{N}$ = total number queries during the observation period, s = percentage number of queries repeated within the workload, r = statistical distribution with which s queries are repeated, t = statistical distribution with which queries are sent, n = number of cache agents in the experiment. For example, a workload <30000, 20, poisson, uniform, 45> describes a workload ($\mathcal{W}$) of 30000 queries; *20%* of queries are repeated in a *poisson* distribution among the workload; inter query arrival rate is set to *uniform* distribution; and number of cache agents = 45.

---

[3] Links to our query generator will be made public later.

We made the following assumptions to maintain the uniformity across all strategies:

- All queries have equal complexity to keep the processing requirements equal.
- All cache units have identical server configuration. They are assumed to be located near to user groups. Hence cache agents can use location preference in their negotiations. Similarly, all data servers are assumed to have identical hardware configuration. We did not consider server-side cache for these experiments.
- Communication network is assumed to be congestion free and transmission lines are always available for data transfers. This assumption is valid to evaluate the performance of a strategy alone.

Average query response time is an important metric to evaluate cache performance. Response time is calculated as the total time elapsed between the time a query is sent from user agent to the time user agent receives response. Hence, response time depends on the data availability at a nearby cache location. Thus, response time indicates the effectiveness of a data placement as well. In a typical scenario several queries are sent simultaneously and the processing takes place in parallel. Here we calculated the average response time for a workload. Each of the experiments were repeated 8 times and median value is calculated below for the comparison study. Time spent for a process to complete is measured in terms of simulated time *ticks*. A tick is a unit time needed to complete it's execution.

$$\text{Response time } = \frac{1}{N} \sum_{i=1}^{n} (\mathcal{D}_i + l_i + d_i + q_{proc}), \tag{1}$$

where, $i = i^{th}$ query, $\mathcal{N} =$ total number queries during the observation period, $\mathcal{D} =$ average processing time at data servers, $l =$ cache latency (time spent at query optimizer + lookup time), $d =$ data transfer time on network and $q_{proc} =$ assemble time of cached data segments and remainder queries.

Average response time for varied query repetition distributions: Average response time was observed in this experiment for varied query repetition distributions as shown in Fig. 5a. For workload $\mathcal{W}_1 = <$ 30000,20,*,uniform,50$>$, each experiment was conducted several times and average was taken. We followed Least Recently Used (LRU) policy to for cache refresh during maintenance. From the results, random and uniform distributions of repetition of queries in the workload (where any particular query repetition pattern is not present) have resulted in the two highest response times across all strategies. This may be due to the deletion of queries based on LRU. Among the strategies, as master/slave does not consider cache agents' preferences, average time for master/slave has the highest response time over every query repetition pattern. Negotiation has exhibited high response times with large communication overhead. While poisson distribution has low response time consistently.

Average response time for varied number of queries: Based on the lower response time for poisson query repetition pattern as shown in Fig. 5a, we focused on the

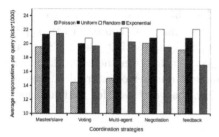

(a) Average response time with workload variation

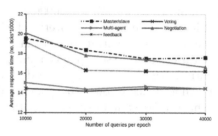

(b) Average response time for poisson workload pattern

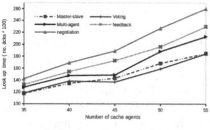

(c) Look up time variation

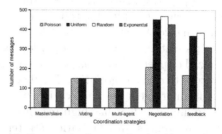

(d) Communication overhead with varying workload patterns

Fig. 5. Experimental evaluation

response time with respect to increasing number of queries in Fig. 5b. With workload W_2 =<*,20,poisson, uniform,50>, almost all strategies stabilize with the increase in number of queries due to the heavy repetition of few number of queries in poisson pattern. Multi-agent and voting have low response times. Negotiation and feedback resulted in high response time and almost similar to Master/slave. But in general they are low as these strategies could find an ideal data placement better than other query repetition distributions. Feedback has shown clear advantage over negotiation. This experiment is to test the scalability of coordination strategies for increased workloads.

Lookup time is another important metric for cache performance and a measure to consider for scaling up of the system. Lookup time is the time needed for query analysis agent to update query index and search for a stored segment due to reordering of data placement after each cache maintenance period. Figure 5c shows the lookup time needed for varying number of cache agents in the system for W_3 =< 30000,20,poisson, uniform, * >. Almost all strategies have linearly increased with increasing number of cache agents. Lookup time for negotiation and feedback are higher than others. This may be due to the higher number of data replacements done by them. Master/slave and voting strategies are quicker in comparison with other strategies and can help to scale the cache system.

The **communication overhead** in terms of number of internal messages needed for a strategy to reach a decision with workload pattern variation is shown in Fig. 5d for $\mathcal{W}_4$ =< 30000,20, *, uniform,50>. Master/slave, voting and multi-agent have the lowest overhead with finite number of communications per cache agent. These strategies are ideal for open systems that uses Internet as applications need to set up huge number of proxy caches over the network. Being iterative, negotiation strategy needed the highest number of internal messages. Though feedback is lower than the negotiation, the worst case for feedback may go up to the maximum similar negotiation.

5   Conclusion and Future Work

In this paper, we have presented a multi-agent system to model distributed cache system and the study of optimal data placement for cached data to achieve higher performance. We chose master/slave, voting and multi-agent planning strategies to represent centralized coordination as well as negotiation to represent decentralized or peer to peer coordination in our study. We introduced a new feedback strategy to refine negotiation. Feedback will help to reduce the message explosion due to inter-agent communications in negotiation. Though master/slave is simple to implement, it has high response time due to the lack of knowledge about user preferences. In negotiation strategy the advantage of considering multiple diagnostics for recommending an ideal place is totally eclipsed by the inter-agent communication overhead. Limitations on the evaluation is not extensively discussed as the main aim of this paper is to present the MAS. In future, we would like to implement other coordination strategies with cache refresh policies. We also plan to incorporate this model in real life applications and compare with existing non multi-agent approaches.

References

1. Bosse, T., Hoogendoorn, M., Treur, J.: Automated evaluation of coordination approaches. In: Ciancarini, P., Wiklicky, H. (eds.) COORDINATION 2006. LNCS, vol. 4038, pp. 44–62. Springer, Heidelberg (2006). doi:10.1007/11767954_4
2. Bussmann, S., Müller, J.: A negotiation framework for cooperating agents. In: Deen, S.M., (ed.) Proceedings of the CKBS-SIG (CKBS 1992) (1992)
3. Consoli, A., Tweedale, J., Jain, L.: An architecture for agent coordination and cooperation. In: Apolloni, B., Howlett, R.J., Jain, L. (eds.) KES 2007. LNCS, vol. 4694, pp. 934–940. Springer, Heidelberg (2007). doi:10.1007/978-3-540-74829-8_114
4. Coulouris, G., Dollimore, J., Kindberg, T., Blair, G.: Distributed Systems - Concepts and Design, 5th edn. Addison Wesley Publishing Company, Reading (2011)
5. Dimakopoulos, V.V., Pitoura, E.: A peer-to-peer approach to resource discovery in multi-agent systems. In: Klusch, M., Omicini, A., Ossowski, S., Laamanen, H. (eds.) CIA 2003. LNCS, vol. 2782, pp. 62–77. Springer, Heidelberg (2003). doi:10.1007/978-3-540-45217-1_5
6. d'Orazio, L., Jouanot, F., Denneulin, Y., Labbé, C., Roncancio, C., Valentin, O.: Distributed semantic caching in grid middleware. In: Wagner, R., Revell, N., Pernul, G. (eds.) DEXA 2007. LNCS, vol. 4653, pp. 162–171. Springer, Heidelberg (2007). doi:10.1007/978-3-540-74469-6_17

7. He, M., Jennings, N.R., Leung, H.-F.: On agent-mediated electronic commerce. IEEE Trans. Knowl. Data Eng. **15**(4), 985–1003 (2003)
8. Hellerstein, J.L., Diao, Y., Parekh, S., Tilbury, D.M.: Feedback Control of Computing Systems. Wiley, New York (2004)
9. Kravari, K., Bassiliades, N.: A survey of agent platforms. J. Artif. Soc. Soc. Simul. **18**, 11 (2015)
10. Kuppili Venkata, S., Keppens, J., Musial, K.: Agent based simulation to evaluate adaptive caching in distributed databases. In: Rovatsos, M., Vouros, G., Julian, V. (eds.) EUMAS/AT -2015. LNCS, vol. 9571, pp. 455–462. Springer, Cham (2016). doi:10.1007/978-3-319-33509-4_36
11. Venkata, S.K., Keppens, J., Musial, K.: Adaptive caching using sub-query fragmentation for reduction in data transfers from distributed databases. In: Lorente, N.P.F., Shortridge, K., (eds.) ADASS XXV, ASP Conference, Series. ASP (2016)
12. Lesser, V., Corkill, D.: Challenges for multi-agent coordination theory based on empirical observations. In: Proceedings of the 2014 International Conference on Autonomous Agents and Multi-Agent Systems, AAMAS 2014 (2014)
13. Lillis, K., Pitoura, E.: Cooperative XPath caching. In: Proceedings of the 2008 ACM SIGMOD International Conference on Management of Data, SIGMOD 2008. ACM (2008)
14. Mahmoud, S., Tyson, G., Miles, S., Taweel, A., Staa, T.V., Luck, M., Delaney, B.: Multi-agent system for recruiting patients for clinical trials. In: International Conference on Autonomous Agents and Multi-Agent Systems, AAMAS 2014 (2014)
15. Marzougui, B., Barkaoui, K.: Interaction protocols in multi-agent systems based on a gent petri nets model. IJACSA **4**(7), 166 (2013)
16. Nwana, H.S., Lee, L.C., Jennings, N.R.: Co-ordination in software agent systems. Br. Telecom Tech. J. **14**(4), 79–88 (1996)
17. Odell, J., Parunak, H.V.D., Bauer, B.: Extending UML for Agents. ERIM, Ann Arbor (2000)
18. Ozsu, T.M., Valduriez, P.: Principles of Distributed Database Systems, 3rd edn. Prentice Hall Press, Upper Saddle River (2007)
19. Sycara, K.P.: Multiagent compromise via negotiation. In: Huhns, M., (ed.) Distributed Artificial Intelligence, vol. 2. Morgan Kaufmann Publishers Inc. (1989)
20. Szalay, A.S., Gray, J., Thakar, A.R., Kunszt, P.Z., Malik, T., Raddick, J., Stoughton, C., van den Berg, J.: The SDSS Skyserver: public access to the sloan digital sky server data. In: Proceedings of the 2002 ACM SIGMOD International Conference on Management of Data, SIGMOD 2002. ACM (2002)
21. Team, T.T.: Mid-tier caching: the TimesTen approach. In: Proceedings of the ACM SIGMOD International Conference on Management of Data, SIGMOD 2002. ACM (2002)
22. Štula, M., Stipaničev, D., Šerić, L.: Multi-agent systems in distributed computation. In: Jezic, G., Kusek, M., Nguyen, N.-T., Howlett, R.J., Jain, L.C. (eds.) KES-AMSTA 2012. LNCS, vol. 7327, pp. 629–637. Springer, Heidelberg (2012). doi:10.1007/978-3-642-30947-2_68
23. Warnier, M., Brazier, F.M.T., Oskamp, A.: Security of distributed digital criminal dossiers. J. Softw. **3**(3), 21–29 (2008)
24. Wooldridge, M., Jennings, N.R., Kinny, D.: The Gaia methodology for agent-oriented analysis and design. Auton. Agents Multi Agent Syst. **3**(3), 285–312 (2000)

Personalised Persuasive Coaching to Increase Older Adults' Physical and Social Activities: A Motivational Model

Helena Lindgren[1(✉)], Esteban Guerrero[1], and Rebecka Janols[2]

[1] Department of Computing Science, Umeå University,
SE-901 87 Umeå, Sweden
{helena.lindgren,esteban.guerrero}@umu.se
[2] Department of Community Medicine and Rehabilitation,
Umeå University, SE-901 87 Umeå, Sweden
rebecka.janols@umu.se

Abstract. The overall aim of this research is to develop an adaptive digital coaching system that gives seniors personalized support for increasing physical activity, and promoting participation in social activity and their own care. The main research question is how can different behavioral and motivational factors of an individual be formally integrated into the knowledge base of a coach agent for generating support tailored to the individual's needs and preferences in a specific situation?

The results include a theory-based motivational model incorporating different person-centric factors, and an algorithm for generating the adaptive and persuasive behavior of the agent that aims to motivate the individual. These are integrated in a mobile coaching application together with a set of theory-based motivating messages targeting primarily physical and social activities. Future work includes the development of methods for handling conflicting motives, and user studies.

Keywords: Agents · Behaviour change · Persuasive technology · Personalisation · Physical activity · Social inclusion · Older adults

1 Introduction

The generic aim of this research is to develop an adaptive digital coach that gives seniors personalized support for increasing physical activity, and promoting participation in social activity and their own care. A basic observation is that such intervention will necessarily aim to change the individual's behavior, which puts particular demands on the design and behavior of the system. *Motivation* is identified as a core factor when changing routines for maintaining or improving health, e.g., adhering to a treatment. Only few Behavior Change Systems are embedding theory-based components of motivation and behavioral change ([20,21]), consequently, it is still largely unknown what effects on activity performance personalized technology can provide that is based on theories on motivation and human activity. This research aims at investigating how particular

© Springer International Publishing AG 2017
Y. Demazeau et al. (Eds.): PAAMS 2017, LNAI 10349, pp. 170–182, 2017.
DOI: 10.1007/978-3-319-59930-4_14

theories may be formalized and applied for personalization purposes for improving health, and whether such theoretical models may be consistent and useful in a realistic setting. A particular aim is to explore how different behavioral and motivational factors of an individual can be formally integrated into a agent-based coaching system for generating support tailored to a specific situation. This was done by:

1. developing a theory-based *motivational model* incorporating different person-centric factors,
2. developing a *personalization module* for generating the adaptive behavior of the agent that aims at motivating the individual, and
3. integrating a set of *motivational messages* categorized based on theory targeting primarily physical and social activities, which forms the motivating content of dialogues between the user and the agent [10].

For developing the adaptive behavior of the system the perspective was taken of autonomous, intelligent and assistive agents [5,9,12], cooperating with the human in the different activities to be conducted: first the baseline assessment of functioning, ability and health; then the iterative cycle of adapting the intervention, which includes (i) the (re-)planning of intervention; (ii) the conduct of the planned activities; and (iii) following up (evaluating) the intervention (Figure 1). The following section introduces the theoretical foundation for adaptation, followed by an introduction to the software in Sect. 3 and an outline of the adaptation strategy in Sect. 4. The generic behavior of a software agent with the role to assist and motivate the individual in these tasks was outlined in a model of goal-based activity (Fig. 1). Key in this process is the agent's aggregation and updating of (i) *the user model* (Sect. 5), (ii) *the motivational model* (Sect. 6), (iii) *its own goal setting* (Sect. 7), (iv) *selection of adaptation strategies* (Sect. 7), and (v) *evaluation of the situation*. The article ends with a brief discussion and an outline of future work in Sect. 8.

2   Theoretical Foundation for Adaptation

A knowledge-based user modeling approach is applied, which is combined with methods for identifying specific individual features [13]. A theory-based approach was applied for developing the motivational model and decision-making framework. Our work that aims to identify specific individual features is based on two main theories: *Activity Theory* (e.g. [11]), which provides systemic models for describing and explaining humans' purposeful behavior in a context, and the *Self-Determination Theory* (SDT) [22] regarding behavioral change and development of motivation in humans.

Activity Theory has in this work been used in the analyses of activity, both the collaborative activity involving the human and the agent, and the agent's activity, consisting of actions and sub-actions (Fig. 1). The prototype applications have the role of common mediating instruments in activities (Fig. 2).

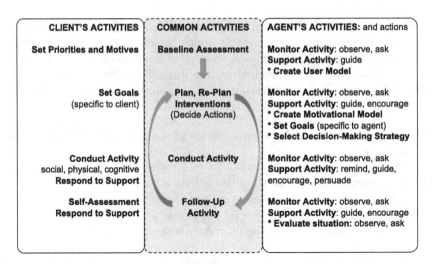

Fig. 1. The cooperating human and software agents' activities in generic terms. The software agent's sub-actions that are marked with (*) are described further.

The SDT concepts *intrinsic* and *extrinsic* motivation, meaning internally motivated or externally motivated activities respectively are applied. Individuals can be motivated because they value an activity with personal commitment (intrinsic motivation) or because there is strong external coercion (extrinsic motivation) [22]. Moreover, intrinsic and extrinsic motivation can be characterized by the importance given to personal goals related to an activity. Following Activity Theory the purposeful activity oriented towards a motive serves to fulfill needs [11], and in this work three particular needs defined by SDT are focussed: *autonomy*, *relatedness* and *competence* [22]. Th hypothesis is made that different types of motivation and consequently activities require different motivating strategies to be mediated by an intelligent coach agent. To create a person-centric and adaptive system for intervention more knowledge is needed about what motivates the individual to change a behavior and translate these into measurable factors, for using them to guide the adaptive behavior of the coach agent. In this work we review and synthesize theories of human occupation and motivation (e.g. [11,17,22]), expertise from the domains of occupational therapy and physiotherapy, and the results from earlier research to form a model of motivation. The model supplements our earlier developed models of human activity and domain knowledge used by agents when aggregating user models in personalized systems for healthcare [1,8,14,18].

3   Platform for Development and Interaction Design

ACKTUS was used as software platform for the development of prototypes [15]. ACKTUS is a web-based content management system that builds upon a core ontology that is extended for different knowledge domains, and a set of services for the execution of applications. ACKTUS is used for managing user authentication and user information, knowledge-based content and structure of the applications in focus for this work. The content, structure and some pre-defined behavior of the prototypes were developed by health professionals and interaction designers by using ACKTUS. This was done by extending a knowledge base developed in earlier studies, which will be further described in Sect. 5. The adaptive behavior of the coach agent embedded in the mobile application *mHemmaVis* is generated by a *personalization module* developed as part of this research.

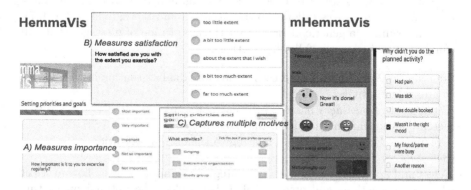

Fig. 2. Examples of baseline questions (A-C), and example of a response by mHemmaVis if the activity has been performed, and a question about reasons when an activity has not been performed. (Color figure online)

HemmaVis is used by the senior as an instrument for the baseline assessment and mHemmaVis is used by the senior for planning activities, setting and adjusting goals, and follow up activities through self-assessment (Fig. 2).

There are three situations with different purposes when the user is invited to become engaged in a dialogue with the agent: (i) to outline planned activities for the current day (breakfast time), (ii) to reflect on the activities of the day and evaluate these (dinner time), and (iii) to revise the plan of activities (dinner time every third day) (Fig. 2).

The planned activities for current day are presented to the user as a checklist with the possibility to mark whether they have performed the activity or not. After the user has reported if (s)he has performed an activity, the activity is augmented with a happy green face for reinforcing the accomplishment in the list of activities, and no face for activities not performed as planned. In both cases an encouraging message is provided and if not conducted, the question about the reason/s for not doing the activity.

4   Outline of the Adaptation Functionality

The agent model follows the BDI format containing Beliefs drawn from the ACKTUS knowledge bases, Desires in the form of goals, and Intentions, forming plans of actions, components which will be described in the following sections.

A generic model of the cooperative agent's behavior was defined that includes a repertoire of goal-oriented actions, and a decision-making strategy for adaptation (Sect. 7). The personalization module takes as input the motivational model relating to the activity to be conducted, which includes the evaluation of earlier performed activity, and the current situation, including self-assessed and, if available, computer-generated assessment of performance and capacity (Sect. 6). The output of the module is a "decision set" of services (i.e. the agent's preferred goal-based actions) tailored to the human and a situation. In our case study the actions are posing questions to collect information and/or providing reminding and encouraging messages tailored to the situation and the individual (Sect. 7).

The following is a generic algorithm for the adaptation of messages that will be further described in the following sections:

- Identify the *Situation* that represents the individual's situation in which (s)he conducts an activity.
- Fetch a set of *messages* based on the current Situation.
- Fetch relevant information from the *User Model*.
- Create the *Motivational Model* relating to the current Situation.
- *Set goals* for the agent.
- Select and apply a decision-making strategy for adaptation (i.e., how to select the optimal actions and create a plan, here select the optimal motivating message).
- Return a decision that includes the motivational message tailored to the person and her/his situation.

5   The User Model

A multi-layered *model of the user* is developed where relationships among physical, environmental, personal and mental factors are defined. This is a generic model generated based on the baseline assessment and updated when new information is collected, e.g. in a followup situation. In situations of specific activity, a tailored *motivational model* is aggregated, which explains the current activity performance and motivates the agent's behavior (Sect. 6).

The information about the user is collected through the *HemmaVis Baseline* assessment protocol, which is a knowledge-based structure modeled in ACKTUS by health professionals. The information is partly based on instruments used in daily occupational therapy practice, and consequently, the HemmaVis Baseline functions as a tool for therapists similar to [4]. An earlier version of this protocol was applied in a study [14], and was modified and further developed in this research, which will be described in this section. The users access the baseline assessment through a web interface, e.g., on a touchpad. HemmaVis mediates the structured protocol containing the questions, and organizes the mediation of person-tailored follow-up questions, also based on the domain experts' modeling. A user model is automatically aggregated based on the information. The user model contains information about the (1) client's preferences and prioritized

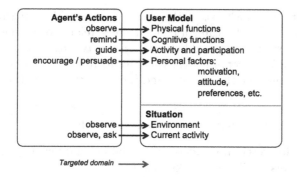

Fig. 3. The actions the software agent selects among have different purposes, either to develop/change or support the client's capacity when performing an activity. Consequently, the actions target different properties of the user, here described from the domains of the user model and situation.

activities, (2) functions and ability to perform the prioritized activities, (3) daily routines and environment, and (4) an activity model containing preference and motivational information associated with each category of activity selected by the individual.

The ACKTUS core ontology, and consequently the information within the user model and motivational model, is partly built upon the terminology model provided by the International Classification of Function, Disability and Health (ICF) provided by the World Health Organization[1], which includes classes for *body functions* and *body structures*, *activity and participation*, *environmental factors* and *personal factors* (Fig. 3). ICF is supplemented with different validated instruments from the rehabilitation domains. The person-specific information that builds the user model is associated to items in the knowledge base, and stored in the Actor Repository. A user model is described as a tuple

$$UM = \langle G,\ AM,\ PF,\ PH,\ COG,\ ENV \rangle$$

where G is a set of the individual's goals relating to the activities in AM, AM is the set of selected activities that builds the activity model including preferences and motivation, PF the set of personal factors including motivation levels, PH is the set of physical functions, COG is the set of cognitive functions, and and ENV is the set of environmental factors (see Fig. 3). The information is categorized based on what concept in the ontology is associated to the information. The goal for each activity is to complete it in a satisfactory way measured with the same scale as for satisfaction, following a *plan* further described in Sect. 6.

During the baseline assessment conducted using (computer-supported) interviews, the client specifies for each category of activity the following:

1. **Importance:** The degree of importance to the client following a five item scale ranging from *not important* to *most important* (Fig. 2A),

---

[1] http://www.who.int/classifications/icf/en/.

2. **Satisfaction:** To which extent the activity is currently being performed in a satisfactory way. The categories of degrees relate to satisfactory or not satisfactory, here distinguished between *too extensively*, or *too little* (Fig. 2B),
3. **Intervention:** Whether or not the client wants to have support from assistive technology to manage the activity, and thereby define a goal relating to this activity.

In addition, the following information is collected:

- **Personal information:** Gender, age, social factors, living conditions, etc.,
- **Daily routines:** Daily and weekly habits,
- **Activities:** Specific prioritized physical and social activities,
- **Health:** Pain and sleeping conditions.

This information can be used for generating a *personalized model of each activity*, defined in Sect. 6.

The content of the baseline assessment application HemmaVis was developed by modeling structured questions, which were associated with the motivation-related concepts. Content of the applications such as motivational messages were also categorized and formalized by associating each to a type of motivation. The level of physical activity was measured by the International Physical Activity Questionnaire (IPAQ) [6], and the motivational level towards physical activity were measured with The Behavioral Regulation in Exercise Questionnaire (BREQ 2) [16], both instruments were digitized and integrated. The rationale for using these two instruments is to be able to measure changes in the individual's physical activity and in their motivation level. The results from the BREQ 2 were also used to calculate the individuals *Relative Autonomy index* (RAI). The index is used to determine each individuals motivational level. The levels are matched to the four types of motivations defined in SDT. This information is used for selecting a message tailored to the person and to the situations involving exercise activities.

The BREQ 2-based motivation index is supplemented with a simpler index based on questions about how important certain categories of activities are to them. The evaluation is based on a 5-grade scale. A threshold is applied for classifying the person into either intrinsically or extrinsically motivated for each type of activity. An activity is interpreted as externally motivated when the client value its importance low and vice versa.

6   The Motivational Model

Instrumental in the agent's decision-making is the *motivational model*, which the agent needs to aggregate in each situation, and tailor to the particular activity to be conducted, since the person's preferences and conditions may change, which affect also the person's motivation. Consequently, the Motivational model is aggregated based on a *situation*, the individual's *current plan of actions*, and the relevant content of the *user model* defined in previous section. In this section the situation, plans and other information specific for generating the motivational model is presented.

Which activities and goals to focus is determined by the *situation*. The following definition of a Situation is applied:

Definition 1 (Situation)

A representation of an individual's Situation is a tuple $SIT_u = \langle a_u, status, sat_u, t \rangle$ *such that:*

- a_u *is the activity that an individual is conducting: physical and/or social.*
- *status is the state of the activity at a particular moment and can take one of the values: not initiated, or completed.*
- sat_u *is a self-assessed evaluation of the individual's satisfaction with respect to the activity.*
- *t is the time when the information of the Situation is captured (timestamp).*

The person-specific information regarding the activity is specified in the user model, as presented in previous section. The following definition of an Activity Model is applied:

Definition 2 (Activity Model)

A representation of a specific activity in relation to the individual user (Activity Model) is a tuple $am_u = \langle a_u, importance_u, satisfaction_u, goal_u, intervention_u, MotRAI_u, MotSIMP_u \rangle$ *such that:*

- *a is the activity that an individual is conducting: physical and/or social.*
- *importance can take one of five values in the range between: most important, and not important.*
- *satisfaction can take one of the five values too little, a bit too little, satisfactory, a bit too often, too often.*
- *goal is to achieve the activity and measure the performance satisfactory.*
- *intervention is a boolean value whether the activity is desired by the user to be supported by the system or not.*
- *MotRAI is the motivational level based on RAI for physical activities.*
- *MotSIMP is the motivational level based on importance, and is either intrinsic or extrinsic.*

The activities that the user specifies in the baseline assessment builds AM, a set of prioritized activity models.

An individual's plan that is formed in the interaction with the system ($PLAN$) is defined as a set of plans relating to specific activities in AM, where the activity is marked as *intervention = yes*, and that has a *Schedule*: $plan_a = \langle g, Schedule \rangle$ where g is the individual's goal relating to one of the activities. Schedule is a set of days selected by the individual for conducting the activity.

The part of the plan that is relevant for a specific situation ($PLAN_{sit}$) is included in the motivational model, and is based on which activity is specified in SIT, and which activities in $PLAN$ have schedules that includes t, specified in SIT. Consequently, the agent will have information about competing goals that may interfere with performance, or reinforce performance for the activity in focus.

To summarize, based on the *situation* in focus (SIT_{curr}), the *activity model* (AM_{sit}) and *plan* ($PLAN_{sit}$), both relevant to the situation, can be generated. This information forms the core parts of the *Motivational Model*, which is defined as follows:

Definition 3 (Motivational Model)
A representation of the individual's Motivational Model is a tuple $MM_u = \langle SIT_{curr}, SIT_{past}, PLAN_{sit}, AM_{sit}, RES_{sit} \rangle$ such that:

- SIT_{curr} *is the current situation following Definition 3.*
- SIT_{past} *is the past situations following Definition 3.*
- $PLAN_{sit}$ *is the plans relevant to the current situation.*
- AM_{sit} *is the set of activities relevant to the current situation, following Definition 2.*
- RES_{sit} *is other relevant information obtained from the user model.*

In a Situation such as presented in Definition 3, information from past Situations (*i.e.*, previous achieved goals, activities or status) is relevant for an individual, since it affects how the individual adjust his/her preferences and motivation related to activities. As such, it may increase, or decrease motivation. Therefore, an overview is included in the mobile application that shows the user what has been accomplished in the past days SIT_{past} in conjunction with the plan for the current day $PLAN_{today}$, since it is assumed that the information will increase motivation.

The individual's resources (and potential barriers) relating to a particular situation is described as a tuple

$$RES_{sit} = \langle PF_{sit}, PH_{sit}, COG_{sit}, ENV_{sit} \rangle$$

where PF the set of personal factors, PH is the physical functions, COG is the cognitive functions, and and ENV is the environmental factors.

The Motivational Model can be related to the basic needs specified in the Self-Determination Theory (SDT) *autonomy*, *competence* and *relatedness*. Autonomy and competence are mainly dependent on the individual's resources, and are therefore taken into consideration in the Motivational Model. The fulfillment of relatedness is dependent on the settings of a particular activity. Consequently, a subset of the activities selected by the individual is expected to fulfill the need for relatedness, e.g., spending time with family members, or taking walks with friends.

To summarize, the motivational model contains information that can be used for (i) tailoring the immediate response to the current situation, (ii) tailoring the response to the characteristics of the particular activity (importance, satisfaction, motivation), (iii) tailoring the response taking competing or supplementary goals into consideration, (iv) tailoring the response by relating it to past achievements, and (v) tailoring the response taking personal and environmental resources into the argumentation about achievements. In the following section the first two are taken into consideration in an algorithm that selects motivating messages.

Input : Motivation Model MM, Activity Model am_u, set of messages $MSGList$

Output: Personalized message

1 Let $MM = \langle SIT_{curr}, SIT_{past}, PLAN_{sit}, AM_{sit}, RES_{sit} \rangle$ be a motivational model ;

2 Let $am_u = \langle a_u, importance_u, satisfaction_u, goal_u, intervention_u, MotRAI_u, MotSIMP_u \rangle$ be an activity model;

3 Let $MSGList$ be an empty list;

4 Let $motTypes \leftarrow \emptyset$ be the motivation classes in motivation ontology relevant to the person ;

5 *initialization*;

6 $MSGList \leftarrow$ FetchSituatedMessages();   /* returns the messages tailored to situation */

7 $motType \leftarrow MotRAI_u$;   /* gets the current motivational level */

8 $motTypes \leftarrow$ FetchMotTypes();   /* returns the motivation classes tailored to person */

9 $motTypes = \{mot_0, \ldots mot_n\}$ where $n \geq 0$;   /* n is the most generic motivational type in the ontology */

10 **for** $mot_0 \in motTypes$ **to** mot_n **do**

11   **if** $mot_0 \neq \emptyset$ **then**

12       $MSGList \leftarrow$ MatchToProfile(RES_{sit});   /* gets all messages considering RES_{sit} information */

13       $MSGList \leftarrow$ ExcludeDislikedMessage() ;   /* excludes disliked messages */

14       $MSGList \leftarrow$ ExcludeSentMessage() ;   /* excludes already sent messages */

15   **end**

16 **end**

17 **return** GetFirst($MSGList$);   /* returns the first message of $MSGList$ */

Algorithm 1. Selection of the personalized message to be delivered in a situation.

7 Selecting Motivational Messages

The messages were classified into different motivation types and associated to different *situations* [10], e.g., when having accomplished a certain type (social and/or physical) of planned activity (PA messages), or when not (NPA messages). The situations were represented as protocols in ACKTUS containing a set of messages. Each situation was associated to a category of activity, and this information is applied in the algorithm for selecting a message.

In this setting, the problem that the agent has to solve is decide upon and perform the most optimal behavior that promotes a particular activity, for example through motivating using tailored messages.

The following set of actions is defined for the software agent s (Figs. 1, 3):

$$Action_s = \{observe, ask, guide, remind, motivate, persuade\}$$

These actions serve the following goals: (i) collect new information (observe and ask), (ii) optimize activity performance (guide), (iii) enhance cognitive ability and effectuate focus shift (remind), and (iv) change attitudes (motivate, persuade).

Different strategies and combinations of strategies can be defined for solving the problem of finding the most optimal actions. In the current implementation the agent's goal-based actions *remind*, and *motivate* through encouragements and motivating feedback on the activity a_u, tailored to the Situation are applied. The strategy described in Algorithm 1 is to follow the motivational model in the selection of the optimal motivational message in the particular situation where the agent's goal is to motivate. The strategy was chosen in the current implementation for the purpose to collect as many responses as possible to the messages that was optimized to the individuals participating in a pilot user study. The number of alternatives in the individual case is reduced by removing the messages that the user has evaluated as not motivating or disliked. Results showed that the older adults were appreciating the tailored messages, and was entertained while having the dialogues. However, the pilot study focussed primarily on the interaction design and not the motivational model. Further, too few individuals were included with the different motivational profiles, and the application was not used long enough to show any sustainable behavior change.

8   Discussion and Future Work

A coach agent promoting a healthier behavior in a user needs to adapt to the situation including the user's changing motivation, preferences, activity etc. However, research in technology-based health interventions (e.g., treatments), and persuasive and behavior change technology are still in its early stages. Only few Behavior Change Systems are embedding theory-based components of motivation and behavioral change, although motivation is identified as a core factor when changing routines for maintaining or improving health ([20,21]), consequently, it is still largely unknown what effects on activity performance personalized technology can provide that is based on theories on motivation and human activity. Typically, simplistic models of human behavior and technology are forming interventions, often assuming that people will make rational decisions if only they become sufficiently informed in the situation when they need the information [7,12,19]. Although behavior change is essential for improving many aspects of life, our habitual systems, conflicting motives and contextual factors are often preventing change, also in the presence of vital information (e.g., [2,3]). Consequently, a new generation of digital assistants, or software agents, is needed that handles such complexity of human activity. Such agents should be able to *adapt* its behavior to the individual, *motivate, guide* and *cooperate* with the individual in pursuing goals that promote physical, cognitive, mental and social well-being [12,23].

The results of the research presented in this article provides a step forward by forming a theory-based motivational model that captures conflicting motives and preferences, and which serves as instrument for the coach agent in its decision-making. Further, the results includes a strategy for adaptation that will be further developed in future work to also handle conflicting motives. Future work includes the development of theory and methods for tailoring the response taking competing or supplementary goals into consideration, and tailoring the response by relating it to past achievements. User studies conducted over a longer period of time involving groups of users with different types of motivation and goals will be conducted to evaluate the users' experience of interacting with the coach agent, and for measuring the potential effects on behavior change.

References

1. Baskar, J., Lindgren, H.: Cognitive architecture of an agent for human-agent dialogues. In: Corchado, J.M., Bajo, J., Kozlak, J., Pawlewski, P., Molina, J.M., Gaudou, B., Julian, V., Unland, R., Lopes, F., Hallenborg, K., García Teodoro, P. (eds.) PAAMS 2014. CCIS, vol. 430, pp. 89–100. Springer, Cham (2014). doi:10. 1007/978-3-319-07767-3_9
2. Bouton, M.E.: Why behavior change is difficult to sustain. Prev. Med. **68**, 29–36 (2014)
3. Cabana, M., Rand, C., Powe, N., Wu, A., Wilson, M., Abboud, P., Rubin, H.: Why don't physicians follow clinical practice guidelines? A framework for improvement. JAMA **282**, 1458–1467 (1999)
4. Casado, A., Jiménez, A., Bajo, J., Omatu, S.: Multi-agent system for occupational therapy. In: Bajo Perez, J., Corchado Rodríguez, J.M., Mathieu, P., Campbell, A., Ortega, A., Adam, E., Navarro, E.M., Ahrndt, S., Moreno, M.N., Julián, V. (eds.) Trends in Practical Applications of Heterogeneous Multi-Agent Systems. The PAAMS Collection. AISC, vol. 293, pp. 53–60. Springer, Cham (2014). doi:10. 1007/978-3-319-07476-4_7
5. Costa, Å., Heras, S., Palanca, J., Novais, P., Julián, V.: A persuasive cognitive assistant system. In: Lindgren, H., de Paz, J.F., Novais, P., Fernández-Caballero, A., Yoe, H., Jiménez-Ramírez, A., Villarrubia, G. (eds.) ISAmI 2016. Advances in Intelligent Systems and Computing, vol. 476, pp. 151–160. Springer, Cham (2016). doi:10.1007/978-3-319-40114-0_17
6. Craig, C.L., et al.: International physical activity questionnaire: 12-country reliability and validity. Med. Sci. Sports Exerc. **35**, 1381–1395 (2003)
7. Fogg, B.: A behavior model for persuasive design. In: Proceedings of the 4th International Conference on Persuasive Technology, PERSUASIVE 2009, pp. 40:1–40:7 (2009)
8. Guerrero, E., Nieves, J.C., Sandlund, M., Lindgren, H.: Activity qualifiers in an argumentation framework as instruments for agents when evaluating human activity. In: Demazeau, Y., Ito, T., Bajo, J., Escalona, M.J. (eds.) PAAMS 2016. LNCS, vol. 9662, pp. 133–144. Springer, Cham (2016). doi:10.1007/978-3-319-39324-7_12

9. Isern, D., Moreno, A.: A systematic literature review of agents applied in health-care. J. Med. Syst. **40**(2), 43:1–43:14 (2016)
10. Janols, R., Lindgren, H.: A Study on Motivational Messages for Supporting Seniors (2017). UMINF 17.08, Umeå University
11. Kaptelinin, V.: Computer-mediated activity: functional organs in social and developmental contexts. In: Nardi, B. (ed.) Context and Consciousness. Activity Theory and Human Computer Interaction, pp. 45–68. MIT Press (1996)
12. Kennedy, C.M., Powell, J., Payne, T.H., Ainsworth, J., Boyd, A., Buchan, I.: Active assistance technology for health-related behavior change: an interdisciplinary review. J. Med. Internet Res. **14**(3), e80 (2012). doi:10.2196/jmir.1893
13. Kuflik, T., Kay, J., Kummerfeld, B.: Challenges and solutions of ubiquitous user modeling. In: Krüger, A., Kuflik, T. (eds.) Ubiquitous Display Environments. Cognitive Technologies, pp. 7–30. Springer, Heidelberg (2012). doi:10.1007/978-3-642-27663-7_2
14. Lindgren, H., Baskar, J., Guerrero, E., Nieves, J.C., Nilsson, I., Yan, C.: Computer-supported assessment for tailoring assistive technology. In: Proceedings of the 6th International Conference on Digital Health Conference, DH 2016, pp. 1–10 (2016)
15. Lindgren, H., Yan, C.: ACKTUS: A platform for developing personalized support systems in the health domain. In: 2015 Proceedings of the 5th International Conference on Digital Health, DH 2015, pp. 135–142 (2015)
16. Markland, D., Tobin, V.: A modification of the behavioral regulation in exercise questionnaire to include an assessment of amotivation. J. Sport Exerc. Psychol. **26**, 191–196 (2004)
17. Michie, S., van Stralen, M.M., West, R.: The behaviour change wheel: a new method for characterising and designing behaviour change interventions. Implement. Sci. **6**(1), 42 (2011)
18. Nieves, J.C., Lindgren, H.: Deliberative argumentation for service provision in smart environments. In: Bulling, N. (ed.) EUMAS 2014. LNCS, vol. 8953, pp. 388–397. Springer, Cham (2015). doi:10.1007/978-3-319-17130-2_27
19. Oinas-Kukkonen, H.: Behavior change support systems: a research model and agenda. In: Proceedings of the 5th international conference on Persuasive Technology, PERSUASIVE 2010 (2010)
20. Riley, W.T., Rivera, D.E., Atienza, A.A., Nilsen, W., Allison, S.M., Mermelstein, R.: Health behavior models in the age of mobile interventions: are our theories up to the task? Transl. Behav. Med. **1**(1), 53–71 (2011)
21. Ritterband, L.M., Thorndike, F.P., Cox, D.J., Kovatchev, B.P., Gonder-Frederick, L.A.: A behavior change model for internet interventions. Ann. Behav. Med. **38**(1), 18–27 (2009)
22. Ryan, R.M., Deci, E.L.: Self-determination theory and the facilitation of intrinsic motivation, social development, and well-being. Am. Psychol. **55**(1), 68–78 (2000)
23. Spruijt-Metz, D., et al.: Building new computational models to support health behavior change and maintenance: new opportunities in behavioral research. Transl. Behav. Med. **5**(3), 335–346 (2015)

Agent Negotiation Techniques for Improving Quality-Attribute Architectural Tradeoffs

Ariel Monteserin[✉], J. Andrés Díaz-Pace, Ignacio Gatti,
and Silvia Schiaffino

ISISTAN (CONICET - UNCPBA), Campus Universitario, Tandil, Argentina
ariel.monteserin@isistan.unicen.edu.ar

Abstract. A key aspect of software architecture design is to satisfy quality-attribute requirements, such as performance or modifiability. This is usually a complex task, because there are often several candidate solutions meeting the same requirements, and the quality-attribute tradeoffs of those solutions need to be considered by architects. In previous work, we developed an agent-based approach called *DesignBots* to assist architects in the exploration of design solutions driven by quality attributes. The agents performed a local search, each one optimizing a particular quality, but they were limited regarding tradeoff analysis capabilities. In this paper, we propose negotiation techniques for improving the tradeoff analysis of the agents, inspired by how human architects (and stakeholders) normally work in real-life projects when assessing alternative designs. In particular, we develop two negotiation strategies that integrate with the *DesignBots* framework. The experimental results obtained so far with an architectural case-study show that the negotiation can produce more satisfying tradeoffs than those currently provided by *DesignBots*.

Keywords: Software architecture design · Quality attributes · Tradeoff analysis · Multi-agent search and negotiation

1 Introduction

Designing a software system in such a way it meets the main quality-attribute requirements (e.g., performance, modifiability, security) is a complex, and error-prone activity, even for experienced architects. A factor that contributes to this complexity is the existence of multiple alternative solutions for the same requirements. The architectural design process can be seen as a search through a large design space, in which the solution space is n-dimensional and each dimension represents a different quality attribute to be optimized. Along this line, a quality-attribute tradeoff means that a quality is satisfied (by a given architecture of the design space) at the cost of negatively affecting another quality (e.g., modifiability versus performance). In previous work, we developed the *DesignBots* approach to assist architects in architecture exploration [5,6].

© Springer International Publishing AG 2017
Y. Demazeau et al. (Eds.): PAAMS 2017, LNAI 10349, pp. 183–195, 2017.
DOI: 10.1007/978-3-319-59930-4_15

DesignBots provides a framework that divides the architectural knowledge into separate components, i.e., agents called *dbots*, each one focused on optimizing a single quality attribute. Usually, an agent represents the interests of a particular stakeholder regarding the architectural solution. Given an initial architecture, each agent explores (by means of local, heuristic search) different design solutions, but only proposes the best one according to its quality goals. The solutions from all agents are then presented to the user (architect), so that she can make an informed decision about the architecture. A number of tradeoffs naturally emerge from these agent solutions, and these tradeoffs are judged by the architect. Each agent might internally compute and discard many solutions, even if they can be relevant for the tradeoff analysis, or they could be combined with solutions from other agents and lead to more tradeoffs. Thus, despite the advantages of the distributed agent search, the solutions currently returned by *DesignBots* to the architect are limited with respect to a (global) analysis of tradeoffs among alternative architectures.

To tackle this problem, we propose an agent-based negotiation approach in order to generate additional solutions and better tradeoffs, in terms of their acceptance by the architect. Negotiation techniques permit to achieve consensus among proposals generated by different agents or *dbots,* while keeping the modular knowledge-based approach of *DesignBots*. In particular, we used a multilateral version of the monotonic concession protocol (MCP) [7] that integrates performance-versus-modifiability negotiation with the existing search capabilities of the *DesignBots* framework. We chose MCP because it models naturally the way humans seem to negotiate about architectural designs.

Two negotiation strategies were investigated. The first strategy consists of two sequential phases: first the agents search and produce a set of architectural alternatives, and afterwards the agents apply MCP to negotiate over those alternatives until agreeing on a final solution. The second strategy is based on the same two phases, but they are intertwined in an iterative fashion. We report on a series of experiments with an architectural case-study, in which the results show that both strategies can produce more satisfying tradeoffs than those resulting from a schema of pure search (as currently in *DesignBots*).

The rest of the article is organized into 5 sections. Section 2 presents the main concepts of *DesignBots* and its current search capabilities. Section 3 describes the two negotiation strategies proposed in this work. Section 4 reports on a preliminary evaluation of both strategies. Section 5 discusses related work. Finally, Sect. 6 presents the conclusions and outlines future work.

2   DesignBots Overview

The design assistance of *DesignBots* is centered around the notion of design agents called *dbots*. A key principle of the approach is that different types of dbots have competencies (i.e., knowledge) in different quality attributes. This principle captures the usual division of expertise of software architects, and also the competing interests of the system stakeholders. To provide assistance to the

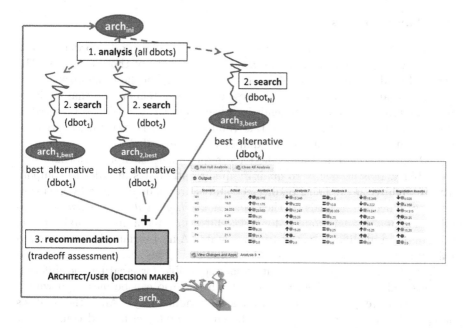

Fig. 1. Main phases in the *DesignBots* cycle of architecture assistance

user (architect), the dbots participate in three phases, as shown in Fig. 1. The first phase is the *analysis* of the architecture, in which each dbot performs an evaluation to determine whether its quality-attribute goals are satisfied with the initial architecture. In the second phase, in case some goals are unsatisfied, the bots *search* for alternative architectures by applying transformations (called tactics) on the initial architecture. At this point, in the *recommendation* phase, the (local) optimal architectures computed by the dbots are presented to the user for a (global) tradeoff assessment. The user can pick any of the proposals as the "new" architecture, and the 3-phase process starts again. This exploration process continues until the user is satisfied with certain architectural alternatives.

The table at the bottom of Fig. 1 shows different architectures and corresponding tradeoffs generated by 4 dbots on a simple initial architecture. The first column lists all the scenarios being pursued by the dbots. The column labeled as "Actual" is the evaluation of the current architecture, and each of the subsequent columns are the analyseis of alternative solutions proposed by the dbots. The color-coded balls indicate whether a scenario is satisfied with a given alternative, as determined by scenario metrics. The arrows (or equal sign) show the variation in the metric between the alternative and the current architecture. An ascending arrow means that the scenario was improved with respect to the previous architecture, and vice versa. The equal sign means that the metric remained (approximately) the same. Note that none of the solutions improve all scenarios, which means that a tradeoff must be made by the architect for choosing a "good enough" architecture. Also note that only 4 solutions are considered, because 4 dbots (M1, M2, M3, and P3) are configured in the tool.

2.1 Main Concepts

There is a number of design concepts that must be understood in order to work with *DesignBots*. In the sequel, be provide a summary of those concepts. The interested reader is referred to [4,6] for a full coverage of the framework.

A *Dbot* is an autonomous agent represented by a system process that analyzes a given architecture and recommends improvements for it. A dbot is targeted to a specific quality attribute and can take (and try to satisfy) several scenarios for that attribute. A dbot can also be equipped with several tactics.

A *Quality attribute* is a non-functional requirement, such as performance or modifiability. It is necessary to quantify quality attributes in order to compare software architectures. Thus, quality attributes are made concrete by means of scenarios, which act as goals for the dbots. A *Quality-attribute scenario* is a representation of a desired property for the architecture that a dbot should achieve. For example, a modifiability scenario may state "A new variable has to be added to the user profile within 15 person days of effort". This scenario is represented by M2 in Fig. 2 (right). The architect is responsible for creating the different scenarios and assigning them to dbots. Each scenario can be measured with a quality metric (e.g., cost in person days for modifiability). After the analysis phase, a dbot evaluates a metric on the current architecture and compares it against a threshold, in order to decide whether the scenario is fulfilled.

An *Architectural tactic* is a design transformation that takes a given architecture and applies changes so as to generate a new architecture (i.e., an alternative solution to the initial architecture). Tactics are used to improve the satisfaction of scenarios, and they are the main operators of the search implemented by the dbots. An example of a tactic consists of inserting an intermediary in between highly coupled modules, as shown in Fig. 2. The initial architecture (A) is transformed into a new architecture (B). Note that the architecture is re-evaluated

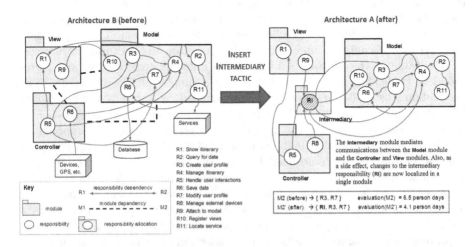

Fig. 2. Application of an architectural tactic for improving a modifiability scenario.

(with respect to scenario M2) after applying the tactic. During tool setup, the architect configures each dbot with a set of tactics. If no tactics are configured in a dbot, it only performs analysis of its scenarios.

2.2   Search of architectural solutions

The dbots are equipped with search algorithms that, departing from an input architecture, can apply and assess the results of different tactics. A given tactic can be instantiated several times on the same architecture. For example, the tactic of inserting an intermediary (Fig. 2) can be applied to different groups of modules. The search works at different levels, that is, for a given alternative, the same dbot (or even other dbots) can apply several tactics, until reaching a predefined depth in the search tree. This "deep" search is based on heuristic algorithms, as they do not perform an exhaustive search over the design space. Furthermore, due to the modular conception of the *DesignBots* framework, each dbot tries to optimize its own metrics provided by its scenarios. Thus, a dbot returns a local and single-quality optimum rather than a global optimum. For instance, the modifiability scenario M2 specifies a cost metric (Fig. 2), which makes dbot M2 search for the solution with the smallest cost via its tactics. Column "Analysis 7" in Fig. 1 comes from inserting an intermediary in the architecture. The combination of the solutions provided by all dbots constitutes an approximation of the Pareto frontier. In principle, it is possible to configure the dbots with search strategies that provide a deeper exploration of the search space. However, the "best" solutions still have to be assessed by the user about their tradeoffs. From a usability perspective, the user should ideally evaluate the most promising solutions. Furthermore, the optimization of scenarios and the tradeoff analysis thereof should take into account that not all scenarios can be equally important to the user. For instance, a user might prefer to improve M2 because it is very valuable for the business, and defer other scenarios to the point of keeping their metrics under predetermined thresholds.

3   Proposed Negotiation Approach

In the approach explained above, each dbot executes its own local (and deep) search and then shares its results with the other dbots (and with the architect). This schema is inspired by how human architects (and stakeholders) would do architecture exploration in real-life project. Nonetheless, a drawback is that *DesignBots* might not provide all solutions and possible tradeoffs, as only a small part of the Pareto frontier is returned by the dbots. Although a table with all the candidate solutions explored by all dbots could be created (i.e., a larger subset of the design space), such a table is likely to produce *information overloading* issues [11] in the user and discourage her from making good decisions. In order to overcome this problem, we argue for a negotiation metaphor able to *enlarge* the current subset of alternatives with satisfying solutions. To arrive to a satisfying solution (in terms of quality-attribute tradeoffs), all the participants (humans, or dbots acting on their behalf) should discuss and negotiate their architectural proposals. This negotiation might rely on priorities of the participants' scenarios, or require additional search for particular solutions. It is unlikely to have a solution that makes everybody happy, but compromises can often be achieved.

In this context, we have developed two negotiation strategies for *DesignBots*, based on the *monotononic concession protocol* (MCP) for multiple parties [7]. These strategies lead to "negotiated" solutions that complement the tradeoff table generated by the dbots. Column "Negotiated Results" in Fig. 1 is an example of a negotiated solution. Details about the two strategies are given next.

3.1   Strategy #1: Sequential Deep Search and Negotiation

Currently, every dbot just presents to the user the best architecture it was able to find when running a local, deep search phase. In this strategy, the outputs of the search phase are subsequently negotiated among the dbots using MCP. More formally, let $DB = \{db_1, db_2, ..., db_N\}$ be a set of N cooperative agents (dbots), and let A be a finite set of architectural solutions (potential agreements) that can be proposed by those agents. The set A can be interpreted as the union of the results of each db when applying tactics over an architecture. Let us assume an initial architecture arq_{ini} (e.g., architecture A in Fig. 2) that must be optimized with respect to 3 scenarios by 3 dbots: db_1 is assigned to modifiability scenario qs_1, db_2 is assigned to modifiability scenario qs_2, and db_3 is assigned to performance scenario qs_3. In this context, each agent applies its search mechanisms and obtains a set of architectural solutions. We denote $A_{i,j}$ to the set of solutions for arq_j computed by db_i. Thus, $A_{1,ini} = \{arq_a, arq_b\}$, $A_{2,ini} = \{arq_l, arq_m, arq_n\}$, and $A_{3,ini} = \{arq_x, arq_y\}$.

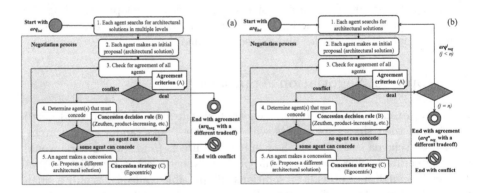

Fig. 3. Steps of MCP for our two negotiation strategies.

The steps of the MCP protocol are summarized in Fig. 3a. At the beginning, each agent makes an initial proposal with its best architectural solution. Then, the proposals are interchanged in order to determine if an agreement on that

Table 1. Utility of architectural solutions according to each agent's utility function

$A_{i,ini}$	$A_{1,ini}$		$A_{2,ini}$			$A_{3,ini}$	
U_i	arq_a	arq_b	arq_l	arq_m	arq_n	arq_x	arq_y
U_1	0.6	0.4	0.4	0.5	0.1	0.2	0.6
U_2	0.3	0.4	0.6	0.5	0.3	0.4	0.4
U_3	0.1	0.5	0.3	0.6	0.7	0.6	0.2

solution can be reached. The notion of *agreement* is defined in terms of the utility of a given proposal for the agents. To do so, a *utility function* $U_i : A \rightarrow \mathbb{R}_0^+$ is assumed in each agent $db_i \in DB$ that maps agreements to non-negative values. The utility function U_i corresponds to a mapping between the scenario metric (sr) of an architectural solution a_j from the point of view of the quality attribute of db_i. A utility function captures the interest of a given stakeholder regarding a particular quality scenario. For instance, if the scenario is about modifiability or performance with cost or latency metrics, respectively; then the utility often increases as the metric decreases. For example, we can have a linear decreasing utility function defined as $U_i(a_j) = (-1/n.ER_i).SR_i(a_j) + 1$, where $SR_i : A \rightarrow \mathbb{R}_0^+$ is a function that computes the metric of an architectural solution; ER is the expected metric (threshold) of the scenario i; and n is a variable that determines when the utility becomes 0 (for example, if $n = 5$, $U_i(a_j) = 0$ when $SR_i(a_j) = 5.ER_i$). In our example, if the utility function of db_1 is linear decreasing with $n = 5$; $ER_1 = 0.2$ and $SR_1(arq_a) = 0.1$, then $U_1(arq_a) = 0.9$. Table 1 shows the utility values of each the solutions in A per agent, assuming that all utility functions are linear decreasing with $b = 1$. Notice that, although the utility function is the same, the utility values of a given solution might vary for each agent since the SR functions are different.

We have an agreement if one agent makes a proposal that is at least as good (regarding utility) for any other agent as their own current proposals [7,14]. If so, the proposal that satisfies all the agents is chosen. In Table 1, after the initial round of proposals, an agreement among the 3 agents is not possible, because each top architectural solution (arq_a for db_1, arq_l for db_2, and arq_x for db_3) in one ranking is marked as low in the two remaining rankings.

After the dbots come up with a list of solutions each, they engage in rounds of negotiation, each one making proposals that need to be assessed by the other agents, until an agreement is reached or the negotiation finishes with a *conflict*. The agents abide by a set of predefined rules that specify the "legal" moves available at any stage of the negotiation process. In MCP, these rules have to do with: (i) the agreement criterion, (ii) which agent makes the next concession, and (iii) how much an agent should concede. The agreement criterion (step 3 of Fig. 3) is a generalization of the agreement for bilateral negotiations [7]: an agreement is reached iff there is a $db_i \in DB$ such that $U_j(a_i) \geq U_j(a_j)$ for all $db_j \in DB$, where a_i is the last proposal of db_i and a_j is the last proposal of db_j.

In case a negotiation round ends up in a conflict, one of the agents must make a *concession* (step 4). A concession means that an agent seeks an inferior proposal (from its own utility perspective) . If no agent can concede, the process finishes with conflict. Several concession strategies are possible. In our example, let us imagine that db_1 decides to make a concession and then proposes arq_b. At this point, the agreement criterion is re-assessed by the agents. However, no consensus is reached yet, since $U_2(arq_b) < U_2(arq_l)$ and $U_3(arq_b) < U_2(arq_x)$ (see Table 1). Then, db_2 concedes and proposes arq_m. Since the latter meets the criterion ($U_1(arq_m) > U_1(arq_b)$ and $U_3(arq_m) = U_3(arq_x)$), the negotiation finishes in agreement. Finally, arq_m is the negotiated architectural solution. Note that the negotiation is not guaranteed to terminate successfully.

Selecting the agent(s) that must concede is determined by the Zeuthen strategy [14] around the concept of *willingness to risk conflict* (WRC) (see [7] for further details). Various strategies are possible for the concession itself, i.e., the new agent proposal [7]. For our work, we selected the *egocentric concession*, in which an agent makes a proposal that is worse for itself. That is, the concession is based on the agent's own evaluation rather than on that of other agents. This strategy does not force the agent to know the utility functions of all agents.

3.2 Strategy #2: Intertwined Search and Negotiation

In this strategy, the idea is to improve the initial architecture by doing several negotiation rounds, in which each intermediate agreement is the input of the next round, as shown in Fig. 3b. This schema works in an iterative fashion and combines (simple) search and negotiation phases. Formally, let us suppose the same $DB = \{db_1, db_2, ..., db_N\}$ that was defined in Subsect. 3.1, and let $A_{i,j}$ be the set of architectural solutions that db_i can reach in iteration j by applying tactics to the architecture selected in the previous iteration $(j-1)$. Based on the same example of the strategy #1, every agent applies its search mechanisms over arq_{ini} and obtains a set of solutions, which leads to $A_{1,0} = \{arq_a, arq_b, arq_c\}$, $A_{2,0} = \{arq_f, arq_g\}$, $A_{3,0} = \{arq_x, arq_y, arq_w, arq_z\}$. Note that an agent only applies its tactics to arq_{ini} and not to the solutions from other agents, like in the deep search phase of strategy #1. Once every agent has its set of alternatives, an MCP instance begins. If the negotiation succeeds, the result is a (satisfying) architecture arq_{neg}^1 for all parties. In the next iteration, the agents repeat all the steps but this time using arq_{neg}^1 (i.e., the output of the previous step) as the input architecture (see Fig. 3b). Thus, in the i-th iteration, the agents run this process taking arq_{neg}^{j-1} as input. This cycle continues for a fixed number of iterations, or until an absolute conflict is reached. In the latter case, the algorithm returns the architectural solution agreed on the previous iteration.

4   Evaluation

The goal of this evaluation was to assess the performance of the 2 negotiation strategies with respect to the pure (deep) search schema of DesignBots. We

Table 2. Quality-attribute scenarios for CTAS case-study.

Modifiability scenarios				Performance scenarios			
Scenario	ER	CR	Priority	Scenario	ER	CR	Priority
M1	28.00	27.68	1	P1	15.00	19.27	1
M2	120.00	70.91	2	P2	9.00	3.75	2
M3	44.00	26.50	10	P3	16.00	31.50	3
				P4	16.00	29.43	4
				P5	8.00	13.38	5

conducted a series of experiments on the CTAS (Clemson's Travel Assistant System) case-study [12], which has been used by other design assistants. Table 2 summarizes the expected responses (ER), current responses (CR) and priorities of 8 CTAS scenarios, which target both modifiability and performance. The initial (input) architecture of CTAS was given in Fig. 2(top).

The experimental procedure consisted of comparing the individual solutions of the dbots and the negotiated ones, under both strategies. We also varied the number of dbots involved in the negotiation (all dbots versus dbots associated to high-priority scenarios). In both cases, we first ran the individual analysis (one per dbot) and then, we ran each of the negotiation strategies.

To consider the priority of particular scenarios during the negotiation process, we defined a utility function where the priority value plays an important role. The rational here was to emphasize a loss in utility for high-priority scenarios, as the cost of the corresponding architectural solutions increase. This means that low-priority scenarios were more concessive than high-priority ones. For this reason, we define a priority-based Boulware function, as described in [8]. This function is defined by $Boulware(cost) = 1 - \left(\frac{cost}{r.er}\right)^{\frac{p}{t}}$, where t is a positive number that indicates how concessive the function is. Thus, if $p < t$ the dbots lose utility quickly when the solution cost of the solutions gets higher. In contrast, if $p > t$ the loss of utility is small when the cost is low but it decreases quickly when cost tends to $r * er$. If $p = t$ the utility function becomes a linear one.

With regards to the dbots involved in the negotiation, we ran experiments with one dbot per scenario described in Table 2, and replicated these experiments but using one dbot per high-priority scenario (scenarios *M1*, *M2* and *P1* with priorities 1 o 2). At last, we computed a priority weighted average (WA) of the improvement obtained by each dbot regarding the metrics of the initial architecture (current response) and the expected metric (expected response).

4.1 Analysis of Results

For the current context of DesignBots (without negotiation), Fig. 4a and b show the improvement rates obtained by the individual analysis (db_{P2} and db_{P5} are omitted because they did not get solutions by applying their tactics for their scenarios). It can be observed that each dbot presented a solution with the best

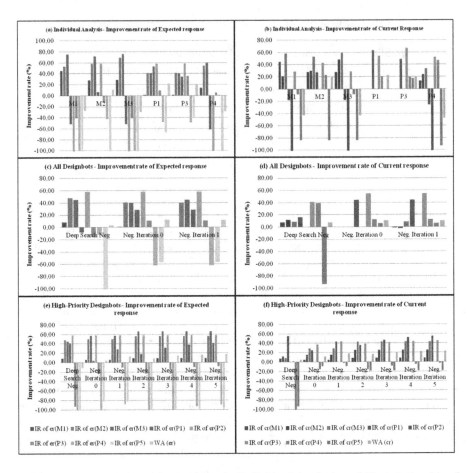

Fig. 4. Improvement rates obtained by the Individual Analysis and Negotiation-based strategies, with all dbots and with high-priority dbots.

improvement in its own scenario. Thus, db_{M1} presented a high improvement for scenario *M1*, but the same solution impoverished the metrics of performance scenarios. In contrast, performance dbots improved their scenarios and kept the modifiability ones unchanged. When it comes to the WA scores, the individual analysis can be divided into two groups according to the metric changes in scenario *P2*. We noticed that db_{M3} and db_{P4} presented solutions that changed the *P2* metric for the worse. However, the solutions of db_{M2}, db_{P1} and db_{P3} did not affect scenario *P2*. In consequence, the WA is higher in the last group. The high WA in *er* obtained by db_{P1} was due to the fact that its solution did not alter the metrics of modifiability scenarios, and also that the actual scenarios responses were below the expected responses (Table 2).

Figure 4c and d show a comparison of the improvement rates obtained by both negotiation-based strategies involving all the dbots. Note that strategy #2

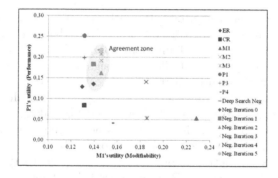

Fig. 5. Architectural solutions according to the utilities of P1 and M1.

ran just two iterations, as the third one finished in conflict mainly due to the large number of dbots involved in the negotiations. However, strategy #2 still obtained better WA results than strategy #1.

Figure 4e and f present the results obtained by the negotiation-based strategies with high-priority dbots. It is worth noticing that reducing the number of agents negatively affected the results of strategy #1. We attributed this situation to a decrease in the number of solutions obtained by strategy #1. In contrast, the results of strategy #2 showed enhancements. In particular, we can see how the solutions from each negotiation iteration improved the WA of the previous iteration. Furthermore, the results obtained with high-priority scenarios were better than the results obtained with all the dbots.

Taking a different perspective, Fig. 5 shows the range of architectural solutions, obtained by the individual analysis and the negotiation-based strategies with high-priority dbots, according to the utility values of db_{P1} and db_{M1} (dbots with the highest priority). It can be seen that the solutions from the individual analysis of db_{P1} and db_{M1} improved the utility in their respective scenarios, while the negotiation strategies exhibited more satisfying tradeoffs (see "Agreement zone"). We think that the negotiated solutions yield a high improvement for because the responses of the modifiability scenarios were under the expected responses in the initial architecture (see Table 2).

5   Related Work

A number of approaches have tackled the optimization of software architectures in function of quality-attribute metrics. A survey and a general optimization process are presented in [2]. Most approaches are often limited to a few quality attributes. Representative examples of architecture optimization platforms are ArchE [3,4], ArcheOpteryx [1], PerOpteryx [9], and AQOSA [10].

ArchE [3,4] is an assistant for architecture design that inspired several design concepts used by *DesignBots*. ArchE searches through the design space via a rule-based engine, using the outputs of quality-attribute modules (called reasoning frameworks) to direct the search towards solutions that satisfy quality scenarios. The analysis of quality-attribute tradeoffs is similar to that of *DesignBots* (without negotiation); thus, the same limitations apply. AQOSA [10] provides tools for component-based systems that allow for design space exploration. Scenario-based analyses for performance, reliability and cost serve to focus the design on particular architectural configurations. The developer can visualize the resulting architectures using Pareto curves, which are used for making design tradeoffs explicit. A drawback of DeSiX is that it does not support automated search, and the developer manually selects configurations to be evaluated by the tool. ArcheOpteryx [1] is an optimization framework targeted to the Architecture Analysis & Design Language (AADL) for embedded systems. The optimization engine is based on genetic algorithms and is amenable to perform multi-objective optimization. The results can be visualized as Pareto diagrams, although the user cannot steer the search for particular quality-attribute tradeoffs, as our negotiation approach aims to do. PerfOpteryx [9] is a variant of Archeopteryx for architectures modeled with the Palladio Component Model (PCM). PerfOpterix is equipped with sophisticated quality-attribute analyzers for performance, reliability and cost. Nonetheless, the conception of PerfOpterix is monolithic in nature, and cannot take advantage of modular or distributed approaches, such as those of ArchE or *DesignBots*.

Another related approach for tradeoff analysis in engineering domains is MATE (Multi-Attribute Tradeoff Exploration) [13]. This approach proposes a system design process based on notions of need identification, architecture exploration, and evaluation, which have direct correspondences with the notions of scenarios, tactics and analysis models of *DesignBots*.

6 Concluding Remarks

In this article, we have presented an approach for managing and improving quality-attribute tradeoffs in architecture exploration activities based on agent negotiation techniques. We have studied two strategies and have experimentally evaluated them in the context of an architectural case-study. The results obtained thus far are promising, since the negotiation strategies produced more satisfying tradeoffs than the one based on pure search mechanisms.

Nonetheless, we still need to assess the strategies with other case-studies and more scenarios in order to determine their pros and cons. On the search side, we can configure different levels of depth in the search tree for each dbot, which affects the number of alternatives generated per dbot, and therefore, can provide more proposals to the negotiation phase. Furthermore, the search heuristic can explore all the possible transformations derived from the tactics associated to the dbots, or alternatively, a faster heuristic can be used, which only tries transformations with good chances of improving the scenario under optimization. On the negotiation side, different utility functions can be employed, for instance, a linear decreasing function. Overall, our future work will study how all these factors can influence the nature of the tradeoff in the solutions and the time it takes to the dbots to compute the candidate solutions. In general, we can see the problem of selecting an architectural solution that satisfies a set of dbots, each one with different goals and preferences, as a group recommendation problem. From this perspective, we plan to investigate how group recommendation techniques can be adapted to work in the *DesignBots* framework.

Acknowledgements. This work is funded by project PIP112-201101-00078 (CONICET, Argentina).

References

1. ICSE Workshop on Model-Based Methodologies for Pervasive and Embedded Software, MOMPES, Vancouver, Canada. IEEE Computer Society (2009)
2. Aleti, A., Buhnova, B., Grunske, L., Koziolek, A., Meedeniya, I.: Software architecture optimization methods: a systematic literature review. IEEE Trans. Softw. Eng. **39**(5), 658–683 (2013)
3. Bachmann, F., Bass, L., Klein, M., Shelton, C.: Designing software architectures to achieve quality attribute requirements. IEE Proc. Softw. **152**(4), 153–165 (2005)
4. Diaz-Pace, A., Kim, H., Bass, L., Bianco, P., Bachmann, F.: Integrating quality-attribute reasoning frameworks in the ArchE design assistant. In: Becker, S., Plasil, F., Reussner, R. (eds.) QoSA 2008. LNCS, vol. 5281, pp. 171–188. Springer, Heidelberg (2008). doi:10.1007/978-3-540-87879-7_11
5. Díaz-Pace, J.A., Campo, M.R.: Using planning techniques to assist quality-driven architectural design exploration. In: Overhage, S., Szyperski, C.A., Reussner, R., Stafford, J.A. (eds.) QoSA 2007. LNCS, vol. 4880, pp. 33–52. Springer, Heidelberg (2007). doi:10.1007/978-3-540-77619-2_3
6. Diaz-Pace, J.A., Campo, M.R.: Exploring alternative software architecture designs: a planning perspective. IEEE Intell. Syst. **23**(5), 66–77 (2008)
7. Endriss, U.: Monotonic concession protocols for multilateral negotiation. In: Proceedings of 5th AAMAS, pp. 392–399 (2006)
8. Fatima, S., Wooldridge, M., Jennings, N.: An agenda-based framework for multi-issue negotiation. Artif. Intell. **152**, 1–45 (2004)
9. Koziolek, A., Reussner, R.H.: Towards a generic quality optimisation framework for component-based system models. In: Proceedings of 14th International ACM Sigsoft Symposium on CBSE, pp. 103–108 (2011)
10. Li, R., Etemaadi, R., Emmerich, M.T.M., Chaudron, M.R.V.: An evolutionary multiobjective optimization approach to component-based software architecture design. In: Proceedings of IEEE CEC, pp. 432–439 (2011)
11. Maes, P.: Agents that reduce work and information overload. Commun. ACM **37**(7), 30–40 (1994)
12. McGregor, J., Bachmann, F., Bass, L., Bianco, P., Klein, M.: Using arche in the classroom: one experience. Technical report CMU/SEI-2007-TN-001, SEI, CMU, Pittsburgh, PA (2007)
13. Ross, A.M., Hastings, D.E.: The tradespace exploration paradigm. INCOSE Int. Symp. **15**(1), 1706–1718 (2005)
14. Zeuthen, F.L.B.: Problems of Monopoly and Economic Warfare. Routledge and Sons, London (1930)

An Agent-Based, Multilevel Welfare Assessment Model for Encompassing Assignment and Matching Problems

Antoine Nongaillard[1] and Sébastien Picault[1,2(✉)]

[1] Univ. Lille, CNRS, Centrale Lille, UMR 9189 – CRIStAL (SMAC),
59000 Lille, France
{antoine.nongaillard,sebastien.picault}@univ-lille.fr
[2] Bioepar, INRA, Oniris, La Chantrerie, 44307 Nantes, France

Abstract. Multi-Agent Systems (MAS) have been applied in recent years to assignment or matching problems in order to enhance privacy in preferences and constraints for individuals, and to facilitate the distribution of solving. A further step in this direction consists in using the organisational structures provided by MAS. Thus, in this paper, we rely upon the capability of Multilevel MAS to reify intermediate viewpoints between the individual and the collective levels, in order to encompass matching or assignment problems. Therefore we define a meta-model for assessing the welfare of agent groups with respect to relevant metrics, so that these groups are able to elaborate solutions that improve the collective well-being without forcing them to disclose all their private information. Finally, we outline the general principles for distributed solvers designed for this type of modelling.

Keywords: Multi-level agent-based modelling · Social choice theory · Assignment and matching problems

1 Introduction

Resource allocation and matching problems are two large and generic families of problems. They have been deeply studied by various methods, both for their modelling and their resolution. They also have been extremely specialised to meet many contexts and heterogeneous application, resulting in an abundance of algorithms, that rival in front of increasingly complex instances.

In this paper, we propose a multilevel agent-based modelling of these problems. We assume that each component of the system modelled is represented by an agent. Moreover, each component is able to calculate its individual satisfaction with respect to its environment, its own constraints and subordinate agents. This approach is intended to elicit objectives and constraints for each system element. We also propose the principles of a distributed solving method, based upon the satisfaction of each agent towards its own constraints, which allows some privacy.

© Springer International Publishing AG 2017
Y. Demazeau et al. (Eds.): PAAMS 2017, LNAI 10349, pp. 196–208, 2017.
DOI: 10.1007/978-3-319-59930-4_16

The paper is organised as follows. In the next section, we review the definition of allocation problems and matching problems. We also discuss the conventional modelling and solving methods. We show the limits of their expressiveness and we present our contribution. We explain the meta-model we propose for measuring multilevel welfare considering all these aspects. Then, we sketch the principles of resolution algorithms. Before concluding, we discuss advantages and limitations of our approach. Eventually, we present the pending questions that requires further works.

2   Literature and Contribution

2.1   Centralised Approaches

A problem of resource allocation aims at distributing a resource set among a population of individuals, optimising a goal defined as the aggregation of individual measures. A matching problem aims at grouping individuals, by optimising a goal defined as the aggregation of assessments made by each individual on other members of their group. In both cases, objectives are often expressed as an aggregation of individual evaluations using the social choice theory [2,3] for instance. While these two families have similarities, they are always addressed as problems of a different nature, in particular because of the possibility or not for "resources" to express preferences towards other members of their group. They are thus resolved by algorithms dedicated to specific families, or even specific sub-problems.

Various paradigms can model these problem families including the constraint satisfaction problem (CSP) multi-objective optimisation (which aims at finding compromise between various potentially conflicting objectives), or multi-criteria optimisation (which seeks to optimise a composite metric).

In terms of resolution, the most common methods are centralised and based on complete information. Indeed, all preferences or constraints are public and manipulated by an overall solver. Among the most known algorithms in this field, we can mention of course the Hungarian algorithm for assigning resources [9] and the Gale-Shapley algorithm for matching problems [8].

These methods usually focus in identifying optimal solutions in absolute terms, by making the strong assumption of a full and public information. Mechanisms for achieving such a solution from a given starting point is not a concern of these methods.

2.2   Distributed Approaches

In recent years, these problems have also been modelled using the multi-agent paradigm. On the one hand, one can consider the problem of resources/tasks allocation within a population of agents: MAS are then just an application area [1,5,18], for which it seems natural to seek distributed solving methods [10]. On the other hand, MAS can be used as a tool to solve allocation or matching problems in a distributed way.

Amongst the latter approaches, some are a mere distribution of computations [4,14] and do not consider the *behaviours* required for agents to achieve a solution, but rather a protocol to set up (e.g., on the assumption of individual rationality) and the solution characteristics (Pareto-optimality, envy-freeness...). Other methods, on the contrary, seek to strengthen the privacy of preferences and constraints: for instance, distributed algorithms guaranteeing privacy of such information were proposed by [15] for allocation problems and [7] for matching problems. In addition, the MAS approach is especially suited to clarify the point of view of each actor involved in the resolution. This "more natural modelling" facilitates the acquisition of expertise on the preferences and constraints, and provides opening towards multi-criteria or multi-objective optimisation. However, the measurement of welfare can only be either individual (agent level) or collective (MAS level).

However, these approaches are primarily a *distribution* under agents of individual preferences and a *distribution* of the allocation/matching solving. In fact, MAS allow to go beyond this mere distribution, taking into account relational aspects for instance (such as networks of acquaintances to specify which agents can negotiate), behavioural aspects (by introducing a variety of strategies in partners or resources selection) and organisational aspects (by the explicit introduction of agent groups sharing some interests). These factors are rarely considered in classic allocation problems or matching problems. Indeed, it presupposes a form of distribution that classic methods exclude, but it is equally rare in MAS methods.

2.3 Contribution

The proposal described here explores a complementary approach. Instead of addressing the very issue of distributing either the preferences or the resolution among a population of agents for a particular problem, we rather try to build a generic multilevel structure which allows the modelling of assignment or matching problems, and the expression of multiple concerns at the same time.

The multilevel agent-based meta-models [6,13,16,17] took a growing importance within MAS in recent years. Indeed, from their origin in the field of simulation, they have spread to other areas, such as distributed constraint solving [12]. Thus, we think that they can also benefit to the types of problems we have discussed above, especially by introducing a capability to represent intermediary stages between "atomic" individuals and the overall system.

In this paper, we propose a multilevel modelling of these problems and lay the foundation of a solving method that clarify goals and constraints of each system element. This distributed solving method is based on the satisfaction by each agent of its own constraints, and consider also some privacy. Our modelling increases the variety of constraints and preferences that can be expressed at every organisation level, using the ability to build composite metrics. Our longer-term objective is to design mechanisms for agents to negotiate a path between an initial situation and a solution displaying desirable properties.

3   Proposed Model

3.1   Multilevel Formalism

In this section, we present the multilevel modelling setting which underlies our approach. Especially, we assume that all relevant entities of the model (e.g. "individuals", "resources", "groups"...) are represented by agents and linked by a belonging relationship. Those relations are not necessarily hierarchical, since for example some problems may imply resource sharing (one resource belonging to several individuals), or allow individuals to be members of several groups at the same time.

In order to implement these features, the formalism we chose is a multilevel agent-based simulation meta-model called "PADAWAN" [16]. It has already been successfully adapted for handling distributed constraint solving in the context of cartographic generalisation [12]. Besides, in the context of allocation or matching problems, some simplifying assumptions can be made. For instance, environments, which are considered a first-order abstraction in simulation, can here be reduced to a mere set of agents, according to the "AgentSet" Design Pattern proposed in [11]. Thus, the key feature in this meta-model is that any agent can contain other agents, and conversely an agent can belong to several agents.

In the rest of the paper, we use the following definitions. The set of all agents is denoted by $\mathbb{A}$; $a_1 \sqsubset a_2$ means that agent a_1 is **contained** by agent a_2 (or a_2 is **host** to a_1). Since the agents can represent individuals as well as resources or groups, the $\sqsubset$ relationship expresses very generic belonging links (in general, a_1 and a_2 have different types, but this is not mandatory). An agent can be contained in several other agents at the same time (in order to represent multiple memberships). The $\sqsubset$ relationship induces a *hosting graph* between the agents, which is an oriented graph. According to the original meta-model hypotheses [16], this graph must be cycle-free. Figure 1 provides an example of such a graph.

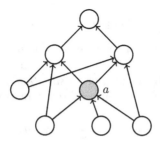

Fig. 1. Example of a hosting graph between agents. The arrow link represents the $\sqsubset$ relation. Agent a belongs to two hosts and contains 3 other agents.

For any agent a we also define its *hosts* and conversely the set of all agents *contained* in a respectively as:

$$hosts(a) = \{a_i \in \mathbb{A} | a \sqsubset a_i\} \tag{1}$$

$$content(a) = \{a_j \in \mathbb{A} | a_j \sqsubset a\} \tag{2}$$

The *level* of an agent in the hosting graph is defined as:

$$level(a) = \begin{cases} 0 & \text{if } hosts(a) = \varnothing \\ 1 + \min_{h \in hosts(a)} level(h) & \text{otherwise} \end{cases} \tag{3}$$

This structuring of the MAS through the belonging relationship leads to an original modelling of the welfare of the agents.

3.2 Multilevel Welfare Model

Our approach consists in grounding the computation of welfare values in the very belonging relations in the MAS. To do so, we decompose the individual welfare of any agent into three contributions which can be aggregated in various ways (depending on the application domain). They represent respectively the agent as *an individual*, as *the neighbour of other agents*, and as the *host to other agents*. Thus we have:

$$w(a) = f_a(\sigma(a), \mu(a), \gamma(a)) \tag{4}$$

The f_a function can be chosen arbitrarily, depending on the situation to be modelled. Since the hosting graph is cycle-free, a consistent computation of the welfare values can be done level by level.

As an Individual. The $\sigma(a)$ contribution ("situation") represents *the satisfaction of agent a as an individual, which is also situated in a given structure.* Thus, this value can be computed from the state of agent a, but also according to the *perceived* properties of its hosts and of their own "ancestors" (as shown on Fig. 2a), and defined as follows:

$$\mathcal{H}(a) = \{h \in \mathbb{A} | a \sqsubset h \vee \exists h' \in \mathcal{H}(a), h' \sqsubset h\} \tag{5}$$

The corresponding value can then be computed by using an operator $\bigoplus^a$, *specific to agent a* (and to be defined for each concrete situation), in order to aggregate the perceptions by agent a of its *situation*, i.e. its own properties and those of all agents that contain a (either directly or transitively):

$$\sigma(a) = \bigoplus_{h \in \{a\} \cup \mathcal{H}(a)}^{a} \chi_a(h) \tag{6}$$

χ_a, here and in what follows, is a way to express the "subjectivity" of agent a, in the sense that, depending on the target application, it can be either properties that can be accurately *measured* by agent a observing other agents, or *estimations* made by agent a.

As a Neighbour. The $\mu(a)$ contribution ("membership") represents the *satisfaction of agent a as member of a group*, in other words the contribution of externalities due to the presence of other agents within the same hosts. Thus, this value must take into account the perception by a of the properties of its *neighbours*, in every host (as shown on Fig. 2b), i.e. the set of agents defined by:

$$\nu(a) = \bigcup_{h \in hosts(a)} content(h) \setminus \{a\} \tag{7}$$

The perceived properties of those neighbours are then aggregated using another operator which we denote by $\odot$:

$$\mu(a) = \underset{n \in \nu(a)}{\odot} \chi_a(n) \tag{8}$$

As a Host. The $\gamma(a)$ contribution ("group representation") represents the *satisfaction of agent a as the representative of a group of agents*, namely in relationship with the agents which are contained in a (i.e., $content(a)$). This satisfaction as a group is intended to measure the *collective welfare* of the agents contained in a, which can be done by aggregating the perceived properties of the agents contained in a, using a third domain-dependent operator, denoted by $\oplus$ (as shown on Fig. 2c):

$$\gamma(a) = \underset{m \in content(a)}{\oplus} \chi_a(m) \tag{9}$$

In most problems, the welfare is computed according to an "ascending" order: the collective welfare, as a measure of the quality of the assignment or matching, is calculated from the individual welfare values. In that case, the "perceived properties" that are relevant to calculate γ are simply the individual welfare of the agents contained in a:

$$\forall m \in content(a), \chi_a(m) = w(m). \tag{10}$$

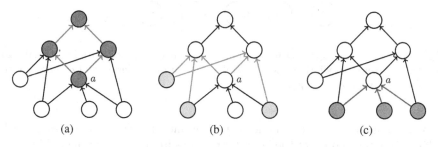

(a)   (b)   (c)

Fig. 2. Contributions to the welfare of agent a: (a) as an individual $\sigma(a)$: a and its direct or transitive hosts; (b) as a neighbour $\mu(a)$: neighbours of a in each of its hosts; (c) as a host $\gamma(a)$: agents contained in a.

To ensure the consistency of this choice, welfares must indeed be calculated by sorting agents in descending order of levels, as defined in Eq. (3).

4   Applications

This example is an overview of the capabilities of our meta-model to represent various points of view (hence, various objectives), specific to each agents family or to each level. It also provides a concrete case of multiple membership.

Here we consider individuals ($\mathcal{I}$) allowed to enrol in several associations ($\mathcal{A}$). These associations can gather into federations ($\mathcal{F}$) and can be funded either by municipalities ($\mathcal{M}$) or by regions ($\mathcal{R}$).

The objectives of such agents are clearly quite different. The individuals seek to maximise their participation in the associations offering their preferred activities, according to private time or budget constraints. The associations and federations intend to assert their size (enrolment) so as to defend their grant requests. The municipalities aim at allocating their available budget as fairly as possible between their local associations. Similarly, the regions try to do the same between municipalities and federations. A typical situation is described by the hosting graph on Fig. 3.

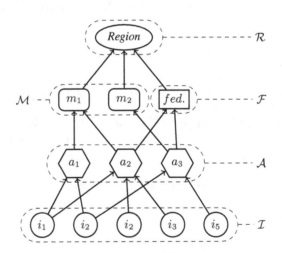

Fig. 3. Hosting graph representing a common associative network, with individuals ($\mathcal{I}$) enrolled in several associations ($\mathcal{A}$), possibly grouped into federations ($\mathcal{F}$) and funded by municipalities ($\mathcal{M}$) or regions ($\mathcal{R}$).

We can assume in this example that the grant allocation is based on a Nash welfare, in order to prevent the largest structures from monopolising the budget, and yet taking their enrolment into account, hence: $\bigoplus_{\mathcal{R}} = \bigoplus_{\mathcal{M}} = \prod$.

An association a which only intends to assert the number of registered members (without consideration for their satisfaction), can simply use $\chi_a(i) = 1$ for every member i and $\bigoplus_{\mathcal{A}} = \sum$. The weight of an association obviously depends on its belonging to a federation, thus for each of its hosts h, we assume $\chi_a(h) = 1$ if $h \in \mathcal{F}$, and $\chi_a(h) = 0$ otherwise, with $\bigoplus_{\mathcal{A}} = \sum$.

The individuals are rather in search of a trade-off between the participation to their preferred activities (e.g. using an affinity model) and the cumulative cost of these activities (which requires a cost matrix $(c_{i,a})$ which reflects the cost for person i to enrol in association a). Again, $\bigoplus_{\mathcal{I}} = \sum$ can be used. But, in addition, people are highly sensitive to their neighbours, i.e. the other individuals enrolled in the same associations. This can again be handled for instance through an affinity-based approach, and an aggregation operator $\bigodot_{\mathcal{I}}$ either optimistic (max), or pessimistic (min).

To summarise, the diversity of objectives within the MAS is made explicit by using a large diversity of metrics, within a structure where all agents are otherwise homogeneous. We show in the next section that this systematisation is the basis for defining generic resolution principles, which can deal with quite different situations, in opposition of classical approaches (either centralised or distributed) where each specific problem is to be solved by its specific method. Indeed, we assume that our meta-model allows the construction of intrinsically multi-agent resolution methods, i.e. relying on local perceptions and interactions between agents, and on generic behaviours subject to context-dependent settings.

5   Solving Method

At this stage, we mainly focused on the *modelling* of assignment or matching problems using a multilevel agent-based formalism. This allows an accurate expression of the viewpoints of every entity involved in the problem. Nevertheless, the advantages of such a modelling have to be also supported by concrete resolution methods.

Most of the time, the specificities of the problem to address, or of the application domain, have a deep impact on the resolution algorithms to use. The approach we propose cannot bypass this issue, and there certainly are many open questions, some of them being discussed in the next section.

Yet, we believe that our meta-model, due to its generic structure, can guide the construction of solving algorithms through the use of generic principles. The guidelines we present below are based on our preliminary work in the matter, and we are currently carrying out a thorough study on this subject.

Besides, a resolution algorithm can be assessed according to a wide range of criteria, from e.g. its computational cost and the size of manipulable instances, to the volume of exchanged messages, or the capability to optimise several metrics at the same time. Thus, searching for a convenient all-purpose method would be quite illusory.

204 A. Nongaillard and S. Picault

5.1 Principles

Instead, we describe below a protocol that allows two agents at the same level to exchange a subset of their content (i.e. other agents). This protocol relies upon some simple principles drawn from [15]:

1. agent s (the *seller*, which starts the negotiation) should be ready to initiate a dialogue by offering "resources" (other agents contained in it) to agent b (the *buyer*, interlocutor of s) – and to do so, *even if this gift is potentially unfavourable*
2. agent b can propose a counterpart, but it does only if it finds this useful
3. to assess the exchange, some principle of subsidiarity applies: if both agents agree upon the favourable or unfavourable nature of the exchange, s and b can take a joint decision; otherwise, they request a mediation from their host.

5.2 A Bilateral Protocol

In what follows, we denote by $\wp(\mathcal{S})$ the power set of set $\mathcal{S}$ (sometimes denoted by $2^{\mathcal{S}}$). $\Delta_a w(+X)$ (resp. $\Delta_a w(-Y)$) denotes the the variation in the welfare of agent a when it adds to (resp. removes from) its *content* the set of agents X (resp. Y). $\Delta_h w(s \overset{X}{\underset{Y}{\rightleftarrows}} b)$ denotes the variation in the welfare of an agent h, host to s and b, when s and b exchange the sets of agents X and Y. We discuss in the next section several methods to assess those values.

On this basis, the protocol for two agents s and b sharing the same host h runs as follows:

1. agent s calculates the "best" non-empty subset $X^\star$ of the agents it contains, which it can part with:

$$X^\star = \arg \max_{X \in \wp(s.content \setminus \varnothing)} \{\Delta_s w(-X)\} \qquad (11)$$

2. if no such subset exists, agent s can propose nothing, the negotiation is over; otherwise, s sends b the message `propose(+X)`.
3. agent b calculates a possible counterpart to the proposal of s:

$$Y^\star = \arg \max_{Y \in \wp(b.content)} \{\Delta_b w(+X - Y)\} \qquad (12)$$

4. if $\Delta_b w(+X - Y) > 0$, agent b sends s the message `offer(-X+Y)`: it is a firm offer, since the exchange of X against Y is favourable to b; otherwise, b sends `propose(-X+Y)`.
5. two "simple" cases can occur:
   - $\Delta_s w(-X + Y) > 0$ and b sent `offer`: in that case, the exchange is favourable to both agents s and b, thus it can be immediately accepted
   - $\Delta_s w(-X + Y) \leq 0$ and b sent `propose`: in that case, the exchange does not benefit anyone, thus it can be immediately rejected
6. in other cases, only one agent benefits from the exchange, thus s asks its host h to pronounce on the collective interest of the exchange. The host calculates $\Delta_h w(s \overset{X}{\underset{Y}{\rightleftarrows}} b)$: the exchange is accepted iff this value is strictly positive.

5.3   Primitives and Experiments

This protocol relies upon primitives which appear to be fully independent from any application domain and from any kind of problem. Basically, in the multilevel meta-model, all agents can be endowed with a capability of adding other agents to their content, of removing other agents from it. From these two building blocks, several primitives can be built, such as a unilateral gift, an exchange, the transfer of agents from one level to another, etc. All these primitives compose a generic basis for the design of agents behaviours aimed at solving particular problems.

For now, this bilateral negotiation protocol, intended for agents sharing the same host, has been successfully tested in the context of a "table assignment problem" , on "small" instances (containing 9 to 15 agents to be able to compare with the optimal assignments). Tables are allowed to interact for exchanging guests, exactly as if they were mere resources: they can be handled like that because the calculation of the welfare of the tables includes the preferences of the guests through the γ contribution. Besides, in order to cope with realistic solutions, we introduced a limitation in the size of the X/Y subsets which are proposed and/or accepted during the negotiations, so as to take into account the number of seats available at each table. This reflects a situation that can occur in many concrete problems, and show that the generic protocol can be easily extended to cope with such constraints, without requiring dramatic changes.

6   Discussion and Future Work

The modelling and resolution principles proposed above are a first step towards a systematic study of distributed solving algorithms for assignment and matching problems modelled through multilevel agent-based representations. We have shown that such a modelling provides a substantial enhancement in the capability of expressing subtle nuances in welfare assessment, and takes explicitly into account the point of view of intermediate organisation levels. This approach to the modelling of assignment or matching problems is generic and requires new resolution methods.

As we built a meta-model which benefits from the intrinsic features of a multilevel MAS, we intend to keep those interesting properties in the solving phase, especially by endowing agents with generic behaviours, based on their local perceptions and belonging or neighbourhood relationships with other agents. The negotiation protocols which can be built under these assumptions are yet unexplored. Then, an extensive work is to be conducted so as to evaluate them in the light of classical criteria, such as the number of operations (moves) to reach a good solution, the nature of the solution itself (optimal or approximate), the volume of exchanged messages, or the quantity of individual information made public.

We have laid out the first blocks in this process by proposing the core principles of any negotiation, presenting a bilateral protocol for agents sharing a same host, and carrying out the corresponding experiments. Our ongoing work on the matter suggests several open questions. We discuss the three main of them below.

The first key issue consists in specifying which agents are allowed to interact with each other so as to exchange part of their content. In the simplest case, which we addressed above, the interacting agents share the same host, which ensures that this host is able to provide an direct arbitration when the negotiating agents disagree about the assessment of a transaction.

But, in some situations, it may be more relevant to allow more agents to interact, using for instance an acquaintance network to specify their potential negotiation partners. In that case, the arbitration mechanism has to be "recursive", i.e. may involve upper levels up to a common host which is able to correctly assess the exchange.

The nature or level of the interacting agents is another aspect of this same question. For now, we assumed negotiation partners at the same level. But, negotiations between agents from different levels are conceivable as well. For instance, in the "table assignment" problem, the guests could be initially contained in the restaurant, which then is in charge of proposing guests to tables; or, the guests contained in the restaurant may be allowed to interact directly with tables. We are currently investigating such inter-level negotiations protocols.

The second key question concerns the capability of agents to assess the variation of their welfare value, induced by a potential exchange (Δw). It is rather difficult to propose an all-purpose solution that would allow a prior evaluation, since it is tightly dependent on the application domain, on the nature of aggregation operators, and on the way the perceived properties are calculated. If prior knowledge is available and if most functions are linear, the variations of welfare may be computed before any effective move.

When prior assessment is not realisable, a general solution consists in a *simulation* of the moves, carried out by the negotiation partners themselves. This process allows each agent to "test" its interest in accepting the exchange, without requiring further communication on its preferences and evaluation functions. The process has of course to be reversible through a "backtrack" mechanisms.

A last point we would like to emphasise, is that a resolution method based on agents behaviours should be able to deal with both static and dynamic problems. Indeed, each agent makes a "local" decision, with regards to its own evaluation of the situation. Thus, from the point of view of the agent, there is no noticeable distinction between a close, static problem where all agents (individuals, resources, groups, etc.) are given once and for all, and an open, dynamic problem where the objectives or properties of the agents, or even the agents themselves, can change over time.

Agent-based resolution methods, in general, are able to operate gradual modifications in response to the reconfiguration of agents, instead of starting the resolution again from scratch. It may prove less efficient of course than a centralised method, but allows to address open systems such as those found in the real world. Hence, in the long term such solving methods can often be transposed to build control mechanisms in distributed systems.

7 Conclusion and Perspectives

In this paper, we proposed a uniform approach to model assignment or matching problems through a multilevel multi-agent system. We have shown on examples the capability of this formalism to express a broad diversity of objectives, representing the viewpoints of the actors of the system. Besides, we started an investigation of the resolution principles and algorithms which can be built for this agent-based structure.

Ongoing work now focuses on the elaboration and evaluation of several protocols based on the nature of the hosting graph between agents, so as to avoid being specific to a problem or to a particular family of problems. This requires to identify couplings between the nature and structure of the addressed problems, and the behaviours to give the agents to enable them build a solution in an incremental way, and should also lead to the development of methodological guidelines.

Finally, we would also mention a long-term, but promising, perspective of our work. As we explained, most agent-based multilevel meta-models were initially developed in the field of simulation. One of the key issues in multilevel agent-based simulation consists in techniques enabling the automatic aggregation or disaggregation of agents, either for reducing the computational cost of the behaviours, or to focus the observation of the simulation on a relevant sub-system, or to enhance the realism of the simulation outcome.

Based on the multilevel decomposition of the satisfaction of the agents proposed in our meta-model, metrics can be built at each level in order to reflect the balance between the state of the simulated entities and external criteria: CPU load, interaction with an observer, compliance of the simulation outcome with reference data, etc. In response to low welfare levels, the agents would decide to aggregate or to disaggregate, in order to enhance their individual or collective satisfaction. We thus think that our multilevel welfare assessment model offers new perspectives to contribute to this issue.

References

1. Airiau, S., Endriss, U.: Multiagent resource allocation with sharable items. JAA-MAS **28**(6), 956–985 (2013)
2. Arrow, K.: Social Choice and Individual Values. Wiley, New York (1963)
3. Arrow, K., Sen, A., Suzumura, K.: Handbook of Social Choice and Welfare, vol. 1. Elsevier, Amsterdam (2002)
4. Brito, I., Meseguer, P.: Distributed stable matching problems. In: Beek, P. (ed.) CP 2005. LNCS, vol. 3709, pp. 152–166. Springer, Heidelberg (2005). doi:10.1007/11564751_14
5. Chevaleyre, Y., Dunne, P., Endriss, U., Lang, J., Lemaître, M., Maudet, N., Padget, J., Phelps, S., Rodriguez-Aguilar, J., Sousa, P.: Issues in multiagent resource allocation. Informatica **30**, 3–31 (2006)

6. Drogoul, A., Amouroux, E., Caillou, P., Gaudou, B., Grignard, A., Marilleau, N., Taillandier, P., Vavasseur, M., Vo, D.A., Zucker, J.D.: GAMA: multi-level and complex environment for agent-based models and simulations. In: Gini, M., et al. (ed.) Proceedings of International Conference on Autonomous Agents and Multi-Agent Systems (AAMAS), pp. 1361–1362 (2013)
7. Everaere, P., Morge, M., Picard, G.: Casanova : un comportement d'agent respectant la privacité pour des mariages stables et équitables. Revue d'Intelligence Artificielle **26**(5), 471–494 (2012)
8. Gale, D., Shapley, L.: College admissions and the stability of marriage. Am. Math. Mon. **69**, 9–14 (1962)
9. Kuhn, H.: The Hungarian method for the assignment problem. Naval Res. Logist. Q. **2**, 83–97 (1955)
10. Macarthur, K., Stranders, R., Ramchurn, S., Jennings, N.: A distributed anytime algorithm for dynamic task allocation in multi-agent systems. In: AAAI Conference on Artificial Intelligence (2011)
11. Mathieu, P., Picault, S., Secq, Y.: Design patterns for environments in multi-agent simulations. In: Chen, Q., Torroni, P., Villata, S., Hsu, J., Omicini, A. (eds.) PRIMA 2015. LNCS (LNAI), vol. 9387, pp. 678–686. Springer, Cham (2015). doi:10.1007/978-3-319-25524-8_51
12. Maudet, A., Touya, G., Duchêne, C., Picault, S.: Representation of interactions in a multi-level multi-agent model for cartography constraint solving. In: Demazeau, Y., Zambonelli, F., Corchado, J.M., Bajo, J. (eds.) PAAMS 2014. LNCS (LNAI), vol. 8473, pp. 183–194. Springer, Cham (2014). doi:10.1007/978-3-319-07551-8_16
13. Morvan, G., Veremme, A., Dupont, D.: IRM4MLS: the influence reaction model for multi-level simulation. In: Bosse, T., Geller, A., Jonker, C.M. (eds.) MABS 2010. LNCS (LNAI), vol. 6532, pp. 16–27. Springer, Heidelberg (2011). doi:10.1007/978-3-642-18345-4_2
14. Netzer, A., Meisels, A., Zivan, R.: Distributed envy minimization for resource allocation. JAAMAS **30**(2), 364–402 (2015)
15. Nongaillard, A., Mathieu, P.: Reallocation problems in agent societies: a local mechanism to maximize social welfare. J. Artif. Soc. Soc. Simul. **14**(3), 5 (2011)
16. Picault, S., Mathieu, P.: An interaction-oriented model for multi-scale simulation. In: Walsh, T. (ed.) 22nd International Joint Conference on Artificial Intelligence (IJCAI), pp. 332–337 (2011)
17. Siebert, J., Ciarletta, L., Chevrier, V.: Agents & artefacts for multiple models coordination: objective and decentralized coordination of simulators. In: Proceedings of ACM Symposium on Applied Computing, pp. 2024–2028 (2010)
18. Weerdt, M., Zhang, Y., Klos, T.: Multiagent task allocation in social networks. JAAMAS **25**(1), 46–86 (2011)

A Multi-Level Multi-Agent Simulation Framework in Animal Epidemiology

Sébastien Picault[1,2]([✉]), Yu-Lin Huang[1], Vianney Sicard[1],
François Beaudeau[1], and Pauline Ezanno[1]

[1] Bioeþar, INRA, Oniris, La Chantrerie, 44307 Nantes, France
{sebastien.picault,yu-lin.huang,vianney.sicard,
francois.beaudeau,pauline.ezanno}@oniris-nantes.fr
[2] Univ. Lille, CNRS, Centrale Lille, UMR 9189 - CRIStAL (SMAC),
59000 Lille, France

Abstract. In order to recommend better control measures in public or animal health, epidemiologists incorporate ever-finer details in their models, from individual diversity to public policies, which often involve several observation scales. Due to the variety of modelling paradigms, it becomes more and more difficult to compare hypotheses and outcomes, all the more that the increased complexity of simulation programs is not yet counterbalanced by design principles nor by software engineering methods. We propose in this paper to use the multi-level agent-based paradigm to integrate existing methods within a common interface, provide a separation between concerns and reduce the part of code devoted to model designers. We illustrate our approach with an application to the Q fever disease in cattle.

Keywords: Epidemiological modelling · Multi-level agent-based simulation · Knowledge and software engineering

1 Introduction

The work presented here takes place within Project MIHMES[1] in the context of cattle epidemiology. To gain a deeper understanding of disease spread processes and to identify efficient control measures, this research studies enzootic livestock diseases at several scales. Various models were developed for either intra-herd or inter-herd spread, using either a compartment-based or individual-based approach, in many programming languages (Scilab, C++, Python, R). They proved relevant to account for field observations and helped designing recommendation strategies to control disease spread. Yet, they lack genericity from a software engineering viewpoint, so that *the exploration of new hypotheses often requires a substantial coding effort*. Besides, the choice of the modelling paradigm is a strong constraint which is the backbone of each simulation program, though

---

[1] http://www6.inra.fr/mihmes.

© Springer International Publishing AG 2017
Y. Demazeau et al. (Eds.): PAAMS 2017, LNAI 10349, pp. 209–221, 2017.
DOI: 10.1007/978-3-319-59930-4_17

it would often be quite useful to replace compartment models by Individual-Based Models (IBM) or vice-versa. This situation is highly representative of the difficulties encountered in epidemiological modelling and thus is taken in the paper as a use-case for testing new software approaches. We believe that Multi-Agent Based Simulations (MABS) are a convenient solution for providing a homogeneous interface to several modelling paradigms. Besides, the concepts and techniques developed in Multi-Level MABS are fully relevant to implement epidemiological models, because of their connection to the issues raised by the multi-level nature of infectious processes, farming techniques, and cattle trade.

The paper is organized as follows: Sect. 2 discusses the main existing paradigms in epidemiological modelling. The design principles and the framework proposed to answer above issues are presented in Sect. 3, and illustrated with an application to Q fever disease in Sect. 4.

2   An Overview of Epidemiological Modelling Paradigms

2.1   Classical Methods: Equations and Compartments

Since the seminal work of Kermack and McKendrick [12], the classical approach to epidemiological modelling relies upon the partition of the population into several *compartments*, each representing a number of individuals sharing a homogeneous state. This strong assumption allows considering only flows of individuals moving among compartments. This is usually described through a flow diagram as the famous "SIR" model (Fig. 1), where three health states are represented: *Susceptible* (S), where individuals can become infected due to the contact with Infectious individuals; *Infectious* (I), where individuals are likely to contaminate others; *Recovered* (R), where individuals are not contagious anymore and cannot be reinfected. The state variables S, I, R, i.e. the amount of individuals in each compartment, are controlled by an Ordinary Differential Equation (ODE) system based on transition rates between compartments. They can be computed either in a continuous, deterministic way, or in a discrete, stochastic way after transforming rates into probabilities and applying multinomial sampling.

Fig. 1. Flow diagram of the classical SIR model. Nodes are compartments measuring number of individuals in each health state; edges are labeled with the flow rates.

This compartment-based paradigm, in addition to allowing analytical insights, is quite flexible. Input and output rates can be used to integrate demographical dynamics. If needed, compartments can easily be subdivided into finergrain boxes, for instance to account for spatial areas or age groups. Several species can also be modelled, e.g. in vector-borne diseases. In addition, the role of environmental contamination can be explicitly introduced through one or more dedicated compartments [14].

Yet, it is not very convenient to account for the individual diversity that is encountered in biological parameters (e.g. in the susceptibility to diseases), or to integrate behavioural considerations, such as seasonal moves, or prevention and control measures. When several concerns are to be taken into account simultaneously in addition to health states, the only possibility offered by compartment-based approaches consists in subdividing compartments again and again (e.g. [14]), which finally resembles very much individual-based models, or to complexify the formalism [18].

2.2   The Rise of Individual and Agent-Based Models

Due to this drawback, a growing number of models use Individual-Based Models (IBM), which allow an explicit integration of the diversity of *individual states* (e.g. [7]), or even to Agent-Based Models (ABM), where the diversity of *individual behaviours* and *interactions* between individuals are native features (e.g. [2,20]). The main advantage of IBM/ABM is to be almost undefinitely extensible, since the introduction of new hypotheses essentially leads to introduct of new agents or behaviours. The dynamics of the model can be studied in details, and domain entities are represented very straightfully by computational entities. Is also easier to represent multifactorial processes and gain a deeper understanding of causal mechanisms of epidemiological systems [15].

As a counterpart, the computational cost is much higher. Not only processing an IBM is generally slower than a compartment model, but the number of repetitions required to study the model is also greater. Indeed, the detail level is at the cost of additional parameters, thus the sensibility analysis has to be carried out more thoroughly. In addition, the enhanced facility for changing hypotheses naturally leads to the temptation of multiplicating the number of scenarios to assess and compare control measures and public policies. Besides, most of these works focus on a practical case and specific pathogens, where Multi-Agent Systems prove a quite convenient tool, but to our knowledge none is dedicated to drawing MAS towards a true paradigm for epidemiological modelling, with a generic methodology and reusable algorithms and architectures.

2.3   The Emergence of Multi-level Simulation

Additional issues are at stake when coming to a regional or national scale, since the spatial dynamics cannot be ignored, and models developed at different scales have to be coupled [4].

A classical approach used to handle epidemiological models at a regional scale is the ecological concept of metapopulation [9]. A metapopulation is a system of interconnected local populations living in isolated patches, each of them endowed with its own epidemic dynamics. Contacts between local populations may occur due to neighbourhood relations, movements, or transport of pathogens via hosts or wind. This method reduces the computational cost that would result from a pure IBM approach, at the expense of a coarse-grained modelling of sub-populations dynamics. This approach is very popular in human epidemiology, since it allows addressing large-scale populations and areas, where contact structures are rather well described. Besides, this approach can be handled either in a deterministic or stochastic way. Yet, compared to equivalent multi-agent based simulations, metapopulations models may lead to overestimate infections [1,11].

Conversely, the computational cost of classical MABS at this scale is quite high. Unless using a massively parallel platform with simple epidemiological assumptions and a high level of software optimizations [17], handling millions of agents is an issue, all the more when repetitions are required to compare scenarios in a credible way.

As it appears from this diversity of modelling paradigms, there is definitely no "ultimate solution" that would fit every situation. On the contrary, a multi-purpose modelling framework should be able to provide tools for allowing a combination of all these methods depending on the target context.

3   A Multi-level Modelling Method and Framework

We first assume that models have to be *designed* from the beginning *as multi-level models*, instead of building for instance an intra-herd model and trying to scale it to the regional scale, or conversely trying to "zoom" within each herd of a metapopulation model by adding finer-grain features. This perspective, far from idealistic, can be achieved through a high degree of modularity concerning two aspects: (1) the structure of models, for which a multi-level agent-based approach seems well suited, and (2) an explicit decomposition of all processes (infectious dynamics, cattle management, trade...) involved in the system. In this section, we present the design principles and the software architecture we propose to answer above issues.

3.1   Structural Modularity: Multi-level Modelling

The number of research works on multi-level agent-based simulations (ML-ABS) is significantly growing in recent years. These simulations use agents to reify organization, observation or scale levels at the same time. In cattle epidemiology, the reification of intermediate entities (e.g. age groups, herds...) between the animal and the population, as well as the use of associated spatial areas (pens, farms, pastures...) is a major advantage to assess fine-grained control measures. Yet, most contributions are designed for specific application fields. Hence, we use one of the very few existing generic multi-level meta-models, PADAWAN [19], which features many design and implementation properties we are seeking for computational epidemiology. Especially, the PADAWAN meta-model enforces a *strong separation between declarative and procedural concerns*, through the independence of behaviours (specified as interaction rules) from the agents that can perform or undergo them. Agents and environments can be associated through two relations: *situation* (agents can interact within several environments) and *encapsulation* (agents can "contain" an environment in order to host other agents). Thus, a multi-level MABS is built as the *combination of a structure* (the architecture and organization of nested agents and environments) *and a function* (an explicit and intelligible description of the processes involved in the system). Since agents can represent any kind of entity, they provide a homogeneous, yet polymorphic interface to integrate multiple modelling paradigms.

3.2 Functional Modularity: Knowledge Engineering

Besides, we argue that field knowledge (parameters, assumptions, processes, data...) introduced in a model must be split with respect to the diversity of concerns, as pointed out by [6]. Therefore, the first task in model design is the identification of distinct processes. We also believe that a multi-level modelling frame intended for epidemiology experts should be *as little intrusive as possible* with respect to their habits, so as to induce only refinements and clarifications of existing methods. Thus, we propose the following principles:

1. *Enhance existing formalisms so as to make them unambiguous, but not abstruse.* For instance, the ODD protocol proposed in [10] is a first step towards the elicitation of expert knowledge, but remains an ambiguous textual template [3]. On the contrary, using powerful formalisms originated from physical multi-scale processes [8], or from molecular biology [13], would be inappropriate as regards epidemiological concerns.
2. *Provide methodological guidelines aimed at identifying typical issues and at answering them with convenient, standardized solutions*, as Design Patterns do in software engineering.
3. *Automate as much as possible the common tasks involved in the simulation process*, so as to let the final users develop only specific, tiny pieces of code.

To stay as close as possible to existing modelling formalisms, we propose to transform the usual flow diagram into a true finite state machine. To do so, we consider that nodes (states) and edges (transitions) can be endowed with additional information (Fig. 2). States are given optional features: (1) a *duration distribution*, which specifies how long an individual is likely to stay in current state, and which is helpful to describe e.g. demographical effects, and (2) *actions* performed when entering the state, being in the state, or leaving the state, e.g. to handle shedding in infectious states. In addition to their label which can represent either a rate, a probability, or an absolute number of individuals,

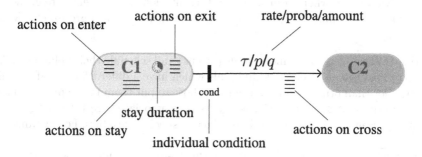

Fig. 2. Enhancements of the flow diagram in a state-machine style.

transitions can be enhanced with: (1) *crossing conditions*, so as to determine which agents from source state are allowed to move towards destination state, and (2) *actions* performed by individuals when crossing the edge, i.e. after leaving the source state and before entering the destination state.

These additions correspond to features that are ordinary hard-coded when coming to the implementation of a model specified through a classical flow diagram. Moving these elements very early in the design process is not much intrusive, contributes to a more accurate view of the whole model, and allows including them in a code-generation process. Moreover, the state-machine diagram can be used indifferently in a compartment-based (deterministic or stochastic) or agent-based approach. All information regarding the processes involved in a model, the corresponding state machines with their states, transitions, conditions, actions, durations and rate/probability/amount parameters can be specified in a YAML configuration file, which is processed to generate the simulation architecture, but can also be used for producing a technical documentation, figures, commenting the sources and assumptions, etc.

3.3   Architecture of the EMuLSion Framework

These design principles have been implemented and experimented through a Python framework, called "EMuLSion"[2]. In this framework, a model is composed of processes (a sequence of actions upon agents), some of them driven by state machines, and using parameters. Parameters include rates, probabilities, amounts, distributions... given either in values, ranges, or expressed as a function of other parameters. They are parsed using a symbolic mathematics library (Sympy) and the consistency of the model is checked automatically.

Class related to agents and to their model-specified behaviours are shown on Fig. 3. All Multi-Level Agents are situated in at least one environment. They are divided into two categories: *atoms* and *groups*. The `AtomAgent` class represents "individuals" (e.g. animals). Its `EvolvingAtom` subclass represents individuals endowed with state-machine driven behaviours. On the contrary, groups of agents can encapsulate a local environment where other agents can be situated. They are themselves composed of two families: *Compartments* and *Aggregations*. The `Compartment` class represents the situation where individuals are homogeneous enough to be aggregated into a simple amount. An `Aggregation` provides a *view* over individuals or other groups, i.e. a representation where agents are gathered according to customizable variables, such as health state, age group, etc. More specifically:

- `SimpleView` agents host individuals (atoms) and schedule their behaviour. An `AdaptiveView` also detects individuals which have a different value of specific variables than others, and ask their own host to put them in the proper place.
- The purpose of `StructuredView` agents is to associate `SimpleView` agents or `Compartment` agents with possible values of specific variables. For instance, in

---

[2] EMuLSion stands for "Epidemiological MUlti-Level SimulatION framework".

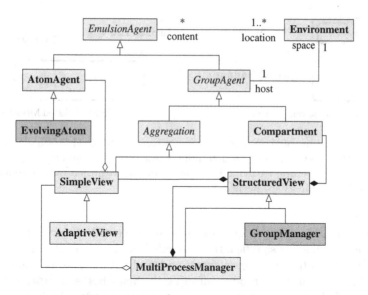

Fig. 3. Class diagram of the multi-level agent hierarchy in the EMuLSion framework. Agent classes with an orange background have a state-machine driven behaviour.

a SIR model, the `health_state` variable can take three values (S, I, R), hence is associated to three `Compartment` agents or to three `SimpleView` agents. The `GroupManager` does the same, but using a state machine to determine how indivuals (or amounts) change their value for those variables.

- Finally, the `MultiProcessManager` can handle several processes in the same simulation. It relies upon at least a `SimpleView` to control all individuals, and a `StructuredView` or `GroupManager` agents to manage the different processes involved in the model.

3.4   Usage Patterns

This composition-based architecture allows representing the modelling paradigms found in computational epidemiology. *Compartment-based models* are built using instances of the `Compartment` class, hosted by a `GroupManager` endowed with a state machine specifying the health states and their transitions (Fig. 4a). `Compartment` agents can adopt a deterministic or a stochastic behaviour on demand. *Individual-based models* are composed of `EvolvingAtom` agents, each endowed with their own state machine(s), and hosted by a `SimpleView` agent (Fig. 4b). Finally, *metapopulations* can be represented using a `StructuredView` or a `MultiProcessManager` holding several agents constructed after one of the latter architectures, with additional processes describing contact structure.

Additional solutions can be built, especially by grouping individuals according to their state. The main advantage of using regroupments of individuals is to provide a straight access to similar individuals, especially when determining which individuals have to change state. For instance, in a stochastic approach,

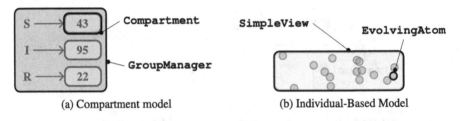

(a) Compartment model   (b) Individual-Based Model

Fig. 4. (a) Structure of a pure compartment-based model. The GroupManager is endowed with a state machine to determine flows between compartments. (b) Pure IBM simulation structure. EvolvingAtoms are endowed with their own state machines and hosted by a SimpleView agent.

one multinomial sample per group can be used instead of one Bernoulli trial per individual, which is significantly more efficient. To do so, the first step consists in building a `GroupManager` agent, endowed with a state machine for one concern, e.g. the infectious process affecting the `health_state` variable (Fig. 5). Each value of the `health_state` is associated with an `AdaptiveView`, containing `AtomAgents`. Atoms move from one state to another according to the state machine. If an external process affects `health_state` of agents, for instance a cure changing "I" into "R", the "I" `AdaptiveView` detects the change and asks the `GroupManager` to put modified atoms in the right place ("R" `AdaptiveView`).

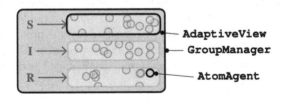

Fig. 5. Structure of an aggregation of individuals into adaptive views. Atoms are grouped according to their common states. The GroupManager is endowed with the state machine to induce state changes in atoms.

The `MultiProcessManager` agent handles a combination of several analogous structures (Fig. 6). This agent is given the list of processes affecting individuals or groupings, and the variables associated with each grouping. If a process is bound to a state machine, it automatically uses a `GroupManager` with the structure described above, otherwise it does the same with a simple `StructuredView`. Each individual is thus accessible from a global list (`SimpleView`) and from each of the groupings.

The current version of EMuLSion counts about 3,200 lines of code (in Python). The framework has been extensively tested on several variations of the theoretical SIR-like models, to check that all usage pattern described above produce equivalent results. In the next section, we show how these usage patterns are deployed for the study of a real disease.

4   Application to Q fever in cattle

To illustrate the interest of our approach, we explain here how it is applied to one of the diseases studied in project MIHMES: Q fever, a zoonosis affecting mainly ruminants. Two specific individual-based models have been already developed for this disease in cattle and are used for comparison, one for the within-herd spread [7], and one for the inter-herd spread [16].

4.1   Q fever model

Our implementation of the Q fever model in dairy herds is based on [7] with 6 health states: susceptible (S), infectious without immune response (I−), infectious with immune response (I+) and bacterial shedding in milk (I+m), and carrier with (C+) or without (C−) antibodies. Contaminations occur through bacterial shedding in the environment. Besides, only adult female cows are taken into account. They follow a farming process ("life cycle") suited for milk production where cows are inseminated, get pregnant (P state), calve (PC) or abort (A) depending on their health state, and wait before new pregnancy (BP). Calving and abortion bring a high level of bacterial shedding.

During each time step, the processes involved at the herd level are the following: (1) bacterial decay in the environment (exponential decrease); (2) culling process to remove cows depending on their parity (i.e. number of calvings); (3) replacement process to introduce new animals in the herd; (4) infection process based on the state machine affecting health state; (5) farm management based on the state machine affecting life cycle; (6) actualization of the grouping of animals by parity.

4.2   Implementation, Tests, and Future Work

To implement this model, we could use a classical IBM approach, but to benefit from the adaptive grouping of individuals, the most suited architecture consists in defining a class for individuals, namely QfeverCow which extends AtomAgent, and one for the herd (QfeverHerd) as a subclass of MultiProcessManager.

The processes involved in the model require that individuals are grouped according to three criteria: parity (for culling), life cycle and health state (both driven by a state machine). The amount of bacteria shedded by infectious animals also depends if they recently calved or not, thus using an additional boolean variable to control the grouping for the infection process is more efficient, all the more than those groups are created only when needed. The resulting architecture is shown on Fig. 6.

The implementation of the Q fever model within the EMuLSion framework was first tested to reproduce the outcomes of the reference intra-herd model [7]. Figure 7 shows the comparison between both on two main outputs (disease prevalence, i.e. proportion of infectious animals, and amount of bacteria excreted in environment). In addition, we are able to test rapidly alternative hypotheses, especially regarding the simplification of the intra-herd model, in order to keep the core mechanisms responsible for the disease spread before introducing inter-herd contamination. This exploratory work will be published in a separate article.

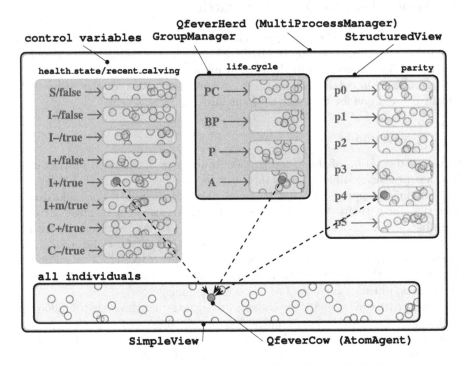

Fig. 6. Structure of the intra-herd model of the Q-Fever disease. Individuals are aggregated according to concern-related variables. Individuals (e.g. the blue one in health state I⁺, life state A and parity 4) can be accessed through each concern or through a global list.

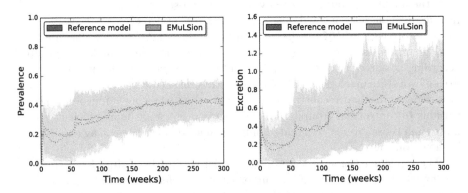

Fig. 7. Average (200 repetitions) and 5–95% percentiles for the prevalence and environmental excretion of bacteria in reference model [7] and in EMuLSion implementation of Q fever.

The original intra-herd [7] and inter-herd [16] models were respectively composed of 1,000 and 2,500 lines of assumption-specific code (in R and Python). The EMuLSion implementation involves a small amount of classes developed for Q fever (circa 250 lines), and a YAML configuration file for describing the state machines, processes, and parameters composed of about 300 key-value pairs, including textual comments.

Ongoing work now focuses on the integration of this model to an inter-herd simulation, using again a `MultiProcessManager` to represent the metapopulation of herds. In Q fever, contamination between herds occurs because of airborne dissemination of bacteria and because of the introduction of infected animals through animal trade. This only affects two processes of the intra-herd model: the renewal process (based on sales and purchases) and the bacterial dispersion. New procedures are currently elaborated to account for these mechanisms, on the basis of existing trade and meteorological data.

5   Conclusion and Perspectives

We have presented a generic approach based on the organization of multi-level nested agents to design and implement epidemiological models. Our method offers a homogeneous way to integrate quite easily classical methods such as compartment-based and individual-based models. Besides, it relies upon a separation of declarative and procedural concerns, first to keep the underlying hypotheses intelligible and revisable, and second to make the simulation engine generic and reliable. Though the development of the framework itself requires advanced skills in computer science, its use for designing and simulating models is made easy for epidemiologists, who have very little code (and simple) to write, and conversely forced to write down their assumptions in detail. This framework has been already applied to re-design the intra-herd model of Q fever and test possible simplifications, in order to build an efficient and relevant between-herd model. Other models developed during the MIHMES project will be re-engineered in a similar way to ensure the sustainability and extensibility of the modelling experience.

More generally, this work is a first step towards the collective elaboration of a common modelling frame to allow an accurate comparison of epidemiological models. The ability to make all assumptions explicit and describe precisely all the processes and interactions involved in a system, and the confidence in a generic, yet versatile simulation engine, are a crucial requirement for scientific reproducibility. Besides, the capability of using indifferently and transparently one paradigm or another paves the way for exploring automatic switch techniques between them, as suggested in [5].

In a wider perspective, we also believe that reducing the duration of design, implementation and testing of new models will be a key stake to answer epidemiological urges (avian or human flu, mosquito-borne diseases), increased by global warming which could lead to a multiplication of unexpected situations.

Acknowledgements. Project MIHMES is funded by the French Research Agency, Program Investments for the Future (ANR-10-BINF-07) and the European fund for the Regional Development (FEDER) of Pays-de-la-Loire. The research work presented here is also funded by the Animal Health Division of the French National Institute for Agricultural Research (INRA).

References

1. Ajelli, M., Gonçalves, B., Balcan, D., Colizza, V., Hu, H., Ramasco, J.J., Merler, S., Vespignani, A.: Comparing large-scale computational approaches to epidemic modeling: agent-based versus structured metapopulation models. BMC Infect. Dis. **10**(1) (2010)
2. Amouroux, E., Desvaux, S., Drogoul, A.: Towards virtual epidemiology: an agent-based approach to the modeling of H5N1 propagation and persistence in north-vietnam. In: Bui, T.D., Ho, T.V., Ha, Q.T. (eds.) PRIMA 2008. LNCS (LNAI), vol. 5357, pp. 26–33. Springer, Heidelberg (2008). doi:10.1007/978-3-540-89674-6_6
3. Amouroux, E., Gaudou, B., Desvaux, S., Drogoul, A.: O.D.D.: a promising but incomplete formalism for individual-based model specification. In: IEEE RIVF International Conference on Computing and Communication Technologies. IEEE (2010)
4. Beaunée, G., Vergu, E., Ezanno, P.: Modelling of paratuberculosis spread between dairy cattle farms at a regional scale. Vet. Res. **46**(1), 1–13 (2015)
5. Bobashev, G.V., Goedecke, D.M., Yu, F., Epstein, J.M.: A hybrid epidemic model: combining the advantages of agent-based and equation-based approaches. In: Winter Simulation Conference (2007)
6. Bui, T.M.A., Stinckwich, S., Ziane, M., Roche, B., Ho, T.V.: KENDRICK: a domain specific language and platform for mathematical epidemiological modelling. In: IEEE RIVF International Conference on Computing and Communication Technologies, pp. 132–137. IEEE (2015)
7. Courcoul, A., Monod, H., Nielen, M., Klinkenberg, D., Hogerwerf, L., Beaudeau, F., Vergu, E.: Modelling the effect of heterogeneity of shedding on the within herd Coxiella burnetii spread and identification of key parameters by sensitivity analysis. J. Theor. Biol. **284**(1), 130–141 (2011)
8. Díaz-Zuccarini, V., Pichardo-Almarza, C.: On the formalization of multi-scale and multi-science processes for integrative biology. Interface Focus **1**(3), 426–437 (2011)
9. Grenfell, B., Harwood, J.: (meta)population dynamics of infectious diseases. Trends Ecol. Evol. **12**(10), 395–399 (1997)
10. Grimm, V., et al.: A standard protocol for describing individual-based and agent-based models. Ecol. Model. **198**(1–2), 115–126 (2006)
11. Keeling, M.J., Danon, L., Vernon, M.C., House, T.A.: Individual identity and movement networks for disease metapopulations. PNAS **107**(19), 8866–8870 (2010)
12. Kermack, W.O., McKendrick, A.G.: A contribution to the mathematical theory of epidemics. Proc. R. Soc. **A115**, 700–721 (1927)
13. Le Novere, N., et al.: The systems biology graphical notation. Nat. Biotech. **27**(8), 735–741 (2009)
14. Marcé, C., Ezanno, P., Seegers, H., Pfeiffer, D., Fourichon, C.: Predicting fadeout versus persistence of paratuberculosis in a dairy cattle herd for management and control purposes: a modelling study. Vet. Res. **42**(1), 36 (2011)
15. Marshall, B.D., Galea, S.: Formalizing the role of agent-based modeling in causal inference and epidemiology. Am. J. Epidemiol. **181**(2), 92–99 (2014)

16. Pandit, P., Hoch, T., Ezanno, P., Beaudeau, F., Vergu, E.: Spread of Coxiella burnetii between dairy cattle herds in an enzootic region: modelling contributions of airborne transmission and trade. Vet. Res. **47**(1) (2016)
17. Parker, J., Epstein, J.M.: A distributed platform for global-scale agent-based models of disease transmission. ACM Trans. Model. Comput. Simul., 2:1–2:25 (2011)
18. Perra, N., Balcan, D., Gonçalves, B., Vespignani, A.: Towards a characterization of behavior-disease models. PLoS ONE **6**(8), e23084 (2011)
19. Picault, S., Mathieu, P.: An interaction-oriented model for multi-scale simulation. In: 22nd International Joint Conference on Artificial Intelligence (IJCAI), pp. 332–337 (2011)
20. Robins, J., Bogen, S., Francis, A., Westhoek, A., Kanarek, A., Lenhart, S., Eda, S.: Agent-based model for Johne's disease dynamics in a dairy herd. Vet. Res. **46**(1) (2015)

Replication-Based Self-healing of Mobile Agents Exploring Complex Networks

Arles Rodríguez[1,2(✉)], Jonatan Gómez[2], and Ada Diaconescu[3]

[1] Fundación Universitaria Konrad Lorenz, Bogotá, Colombia
arlese.rodriguezp@konradlorenz.edu.co
[2] ALIFE Research Group, Universidad Nacional de Colombia, Bogotá, Colombia
jgomezpe@unal.edu.co
[3] Telecom ParisTech, IMT, Paris-Saclay University, Paris, France
ada.diaconescu@telecom-paristech.fr

Abstract. Multi-agent based approaches can offer highly scalable, robust and flexible ways to provide data-collection and synchronisation services in large-scale dynamic distributed environments, ranging from physical terrains to sensor networks, computing Clouds, and the Internet of Things (IoT). The network topology of the targeted distributed system, as well as the agents' exploration algorithm, have an important impact on service performance and consequently on robustness in case of failure-prone agents. In previous works we have proposed a pheromone-based agent exploration algorithm that performs best in most targeted environments. We have also identified the network topology characteristics that are most sensitive to agent failure. In this paper, we propose a replication-based self-healing approach that enables agents to complete a data-synchronisation task even for high-failure rates, in failure-sensitive network topologies. System nodes can learn and estimate time-outs dynamically, so as to minimise false positives. We evaluate overheads incurred by agent replication, in terms of memory consumption and message communication. The reported findings can help design viable multi-agent solutions for a wide variety of data-intensive distributed systems.

Keywords: Replication · Multi-agent systems · Distributed system · Complex networks · Exploration · Data synchronisation · Self-healing failures

1 Introduction

Multi-agent based approaches can offer highly scalable, robust and flexible ways to provide data-collection and synchronisation services in large-scale dynamic distributed environments, ranging from physical terrains to sensor networks, computing Clouds, and the Internet of Things (IoT). In previous works we have shown that both the network topology of the targeted distributed system, and the agents' network exploration algorithm, are key to service performance, and, consequently, to robustness in case of failure-prone agents. In [1] we have proposed a pheromone-based agent exploration algorithm that performs best for

© Springer International Publishing AG 2017
Y. Demazeau et al. (Eds.): PAAMS 2017, LNAI 10349, pp. 222–233, 2017.
DOI: 10.1007/978-3-319-59930-4_18

collecting data from physical environments with various topologies. The performance of this algorithm was also confirmed for distributed computing systems, where the exploration space was a complex network (rather than a uniform surface) [2]. These findings are consistent with related works that also correlate complex network topology to distributed task performance [3–5].

Performance also impacts robustness, since faster agent exploration provides better resistance to agent failure (i.e. the task is completed before all agents fail). In [2], we identified the characteristics of network topologies most sensitive to agent failure, when using our pheromone-based algorithm. Namely, the agents' success was inversely correlated to the variance of the betweenness centrality among nodes – e.g. Small World or Hub & Spoke topologies were the most fragile. To improve the robustness of our exploration algorithm in such topologies, we propose here a self-healing approach based on localised agent replication.

Replication is a well-known strategy based on object copy creation (e.g. files, databases, sensor information) [6]. It helps deal with component failures and hence ensure better performance and dependability. In distributed systems, time-outs are commonly used to detect node failures and trigger replication. Nodes repeatedly exchange ping messages (or heart-beats) and the lack of a node's response within a delay indicates the node's failure [7,8]. One difficulty here is to estimate time-out values, so as to avoid false positives and node over-replication. Another difficulty is system scalability, as the number of monitoring messages may grow exponentially with the system size. Several strategies are available to limit communication to local domains [9,10].

In the presented study, agents aim to complete the collective task of synchronising data across all nodes of a distributed system. Each node is initialised with different data, which is only updated by agents (this is a simplifying assumption that can be lifted in future works). Agents explore the system and progressively collect, merge and deposit data at each node, until all nodes contain the same data aggregate. Agents can fail with a predefined probability, meaning they are removed from the system. The self-healing technique proposed here aims to replicate agents so as to: (i) ensure task completion, even for relatively high failure rates; and, (ii) avoid false positives and over-replication, when time-outs are initially unknown (e.g. vary dynamically).

In short, each node keeps references of agents that leave the node for a neighbour node. Once arrived, the agent notifies the node that it left from. If the node does *not* receive a notification from an agent within an expected delay, then the node creates a new agent and injects the latest local data aggregate into it. The time-out is the estimated delay for an agent's transfer from the current node to its neighbour node. To avoid over-replication, if a notification arrives after a replica has already been created, then the node picks one of the next arriving agents, merges its data with the local aggregate, then removes the agent. The node also updates its time-out delay accordingly, hence learning and adapting to local communication delays on each of its network links.

This replication technique applies to tasks performed by identical agents, where differing agent states (i.e. partial data aggregates) can be reloaded from the local nodes. Possible applications include ad-hoc networks or sensor networks where agents can be lost during communication and in re-designing services like traditional DNS using peer-to-peer protocols when network partitions can produce disruptions in internet services and high performance is required [11]. Additionally, future work will aim to enable agents to handle node and link failures in a local fashion (e.g. partial failures, where agents provide altered data [12] or node crashes in cloud environments where the topology must be maintained and node instances can be created and interconnected dynamically).

The remaining of this paper is organized as follows: Sect. 2 presents the agents' data-replication collective task, the complex network topologies studied and the agent design. Section 3 presents the replication technique and Sect. 4 details the experimental settings (i.e. complex network topology, failure rates and replication algorithm configuration) and discusses results. Finally, Sect. 5 presents conclusions and future works.

2   Data Replication Problem

Agents must explore nodes interconnected via a complex network. Initially, each node holds different data. The agents collect and replicate data across the nodes until all nodes hold the same data aggregate. Agents can fail, with a probability p_f (e.g. $p_f = 0.1$ means that an agent can crash in one of ten simulation steps).

The agent implementation is based on [2], in turn inspired by previous approaches [13,14]. Each agent is endowed with a collection of perceptions $P = \{pheromone, data, node, neighbors, msg\}$ and actions $A = \{Move(k), Collect, Send(msg), Recv\}$. In the collection P, pheromone is a vector of real numbers with values in $[0, 1]$ that represent the amount of pheromone in the agent's vicinity (i.e. nodes adjacent to the current location); *data* stores a data copy on the current node; *neighbour* returns the identities of agents in the same vertex; *msg* stores messages from other agents; and *node* returns the agent's location (current node). In the actions, $Move(k)$ moves the agent to a node k and copies the agent's data in k; *Collect* copies data from current node in the agent's memory; and *Send* and *Recv* exchange information with other agents.

Simulation is performed in rounds, where each round defines the time in which each agent senses its local environment (current node, data in current node, co-located agents and adjacent nodes); decides an action (e.g. move to determined vertex based on the amount of pheromone) and execute it [13].

Complex networks have a large number of interconnected nodes with some special features, like relatively small *distances* among nodes, power-law degree distributions and non-trivial topological properties [4]. For the experiments, we selected complex networks that were challenging for completing a data-collection task, as shown in [2]: a *Small-World*, *Scale-free*, *Community* network and *Hub & Spoke* (Fig. 1).

For the Small-World (Fig. 1-a), we used the model of Watts-Strogatz [15,16]. In this model, a regular ring lattice network with n vertices and k edges per vertex is created. Then each edge in the network is rewired with a probability β. The β parameter determines how regular the final network will be: $\beta = 0$

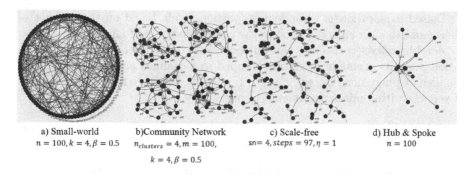

a) Small-world
$n = 100, k = 4, \beta = 0.5$

b)Community Network
$n_{clusters} = 4, m = 100,$
$k = 4, \beta = 0.5$

c) Scale-free
$sn = 4, steps = 97, \eta = 1$

d) Hub & Spoke
$n = 100$

Fig. 1. Complex network topologies selected for experiments.

generates a regular network, $\beta = 1$ a random network, and in-between values a Small-World network [17]. The Community network in this paper (Fig. 1-b) were generated using a $n_{clusters}$ parameter to define the number of groups in the network and adding a single connection between nodes of different groups. Each group was generated as a Small-World network (with its own k, β, and $n = m/n_{clusters}$, where m is the number of nodes in the network). In this paper, a Community network with four clusters is connected via a circle formed by pairs of nodes selected randomly from different groups. The Scale-free network (Fig. 1-c),was modelled by starting with sn nodes and η connections. At each step, a new node is added and connected via η links to existing nodes, giving priority to nodes with higher degrees [18]. The probability to connect to an existing node is defined by $p_i = \frac{k_i}{\sum_j (k_j)}$, where k_i is the degree of node i [16,19,20]. Hub & Spoke corresponds to a Star configuration of a central node and $n - 1$ adjacent nodes. Hub & Spoke networks are applied for obtaining high availability and reliable computing services by expansion of individual cloud instances [21].

2.1   Agent Exploration Strategy

To implement the agents' exploration strategy, we adopt the pheromone-based approach presented in [2], which is an adaptation for complex network exploration of the algorithm in [1], in turn inspired by Ant Colony Systems (ACS). In this strategy, agents choose the nodes with the minimum amount of pheromone as exploitation rule. If more than one node have the same minimum amount, the next location is selected at random.

When a simulation starts, the initial value of pheromone in each node is $\tau_v = 0.5$. As in ACS [22], the decision of exploring or exploiting new nodes is based on a pseudo-random variable $q \in [0, 1]$ (Eq. 1):

$$dir = \begin{cases} \text{exploitation rule} & \text{if } q \leq 0.9 \\ \text{biased exploration} & \text{otherwise} \end{cases} \tag{1}$$

Biased exploration is a random-proportional rule based on the amount of pheromone in each adjacent node to the current location of an agent i.

$neighbourhood(i)$ includes the vertices connected to vertex i. Biased exploration prevents agents from getting trapped in a confined area (e.g. agents surrounded by pheromone traces). $\tau'_v(v) = 1 - \tau_v(v)$ is defined to reward the selection of vertices with a minimum amount of pheromone.

$$p_d(x, y) = \frac{\tau'_v(v)}{\sum_{(k) \in \text{neighbourhood(i)}} \tau_v(k)} \tag{2}$$

In each round t, each agent i updates its internal pheromone value $\tau_{a_t}(i)$ (as in Eq. 3) and the pheromone amount in its current node $\tau_v(v)$ (as in Eq. 4).

$$\tau_{a_t}(i) = (\tau_{a_{t-1}}(i) + 0.01 * (0.5 - \tau_{a_{t-1}}(i))) \tag{3}$$

$$\tau_{v_t}(v) = \tau_{v_{t-1}}(v) + 0.01 * (\tau_{a_{t-1}}(i) - \tau_{v_{t-1}}(v)) \tag{4}$$

If an agent i finds or receives new information, then its internal pheromone value is updated to its initial value of $\tau_{a_t}(i) = 1$. In this case, Eq. 3 decreases the internal pheromone value at each round; and Eq. 4 increases the amount of pheromone in the locations that the carrier agent explores.

Additionally, a passive exploration strategy is added to avoid stagnation, allowing re-exploration of routes of agents that failed without sharing information [23]. The environment performs pheromone evaporation on all nodes V of the complex network G, using the definition in [24] with evaporation rate $\rho = 0.01$: $\tau_{v_i} = (1 - \rho)\tau_{v_{i_{(t-1)}}}$, for $\forall_i \in \{V, G = (V, E)\}$

3   Agent Replication Approach

To deal with agent failure, we propose a replication strategy that enables nodes to create new agent instances. Agents can fail when moving between nodes (e.g. unreliable communication); node crashes will be addressed in future work. In the proposed model, each node is responsible for a dynamic set of agents, called $followedAgents = \{a1, a2, a3, ..., a_n\}$, which it monitors and possibly replicates.

When an agent departs from a node, it sends a message *departing* to its current node, including the agent id and node destination. When an agent arrives at a node destination, it sends a message *freeresp* back to its previous node. Each time a node receives a *departing* message, it assumes responsibility for the corresponding agent, adding it to the $followedAgents$ set. When a node receives a *freeresp* message, it deletes the agent from $followedAgents$.

Each node has an internal round counter, $nodeAge$, for calculating the round difference between the *departing* and *freeresp* messages for each agent k in its $followedAgents$ set. All differences are stored in a special-purpose data structure, $expectedMsgtime$, separately for each neighbour node:

expectedMsgtime(destination(k)) ← getRound(freeresp) − getRound(departing).

Algorithm 1 defines how nodes decide when to create an agent replica, for each agent in $followedAgents$. The variable $wsize$ is introduced to calculate the median and standard deviation of the last n elements in $expectedMsgtime$, and used to calculate the expected time-out. When the time-out expires, the node creates an agent replica and injects its local data aggregate into it. When a node detects a false positive – i.e. receives a $freeresp$ after creating a replica – the node deletes the next arriving agent (after collecting its data).

Algorithm 1. Replication algorithm

```
1: for each Agent a ∈ followedAgents do
2:     dest ← getDestination(a)                          ▷ gets next location of agent a
3:     mRounds ← median(expectedMsgtime(dest), wsize)
4:     sRounds ← stdev(expectedMsgtime(dest), wsize)
5:     if nodeAge − getRoundDepartMsg(a) > mRounds + 3 * sRounds then
6:         createReplica(a)
7:         followedAgents.remove(a)
8:     end if
9: end for
```

---

4   Experiments and Results

Experiments aimed to: (i) determine whether the proposed replication strategy is able to deal with agent failures, so as to complete the data-replication task; (ii) to assess the time taken in rounds, and the induced overheads in terms of memory consumption and communication messages; and, (iii) to show how the system could learn to approximate communication time-outs and avoid over-replication, by alternating simulations without and with agent movement delays.

Each experiment was performed 30 times. Agents start from random locations, selected separately for each topology (but the same ones for all 30 repetitions in any one topology). In addition, each network consists of 100 nodes and is explored by 10 agents (in a relation 10 to 1).

An experiment is a combination of: agents that replicate data (10 agents are defined); A failure probability: $p_f = \{0, 1e-3, 3e-3, 5e-3, 7e-3, 9e-3, 1e-2, 3e-2, 5e-2\}$; activation or deactivation of the replication algorithm; and one complex network (Small-World $n = 100$, $k = 4$, $\beta = 0.5$, Community Network $n_{clusters} = 4$, $m = 100$, $k = 4$, $\beta = 0.5$, Scale-free $sn = 4$, $steps = 97$, $\eta = 1$ and Hub & Spoke: $n = 100$).

The parameters of the replication algorithm are: time-out of $t = 10$ rounds assigned initially to each element in $expectedMsgtime$ and $wsize = 10$.

$expectedMsgtime$ is stored in each simulation to have a history and use this values in the next simulation allowing learning of the time-outs.

4.1   Experiments *Without* Agent Movement Delays

These experiments were performed without agent movement delays between nodes. The first comparison is between experiments with and without replication. With replication, all experiments are successful even with a $p_f = 0.5$, as

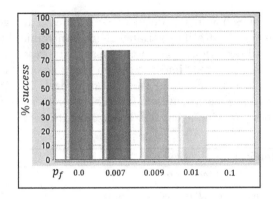

Fig. 2. p_f vs. success rates for community network $n = 100$, $\beta = 0.5$, $degree = 4$ with no replication.

the agents complete the task for all analysed complex networks. Without replication, success rates drop with the increase of p_f (Fig. 2). Hence, there are no successful experiments for a $pf \geq 0.1$ in the Community, Small-World and Hub & spoke networks; and for $pf \geq 0.003$ in the selected Scale-free network.

In terms of number of replicas created, we sorted the 30 simulations by date and obtained maximum, median and minimum number of agents in each simulation. As expected, without replication, the median and minimum number of agents reduces when p_f increases (Fig. 2). Figure 3 shows the results with replication. For a $p_f = 0$, the initial number of agents is maintained (i.e. 10 agents), as there is no need to create replicas. For increasing p_f (i.e. 0.1, 0.3, 0.5), the minimum and median numbers are lower, showing the need for replication. Additionally, the system learns the time-out and hence increases the minimum number of agents, making the median to tend to the initial number, for all p_f values. The same behaviour is observed for all tested complex networks.

Table 1. False positives with replication and without delay

Complex network	Number of false positives
Small-World $\beta = 0.5$, $n = 100$, $degree = 4$	0
Hub & Spoke	0
Scale-free $sn = 4$, $eta = 1$, $numSteps = 97$	1
Community $\beta = 0.5$, $degree = 4$, $clusters = 4$	4

Table 1 presents the total number of false positives in the 30 experiments by each topology and all the values of p_f. From this table it is observed how the number of false positives is small. For the Scale-free one false positive is presented with a $pf = 0.5$ and for Community network there are two for a $pf = 0.007$ and a $pf = 0.3$.

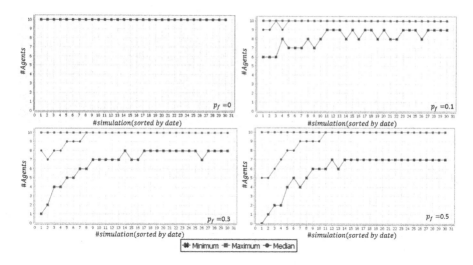

Fig. 3. Simulation sorted by date vs number of agents (max, median, min) in a Small-World network $n = 100$, $\beta = 0.5$, $degree = 4$.

4.2   Experiments *with* Agent Movement Delay

A delay of 1000 ms is added in each agent movement, and the initial time-out of 10 rounds is maintained. This time-out is too small compared to the actual agent movement delay, hence initially producing a lot of false positives. Figure 4 shows how time-out values adapt, reducing the number of replicas from one simulation to another. Time-out learning can be faster if p_f tends to zero. Additionally, in all cases using replication, success rates are 100%. For higher p_f values, results shown that the number of agents reduces, yet this takes more time since agents fail continuously (Fig. 4).

As shown in Fig. 5-a, a higher p_f implies lesser agents moving in the network and a higher time to estimate the real time-out. However, even with high failure rates the system adapts and reduces false positives over time.

4.3   Results in Terms of Round Number

These results compare the differences in rounds for the experiments with and without replication for $p_f = 0$. The null and alternative hypothesis for a determined topology are the following:

- $H0$: the means of the round number with and without replication are equal for a network G;
- $H1$: the means of round number for the two algorithms are different for a network G indicating correlation between the application of replication and the round number.

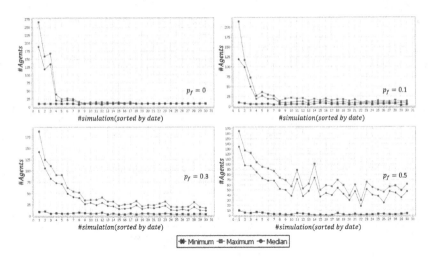

Fig. 4. Simulations sorted by date vs number of agents (max, median, min) in a Small-World network $n = 100$, $\beta = 0.5$, *degree* $= 4$ with delay.

As shown in Table 2, for Small-World and Community networks there is no significant difference between means (*pval* > 0.05). For Hub & Spoke, the mean and median of the round number is lesser with replication than without replication, with a significant difference. However, for a Scale-free network there is the greatest difference in means, as the replication algorithm spends more time with replication compared to other complex networks.

Figure 5-b shows a box-plot of p_f vs round number for a Small-World network. As p_f increases, the round number for task completion increases. This can be because for $p_f \geq 0.1$ agents fail more frequently requiring more replicas to complete the task (for $p_f = 0.1$ there are no successful experiments without replication).

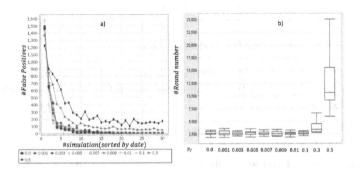

Fig. 5. (a) Simulation sorted by date vs false positives (b) Number of rounds necessary to successfully complete a simulation versus pf - Small-World network $\beta = 0.5$, *degree* $= 4$ with replication.

Table 2. Differences in rounds of replication with delay and no replication with a $p_f = 0$

	$p - value$	Repl	No repl
Small-World	0.6891	2828.034 ± 742.79	2636.448 ± 250.54
Community network	0.6856	4927.552 ± 1126.13	5050.655 ± 1380.60
Scale-free	3.725e−09	103529 ± 46554.29	28640.9 ± 7469.88
Hub & Spoke	0.003511	5371.52 ± 584.27	5855.14 ± 485.43

4.4   Results in Terms of Memory Consumption

To evaluate memory consumption we choose the scenario with delay, because it generates a greater number of replicas, and compare the simulation with a $pf = 0$. As shown in Fig. 6, there is not a difference of more than 2MB in memory consumption after the system learns the time-out for Small-World, Community and Hub & Spoke. The Scale-free network features the highest difference in terms of memory consumption. This can be because this network topology takes more time to complete the task, with the agent exploration algorithm proposed.

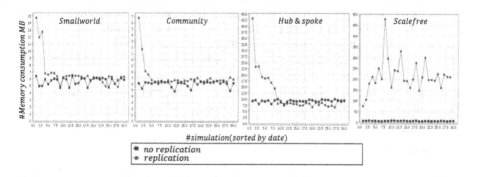

Fig. 6. Simulation sorted by date vs memory consumption.

5   Conclusions and Future Work

In this paper, we proposed a replication approach to deal with failures in mobile agents. This approach allows a system to complete a distributed task even with high failure rates. Nodes and agents have been modelled as agents that communicate between them, agents with a data-replication task, and nodes that store information and also can create new agents and learn the delay necessary to create a new agent copy allowing the system to self-recover.

The proposed approach only stores in local node memory the identities of departed agents, rather than entire agent replicas, taking advantage of the monotonically increasing synchronisation of information on each node, over time. When a new agent replica is created, it receives the information available in the local node, which is the same or more up-to-date than the information of the failed agent. This helps save node memory and increase task competition speed.

Experimental results show that the system approximates the number of replicas to create by obtaining the initial number of agents. By replication, it is possible to have 100 percent of success for the task, in performed experiments. However, experiments suggest that the time in rounds taken to complete the task increases with the failure probability (if $pf \geq 0.1$).

Additionally, results show how for a Small-World, Community and Hub & Spoke network, the memory consumption reduces as time-out is learned. However, a high memory consumption and the highest round numbers are observed in the experiments with a Scale-free network, since agents normally take more time to complete the task. Results suggest a possible relationship between the type of complex network selected, the speed of data replication and the movement algorithm. As shown in [2], better results were obtained with an Small-World and a Community network. The slowest topology was the Scale-free with addition of only one edge by step. This topology is characterized by difficult exploration because there are hubs with a higher degree of connection that slow-down agent exploration. However, even with this configuration, success is achieved in all the experiments performed with agent replication.

Future work will focus on another important challenge in self-healing: recovering failing nodes and addressing data integrity problems. We hope that obtained results can provide useful insights into the behaviour of data management applications with different execution environments, and help design distributed protocols for data replication in server clouds, clusters and different kinds of distributed devices (IoT). More information regarding experiments, including complete measurements, tables and source code are available at http://www.alife.unal.edu.co/%7Eaerodriguezp/networksim/

References

1. Rodriguez, A., Gomez, J., Diaconescu, A.: Foraging-inspired self-organisation for terrain exploration with failure-prone agents. In: 2015 IEEE 9th International Conference on Self-Adaptive and Self-Organizing Systems, pp. 121–130. IEEE, October 2015
2. Rodriguez, A., Gomez, J., Diaconescu, A.: Exploring complex networks with failure-prone agents. In: Verlag, S., (ed.) 15th Mexican International Conference on Artificial Intelligence, MICAI 2016. Lecture Notes in Computer Science (2016)
3. Van Der Hofstad, R.: Random Graphs and Complex Networks, vol. 1 (2016). http://www.win.tue.nl/rhofstad/NotesRGCN.pdf
4. Boccaletti, S.: The Synchronized Dynamics of Complex Systems. Elsevier, Florence (2008)
5. Grabow, C., Hill, S.M., Grosskinsky, S., Timme, M.: Do small worlds synchronize fastest? EPL Europhys. Lett. **90**, 48002 (2010)
6. Renesse, R., Guerraoui, R.: Replication techniques for availability. In: Charron-Bost, B., Pedone, F., Schiper, A. (eds.) Replication. LNCS, vol. 5959, pp. 19–40. Springer, Heidelberg (2010). doi:10.1007/978-3-642-11294-2_2

7. Tanenbaum, A., Steen, M.V.: Distributed Systems: Principles and Paradigms. Prentice-Hall, Upper Saddle River (2006)
8. van Renesse, R., Guerraoui, R.: Replication. Springer, Heidelberg (2010)
9. Satzger, B., Pietzowski, A., Ungerer, T.: Autonomous and scalable failure detection in distributed systems. Int. J. Auton. Adapt. Commun. Syst. **4**, 61 (2011)
10. Horita, Y., Taura, K., Chikayama, T.: A scalable and efficient self-organizing failure detector for grid applications. In: The 6th IEEE/ACM International Workshop on Grid Computing (2005). 9 pp
11. Cox, R., Muthitacharoen, A., Morris, R.T.: Serving DNS using a peer-to-peer lookup service. In: Druschel, P., Kaashoek, F., Rowstron, A. (eds.) IPTPS 2002. LNCS, vol. 2429, pp. 155–165. Springer, Heidelberg (2002). doi:10.1007/3-540-45748-8_15
12. Nguyen Vu, Q.A., Hassas, S., Armetta, F., Gaudou, B., Canal, R.: Combining trust and self-organization for robust maintaining of information coherence in disturbed MAS. In: Proceedings - 2011 5th IEEE International Conference on Self-Adaptive and Self-Organizing Systems, SASO 2011, pp. 178–187 (2011)
13. Russell, S.J., Norvig, P.: Artificial Intelligence: A Modern Approach, vol. 9. (1995)
14. Balaji, P.G., Srinivasan, D.: An introduction to multi-agent systems. In: Srinivasan, D., Jain, L.C. (eds.) Studies in Computational Intelligence, vol. 310, pp. 1–27. Springer, Heidelberg (2010)
15. Watts, D.J., Strogatz, S.H.: Collective dynamics of 'small-world' networks. Nature **393**, 440–442 (1998)
16. White, S.: Analysis and visualization of network data using JUNG. J. Stat. Softw. **10**, 1–35 (2005)
17. Mori, H., Uehara, M., Matsumoto, K.: Parallel architectures with small world network model. In: 2015 IEEE 29th International Conference on Advanced Information Networking and Applications Workshops, pp. 467–472 (2015)
18. Li, L., Alderson, D., Doyle, J.C., Willinger, W.: Towards a theory of scale-free graphs: definition, properties, and implications. Internet Math **2**, 431–523 (2006)
19. Small, M.: "Scale-Free Network" - MathWorld-A Wolfram Web Resource (2016)
20. Takemoto, K., Oosawa, C.: Introduction to complex networks: measures, statistical properties, and models. In: Statistical and Machine Learning Approaches for Network Analysis, pp. 45–75. Wiley, Hoboken, NJ, USA (2012)
21. Mahmood, Z., Hill, R. (eds.): Cloud Computing for Enterprise Architectures. Computer Communications and Networks. Springer, London (2011)
22. Dorigo, M., Gambardella, L.: Ant colony system: a cooperative learning approach to the traveling salesman problem. IEEE Trans. Evol. Comput. **1**, 53–66 (1997)
23. Bell, J.E., McMullen, P.R.: Ant colony optimization techniques for the vehicle routing problem. Adv. Eng. Inform. **18**, 41–48 (2004)
24. Dorigo, M., Stutzle, T.: Ant Colony Optimization, vol. 1. MIT Press, Cambridge (2004)

Soil: An Agent-Based Social Simulator in Python for Modelling and Simulation of Social Networks

Jesús M. Sánchez, Carlos A. Iglesias$^{(\boxtimes)}$, and J. Fernando Sánchez-Rada

Intelligent Systems Group, DIT, E.T.S. de Ingenieros de Telecomunicación,
Universidad Politécnica de Madrid, 28040 Madrid, Spain
jesusmanuel.sanchez.martinez@alumnos.upm.es,
{cif,jfernando}@dit.upm.es
http://www.gsi.dit.upm.es

Abstract. Social networks have a great impact in our lives. While they started to improve and aid communication, nowadays they are used both in professional and personal spheres, and their popularity has made them attractive for developing a number of business models. Agent-based Social Simulation (ABSS) is one of the techniques that has been used for analysing and simulating social networks with the aim of understanding and even forecasting their dynamics. Nevertheless, most available ABSS platforms do not provide specific facilities for modelling, simulating and visualising social networks. This article aims at bridging this gap by introducing an ABSS platform specifically designed for modelling social networks. The main contributions of this paper are: (1) a review and characterisation of existing ABSS platforms; (2) the design of an ABSS platform for social network modelling and simulation; and (3) the development of a number of behaviour models for evaluating the platform for information, rumours and emotion propagation. Finally, the article is complemented by a free and open source simulator.

1 Introduction

Social Networks (SNs) have a great impact in our lives. While they started to improve and aid communication, nowadays they are used both in professional and personal spheres, affecting different aspects ranging economic [11] to health outcomes [22].

The emergence of social computing [45] has raised the interest in the design, analysis and forecasting of social systems. To this end, Social Computing is a cross-disciplinary field with theoretical underpinnings including both computational and social sciences, as well as research from areas such as social psychology, human computer interaction, Social Network Analysis (SNA), anthropology, sociology, organization theory, and computing theory.

One of the fields where ABSS has been applied is the analysis and simulation of social networks, in applications such as viral marketing [40], innovation diffusion [20], rumour propagation [23]. In fact, some authors [33] propose that the use of social media in agent based simulations can leverage the input data

© Springer International Publishing AG 2017
Y. Demazeau et al. (Eds.): PAAMS 2017, LNAI 10349, pp. 234–245, 2017.
DOI: 10.1007/978-3-319-59930-4_19

problem in ABSS, since capturing data from individuals is an expensive and difficult task in longitudinal studies.

Nevertheless, there is a lack of ABSS platforms that provide support for social network modelling. Thus, we aim at bridging this gap by designing and developing an ABSS in Python specifically designed for social networks which benefits from the wide number of available Python libraries for network analysis and machine learning.

The remainder of the article is organised as follows. First, we review existing ABSS platforms to justify why they are not suitable for our problem in Sect. 2, as well as applications of ABSS to social network analysis. Based on this, we present a set of requirements for the desired platform in Sect. 3. Then, the proposed model, architecture and simulation workflow are presented in Sect. 4. The platform has been evaluated through the development of a library of models which is described in Sect. 5. We conclude with Sect. 6 and provide an outlook of future work.

2   Review of ABSS Platforms for Modelling SNs

In recent years numerous ABSS have been developed, as shown by Railsback et al. [34] and Nikolay et al. [31]. Based on this latter work that reviews 55 ABSS platforms, we have reviewed ABSS platforms to evaluate their suitability for modelling social networks, attending to the following aspects: (i) type of platform (general purpose or domain specific), (ii) programming language, (iii) expertise in its application to SNs, (iv) whether the framework provides SNA facilities and (v) whether the license is Open Source (OS). Table 1 summarizes the platforms and the reviewed aspects.

From the initial list provided in [31] we have filtered out platforms that are under a commercial license (e.g. cougaar), not actively developed (e.g. ABLE), focused on training (e.g. AgentSheets), or otherwise not directly focused on simulation (e.g. ECJ or Jade). The resulting set of platforms is Common-Pool Resources and Multi-Agent Systems (Cormas) [7], Madkit [14], Mason [24], NetLogo [35], Repast [32], SeSam [16] and Swarm [27]. Based on our literature research, we have added some additional platforms: UbikSim [9], EscapeSim [41], HashKat [38], Mesa [28], Krowdix [6] and Multi-Agent Scalable Runtime platform for Simulation (MASeRaTi) [2].

Cormas [7] is a general ABSS platform dedicated to natural and common resource management. There is a work [36] that models a social network of innovation diffusion in the medical domain. Madkit [14] is a general multiagent platform which relies on organization concepts and includes simulation facilities. Kodia et al. [21] describe a model where investors are tied by relationships such as friendship, trust and privacy. Mason [24] is a popular multiagent simulation. There is an extension *socialnets* that provides simple network statistics and a bridge to the Java Graph library Jung.[1] Some authors [40] have used Mason for

---

[1] http://jung.sourceforge.net/.

Table 1. Review of ABSS platforms

Name	Domain	Language	SNs	SNA	OS
Cormas	Generic	VisualWorks	✓	✗	✓
NetLogo	Generic	NetLogo, Scala & Java	✓	✗	✓
Swarm	Generic	Objective-C, Java	✓	✗	✓
MadKit	Generic	Java	✓	✗	✓
MASON	Generic	Java	✓	✗	✓
Repast	Generic	Java	✓	✓	✓
SeSam	Generic	Java	✗	✗	✓
MASeRaTi	Generic	Java	✗	✗	✓
Mesa	Generic	Python	✗	✗	✓
UbikSim	AmI	Java	✗	✗	✓
EscapeSim	Evacuation	Java	✗	✗	✓
HashKat	Social networks	C++	✓	✓	✓
Krowdix	Social networks	Java	✓	✓	✗
Soil	Social networks	Python	✓	✓	✓

modelling viral marketing in Twitter. To this end, authors usually complement Mason with other libraries and tools e.g. GraphStream[2] for synthetic network generation and dynamic network visualisation, iGraph[3] for centrality and network measures, and Gephi[4] for detailed analysis of the network. NetLogo [35] is a multiagent programming and simulation environment. It includes facilities for network representations although not for network analysis. An outdated extension to NetLogo is described in [5], where the network analysis and visualisation tool Pajek[5] is integrated. In addition, there are some available models of social networks (e.g. Social circles [15]), but they do not provide facilities for analysing or building new models. Repast [32] is an agent based simulation platform that provides a large library of simulation models. Repast has been extended for SNA [19]. The library Repast Social Network Analysis (ReSoNetA) adds network functionality to RepastJ. It provides a number of network metrics (centrality, prestige and authority) based on the graph Java library Jung as well as visualisation facilities. This library exploits Repast's built-in facilities for network modelling. In addition, other works such as van Maanen [25] have used Repast for modelling social influence in Twitter. SeSam [16] provides a generic environment for agent based simulations but it has not been applied for social network modelling. Swarm [27] is a well known agent-based simulator that has been applied to social network problems such as open source project dynamics [27].

---

[2] http://graphstream-project.org/.
[3] http://igraph.org/.
[4] https://gephi.org/.
[5] http://mrvar.fdv.uni-lj.si/pajek/.

While the previous ABSS platforms were designed for its application to a wide variety of domains, other platforms, such as UbikSim [9] and EscapeSim [41] has been specifically designed for a particular domain, such as Ambient Intelligence (AmI) and evacuation.

HashKat [38] is a C++ ABSS platform specifically designed for the study and simulation of social networks. It includes facilities for network growth and information diffusion, based on a kinetic Monte Carlo model. It exports information to be processed by machine learning libraries such as NetworkX[6] or R's iGraph and network visualisation with Gephi.

Mesa [28] is an ABSS platform that aims at providing a Python alternative to traditional Netlogo, MASON or Repast. It enables in-browser visualisation and takes advantage of Python ecosystem. Krowdix [6] is a Java ABSS for social networks but it is not open source. It uses JUNG for network functions and JFreeChart[7] for visualisation. The simulation model considers users, their relationships, user groups and interchanged contents. It has been applied to Twitter and Facebook. MASeRaTi [2] is a distributed and scalable ABSS that uses the Belief-Desire-Intention (BDI) framework lightjason [3], that extends the agent-oriented programming language AgentSpeak.

To summarise, except for HashKat and Krodix, ABSS platforms do not provide support for the analysis of social networks, although some platforms have already been used for this purpose. Moreover, most ABSS platforms are programmed in Java. MASeRaTi follows a different approach where agents can be programmed based on a BDI model. Main challenges for applying existing platforms to social networks come from their underlying models, frequently tied to spatial models.

3   ABSS Requirements for Social Networks

Based on the previously presented review of ABSS platforms and their application to SN analysis and simulation, we have identified the requirements listed below, which are structured in network and agent model.

Network model. The network level groups all the functionalities related to the structural aspects of the social network. The following requirements have been identified:

- *Generation of synthetic graphs.* Even though accessing real social network graphs is critical, real datasets have a number of disadvantages [39]. First, sharing large social graphs is challenging, since they should be anonymised and there are limitations in the way they can be shared (for example, only tweet ids can be shared in Twitter, which requires collecting the dataset with API restrictions and difficulties in reproducing the original dataset since some tweets could be no longer available). Second, the availability of a small number of social graphs can limit the statistical confidence in the experimentation

---

[6] https://networkx.github.io/.

[7] http://www.jfree.org/jfreechart/.

results. Finally, obtaining real datasets suitable for the desired experimentation can be difficult and require a great effort. Thus, synthetic graph generated by measurement-calibrated graph models [39] so that graph models are fitted to a real social graph, and the simulation are realistic. The platform should provide implementation of classical social graph models [39] (e.g. Barabasi-Albert model [4], Random Walk [44], etc.) and should be extensible to innovative models.

- *Graph traversing and visualisation.* The platform should provide functionalities for traversing social graphs and visualising social structure, in order to be applied to diffusion models [13].
- *SNA functionalities.* Several functionalities should be available for the analysis of the social graph, such as calculation of social metrics (e.g. centrality, betweenness, etc.) as well as algorithms for community detection.
- *Export and import of network model.* There should be facilities for importing and exporting social graphs, based on popular formats such as Graph Modelling Language (GML) [18], GraphML [8] and Graph Exchange XML Format (GEXF) [12].

Agent model. The agent level models the agent characteristics, their state, how agent state evolves in every simulation step. Following the modelling steps proposed by Macal and North [26], we outline the requirements for social network modelling. Platform should allow users to: (i) define agent type definition and attributes (e.g. sentiment, frequency of tweeting, number of followers, etc.); (ii) define interactions with the environment, that represent external factors to agent decision, such as news or market evolution; and (iii) specify methods to update agent state based on their interaction with other agents and the environment. This include the capability to update the agent social network (i.e. creation or modification of social links).

Non functional requirements. Regarding non functional requirements, several aspects have been considered. First of all, the *programming language* is an important decision. In order to provide a homogeneous programming environment, network and machine learning libraries should be available. Both Java and Python fulfill these requirements, as we have introduced previously. As previously outlined, it is very important that ABSS provide *interactive experimentation facilities* that enable researchers to run and define their experiments. In this regard, most platforms ABSS platforms such as Mason or Repast provide configurable and extensible *configuration facilities* [43]. *Scalability* has been recently addressed by a number of researchers [1,2]. The ability to distribute agents across machines or big data processing infrastructures can be required for the simulation of large scale social networks. Finally, *extensibility and reusability* of simulation models should be encouraged [37], so that researchers can benefit from a library of tested simulation models that can be used, extended and adapted to model new behaviours.

4   Soil Platform

4.1   Design Decisions

The first design decision is the selection of Python [30], given its increased popularity, its very gradual learning curve, readability, clear syntax and availability of libraries for network processing and machine learning. In addition, we consider the interactive analysis of the IPython interface[8] very beneficial for simulation. From the reviewed platforms, only one platform is available in Python, Mesa, but it does not provide network facilities yet and is still in constant evolution. Hence, we evaluated different options to extend Mesa for this scenario. Another alternative was to extend nxsim[9], a Python library that provides a basic ABSS framework, based on Simpy [29]. We eventually chose nxsim due to its simplicity and robustness.

Regarding the network model, we have opted for NetworkX, which is the de-facto standard library for SNA analysis of small to medium networks. For massive networks, the transition to NetworkKit [42] is straight forward. NetworkX provides functionalities for manipulating and representing graphs, generators of classical and popular graph models, and graph algorithms for analysing graph properties. In addition, NetworkX is interoperable with a great number of graph formats, including GML, GraphML JSON and GEXF.

For network visualization, we have selected Gephi, an open-sourced software for network and graph interactive analysis. Gephi is able to render in 3D and real-time large and complex networks. In addition, both NetworkX and Gephi support the format GraphML, so a graph generated with NetworkX can be explored with Gephi in every simulation step. Finally, configurability will be achieved with configuration files.

4.2   Simulation Model for Social Networks

We propose a simulation model of SNs consisting of users represented by agents and a network that represents the social links between users. Agent are characterised by their state (e.g. infected) and the behaviours they can carry out in every simulation step, usually depending on the user state. Each behaviour defines the actions carried out (e.g. tweeting, following a user, etc.) and how the agent state evolves, depending on external factors (e.g. news about a topic) or social factors (e.g. opinion of their friends). Probabilities defined in the configuration control the frequency of actions in every behaviour.

This simulation model has been implemented in the architecture shown in Fig. 1 and consists of four main components.

The *NetworkSimulation* class is in charge of the network simulator engine. It provides forward-time simulation of events in a network based on nxsim and Simpy. Based on configuration parameters, a graph is generated with NetworkX

---

[8] https://ipython.org/.
[9] https://pypi.python.org/pypi/nxsim.

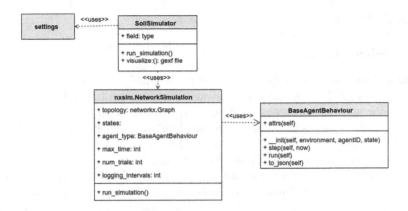

Fig. 1. Simulation components

and an agent class is populated to each network node. The main parameters are the network type, number of nodes, maximum simulation time, number of simulations and timeout between each simulation step.

The *BaseAgentBehaviour* class is the basic agent behaviour that should be extended for each social network simulation model. It provides a basic functionality for generation of a JSON file with the status of the agents for its analysis with machine libraries such as Scikit-Learn.

The *SoilSimulator* class is in charge of running the simulation pipeline defined in Sect. 4.3, which consists in running the simulation and generating a visualisation file in GEXF which can be visualised with Gephi. In addition, interactive analysis can be done through IPython notebooks.

Settings groups the general settings for simulations and the settings of the different models available in Soil's simulation model library.

4.3   Simulation Workflow

An overview of the system's flow is shown in Fig. 2. The simulation workflow consists of three steps: configuration, simulation and visualization.

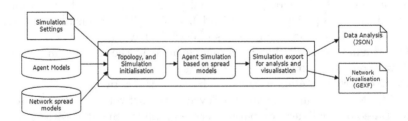

Fig. 2. Social simulator's workflow

In the first step, the main parameters of the simulation are configured in the *settings.py* file. The main parameters are: network graph type, number of agents, agent type, maximum time of simulation and time step length. In addition, the parameters of the behaviour model should be configured (e.g. initial states or probability of an agent action). Agent behaviours should be selected from the provided library or developed extending the *BaseAgentBehaviour* class.

Once the simulation is configured, the next step is the simulation, that can be done step by step or a number of steps. The class *BaseAgentBehaviour* stores the status of every agent in every simulation step into a JSON file to be exported once the simulation is finished. This allows us to automatise the process of generating the .gexf file.

Finally, users can carry out further analysis with the JSON file as well as visualize the evolution the simulation with the generated .gexf file with the tool Gephi, as shown in Fig. 5.

5   Test Cases

We have evaluated Soil in the development of a number of simulation models. In these experiments, we have used the Barabasi-Albert network generation model [4].

The models included in the library deal with viral marketing in Twitter [40], infection (SISa [17]), sentiment correlation the social network Weibo [10], Bass model [35] and Independent Correlation Model [35] of information diffusion in social networks.

In order to illustrate the functionalities of Soil, we review the Viral Marketing model [40], which is based on rumour propagation models. In it, agents have four potential states: neutral, infected, vaccinated and cured. This model includes the fact that infected users who made a mistake believing in the rumour will not be

```
class ControlModelM2(BaseBehaviour):
# init states
def step(self, now):
if self.state['id'] == 0:   #Neutral
self.neutral_behaviour()
elif self.state['id'] == 1:  #Infected
self.infected_behaviour()
...
def infected_behaviour(self):
# Infected
neutral_neighbors = self.get_neighboring_agents(state_id=0)
for neighbor in neutral_neighbors:
if random.random() < self.prob_infect:
neighbor.state['id'] = 1  # Infected
```

Fig. 3. Code snippet of an infected behaviour

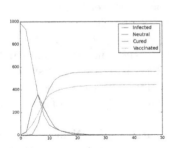

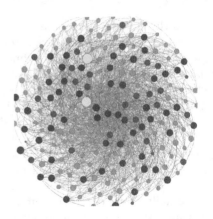

Fig. 4. Agent evolution   **Fig. 5.** Network visualization

in favour of spreading their mistakes through the network. A example of how behaviours are programmed is shown in Fig. 3. This behaviour shows that an infected agent first selects its neutral neighbours and infects them with a given probability. Figures 4 and 5 show the evolution of agent states and network visualisation, respectively.

6   Conclusions and Outlook

While generic ABSS provide a suitable framework, we think that further research on ABSS platforms for specific domains is needed. In this paper we have reviewed the existing frameworks and the requirements for modelling and simulation of social networks.

Soil is a modern ABSS for social networks developed in Python that benefits from the Python ecosystem. It has been applied to a number of social network simulation models, ranging from rumour propagation to emotion propagation and information diffusion. Additionally, it is fully open source, cross-platform and produces outputs compatible with SNA packages and network visualisation tools. The platform has been designed for research purposes, and has focused on simplicity of developing new simulation models. Soil allows the generation of dynamic networks and its animation thanks to the use of Gephi. In spite of the growing development of the Python ecosystem, there are still some functionalities, such as Exponential Random Graph Model (ERGMs) which are better supported in other environments such as R with the statnet[10] package, which provides a wide range of functionality for the statistical analysis of social networks. In particular, these models are very interesting for fitting models given a network data set. As future work, we aim at evaluating and integrating implementations such as ergm[11].

---

[10] http://statnetproject.org.
[11] https://github.com/jcatw/ergm.

Lastly, Soil is work in progress. We aim at improving the experimentation and visualisation facilities provided by the platform, and improve the platform through its application in more use cases and through the collaboration with other research groups.

Acknowledgements. This work is supported by the Spanish Ministry of Economy and Competitiveness under the R&D projects SEMOLA (TEC2015-68284-R) and Emo-Spaces (RTC-2016-5053-7), by the Regional Government of Madrid through the project MOSI-AGIL-CM (grant P2013/ICE-3019, co-funded by EU Structural Funds FSE and FEDER), and by the European Union through the project MixedEmotions (Grant Agreement no: 141111).

References

1. Aaby, B.G., et al.: Efficient simulation of agent-based models on multi-GPU and multi-core clusters. In: Proceedings of the 3rd International ICST Conference on Simulation Tools and Techniques, SIMUTools 2010, Torremolinos, Malaga, Spain. ICST (2010)
2. Ahlbrecht, T., Dix, J., Köster, M., Kraus, P., Müller, J.P.: A scalable runtime platform for multiagent-based simulation. In: Dalpiaz, F., Dix, J., Riemsdijk, M.B. (eds.) EMAS 2014. LNCS, vol. 8758, pp. 81–102. Springer, Cham (2014). doi:10.1007/978-3-319-14484-9_5
3. Aschermann, M., et al.: LightJason: a BDI framework inspired by Jason. Technical report IfI-16-04, Depart. Department of Computer Science, TU Clausthal, Germany (2014)
4. Barabáasi, A.-L., Albert, R.: Emergence of scaling in random networks. Science **286**(5439), 509–512 (1999)
5. Berryman, M.J., Angus, S.D.: Tutorials on agent-based modelling with NetLogo and network analysis with Pajek. In: Complex Physical, Biophysical and Econophysical Systems, vol. 1. World Scientific, Hackensack (2010)
6. Blanco-Moreno, D., Cárdenas, M., Fuentes-Fernández, R., Pavón, J.: Krowdix: agent-based simulation of online social networks. In: Bazzan, A.L.C., Pichara, K. (eds.) IBERAMIA 2014. LNCS, vol. 8864, pp. 587–598. Springer, Cham (2014). doi:10.1007/978-3-319-12027-0_47
7. Bommel, P., et al.: Cormas, an agent-based simulation platform for coupling human decisions with computerized dynamics. In: ISAGA 2015: Hybrid Simulation and Gaming in the Network Society (2015)
8. Brandes, U., et al.: Graph markup language (GraphML). In: Handbook of Graph Drawing and Visualization 20007 (2013)
9. Campuzano, F., Garcia-Valverde, T., Garcia-Sola, A., Botia, J.A.: Flexible simulation of ubiquitous computing environments. In: Novais, P., Preuveneers, D., Corchado, J.M. (eds.) Ambient Intelligence - Software and Applications. AINSC, vol. 92, pp. 189–196. Springer, Heidelberg (2011)
10. Fan, R., et al.: Anger is more influential than joy: sentiment correlation in Weibo. In: CoRR abs/1309.2402 (2013)
11. Granovetter, M.: The impact of social structure on economic outcomes. J. Econ. Perspect. **19**(1), 33–50 (2005)
12. Group, G.W.: GEXF file format. GEXF Working Group (2009)

13. Guille, A., et al.: Information diffusion in online social networks: a survey. ACM SIGMOD Rec. **42**(2), 17–28 (2013)
14. Gutknecht, O., Ferber, J.: The MADKIT agent platform architecture. In: Wagner, T., Rana, O.F. (eds.) AGENTS 2000. LNCS, vol. 1887, pp. 48–55. Springer, Heidelberg (2001). doi:10.1007/3-540-47772-1_5
15. Hamill, L., Gilbert, N.: Social circles: a simple structure for agent-based social network models. J. Artif. Soc. Soc. Simul. **12**(2), 3 (2009)
16. Herrler, R., Fehler, M.: SeSAm: implementation of agent based simulation using visual programming. In: Components (2006)
17. Hill, A.L., et al.: Emotions as infectious diseases in a large social network: the SISa model. Proc. Roy. Soc. Lond. B Biol. Sci. **277**(1701), 3827–3835 (2010)
18. Himsolt, M.: GML: a portable graph file format. Technical report. Universität Passau (1997)
19. Holzhauer, S.: Developing a Social Network Analysis and Visualization Module for Repast Models, vol. 4. Kassel University Press GmbH, Kassel (2010)
20. Kiesling, E., et al.: Agent-based simulation of innovation diffusion: a review. CEJOR **20**(2), 183–230 (2012)
21. Kodia, Z., Said, L.B., Ghedira, K.: Stylized facts study through a multi-agent based simulation of an artificial stock market. In: Li Calzi, M., Milone, L., Pellizzari, P. (eds.) Progress in Artificial Economics. Lecture Notes in Economics and Mathematical Systems, vol. 645, pp. 27–38. Springer, Heidelberg (2010). doi:10.1007/978-3-642-13947-5_3
22. Korda, H., Itani, Z.: Harnessing social media for health promotion and behavior change. Health Promot. Pract. **14**(1), 15–23 (2013)
23. Liu, D., Chen, X.: Rumor propagation in online social networks like twitter - a simulation study. In: 2011 Third International Conference on Multimedia Information Networking and Security, November 2011
24. Luke, S.: MASON: a multiagent simulation environment. Simulation **81**, 517–527 (2005)
25. van Maanen, P.-P., van der Vecht, B.: An agent-based approach to modeling online social influence. In: Proceedings of the 2013 IEEE/ACM International Conference on Advances in Social Networks Analysis and Mining. ACM (2013)
26. Macal, C.M., North, M.J.: Tutorial on agent-based modeling and simulation. In: Simulation Conference, 2005 Proceedings of the Winter. IEEE (2005)
27. Madey, G., et al.: Agent-based modeling of open source using Swarm. In: AMCIS 2002 Proceedings (2002)
28. Masad, D., Kazil, J.: MESA: an agent-based modeling framework. In: Proceedings of the 14th Python in Science Conference (SCIPY 2015) (2015)
29. Matloff, N.: Introduction to discrete-event simulation and the Simpy language. In: Davis, CA. Dept of Computer Science. University of California at Davis. Retrieved 2 Aug 2008
30. McKinney, W.: Python for Data Analysis. O'Reilly, Sebastopol (2012)
31. Nikolai, C., Madey, G.: Tools of the trade: a survey of various agend based modeling platforms. J. Artif. Soc. Soc. Simul. **12**(2), 2 (2009)
32. Ozik, J., Collier, N., Combs, T., Macal, C.M., North, M.: Repast simphony statecharts. J. Artif. Soc. Soc. Simul. **18**(3), 11 (2015). http://jasss.soc.surrey.ac.uk/18/3/11.html
33. Padilla, J.J., et al.: Leveraging social media data in agentbased simulations. In: Proceedings of the 2014 Annual Simulation Symposium. Society for Computer Simulation International (2014)

34. Railsback, S.F., et al.: Agent-based simulation platforms: review and development recommendations. Simulation **82**(9), 609–623 (2006)
35. Rand, W., Wilensky, U.: An Introduction to Agent-Based Modeling: Modeling Natural, Social, and Engineered Complex Systems with NetLogo. MIT Press, Cambridge (2015)
36. Ratna, N.N., et al.: Diffusion and social networks: revisiting medical innovation with agents. In: Qudrat-Ullah, H., Spector, J.M., Davidsen, P.I. (eds.) Complex Decision Making, pp. 247–265. Springer, Heidelberg (2008)
37. Robinson, S., et al.: Simulation model reuse: definitions, benefits and obstacles. Simul. Model. Pract. Theory **12**(7), 479–494 (2004)
38. Ryczko, K., et al.: Hashkat: large-scale simulations of online social networks. In: arXiv preprint arXiv (2016)
39. Sala, A., et al.: Measurement-calibrated graph models for social network experiments. In: Proceedings of the 19th International Conference on World Wide Web. ACM (2010)
40. Serrano, E., Iglesias, C.A.: Validating viral marketing strategies in Twitter via agent-based social simulation. Expert Syst. Appl. **50**(1), 140–150 (2016)
41. Serrano, E., et al.: Towards a holistic framework for the evaluation of emergency plans in indoor environments. Sensors **14**(3), 4513–4535 (2014)
42. Staudt, C., et al.: NetworKit: an interactive tool suite for high-performance network analysis. In: CoRR abs/1403.3005 (2014)
43. Szufel, P., et al.: Controlling simulation experiment design for agent-based models using tree representation of parameter space. Found. Comput. Decis. Sci. **38**(4), 277–298 (2013)
44. Vázquez, A.: Growing network with local rules: preferential attachment, clustering hierarchy, and degree correlations. Phys. Rev. E **67**(5), 056104 (2003)
45. Wang, F.Y., et al.: Social computing: from social informatics to social intelligence, March 2007

Agents as Bots – An Initial Attempt Towards Model-Driven MMORPG Gameplay

Markus Schatten, Bogdan Okreša Đurić[✉], Igor Tomičić, and Nikola Ivković

Artificial Intelligence Laboratory, Faculty of Organization and Informatics,
University of Zagreb, Zagreb, Croatia
{markus.schatten,dokresa,igor.tomicic,nikola.ivkovic}@foi.hr
http://ai.foi.hr/modelmmorpg

Abstract. Massively multi-player on-line role-playing games (MMO-RPGs) present a large-scale, digital environment that fosters organizational behaviour of players in which multi-agent systems (MASs) can be used for various purposes including but not limited to automated testing, bot detection or analysis of social player behaviour and human – artificial agent interaction. A work-in-progress model-driven MAS development environment for such games is presented. An open-source MMORPG called The Mana World (TMW) is used as an example scenario on which the various components of the system are tested.

Keywords: MMORPG · Agents · Model-driven development · Agent organizations

1 Introduction

MMORPGs offer a natural application domain for MASs, and especially large-scale MASs (LSMASs). MMORPGs are on-line games in which large numbers of players interact both collaborating and competing with each other by solving various quests or tasks. Not only (human) players interact, but also artificial entities including non-playing characters (NPCs), various mobs (the enemies or monsters to be fought), and some times even bots (artificial players), albeit in most cases illegally.

During the ModelMMORPG project[1] we have set our objective to study MMORPGs from an agent-based perspective in order to develop methods and tools that will enable us to solve interesting problems bound to these games. Some of these problems include (1) automated gameplay testing – e.g. development of bots/agents that will play the game and deliver possible bottlenecks, (2) load testing – MMORPG servers have to be robust under potentially very heavy loads of simultaneous players, (3) bot detection – on most MMORPGs forbid the use of automated player bots often used by players to acquire resources and use various automated and semi-automated Turing tests to recognize bots,

---

[1] See http://ai.foi.hr/modelmmorpg for details.

© Springer International Publishing AG 2017
Y. Demazeau et al. (Eds.): PAAMS 2017, LNAI 10349, pp. 246–258, 2017.
DOI: 10.1007/978-3-319-59930-4_20

(4) design of human-artificial agent interfaces – in such games players interact with numerous artificial entities like the mentioned NPCs and mobs, (5) analysis of social human on-line behaviour – players interact through various chatrooms and VoIP technologies, fight each other, organize into parties or guilds, create their social network etc., and all these data is often stored and available for analysis, (6) simulation of human on-line behaviour – using the previous mentioned data, (agent based) models of behaviour can be established.

The workplan of the ModelMMORPG project was to firstly study human behaviour in MMORPGs by developing a special quest for an open-source MMO-RPG called The Mana World (TMW) that would especially foster organizational behaviour between players. Results of this study that featured social network analysis and natural language processing methods, were presented in [1]. Additionally, and in-depth literature review was conducted to identify most valuable organizational design patterns that can be used in developing LSMAS [2]. Afterwards, a number of MMORPG modelling methods were identified [3] and a meta-model for LSMAS development was developed [4]. Finally, on the foundations of this meta-model, we are building a graphical modelling tool and model-driven LSMAS application generator that will allow us to generate LSMAS templates based on their organizational model. We will test this modelling tool and generator on MMORPGs on a number of scenarios. In this paper we shall report on the current state of development of this tool.

2 Related Work

MMORPGs continually prove to be a modern concept of applied information technologies providing users with a wide arrange of services, ranging from entertainment, relaxation, or action, over education, reflex, and reaction building, to research, experiment field, and a source of huge amounts of data. The impact of MMOGs (Massively Multiplayer Online Games) on modern-day market and life is undeniable [3], both in commercial and player context.

Automated playing agents are usually frowned upon by the gaming community which is reflected in the literature mostly dealing with techniques of preventing bots from playing MMO games (like [5–7]). Therefore the attempts at creating a virtual simulated world comprising artificial intelligent agents, such as presented within this research, is a rather unique task. There were only few attempts to create automated testing environments for large-scale settings like in [8] Jung et al. which in order to ensure game stability developed the VENUS simulator and an efficient method for simulating large numbers of virtual clients in on-line games. Also [9, 10] propose the VENUS II system allowing for blackbox and scenario-based testing by generating game grammar based user behaviour packages to facilitate various game-related scenarios.

3 The Mana World

TMW is a free 2D open source MMORPG licensed under GPL, with the visuals reminding of classic RPG games of the 1990s like Zelda or Final Fantasy.

Players of TMW are able to connect to one of several officially available game servers or install their own local server with optional customizations. From within the game, players are able to interact with each other by using a number available mechanisms such as chat, fights, trade, or creating social network communities (including friends, enemies, etc.) and organizing into parties of players. The game story itself is emerging from the quests and the numerous interactions, both of which are of crucial importance to this work – quests encourage forming parties, which are establishing their own inner interactions, mechanics, responsibilities, delegations, community feel, and other aspects of such social groups aiming to reach their common goal.

We have chosen to use TMW as our main development and testing playground since it is open source and has a very helpful community.

4   System Architecture

There have been numerous attempts in establishing model driven game development frameworks (see [11,12] for a good overview) as well as model driven MAS development (see for example [2,13,14]). Besides of [15] there have been very few studies dealing with agent-based game development, and even less with model driven agent-based game development.

One of the objectives of the mentioned ModelMMOPRG project was to establish an agent-based framework for the development of LSMASs with special regard to MMORPGs as an initial application domain. With this in mind, we have designed a complex development system which is general in terms of allowing to develop LSMASs regardless of applicative domain and have specialized it for MMORPGs through a plug-in system which allows us to connect various additional domain specific tools and libraries, depending on the problem at hand.

Figure 1 gives an outline of the system architecture which consists of three components, some having a number of sub-components: (1) an ontology defining the most important concepts LSMASs' organizations (see [16,17] for more details); (2) the modelling tool comprising a metamodel (derived from the previously mentioned ontology [4]), a graphical user interface and an application

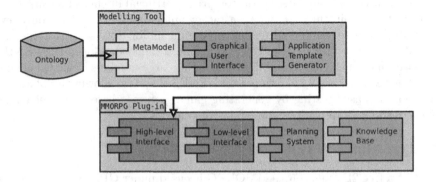

Fig. 1. System architecture

template generator; and (3) a MMORPG plug-in which allows generating models for the use with TMW, consisting of a high-level interface, a low-level interface, a knowledge base and a planning system. Individual agents that are modeled as a part of the system using the modeling tool are detailed and instantiated in the latter part of the described architecture.

These components are described in more detail in the following sections.

4.1   Modeling Tool

The modeling tool is implemented using AToM^3 metamodeling environment for several reasons, main of which are: AToM^3 is an open source tool freely available for download and use, meaning that possibly needed modifications can be introduced rather easily to the already available environment; AToM^3 is inherently designed for modeling and metamodeling processes, therefore is highly suitable for the set goals of this research; programming language used to develop AToM^3 is Python, a widely used language that is suitable for this research because it allows for easy integration with other parts of the described research, and is highly customizable and extensible using many libraries available.

The basis upon which this modeling tool was built is a work-in-progress organizational metamodel for LSMAS [4]. The current version of the metamodel[2] features several concepts that can be used for modeling a MAS: Organizational unit, Role, Objective, Individual knowledge artifact, Organizational knowledge artifact, Process, and various properties between the stated concepts. Additionally, to take into consideration organizational dynamics and agent interaction graph grammars and temporal logic are partially supported by the modeling tool.

The first step in developing the mentioned metamodel and subsequently the modeling tool for this research was to select concepts to be modeled. The concept set was not introduced randomly, but based on the already available OOVA-SIS ontology [16] comprising organizational concepts useful for LSMAS, and a short review [18] of some of the prominent MAS and LSMAS models that are described and published thus far. Furthermore, selection procedure for the concepts to be included in the meta-model was based on observing and testing various MMORPGs and the elements they feature.

Established core concepts are those that represent individuals, i.e. individual player-agents, and those that represent roles, i.e. grouped sets of organizational, behavioural, and normative constraints. Several other concepts of high importance were identified when populating the set of concepts to be included in the metamodel as follows:

- Quest - MMORPG players are often motivated to advance through the game by quests, objectives consisting of smaller tasks that have to be achieved in order to successfully complete the given quest, since they are rewarded for quest completion either by receiving some important items, experience points (accumulation of which is vital to player's character progression), or another kind of a reward;

---

[2] The modeling tool is available at https://github.com/Balannen/LSMASOMM.

- Party - since the element of socialization is of great importance in MMO-RPGs, players often form groups (parties, guilds etc.) that help them utilize the power of cooperation when completing various quests, facing enemies, advancing through the game in general, or accessing parts of the game that would be inaccessible otherwise;
- Actions - since the system often used in MMORPGs grants specialization enhancements to players using the concept of roles, roles are used in the metamodel being developed as the way of defining various available actions that can be conducted by players playing various roles, and which are grouped into processes that can successfully complete a specific task, therefore proving to be vital for a specific quest the particular task is a part of.

It is worth noting that one of the objectives of the metamodel is to utilize a certain level of abstraction. Therefore no concepts are included that would allow a user to model details of a player agent, or many details of a role the players could play, or a specific way of defining a quest, etc. What the metamodel is designed for is a high-level description of a system of agents playing a particular game, providing users with features that allow them to generate a programing code outline for the modeled system.

One of the more practical features of the modeling tool is programing code-generating of the modeled system, described in the following section.

4.2   Application Template Generator

While the metamodel offers its users an environment for describing and modeling a system of agents in an MMORPG, the application template generator brings the modeled system closer to life. The application template generating feature of the final modeling tool will allow the user to generate basic elements needed for implementing the modeled system. This feature is a work in progress at the moment, but it can already serve for receiving essential programing code structure for Smart Python Agent Development Environment (SPADE) [19] agents. SPADE is the environment of choice since it is developed in and uses Python which makes it easy to integrate it with various additional modules (the modeling tool included) that help its integration with TMW, and because it allows for easy definitions of agents in a multiagent environment that use advanced deductive knowledge bases.

The generator uses enhanced native features of AToM^3 for storing and printing nodes of a model. Implementation is based on the Zope Object Database (ZODB), an object-oriented database for transparently and persistently storing Python objects. The use of ZODB is motivated by further development of the metamodel, in a multi-model modeling direction that would allow a user to model a system using several different models representing various layers or perspectives of the same system, therefore using the same elements.

Essential information was therefore extracted from the elements of a model, and stored in ZODB in custom format. Saved data is then converted using the current version of the application template generator into essential programing code for a system comprising SPADE agents.

4.3   High-Level Interface

The high-level interface[3] implements a belief-desire-intention (BDI) agent model using SPADE. In it's current state, it defines an artificial player with a number of agent behaviours in which the agent observes it's environment (observation is provided by the low-level interface and stored in the agent's knowledge base described below), contemplates about current objectives it wants to achieve (actual quests provided by various NPCs from the game), plans it's future actions based on knowledge about the world (using a STRIPS [20] based planner described below) and goes on to take actions to implement the current plan (using basic actions provided by the low-level interface).

The high-level interface is the least finished component of the whole system, due to the fact that it provides the intersection between the modelling tool and application template generator above and the low-level interface, knowledge base and planning system below. Thus, it had to be developed last and has to integrate almost all other components. While the connection to the lower layers (low level interface, knowledge base, planner) is more or less well established (the low level interface is a Python module easily imported into the high level interface; the knowledge base and the planner are SWI Prolog modules easily interfaced through SPADE's knowledge base features), the connection to the upper layers (modelling tool and application template generator) need to be developed further to be fully functional.

4.4   Knowledge Base and Planning System

The knowledge base and the planning systems have been partially described in [21]. The knowledge base consists of a TMW ontology that defines the basic entities and actions available in the game (NPCc, items, mobs, maps etc.) as well as detailed descriptions on possible quests. The quest descriptions were derived from the TMW wiki and coded into Prolog, while the map descriptions were parsed from the actual XML map descriptions from TMW code. Herein we have chosen to use SWI Prolog to implement the knowledge bases and planner, mainly due to the fact that SWI is the most complete and available Prolog system. Still, other options like XSB, ECLiPSe or Flora-2 are possibilities. The planning system is a STRIPS-based planner which consists of a set of rules which model the various quests provided by NPCs in the game. For example, the following listing defines the "Trade skill" quest in which a player can learn to trade items with other players by giving a trader in the city of Tulimshar 5 gold coins.

---

[3] The MMORPG plug-in including the high-level interface are available at https://github.com/tomicic/ModelMMORPG.

```
do_quest(A, trade_skill) :-
%  Preconditions:
      location(trader_in_tulimshar ,XTT,YTT),
      level(A,La), La>=1,
      \+ done_quest(A,done_trade_skill),
      money(A,Ma), Ma>=5,
%  Deletions:
      retract(money(A,Ma)),
%  Additions:
      walk_to_location(A,XTT,YTT),
      assert(plan(talk(A,trader_in_tulimshar , 'Do_you_have_anything_for_me
            ?'))),
      NewMa is Ma-5, assert(money(A,NewMa)),
      assert(ability(A, trade_ability)),
      assert(done_quest(A, done_trade_skill)).
```

Listing 1. Example planning rule

4.5   Low-Level Interface

The main architecture of TMW is build around three servers and a client. The servers carry out the following functions:

- Managing accounts and connections to character server (login server - the first server the client connects to);
- Managing characters, connecting them to the map server, handling saving and loading of character data (character server);
- Managing game content (such as monsters, items, maps, etc.) and the interaction of game content with players (map server).

Communication between TMW server and client is implemented by custom application layer messages on the top of TCP transport layer protocol. Both the client and the server are implementing finite state machines that are changing their states in response to messages which are being sent and received between them. The messages are mostly defined with fixed length binary fields, but some messages contain variable length fields. Unfortunately, only several message types are fully documented, and the others merely pointed to the locations of C++ source code where they should have been implemented.

We have reverse engineered the structure of the messages by analyzing the source code and the real-world network traffic by using the network protocol analyzer Wireshark. To make the network traffic analyses easier we have developed a basic packet dissector for Wireshark using the Lua programming language and semiautomated tools in spreadsheet processing applications. Since TCP deals with streams of bytes it is up to the programmer to discover borders between different Mana messages. More than one Mana message can arrive in the same TCP segment, but also one message can be separated into multiple TCP segments. Based on the value at the beginning of the message, the type and the structure are inferred. Especially hard to decode are the messages that do not obey byte boundaries, e.g. 12-bit integers.

The main challenge in the Low-Level Interface development was to identify, locate, interpret and rewrite un-documented packets and functions written in C++ to the Python environment. The main idea is to "simulate" the actions of the human player within the game by using the Python script based on TMW client implementation code. Starting with the most basic functions such as character creation, server login request, server connection, character choice, etc., the interface progressed to imitate in-game functions such as moving the character on the map, attacking other creatures, picking up and equipping items, chatting with other players, creating and joining/leaving parties, following other players, trading, etc.

Figure 2 shows a sample session of the implemented interface in which the current player picks up an item.

Fig. 2. Python client: collecting items on the map

The logic of the Python client is detailed within four key Python classes, namely:

- Character - manages all relevant data of a TMW character;
- Connection - manages a connection to the three TMW servers and provides a low level interface to control a character (moving, attacking, creating parties, chatting, taking items, etc.);
- Packet - manages data about a given packet; interprets packets received from the server;
- PacketBuffer - deals with incoming packets from a given socket server.

Packets are implemented as Python dictionaries, which store hexadecimal codes of packets as keys, and packet length and packet name as values in tuples.

Core player manipulations are implemented in *Connection* Class methods, such as the following:

```
def takeAllDroppedItems(self):
    for key, value in Packet.droppedItemDict.items():
        itemID = key
        debug( "ItemID:_%d" %itemID )
        x = value[1]
        debug( "x_coord:_%d" %x )
        y = value[2]
        debug( "y_coord:_%d" % y )
        c.setDestination(x−1, y, 2)
        time.sleep(2)
        c.itemPickUp(itemID)
        time.sleep(0.5)
```

Listing 2. Example interface method

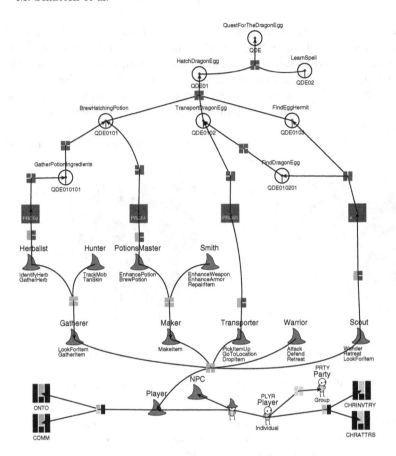

Fig. 3. Model of the quest for the Dragon Egg example in TMW domain (Color figure online)

The listing illustrates an example of a Python client method *takeAllDropped-Items* which allows an agent to pick up all items that were recently dropped possibly by some monster that has just been defeated. The method makes use of two other methods: *setDestination* which allows moving the character in a 2D space and *itemPickUp* that allows picking up items which are within reach.

5 Example Model

The model developed within this example is based on the quest developed in early stages of the ModelMMORPG project: *The Quest for the Dragon Egg*. The quest was developed for TMW, and features several NPCs, various items, and demands that players use different kinds of actions and utilize socialization features of the game.

The quest requires the player to seek the *Dragon Egg* item in one of three random possible locations in *The Mana World*, retrieve the egg, hatch it using the brewed *Hatching Potion* with the helping hand of the *Hermit* NPC, and visit the *Arch Wizard* NPC to finally receive the ultimate prize of the quest – a spell to invoke a powerful dragon to their side.

Finishing the quest is not as straightforward as it seems from this high level description though, as many additional constraints are introduced. The quest is valid for 24 h of real-world time only, i.e. the egg is rendered useless 24 h after being created in the world. The egg is guarded by many violent monsters. Once the *Dragon Egg* item is picked up by a player, the only way to transport the item to the *Hermit* NPC is by the constant cooperation of three players. Furthermore, the *Hatching Potion* item is difficult to create, since the ingredients are not easily found. Once the egg is hatched, the given player must visit the *Arch Wizard* NPC in order to finally complete the quest.

Some of the above stated sub-tasks (e.g. potion hatching, egg finding, egg taking) implicitly require various roles in order to be successfully finished. The described quest, and roles necessary for its completion, along with the individual player class, are modeled using the current version of the described modeling tool as shown in Fig. 3.

Individual player-agents are instantiated from the definition of an individual player shown as stickmen in Fig. 3. Players can form a group of players, called a party in MMORPG domain, and each player has access to some individual knowledge, shown to the right of the modeled player. Every player agent plays one of the two high level roles: Player or NPC. When playing the Player role, the individual player can play any of the available roles, shown as blue hats in Fig. 3. Each role can access some organizational knowledge, shown in the lower-left corner of Fig. 3. Additionally, each role has some defined actions, shown to the right of each of the roles in Fig. 3 (e.g. role Warrior has actions Attack, Defend, and Retreat), that can be combined into processes, shown as green squares in Fig. 3, that can be used to successfully complete some tasks (shown circular in Fig. 3). A quest, visible as the topmost element in Fig. 3, is divided into simpler sub-tasks that make the original quest reachable by the agents of the system.

The generated code of the modeled system is shown in the following listings. Listing 3 shows generated code for player agent class using the *tabula rasa* approach, i.e. every player starts only with a behavior that enables them to change their role and thus gain actions and personal features.

```
import spade
from RoleBehaviours import *

class OrgUnit45Player(spade.Agent.Agent):
    class ChangeRole(spade.Behaviour.OneShotBehaviour):
        def _process(self):
            print 'Player:_behaving_ChangeRole'

    def _setup(self):
        self.addBehaviour(self.ChangeRole(), None)
```

Listing 3. Generated code for SPADE Player agent

Behaviors that can be used by playing a particular role are described in Listing 4. Only essential elements of a behavior (i.e. an action named using

SPADE naming scheme) are presently generated by the generating feature of
the metamodel.

```
class PickItemUp(spade.Behaviour.OneShotBehaviour):
    def _process(self):
        print 'Transporter:_behaving_PickItemUp'
...
class BrewPotion(spade.Behaviour.OneShotBehaviour):
    def _process(self):
        print 'PotionsMaster:_behaving_BrewPotion'
...
class Attack(spade.Behaviour.OneShotBehaviour):
    def _process(self):
        print 'Warrior:_behaving_Attack'
```

Listing 4. Excerpt from generated code for SPADE behaviors

These generated templates can now be extended using application specific
programming. For example the behaviour PickItemUp from Listing 4 could be
extended with high-level and low-level interface code in a way similar to the
following:

```
class PickItemUp(spade.Behaviour.OneShotBehaviour):
    def _process(self):
        print 'Transporter:_behaving_PickItemUp'
        for r in self.myAgent.ask('position(X,Y),itemNear(X,Y,Item)'):
            self.myAgent.itemPickup(r['Item'])
        sleep(1)
```

Listing 5. Generated code extended with high- and low-level interface code

As one can see in Listing 5, the behaviour firstly queries the current agent's
knowledge base for near items. Then it uses the agent's itemPickup method to
pick up one item after another.

6   Conclusions and Future Work

In this work in progress paper we have reported on the current state of development of a model driven and agent based MMORPG development platform.
This platform is part of a broader scope LSMAS development framework which
has been specialized with a plug-in system that allows us to model MMORPG
related scenarios.

As of the time of writing, the presented system has a fully developed ontology,
partially developed modelling tool (one of the three components, namely the
application template generator, needs to be developed more maturely) and a
partially developed MMORPG plug-in (also, one of the four components, namely
the high-level interface, needs to be developed further and integrated with the
application template generator).

The provided example model shows some of the possibilities of the developed
system. A graphical model is transformed into an application template, that can
then be extended using the developed MMORPG plug-in.

Our future work is dedicated to finishing the planned work and enriching
some of the components to allow for easier transition from model to application
as well as dealing with performance related issues. We are planning to achieve

this through tighter integration of the application template generator of the modelling tool and the high level interface of the MMORPG plug-in.

Acknowledgment. This work has been supported in full by the Croatian Science Foundation under the project number 8537. We would also like to acknowledge TMW development team which often helped us with various implementation specific details. Additionally, we would like to thank our students Marin Rukavina, Dario Belinić and Lovro Predovan and prof. Marko Maliković who helped in developing parts of the knowledge base, planning system and server components respectively.

References

1. Schatten, M., Ðurić, B.O.: Social networks in "the mana world"-an analysis of social ties in an open source MMORPG. Int. J. Multimedia Ubiquit. Eng. **11**(3), 257–272 (2016)
2. Schatten, M., Ševa, J., Tomičić, I.: A roadmap for scalable agent organizations in the internet of everything. J. Syst. Softw. **115**, 31–41 (2016)
3. Schatten, M., Tomičić, I., Ðurić, B.O.: Multi-agent modeling methods for massivley multi-player on-line role-playing games. In: MIPRO, Opatija, HR (2015)
4. Ðurić, B.O.: Organizational metamodel for large-scale multi-agent systems. In: de la Prieta, F., et al. (eds.) Trends in Practical Applications of Scalable Multi-Agent Systems, the PAAMS Collection. AISC, vol. 473, pp. 387–390. Springer, Cham (2016). doi:10.1007/978-3-319-40159-1_36
5. Yan, J.: Bot, cyborg and automated turing test. In: Christianson, B., Crispo, B., Malcolm, J.A., Roe, M. (eds.) Security Protocols 2006. LNCS, vol. 5087, pp. 190–197. Springer, Heidelberg (2009). doi:10.1007/978-3-642-04904-0_26
6. Golle, P., Ducheneaut, N.: Preventing bots from playing online games. Comput. Entertainment (CIE) **3**(3), 3 (2005)
7. van Kesteren, M., Langevoort, J., Grootjen, F.: A step in the right direction: botdetection in MMORPGs using movement analysis. In: Proceedings of the 21st Belgian-Dutch Conference on Artificial Intelligence (BNAIC 2009), pp. 129–136 (2009)
8. Jung, Y.W., Lim, B.-H., Sim, K.-H., Lee, H.J., Park, I.K., Chung, J.Y., Lee, J.: VENUS: the online game simulator using massively virtual clients. In: Baik, D.-K. (ed.) AsiaSim 2004. LNCS, vol. 3398, pp. 589–596. Springer, Heidelberg (2005). doi:10.1007/978-3-540-30585-9_66
9. Cho, C.-S., Sohn, K.-M., Park, C.-J., Kang, J.-H.: Online game testing using scenario-based control of massive virtual users. In: 2010 The 12th International Conference on Advanced Communication Technology (ICACT), vol. 2, pp. 1676–1680. IEEE (2010)
10. Cho, C.-S., Lee, D.-C., Sohn, K.-M., Park, C.-J., Kang, J.-H.: Scenario-based approach for blackbox load testing of online game servers. In: 2010 International Conference on Cyber-Enabled Distributed Computing and Knowledge Discovery (CyberC), pp. 259–265. IEEE (2010)
11. Reyno, E.M., Cubel, J.Á.C.: Model driven game development: 2D platform game prototyping. In: GAMEON, pp. 5–7. Citeseer (2008)
12. Tang, S., Hanneghan, M.: State-of-the-art model driven game development: a survey of technological solutions for game-based learning. J. Interact. Learn. Res. **22**(4), 551 (2011)

13. Gascueña, J.M., Navarro, E., Fernández-Caballero, A.: Model-driven engineering techniques for the development of multi-agent systems. Eng. Appl. Artif. Intell. **25**(1), 159–173 (2012)
14. Pavón, J., Gómez-Sanz, J., Fuentes, R.: Model driven development of multi-agent systems. In: Rensink, A., Warmer, J. (eds.) ECMDA-FA 2006. LNCS, vol. 4066, pp. 284–298. Springer, Heidelberg (2006). doi:10.1007/11787044_22
15. Li, Y., Musilek, P., Wyard-Scott, L.: Fuzzy logic in agent-based game design. In: IEEE Annual Meeting of the Fuzzy Information. Processing NAFIPS 2004, vol. 2, pp. 734–739. IEEE (2004)
16. Schatten, M.: Organizational architectures for large-scale multi-agent systems' development: an initial ontology. In: Omatu, S., Bersini, H., Corchado, J.M., Rodríguez, S., Pawlewski, P., Bucciarelli, E. (eds.) Distributed Computing and Artificial Intelligence, 11th International Conference. AISC, vol. 290, pp. 261–268. Springer, Cham (2014). doi:10.1007/978-3-319-07593-8_31
17. Đurić, B.O., Schatten, M.: Defining ontology combining concepts of massive multi-player online role playing games and organization of large-scale multi-agent systems. In: 2016 39th International Convention on Information and Communication Technology, Electronics and Microelectronics (MIPRO), pp. 1330–1335. IEEE (2016)
18. Abbas, H.A., Shaheen, S.I., Amin, M.H.: Organization of multi-agent systems: an overview. arXiv preprint arXiv:1506.09032 (2015)
19. Gregori, M.E., Cámara, J.P., Bada, G.A.: A jabber-based multi-agent system platform. In: Proceedings of the Fifth International Joint Conference on Autonomous Agents and Multiagent Systems, pp. 1282–1284. ACM (2006)
20. Fikes, R.E., Nilsson, N.J.: Strips: a new approach to the application of theorem proving to problem solving. Artif. Intell. **2**(3), 189–208 (1972)
21. Maliković, M., Schatten, M.: Artificial intelligent player's planning in massively multi-player on-line role-playing games. In: 26th Central European Conference on Information and Intelligent Systems (2015)

Improvement of Robustness to Environmental Changes by Autonomous Divisional Cooperation in Multi-agent Cooperative Patrol Problem

Ayumi Sugiyama[✉] and Toshiharu Sugawara[✉]

Department of Computer Science and Engineering,
Waseda University, Tokyo 1698555, Japan
sugi.ayumi@ruri.waseda.jp, sugawara@waseda.jp

Abstract. We propose a learning and negotiation method to enhance divisional cooperation and demonstrate its robustness to environmental changes in the context of the multi-agent cooperative problem. With the ongoing advances in information and communication technology, we now have access to a vast array of information, and everything has become more closely connected due to innovations such as the Internet of Things. However, this makes the tasks/problems in these environments complicated. In particular, we often require fast decision making and flexible responses to adapt to changes of environment. For these requirements, multi-agent systems have been attracting interest, but the manner in which multiple agents cooperate with each other is a challenging issue because of the computational cost, environmental complexity, and sophisticated interaction required between agents. In this work, we address a problem called the *continuous cooperative patrol problem*, which requires high autonomy, and propose an autonomous learning method with simple negotiation to enhance divisional cooperation for efficient work. We also investigate how this system can have high robustness, as this is one of the key elements in an autonomous distributed system. We experimentally show that agents with our method generate role sharing in a bottom-up manner for effective divisional cooperation. The results also show that two roles, specialist and generalist, emerged in a bottom-up manner, and these roles enhanced the overall efficiency and the robustness to environmental change.

Keywords: Divisional cooperation · Multi-agent system · Continuous patrolling

1 Introduction

Autonomous decision making and collaboration by multiple agents have been required in various fields. Ongoing developments in information and communication technology now enable us to easily obtain almost any information we desire, and everything is now more closely connected due to innovations such as the Internet of Things. These developments have dramatically increased the

© Springer International Publishing AG 2017
Y. Demazeau et al. (Eds.): PAAMS 2017, LNAI 10349, pp. 259–271, 2017.
DOI: 10.1007/978-3-319-59930-4_21

amount of information to be processed and cause frequent changes of environments. It is difficult to adapt to these changes with top-down and centralized control systems because the environments are constantly growing and problems and systems are becoming complicated.

In this work, we address one of the more sophisticated problems that require high agent autonomy; the *continuous cooperative patrolling problem* (CCPP), in which multiple autonomous agents continuously move around a given area without any definitive determination of the optimal route such as a method based on the traveling salesman problem. A good solution to CCPP would be expected of enormous benefit in a variety of applications such as security surveillance and cleaning tasks, so CCPP and similar problems are being actively studied. David and Rui [3] systematically summarized recent several cooperative patrolling methods.

Research on multi-agent systems to resolve these problems in a bottom-up and distributed manner by autonomous agents has been attracting attention. The key issues in terms of improving the overall work efficiency in CCPP are appropriate divisional cooperation and division of labor. For example, there have been studies on how divisional cooperation based on the swarm system and social insects is achieved in environments where no centralized manager exists [5,10]. However, the methods in these works focus on the foraging activity and adjust the ratio of agents equally to each task or food under the assumption that the appropriate ratio of agents to be deployed in each location has been given in advance. Talita et al. [11] proposed a negotiation algorithm based on an auction mechanism for patrolling. In their method, the appropriate ratio of agents to be allocated individual tasks is not given but is decided by auction. However, its computational cost for negotiation is high.

One important issue for CCPP by cooperative agents is how to allocate the locations for visiting to individual agents, and two approaches to this issue can be considered. The first is partitioning an area into disjoint subareas, each of which is allocated to one or a few agents as responsible areas [1,4,6,10]. Although this approach can easily prevent agent competition, it is not robust enough to changes of environment because the convergence speed decreases as the number of agents or the size of environment increases. The second approach is not dividing the area but having the agents generate their own targets and planning/behavior strategies for moving around the environments [2,7]. This approach aims at establishing bottom-up cooperation in a whole system by a simple policy to action, and it can be expected to have high flexibility for changes. However, the mutual influence between agents for autonomous decision making becomes complicated and the effect of the agents' behavior on the environment becomes unforeseeable, and thus, no optimal method has yet been clarified. We have also focused on the second approach to solve CCPP and previously proposed an autonomous learning meta-strategy to find the appropriate strategy in accordance with the an environment [12] and a method with which agents indirectly learn the behavior of other agents by learning the importance of location in the environment [9]. We also introduced a range of responsibility to agents and simple negotiation to enhance divisional cooperation in a bottom-up manner [8]. However, these earlier works focused on efficient team formation and task allocation, and did not consider robustness to environmental changes, which is an important issue in real-world applications.

Thus, here we define the robustness as the ability to maintain work efficiency even when some agent in the environment stops and extend our previous works [8,9] to improve the robustness in CCPPs. We clarify the characteristics of our proposed method by investigating the relationships between autonomous divisional cooperation and robustness of the system's change. We conducted experiments where a number of agents suddenly stopped and found that the proposed method can adapt to such sudden changes. An analysis of the experimental results showed that our method generated the role sharing by mutual effect through autonomous learning and simple negotiation and exhibited a good robustness to the issue of agent stoppage. This paper clarifies which elements are required for and contribute to the robustness to changes in multi-agent systems.

This paper is organized as follows. In Sect. 2, we describe our model of environment and agent based on CCPP. Section 3 describes our method, in which agents decide which nodes they are their responsible for by using, simple negotiation, and (re)learning of importance of location. Section 4 evaluates our method in the case of some agents suddenly stopping, and we show the high robustness of our method and explain our analysis of the factors improve the robustness. We conclude with a brief summary in Sect. 5.

2 Model

In CCPP, events occur at each node with different frequency and agents move around to detect the events in the environment. Here, we explain the model based on CCPP used in this study. Our model is an extension of the one by Sugiyama and Sugawara [9].

2.1 Environment

We introduce discrete time with units called *ticks* in which events occur and agents move and decide their strategy. An environment for agents to patrol is described by $G = (V, E)$ that can be embedded into $\mathbb{R}^2$. $V = \{v_1, \ldots v_m\}$ is the set of nodes to visit, and v has coordinates as $v = (x_v, y_v)$. E is the set of edges. Agents can move to an adjacent node connected by the edge, but if an obstacle $R_o \subset \mathbb{R}^2$ exists on the node v, agents cannot move to that node. All nodes have a value of the *probabilities of event occurrence* $p(v)$ ($0 \leq p(v) \leq 1$). A high value of $p(v)$ means the event will frequently occur. The number of neglected events without visiting (or monitoring) v at time t is expressed by $L_t(v)$. $L_t(v)$ is updated based on $p(v)$ at every tick by

$$L_t(v) \leftarrow \begin{cases} L_{t-1}(v) + 1 & \text{(if an event occurs)}, \\ L_{t-1}(v) & \text{(otherwise)}. \end{cases} \tag{1}$$

When an agent visits node v at time t, the neglected events at v are cleared and $L_t(v)$ is set to 0.

The requirement of CCPP is to minimize the values of $L_t(v)$ by visiting important nodes. Therefore, we define the performance measure D_{t_s,t_e} during the interval from t_s to t_e to evaluate our method as

$$D_{t_s,t_e}(s) = \sum_{v \in V} \sum_{t=t_s+1}^{t_e} L_t(v), \tag{2}$$

where $t_s < t_e$ and s is the strategy selected by agents. We explain this strategy in Sect. 2.3. $D_{t_s,t_e}(s)$ expresses the cumulative neglected duration for interval $(t_s, t_e]$ when agents use strategy s, so a smaller D_{t_s,t_e} indicates a better system performance.

2.2   Agent

In this research, we make two assumptions that simplify the problem so as to focus on cooperation among agents and the influence of divisional cooperation on robustness. First, multiple agents can be at the same node. This may be impossible in two-dimensional space, but many notable collision avoidance algorithms have been proposed, so we believe we can use it. Second, agents know their own and others' locations. We believe this is a reasonable assumption because recent positioning technology such as the global positioning system is high-precision and outer observable information such as location is easier to understand than inner information.

Let $A = \{1, \ldots, n\}$ be a set of agents. The position of agent i at time t is represented as $v_t^i \in V$. Agent i has a battery with a limited capacity, so i must periodically return to its charging base v_{base}^i to charge its battery for continuous patrolling (the control algorithm is outside the scope of this paper) [9]. Agent i learns and estimates a degree of *importance* $p^i(v)$ of node v and i has a set of these importance as $P^i = \{(v, p^i(v)) | v \in V\}$. The importance can be expressed as a numerical value, and differs from $p(v)$ in that each agent has a different belief for $p^i(v)$: namely, if some agents frequently visit a node, the importance of the node is low for other agents. Agent i estimates the priority to visit at time t as $EL_t^i(v)$ using $p^i(v)$. We explain how agents learn it in Sect. 3.

Communication between agents is often limited, and frequent communication is costly, so we consider these factors to model communications between agents. We denote Euclidean distance between agents i and j as $m(v^i, v^j)$. Agents have the *communication range*, d_{com} (>0), and i can communicate with agent j at time t only when $m(v_t^i, v_t^j) < d_{com}$. To avoid cost increase due to excessive communication, we also define the minimum interval T_{limit} (>0). Agent i store last communication time with j as $T_{last}^{i,j}$ and if $T_{limit} \geq t - T_{last}^{i,j}$ at current time t, i does not communicate with j.

2.3   Planning in Agents

Agent i patrols by repeating the following flow. First, i decides the target node, v_{tar}^i, according to *target decision strategy s*. Second, i generates the path to v_{tar}^i according to a *path planning strategy*. Finally, i goes to v_{tar}^i using the generated path.

We introduce some target decision strategies below. We briefly explain these strategies; the details are discussed in [8, 12].

Random selection (R): i randomly selects v_{tar}^i from V.

Probabilistic greedy selection (PGS): i randomly selects v_{tar}^i from N_g highest nodes according to the values of estimated priority $EL_t^i(v)$.

Prioritizing unvisited interval (PI): i selects v_{tar}^i that was not recently visited; it selects from the N_i highest nodes according to the interval $I_t^i(v)$ in V.

Balanced neighbor-preferential selection (BNPS): i first selects nearby node whose $EL_t^i(v)$ is large. After i move around nearby nodes, it selects v_{tar}^i by PGS.

Adaptive meta target decision strategy (AMTDS) [12]: i learns the appropriate strategy from a given set of strategies $S = \{s_1, \ldots, s_n\}$. Agents with AMTDS change their strategy according to the situation of the environment. They can obtain $p(v)$ before patrolling and set the value as $p^i(v)$ all the times. In this paper, we set S as $S = \{R, PGS, PI, BNPS\}$.

AMTDS with learning of dirt accumulation probability (AMTDS/ LD) [9]: AMTDS/LD is an extension of AMTDS. Agents with AMTDS/ LD also change their strategy but they cannot obtain $p(v)$ before patrolling. They learn $p^i(v)$ due to their patrolling.

We introduce two path planning strategies. The first is the shortest path strategy using Dijkstra's algorithm. The second is the *gradual path generation* (GPG) method. An agent with the CPG method generates the shortest path and then, if it estimates there are some nodes where many events are ignored near the shortest path, it visits them. We found that the CPG method usually outperformed the simple shortest path strategy, so we only used GPG in our experiment. The details of these algorithms are also described in [12].

3 Proposed Method

Our objective in proposing this method is to enhance effective flexible divisional cooperation from micro-behaviors such as autonomous learning and one-on-one negotiation. We call our method *AMTDS with learning of event probabilities and enhancing divisional cooperation* (AMTDS/EDC). The basic idea of our method is that each agent independently judges which it is responsible for by learning of the importance of each node. For this purpose, we introduce a set of *responsible nodes* and a simple negotiation algorithm that uses the size and center of responsible nodes to enhance divisional cooperation. The proposed model and method are based on that in [8], but we extend it for robustness to environmental changes.

The significant difference from the existing methods like TSP based approach and contract net protocol of our method is that agents with our method do not fully determine the responsibility by negotiation. A strict decision making and reasoning require high costs, so we considered the patrolling method which agent did not communicate with each other in [9]. However, very simple communication that does not require high cost can sometime greatly improve the overall efficiency. Thus, we propose the simple negotiation method without strict decision making and reasoning to enhance the efficiency.

3.1 Learning Importance and Responsible Node

Agent i can learn the time at which any agent visits node v most recently because of the assumption explained in Sect. 2.2, and i can be used to calculate an elapsed time $I_t^i(v)$ from t_{visit}^v to current time t as

$$I_t^i(v) = t - t_{visit}^v. \tag{3}$$

Then, when agent i visits node v, $p^i(v)$ is updated from $I_t^i(v)$ as

$$p^i(v) \leftarrow \begin{cases} (1-\beta)p^i(v) + \beta\dfrac{1}{I_t^i(v)} & \text{(if events on } v \text{ are cleared),} \\ (1-\beta)p^i(v) \text{ (otherwise),} \end{cases} \tag{4}$$

where α $(0 < \beta \le 1)$ is the learning ratio.

Here, we introduce the set of *responsible nodes* V_{self}^i $(\subset V)$. Agent i basically decides its next target v_{tar}^i from V_{self}^i (not V), but when i selects R or PI as the target decision strategy, it decides v_{tar}^i from V, since the purpose of these strategies is exploration. Agent i updates V_{self}^i when i returns to the charging base. i sorts the elements of P^i in descending order of $p^i(v)$ and defines V_{self}^i as the set of the first N_{self}^i nodes in P^i, where N_{self}^i expresses the size of V_{self}^i. If the values of $p^i(v)$ are identical for different nodes, one of them is selected randomly. We set the initial value of V_{self}^i as $V_{self}^i = V$, so N_{self}^i initially equals $|V|$ and is adjusted through the negotiation.

In addition, we introduce just two parameters calculated from V_{self}^i for negotiation. The first parameter is the *total amount of importance* of its responsible nodes p_{sum}^i (≥ 0) and is calculated as

$$p_{sum}^i = \sum_{v \in V_{self}^i} p_t^i(v).$$

p_{sum}^i expresses the total burden of tasks for which i is responsible because a node with high $p^i(v)$ requires frequent visits. The second parameter is the *barycenter*, $C^i = (x_c^i, y_c^i)$ of V_{self}^i, that is the node in V closest to (x_c^i, y_c^i), where x_c^i and y_c^i are calculated as

$$x_c^i = \sum_{v \in V_{self}^i} \frac{p^i(v)}{p_{sum}^i} x_v, \text{ and } y_c^i = \sum_{v \in V_{self}^i} \frac{p^i(v)}{p_{sum}^i} y_v. \tag{5}$$

When we define the shortest path length from node v_p to v_q as $d(v_p, v_q)$, if $d(C^i, v) < d(C^j, v)$, the cost of agent i to visit node v is smaller than that of j. Note that distance d is the length between nodes and different from Euclidean distance that is used to define communication range.

3.2   Negotiation Between Agents

Agents with our method individually try to improve the elements of each V^i_{self} by simple negotiation for more effective patrolling. In this negotiation, agents do not fully decide who is responsible for the node; rather agent i entrusts a number of important nodes to j if j is more appropriate to handle them.

We introduce two types of negotiation. The first is negotiation for balancing responsibility, in which agents try to balance the learned responsibility when their amounts of responsibility are very different: Agent i with larger responsibility delegates the importance of some nodes that are not important for agent i to agent j with lower responsibility, and thus, i concentrates more on the important tasks and j will be able to widely explore locations considered important. The second negotiation is for improving the performance and agents carefully trade of the responsible nodes between agents when their p^i_{sum} is almost the identical. Hence, agent i delegates the importance of some nodes that are important for agent i and another agent j can visit to the nodes at a lower cost, and thus both agents i and j can decrease the cost to patrol in their responsible nodes.

Negotiation for Balancing Tasks. If condition

$$1 + T_c < p^i_{sum}/p^j_{sum} \tag{6}$$

is satisfied, agents i and j negotiate to balance the learned responsibility. T_c ($0 < T_c \ll 1$) is the threshold value to judge it there is a difference of responsibility between i and j. Then, i calculates the ordered set

$$V^{i,j}_{self} = \{v \in V^i_{self} \mid d(C^i, v) > d(C^j, v)\},$$

where the elements are sorted by $p^i(v)$ in descending order. Then, i selects the smallest e_g (positive integer) nodes the nodes that are not so important to i— in $V^{i,j}_{self}$ (i.e., from the tail), and i delegates its $p^i(v)$ to j as

$$p^j(v) \leftarrow p^j(v) + p^i(v) \times \delta, \tag{7}$$
$$p^i(v) \leftarrow p^i(v) \times \delta, \tag{8}$$

where $\delta (0 < \delta < 1)$ is the ratio to delegate. e_g is determined on the basis of the ratio of p^i_{sum} to p^j_{sum}:

$$e_g = \min\left(N^i_{self} - 1, N^i_{gmax}, \left\lfloor \frac{p^i_{sum}}{p^j_{sum}} \times \gamma \right\rfloor\right), \tag{9}$$

where N^i_{gmax} ($0 < N^i_{gmax} < N^i_{self}$) is the upper limit to prevent big fluctuations. After giving and receiving information, agents i and j update their sizes of responsible nodes by

$$N^i_{self} \leftarrow N^i_{self} - e_g \tag{10}$$
$$N^j_{self} \leftarrow \min(|V|, N^j_{self} + e_g). \tag{11}$$

Negotiation for Trade-Off of Responsibility. If condition

$$1 - T_c < p^i_{sum}/p^j_{sum} < 1 + T_c \tag{12}$$

is satisfied, they negotiate to improve their V^i_{self} by swapping responsibility of a number of nodes. i selects the first N^i_{cmax} nodes from the head of $V^{i,j}_{self}$ and then i delegates those $p^i(v)$ to j according to Eqs. 7 and 8. Then, e_g is determined as

$$e_g = \min\left(N^i_{self} - 1, N^i_{cmax}\right), \tag{13}$$

where $N^i_{cmax}(> 0)$ is the upper limit. Note that nodes with high $p^i(v)$ incur relatively high burdens, so N^i_{cmax} must be a small constant and much less than N^i_{gmax}. After exchanging information, they update their sizes of responsible nodes by Eq. 10. When Eq. 12 is satisfied, agent j is also likely to send parts of the learned information to i, so these processes occur in the opposite direction.

4   Experiments and Discussion

Experimental Setting. To evaluate our method, we prepared a large environment for agents to patrol (Fig. 1) that consists of six rooms indicated by *Room N* (where $N = 0, \ldots, 5$), a corridor, and a number of dirty regions. It was represented by a 101×101 2-dimensional grid space with several obstacles. We made the environment using C#. We set $p(v)$ for $v \in V$ as

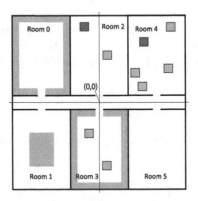

Fig. 1. Experimental environment. (Color figure online)

$$p(v) = \begin{cases} 10^{-3} \text{ if } v \text{ was in a red region,} \\ 10^{-4} \text{ if } v \text{ was in an orange region, and} \\ 10^{-6} \text{ otherwise,} \end{cases} \tag{14}$$

Table 1. Values of the parameters used in Sect. 2

Model	Parameter	Value
PGS	N_g	5
PI	N_i	5
AMTDS/LD	α	0.1
	β	0.05
	ε	0.05
Communication	d_{com}	5
	T_{limit}	10800

Table 2. Value of the parameters used in Sect. 3

Strategy	Parameter	Value
AMTDS/EDC	N_{gmax}	100
	N_{cmax}	10
	T_c	0.05
	γ	10
	δ	0.5

where the colored regions are as shown in Fig. 1. We set the number of agents, $|A|$, to 20 and set their charging base, v_{base}^i, as $v_{base}^i = (0,0)$ for $\forall i \in A$. Agents start their patrol from their v_{base}^i and must periodically return to v_{base}^i before their battery runs out. The capacity of the battery in each agent enables them to move at most 900 ticks, and it requires 2700 ticks for a full charge when the battery is completely empty. The maximum cycle of movements and charges is 3600 ticks, so we measure $D_{t_s,t_e}(s)$ at every 3600 ticks. In this experiment, agents selected AMTDS/LD or AMTDS/EDC as the target decision strategy. The parameter values used in the model and our method are listed in Tables 1 and 2.

Robustness Evaluation. Due to the page limitation, we only show the result of the experiment where some part of the agents suddenly stopped operating in order to investigate which had better robustness, AMTDS/EDC or AMTDS/LD, and the effect of divisional cooperation on robustness. Note that agents with AMTDS/EDC had a limited range of responsibility and agents with AMTDS/LD were responsible for the whole environment. We stopped ten agents selected randomly at 1,000,000 ticks and then they restarted at 2,000,000 ticks. Stopped agents could not move and communicate with others when they were stopped and other agents could not know they were stopped. Figure 2 plots the improvement to $D(s)$ over time. Compared to AMTDS/LD, AMTDS/EDC greatly prevented the deterioration of efficiency after the stoppage, where $D(s)$ decreased by 36.6% at the peak. Moreover, AMTDS/EDC outperformed AMTDS/LD before/after agents stopped at all times. The beginning part of Fig. 2 (before 1,000,000 ticks) indicates that AMTDS/EDC outperformed AMTDS/LD when the environment had no change. The difference in efficiency between AMTDS/EDC and AMTDS/LD is also discussed in [8] in more detail.

Figure 3 plots the working time of agents with AMTDS/LD or AMTDS/EDC in individual rooms during the last 1,000,000 ticks and the 20 agents in Fig. 3 are sorted in descending order of working time in Room 3. We can see that agents with AMTDS/EDC mainly worked in one or two rooms having more bias than AMTDS/LD. Agents with AMTDS/EDC tried to improve their responsibility by the learning and negotiation, and thus they could create regional segmentation in a bottom-up manner.

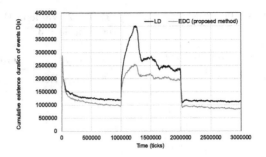

Fig. 2. Improvement in $D(s)$ over time.

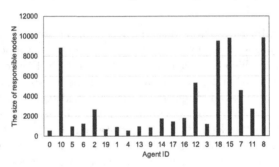

Fig. 3. Distribution of working time during last 1,000,000 ticks.

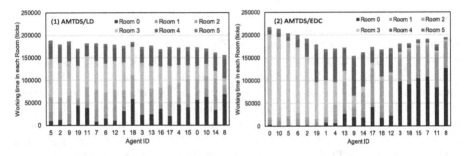

Fig. 4. Size of responsible nodes N_{self}^i at 3,000,000 ticks.

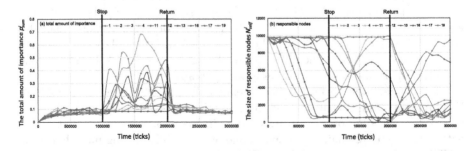

Fig. 5. Change of p_{sum}^i and N_{self}^i.

Role sharing also occurred in the size of responsibility. Figure 4 plots the size of responsible node N_{self}^i at 3,000,000 ticks in agents. This figure indicates that some agents focused on specific nodes, like *specialists*, and some agents moved around a larger area like *generalists*. Agents like specialists could move around with high accuracy in their responsible nodes because these agents focused on a specific area and could learn well. Agents like generalists could explore in a larger area and they did not need to visit high $p(v)$, nodes because the specialists frequently visited, instead. We consider these role sharing raised the efficiency of the patrols as divisional cooperation.

Next, we discuss robustness. As mentioned above, the role of the specialist who has responsibility to only specific areas is generated by AMTDS/EDC. Thus, we can say that agents could autonomously segment the regions to themselves, so intuitively, it takes more time to cover the task for which the specialist has great responsibility if the specialist stops. However, Fig. 2 indicates that AMTDS/EDC has higher robustness to environmental change.

We analyzed how agents with AMTDS/EDC flexibly reacted to the stop of agents. Figure 5(a) shows the change of p_{sum}^i of agents that did not stop and Fig. 5(b) shows the change of N_{self}^i of these agents in an experimented trial. Note that the this experimental trial was randomly selected from thirty trials without any intentions, and similar characteristics were observed in other trials. Figure 5(a) shows that the value of p_{sum}^i greatly changed after some agents stopped. This is because the agents discovered and learned a remaining task that a stopped agent was primarily responsible for. Similarly, Fig. 5(b) shows that agents changed their value of N_{self}^i by negotiation according to the change of the value of p_{sum}^i after some agents stopped. Interestingly, some generalists (agents 1, 3, 12) were drastically decreasing the value of N_{self}^i and some specialists (agents 2, 4) were drastically increasing it. We conclude that generalists who widely move around could quickly find remaining uncovered tasks and that the value of p_{sum}^i of specialists became relatively smaller than other agents that quickly detected the change. In this way, agents with AMTDS/EDC have high robustness by flexibly changing the range of responsibility, N_{self}^i, and its role.

From these results, we formulated the hypothesis that generalists are important because they have high robustness to stopping agents. To confirm this hypothesis, we conducted an additional experiment in which the top ten (generalist) or bottom ten (specialist) N_{self}^i agents were stopped. Figure 6 plots the improvement in $D(s)$ of the average of 30 trials. It shows that it is inefficient when the generalists stopped. This result supports our hypothesis. As specialists focus on specific nodes, other agents can greatly reduce switching costs to visit there and improve overall efficiency. In contrast, generalists are responsible for a wide range of environment and can respond quickly when there is a change in the environment. Therefore, both roles are important for robustness, and agents with our method can decide and adjust their roles automatically.

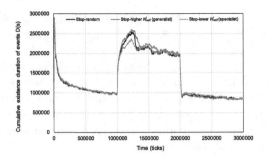

Fig. 6. Improvement in $D(s)$ over time when specialist or generalist stopped

5   Conclusion

We focused on CCPP, which requires higher autonomy and cooperation between agents, and investigated how autonomous divisional cooperation affects robustness. First, we proposed a method in which agents do not fully decide who is responsible for the node to enhance divisional cooperation by autonomous learning importance of each task and simple negotiation. Experimental evaluation revealed that our method enhanced divisional cooperation. We also found that our method generated two roles in agents, specialist and generalist, and that agents were able to move around with different patterns; thus, our method outperformed the previous one. Second, we investigated the relationship between divisional cooperation and robustness by an experiment where some agents suddenly stopped. The results suggest that divisional cooperation improves the robustness to stopping agents because agents flexibly change their roles and responsibility. In particular, we found that the generalist is more important for robustness because the generalist can quickly find and deal with tasks that stopped agents were responsible for, so other agents were not greatly swayed by the change.

We plan to compare with deterministic method like TSP based approach, and we will clarify the effective environmental structure for our method in our next research.

Acknowledgment. This work was, in part, supported by JSPS KAKENHI Grant Number 25280087 and Grant-in-Aid for JSPS Research Fellow (JP16J11980).

References

1. Ahmadi, M., Stone, P.: A multi-robot system for continuous area sweeping tasks. In: Proceedings of the 2006 IEEE International Conference on Robotics and Automation, pp. 1724–1729 (2006)
2. Cheng, K., Dasgupta, P.: Dynamic area coverage using faulty multi-agent swarms. In: IEEE/WIC/ACM International Conference on Intelligent Agent Technology, pp. 17–23 (2007)

3. Portugal, D., Rocha, R.: A survey on multi-robot patrolling algorithms. In: Camarinha-Matos, L.M. (ed.) DoCEIS 2011. IAICT, vol. 349, pp. 139–146. Springer, Heidelberg (2011). doi:10.1007/978-3-642-19170-1_15

4. Elor, Y., Bruckstein, A.M.: Multi-a(ge)nt graph patrolling and partitioning. In: Proceedings of the 2009 IEEE/WIC/ACM International Joint Conference on Web Intelligence and Intelligent Agent Technologies, pp. 52–57 (2009)

5. Jones, C., Mataric, M.J.: Adaptive division of labor in large-scale minimalist multi-robot systems. In: Proceedings of the 2003 IEEE/RSJ International Conference on Intelligent Robots and Systems (IROS 2003), vol. 2, pp. 1969–1974 (2003)

6. Kato, C., Sugawara, T.: Decentralized area partitioning for a cooperative cleaning task. In: Boella, G., Elkind, E., Savarimuthu, B.T.R., Dignum, F., Purvis, M.K. (eds.) PRIMA 2013. LNCS, vol. 8291, pp. 470–477. Springer, Heidelberg (2013). doi:10.1007/978-3-642-44927-7_36

7. Sampaio, P., Ramalho, G., Tedesco, P.: The gravitational strategy for the timed patrolling. In: 22nd IEEE International Conference on Tools with Artificial Intelligence, pp. 113–120 (2010)

8. Sugiyama, A., Sea, V., Sugawara, T.: Effective task allocation by enhancing divisional cooperation in multi-agent continuous patrolling tasks. In: IEEE 28th International Conference on Tools with Artificial Intelligence, pp. 33–40 (2016)

9. Sugiyama, A., Sugawara, T.: Meta-strategy for cooperative tasks with learning of environments in multi-agent continuous tasks. In: Proceedings of the 30th Annual ACM Symposium on Applied Computing, pp. 494–500 (2015)

10. Suseki, K., Mizuguchi, T., Sugawara, K., Kosuge, K.: Proportion regulation for division of labor in multi-robot system. In: Proceedings of the 2005 IEEE/RSJ International Conference on Intelligent Robots and Systems, pp. 2339–2344 (2005)

11. Menezes, T., Tedesco, P., Ramalho, G.: Negotiator agents for the patrolling task. In: Sichman, J.S., Coelho, H., Rezende, S.O. (eds.) IBERAMIA/SBIA -2006. LNCS (LNAI), vol. 4140, pp. 48–57. Springer, Heidelberg (2006). doi:10.1007/11874850_9

12. Yoneda, K., Sugiyama, A., Kato, C., Sugawara, T.: Learning and relearning of target decision strategies in continuous coordinated cleaning tasks with shallow coordination. Web Intell. **13**(4), 279–294 (2015)

Multi-Agent Parking Place Simulation

Thomas Vrancken, Daniel Tenbrock, Sebastian Reick, Dejan Bozhinovski,
Gerhard Weiss, and Gerasimos Spanakis$^{(\boxtimes)}$

Department of Data Science and Knowledge Engineering,
Maastricht University, Maastricht, The Netherlands
{t.vrancken,d.tenbrock,s.reick,
d.bozhinovski}@student.maastrichtuniversity.nl,
{gerhard.weiss,jerry.spanakis}@maastrichtuniversity.nl

Abstract. Parking in large urban areas is becoming an issue of great
concern with many implications (environmental, financial, societal, etc.).
In our research we investigate automated dynamic pricing (ADP) as a
mechanism for regulating parking place allocation. ADP means that the
price for staying in a parking facility for a certain amount of time will
fluctuate depending on the day and time of the week. In this paper, such
a scenario is explored using multi-agent based simulation. Two kinds
of agents are considered: drivers and parking facilities. Experiments are
conducted in a real city environment in order to observe the impact of
dynamic pricing, competition and demand increase. Results show that
dynamic pricing application leads to better results (in terms of profit
margin) for the parking facilities while it decreases drivers' utility.

1 Introduction

One of the arising problems of metropolitan areas is how to structure traffic
flow and more specifically how to spread demand for parking so that is not
concentrated in the city center, where most of the drivers want to go. A proposed
solution would be the application of dynamic pricing, i.e. price fluctuation of
parking depending on the day/time of the week. The desired outcome would be
less traffic concentration in specific areas and homogeneous capacity filling at
various car parks. Dynamic pricing has been already proposed in the parking
space allocation domain ([2,5]). Reaction of drivers to such techniques has also
been studied ([4,6,8,9]) but not in a thorough way and not using a multi-agent
based model.

Goal of this paper is to build a multi-agent based simulation environment that
will inspect the application of dynamic pricing and assess any changes in social
welfare and parking agency profits. For this purpose, REPAST suite[1] is utilized
in order to implement two kinds of agents (drivers and parking facilities) and
simulate the demand and supply of parking resources. Advantage of multi-agent

---

T. Vrancken, D. Tenbrock, S. Reick and D. Bozhinovski—Denotes equal
contribution.

[1] https://repast.github.io/.

© Springer International Publishing AG 2017
Y. Demazeau et al. (Eds.): PAAMS 2017, LNAI 10349, pp. 272–283, 2017.
DOI: 10.1007/978-3-319-59930-4_22

approach is that we are able to model interactions between the different parties in an intuitive way. Without loss of generality, the studied context was the city of Maastricht, Netherlands and the simulation was examined from the perspective of the parking agency that owns most of current parking facilities in the city, namely Q-Park. This offered the opportunity to assess the effect of dynamic versus static pricing and then inspect the effect of competition and of a drastic demand increase. Results of different simulations confirm that applying dynamic prices increases consequently the profits of the car parking facility, though it does not improve social welfare. Increasing competition however does increase social welfare while decreasing Q-Parks profits. Finally, increasing demand will drastically increase profits while decreasing social welfare.

The remainder of the paper is organized as follows. Section 2 will present the context of the simulation while Sect. 3 will then present the multi-agent model part. Experiments and results are presented in Sect. 4 while lastly, Sect. 5 concludes the paper.

2   Context and Data Generation

The simulated environment represents the city center of Maastricht, Netherlands. The simulation is run on a grid which is laid upon the city map. Each grid field is approximately 22 m x 22 m wide and the simulated environment holds 120×80 of those grid fields. While in real life, drivers will only use those grid fields which match with streets, this restriction was ignored for the simulation in order to keep the multi-agent approach to dynamic pricing in a topic related context. Therefore a street simulation was not planned for the purpose of this paper. There are in total 13 car parks in Maastricht (owned by Q-Park) and they are included as parking facilities on the map and positioned at respective grid fields which correspond to their actual position.

Both capacity and pricing of the real parks are used as initial variables for the car park agents and also as a comparison between static and dynamic pricing. They are presented in Table 1 (Fig. 1).

While data for parking agencies could be retrieved, this was not the case for driver data (i.e. number of drivers, desired destination, price ideas, planned duration of stay, preferred walking distance). In order to still run the simulation on a close-to-realistic set of drivers, the dataset for the drivers was generated by gathering ideas about realistic values and adding a randomization. In order to make the driver data easily extendable for additional parameters, the following CSV (comma separated values) format was used:

ID, start.X, start.Y, destination.X, destination.Y, arrival, max. price per hour, duration of stay, max. walking distance, initial time, day

Each driver has an ID which is unique for the day it spawns on the map. The starting point of the driver is random (denoted by start.X and start.Y), while the destination of the driver is normally distributed around the center of the map (destination.X and destination.Y). The distribution is ellipsoidal with a maximum of 1/3 of the grids width in direction of x and a maximum of 1/3 of the grids heights in direction of y.

Table 1. Q-Park facilities of Maastricht

Name	Capacity	Price per hour	Max. price per day
Cabergerweg	698	1.43€	9.00€
Sphinx-terrein	500	2.22€	13.00€
De griend	351	2.22€	13.00€
Bassin	407	2.73€	25.00€
P + R station Maastricht	335	1.89€	13.00€
Mosae forum	1082	2.73€	25.00€
Vrijthof	545	3.53€	35.00€
P + R meerssenerweg	65	1.89€	13.00€
O.L. vrouweparking	350	2.73€	25.00€
Plein 1992	449	2.22€	13.00€
De colonel	297	2.22€	13.00€
Bonnefantenmuseum	303	1.43€	25.00€
Brusselse poort	610	1.43€	25.00€

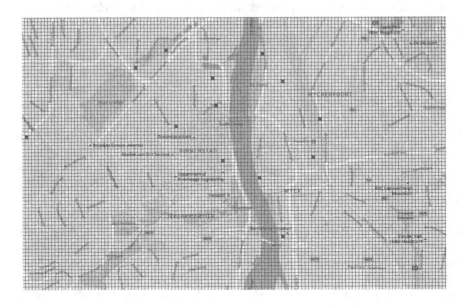

Fig. 1. Spreading of car parks (red squares). (Color figure online)

For a timestamp T a (random) number of driver N_T spawns at T minus 90 min in order to give the drivers enough time to reach their destination (i.e. time T is the desired time for the drivers to arrive at their destinations). Duration of stay for these drivers is also random. Timestamps are measured in minutes and represent the clock time for a specific day. The desired arrival time of the

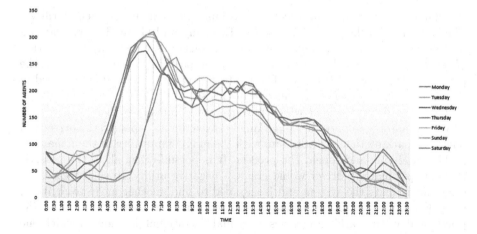

Fig. 2. Number of driver agents per day of the week

drivers is spread $+/-15$ minutes around T. Every driver will try to reach their destination on time, while choosing their parking location according to their preferred maximal price per hour and maximal walking distance. These two variables are influenced by a random factor as well, resulting the maximal price per hour to span from 0.80€ to 1.20€ and the walking distance from 800 to 1200 m for every driver.

Note that the arrival time and duration of stay of the drivers are randomized to reflect reality. That is, during the week, more drivers spawn in the morning to represent workers wanting to arrive to their workplace. Those have a duration of stay randomized between 7.5 and 8.5 hours, which should fit the average worker's schedule. During weekends, drivers are expected to show up later. They will also be more spread over the day, which means that more drivers will enter the system during the afternoon. The peak that was previously at 7:00 is postponed to around 9:00. Overall, there are less drivers than for the workdays. The driver data for weekdays can be seen in Fig. 2.

3   Model Implementation

The simulation uses two kinds of agents: drivers and parking facilities. Drivers can have two kinds of behavior: guided or explorer. This section will present how those agents behave and what assumptions were used to model them.

3.1   Driver Agents

Drivers can behave in two possible ways. They can either be guided drivers or explorer drivers. Guided drivers are assumed to behave rationally and to have total knowledge about prices and locations of all of the parking facilities in the environment. Thus, the first thing such a driver does when appearing in the simulation system is to select the parking that maximises their "utility". The concept of utility is widely used in Economy and Game Theory and is a representation of the happiness of an agent (or consumer, here both) as a function of several parameters (here mainly price of the parking and distance from the parking to their destination) [7]. The model for drivers' utility function used in this simulation is presented at the end of this subsection.

Once the driver decided which parking would maximise their utility, they move to it and try to park. If the parking is at maximum capacity, the driver will select the parking that provides him with the maximum utility in the remaining parking available and repeat the process. It is possible that all of the possible parking options for a driver would create a negative utility. In such a case, the driver agent exits the system and is assumed to find another mean to arrive to their destination. Intuition behind the guided drivers is that as they know the prices of all of the parking agencies, they make a rational decision on which one to choose and they will react to change in prices rather fast.

On the other hand, explorer drivers behave more like real life parking consumers, having less knowledge about what parking options are available to them. Their difference from guided drivers is that they are driving around until they find a parking spot (i.e. they drive to the parking place closest to them) and check if there is a place left and if the price and location of the parking creates a utility for them. If not, then they find another parking and the process is repeated. Intuition behind explorer drivers is that they will slow down the reaction in demand for a parking if the prices increase. Note that the utility is calculated using the same utility function as for the guided drivers (see below), though in the case of explorer drivers it is calculated only to check whether it is worth it for the explorer to use the parking facility just found.

As stated earlier, each driver must be able to derive how happy they would be from parking in a certain facility, i.e. the *utility* from that outcome. The utility function of a certain driver i to park in a certain parking facility j is defined using the following Equations.

$$u_{i,j} = C_i - pr_i \cdot (P_{i,j})^u - w_i \cdot (W_{i,j})^v \tag{1}$$

$$P_{i,j} = \alpha \cdot price_j \cdot duration\_of\_stay_i \tag{2}$$

$$W_{i,j} = \beta \cdot distance\_to\_destination_{i,j} \tag{3}$$

In this model, C_i is the constant representing the utility the driver would receive by arriving to their destination, without having to walk or to pay for a parking place. It is a random value attributed to each driver agent. $P_{i,j}$ is a value representing how much driver i will have to pay to park for their entire duration in parking j, scaled by the constant α. Similarly, $W_{i,j}$ represents the effort from driver d_i to walk from the parking p_j to his destination, scaled by β. The constants' α and β are used to enable a fair comparison of the impact of meters and euros on the utility.

The coefficients pr_i and w_i represent the emphasis of agent i on paying a certain amount of money and walking a certain distance respectively.

Indeed, every agent is not assumed to have the same change in utility from walking a certain distance or paying a certain price. That is, another agent, say k might be willing to have a lower utility function for the same price. Agent k will then have a higher price emphasis pr_k, that is $pr_k > pr_i$. The walking emphasis w_i is used in the same way. Both are randomly assigned to each driver and range between 1 and 1.5. It represents the agent personality and this heterogeneity in driver agent's personalities improves the realistic depiction of the simulation. Note that the distribution of coefficients pr_i and w_i can be changed to reflect a different environment (e.g. another city).

The powers u and v are both set to 0.9. They create non-linearity in the impact of price and effort on the walking distance. Indeed, it is fair to assume that a fixed increase in price (e.g. a 1€ increase) would have more impact on a customer whose original price to pay was low (e.g. original price of 2€) than on a customer whose original price to pay was higher (e.g. original price of 200€). The concavity of the utility function, ensured by setting $u \in (0, 1)$ and $v \in (0, 1)$, will reflect this concept in the driver's decision process.

3.2 Parking Agents

Parking agents were used to represent two different kinds of parking facilities. The parking agents can either be operated by the sole owner of parking facilities (in the case of Maastricht that is Q-Park) and their goal is to adapt their prices in order to optimize their profit, or they can be a competitor which just uses a static pricing model (in the case of Maastricht that can be the parking at municipality's public places). A parking facility in the real world can be described by location, name, price, capacity and operator. Name, location, capacity and operator are assigned to the agent during initialisation and are fixed.

Every parking agent can apply seven pricing schemes. Each scheme is mapped to one specific day of the week and is fully independent from the other pricing schemes. Parking facilities can react to the driver agents, but do not interact with them (i.e. there is no negotiation). The parking facilities possess an internal clock used for keeping check of the parked drivers and to decide which pricing scheme to apply. Once a driver checks in at a car park, the id of the driver and their duration of stay are saved in a list. Similarly, car park agents check whether drivers have to be checked out using that list. If the parking facility is applying dynamic pricing, then at the end of every week they will update their pricing model in order to improve their profit. This process is described in the following Subsection.

3.3 Pricing Scheme

The final price paid by the driver will be computed based on three parameters: the price per minute (most important), a minimal price every customer has to pay for the stay and a maximum price one would have to pay (i.e. staying a full day might have a fixed price lower than the hourly computed price of staying that amount of time). On top of that, there is a in- and deflation parameter defining the price per minute. The default value for this factor is 1 and the intuition is that if the value becomes lower or higher than 1 during optimisation, this will result in the price changing with every successive hour stayed in the parking facility. For example, if the price per hour is 1 euro and the inflation value is 1.10 then the driver will pay, according to what can be seen in Table 2.

Table 2. Price adjustment with inflation

Hour	Price for that hour	Full price
1	1	1
2	1.1	2.1
3	1.21	3.31
4	1.331	4.641

The final price can also be scaled depending on the current capacity of the parking. The normal price will be payed if the capacity of the car park is between 30% and 70%. If the capacity moves out of these boundaries the price will be linearly adjusted to increase the price according to the parameter. For instance, At 0% or a 100% the price will change by the percentile amount of the parameter.

The parameters are updated using gradient decent. To do this, the parking agent decides to update one parameter each week. The update method is given the percentile change in revenue. The standard equation for an update, if the last update increased the size, can be seen in Eq. 4. If the price was decreased in the last update, Eq. 5 is used. In these Equations, δ denotes the learning rate and γ denotes the percentile change in revenue in comparison to last week.

$$x_{i+1} = x_i + \delta \cdot x_i \cdot (\gamma - 1) \tag{4}$$

$$x_{i+1} = x_i - \delta \cdot x_i \cdot (\gamma - 1) \tag{5}$$

Every parameter is updated five times in a row before the next parameter will be updated. The default value for the δ is empirically set to 0.3. If δ is assigned a value too high, it can lead to rapid price changes and the algorithm will fail to converge. Setting the δ too low will increase the convergence time. Parameters are not allowed to fall below 0 (such updates are not possible). For improved convergence speed and more robust gradient decent (e.g. against ill chosen learning rates), Adaptive Moment Estimation (ADAM) [3] is implemented within REPAST. ADAM is a method to compute adaptive learning rates for parameters by storing a exponentially decaying average of past squared gradients.

4   Simulation Results

This Section will present three experiments that were conducted with the developed simulation. Performance measures will be profits for the parking owner(s), social welfare and average price.

Profits of the owner of certain parking facilities are the sum of the profits for all of those parking facilities. Note that for experiments 1 and 3 there is a unique parking owner (namely Q-Park). Profits are defined as the revenues minus the costs [7]. Without loss of generality we considered a fixed value for costs, so revenues and profits are directly analogous.

Social welfare is calculated as the sum of the utilities of all of the drivers in the system. It is the synonym of consumer welfare (which is actually shown to fluctuate in the economic way it theoretically should). The program is set to add a utility of -10000 to the social welfare for each of the drivers that do not manage to find a parking providing them with a positive utility, hence that exit the system. This high value represents that one has a greater loss in utility by not finding a parking at all than by finding one that is just relatively too expensive.

4.1 Experiment 1: Dynamic Pricing vs. Static Pricing

The first experiment conducted is meant to study the impact of dynamic pricing on the profits of the sole car park owner (Q-Park) and the social welfare. For this purpose, two simulations were run, one using the original static prices and one using dynamic pricing. The simulation ran for 34 (simulated) weeks in total. For the static pricing run, all car parks agents solely used the static prices presented in Table 1. In comparison to this, the same time span was covered in a second run, but with all car park agents defined to update their pricing according to the dynamic pricing approach. Price adjustment happens on a weekly basis, as explained in Sect. 3. For both runs, the same set of drivers with the same predefined preferences and destinations was used in order to compare just the performance of static pricing against dynamic pricing. The amount of drivers as well as their desired duration of stay corresponds to the graphs and tables from Sect. 2.

The results of these simulations are presented in Figs. 3 and 4. The first conclusion is that dynamic pricing increases the profits for Q-Park. Figure 3 shows that, after 35 weeks of adaptation, the profits using ADP are about 23 000€ higher than the ones using static pricing. This represents a 32% increase in profit which shows that it is really profitable for car park agencies to apply dynamic pricing. The fluctuations in profits under dynamic pricing are due to the time that parking agents need to adapt the prices to demand. This effect decreases in the long run (prices fluctuate less in the long run, considering stable demand).

Yet, social welfare turned out to be always slightly lower using dynamic pricing. Note however that this model of social welfare does not include utility for regulating traffic flow, avoiding traffic jams, etc. For example, it is expected that dynamic pricing will spread demand for parking across the town, hence making the traffic flow more homogeneous. It is fair to assume that this effect should increase social welfare. Furthermore, there is no utility penalty for arriving to a parking facility that attained its maximum capacity and having to drive to another facility. Such a situation occurs way less often under dynamic pricing.

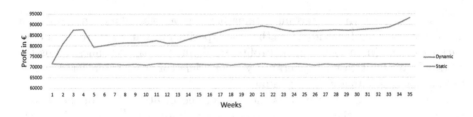

Fig. 3. Profits with dynamic vs static pricing scheme

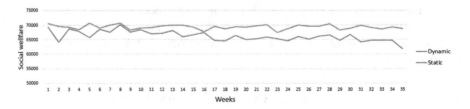

Fig. 4. Social welfare with dynamic vs static pricing scheme

4.2   Experiment 2: Competition vs. Monopoly

The second experiment will measure the impact of increased competition. That is, we relax the assumption that all car parks belong to the same owner and instead, there are some competitors which try to maximize their *summed* profits. In this case, we assumed that 5 of the main parking facilities belong to a competitor. Those 5 parking facilities were selected to be located near the center, hence bringing them leverage to attract drivers. These five car parks will use static pricing, while the rest of the car parks will use dynamic prices and aim at maximising their accumulated profits (obviously without considering the profits of the static car parks).

Figure 5 shows the average price per week of the 8 car parks that always apply dynamic pricing, under the scenario that the other do as well and under the scenario that they do not. One can observe that those 8 car parks have to set their prices much lower when there is competition. The insight is straightforward: Under monopoly, they can coordinate their prices and set them high, while under competition they have to follow the lowest prices in order to still attract customers.

On the other hand, Fig. 6 shows that social welfare drastically increases with competition. This follows the fact that the "outer-city" car park facilities that are assumed to still belong to one owner had to decrease their price in order to steal customers from the competition. This accords with a fundamental principle of free trade economy. Increasing competition will force the suppliers to bring down their price, hence increasing consumers welfare. That is why free trade and competitive markets are enforced in many economies. As a matter of fact, the European Commission already fined some companies that undertook some actions to settle them as monopolies [1].

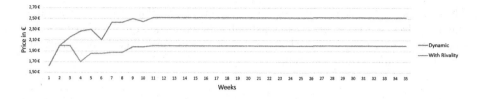

Fig. 5. Prices with competition vs monopoly

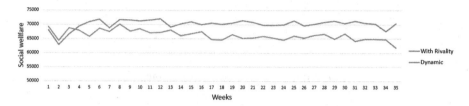

Fig. 6. Social welfare with competition vs monopoly

4.3 Experiment 3: High Amount vs. Normal Amount of Drivers

The last experiment tested the dynamic and static run from the first scenario on a bigger driver dataset. For this purpose, the amount of drivers from experiment 1 was increased to approximately 3 times as much as before. The situation for the car parks does not differ from experiment 1. The insight behind this test is to observe the consequences of a drastic increase in demand.

Figure 7 shows the profits of static and dynamic pricing under the assumption of higher demand ("many drivers" line) and normal demand ("normal drivers" line, referring to normal number of drivers). One can observe a drastic increase in the profits of the sole car park owner with higher demand and this is not surprising since higher demand means higher profits. The difference in profit is also higher in the case of dynamic pricing. Furthermore, it is more valuable to be able to spread demand over the different parking facilities when there is a high demand. Indeed, one of the positive aspect of dynamic pricing is that the parking owner can distribute better the demand. That is, ensuring to minimise the number of parking facilities that become full by spreading demand over the different parking facilities by increasing the prices where there is a high demand or decreasing the prices where there is a low demand. That aspect is of course more valuable when there are much more drivers, as a full parking situation is more likely to happen.

Figure 8 shows the change in the social welfare following this experiment. Recall that when a driver finds no available spot that yields a positive utility, then they exit the system *and* adds a −10000 utility to the social welfare. With three times more drivers, we have two consequences: Firstly, the prices of parking facilities increase and secondly, parking facilities will become full much faster, especially where there is high demand. This forces some drivers to consider parking facilities further away from the city center (i.e. their destination).

Those parking facilities will also have higher prices. These effects combined (higher prices and fewer options) drastically increase the number of drivers that cannot find a parking facility that suits their bound on utility. Hence, it drastically brings down the social welfare.

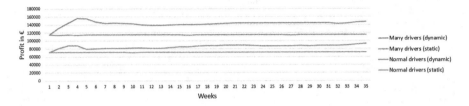

Fig. 7. Profits with competition vs monopoly

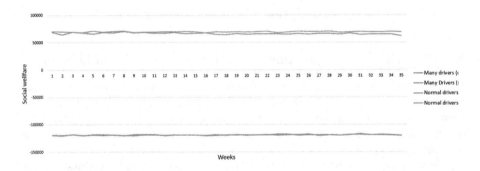

Fig. 8. Social welfare with competition vs monopoly

5   Conclusion

In this paper, a simulation environment to assess effectiveness of dynamic pricing to parking space allocation was presented. By carefully implementing the agents' behavior (drivers and car parks), it was shown that a multi-agent simulation is possible to be used to examine market's reaction to different effects. The conducted experiments lead to some interesting conclusions. First of all, using dynamic pricing can be very profitable for a car park agency. Moreover, dynamic pricing has a larger impact on profits when the supplier is in a monopoly situation and/or when there is high demand. The results are interesting in as far as they indicate that, because of the possibly negative implications of automated dynamic pricing on the benefits for the car drivers (i.e. social welfare), ADP calls for regulatory measures, which are to be specified in negotiation with the private parking agencies by the city authorities or even are to be regulated by law at a national level. Such regulations may take into account factors such as environmental pollution, traffic flow/jams, etc. in order to counter-balance purely economic factors. Experiments are also in accordance with the related economic principles. Note as well that such simulation could be used to assess the potential of applying dynamic pricing to a whole range of other services.

In this paper, real data for costs of each car park or for the drivers were not available in order to bring simulation closer to reality. Having such information would severely improve the validity of the results. Another improvement would be to assess the effect of simulation (which in any case is generically designed) on an environment with more competitors and also higher amount of drivers that exceed the total limit of parking slots. This could lead to some potentially interesting results of how market will react.

Finally, the behaviour of agents (both car park and driver agents) can be further improved by extending the artificial data or using real data from actual traffic. This especially refers to the assumption that drivers can drive on every grid field. By limiting the movement to grids that represent actual streets, the simulation could also be used to simulate traffic and maybe even used to spread the traffic flow across the city by making use of the dynamic pricing for the different car park. This is a promising future research direction with much greater impact on many interested stakeholders (city, drivers, car parks).

References

1. European Commission Press Release: Competition activity run high in (2000). http://europa.eu/rapid/press-release_IP-01-698_en.htm?locale=en. Accessed 06 Feb 2017
2. Amir, K., Yao-Chun, S., Xu, Z., Yi, H.: iParker-a new smart car-parking system based on dynamic resource allocation and pricing. IEEE Trans. Intell. Transp. Syst. **17**(9), 2637–2647 (2016)
3. Kingma, D.P., Ba, J.: ADAM: a method for stochastic optimization. In: International Conference on Learning Representations. arXiv preprint arXiv:1412.6980 (2015)
4. Mackowski, D., Bai, Y., Ouyang, Y.: Parking space management via dynamic performance-based pricing. Transp. Res. Procedia **7**, 170–191 (2015)
5. Meier, R.: Mechanisms for Stability and Welfare: Increasing Cooperation Among Self-Interested Agents. AI Access (2014). ISBN:978-1-291-97962-6
6. Silva, M., Martín, G.: Agent-based parking occupancy simulation (2015)
7. Perloff, J.M.: Microeconomics New Myeconlab Access Card: Theory and Applications with Calculus. Prentice Hall, Upper Saddle River (2011)
8. Steenberghen, T., Dieussaert, K., Maerivoet, S., Spitaels, K.: SUSTAPARK: an agentbased model for simulating parking search. URISA J. **24**(1), 63–77 (2012)
9. Xu, H., Zhou, J., Xu, W.: A decision-making rule for modeling travelers' route choice behavior based on cumulative prospect theory. Transp. Res. Part C: Emerg. Technol. **19**(2), 218–228 (2011)

KRISTINA: A Knowledge-Based Virtual Conversation Agent

Leo Wanner[1,2(✉)], Elisabeth André[3], Josep Blat[2], Stamatia Dasiopoulou[2],
Mireia Farrùs[2], Thiago Fraga[4], Eleni Kamateri[5], Florian Lingenfelser[3],
Gerard Llorach[2], Oriol Martínez[2], Georgios Meditskos[5], Simon Mille[2],
Wolfgang Minker[6], Louisa Pragst[6], Dominik Schiller[3], Andries Stam[7],
Ludo Stellingwerff[7], Federico Sukno[2], Bianca Vieru[4], and Stefanos Vrochidis[5]

[1] ICREA, Barcelona, Spain
leo.wanner@upf.edu
[2] Universitat Pompeu Fabra, Barcelona, Spain
[3] Universität Augsburg, Augsburg, Germany
[4] Vocapia Research, Orsay, France
[5] CERTH, Thessaloniki, Greece
[6] Universität Ulm, Ulm, Germany
[7] Almende, Rotterdam, The Netherlands

Abstract. We present an intelligent embodied conversation agent with
linguistic, social and emotional competence. Unlike the vast majority
of the state-of-the-art conversation agents, the proposed agent is constructed around an ontology-based knowledge model that allows for flexible reasoning-driven dialogue planning, instead of using predefined dialogue scripts. It is further complemented by multimodal communication
analysis and generation modules and a search engine for the retrieval of
multimedia background content from the web needed for conducting a
conversation on a given topic. The evaluation of the 1st prototype of the
agent shows a high degree of acceptance of the agent by the users with
respect to its trustworthiness, naturalness, etc. The individual technologies are being further improved in the 2nd prototype.

Keywords: Conversation agent · Multimodal interaction · Ontologies ·
Dialogue management

1 Introduction

The need for intelligent conversation agents as social companions that are able to
entertain, coach, converse, etc. with those who feel, e.g., lonely or overstrained
is on the rise. However, in order to be able to act as a social companion, an
agent must be eloquent, knowledgeable, and possess a certain cultural, social
and emotional competence. Considerable advances have been made to increase
the agent's affective and social competence; see., e.g., [4,26,37]. However, most
of the current proposals in the field still do not rise up to the challenge as a
whole. Thus, they usually follow a predefined dialogue strategy (which cannot

© Springer International Publishing AG 2017
Y. Demazeau et al. (Eds.): PAAMS 2017, LNAI 10349, pp. 284–295, 2017.
DOI: 10.1007/978-3-319-59930-4_23

be assumed when interacting with, e.g., elderly); they do not take into account cultural idiosyncrasies of the addressee when planning their actions; they are not multilingual to be able to intermediate between a migrant and a native from the host country; etc. See, e.g., [1, 36] for some representative examples. To essentially improve on the capacity of a conversational agent to conduct a versatile emotionally and culturally sensitive dialogue, the role of the knowledge model underlying the agent must be reconsidered. An advanced ontology-based knowledge model is capable of capturing the content of the multimodal (verbal, facial, and gestural) communication input of the user in terms of abstract interpretable structures. Furthermore, it facilitates the interpretation of the input of the user and the decision on the next move of the agent by means of a variety of reasoning mechanisms. And, obviously, it also facilitates the dialogue history bookkeeping, the representation of the cultural and social specifics of a user, as well as domain-specific and common sense knowledge.

In what follows, we present the design and first prototypical implementation of an agent (henceforth referred to as "KRISTINA") in which the knowledge model is central. KRISTINA is projected as an embodied companion for (elderly) migrants with language and cultural barriers in the host country and as a trusted information provision party and mediator in questions related to basic care and healthcare. Consider an excerpt of a sample dialogue as targeted by KRISTINA:

K: *You look downhearted today. What is wrong?*
U: *I feel sad. Because of my eyes, I even can't read the newspaper anymore.*
K: *Shall I read the newspaper aloud for you?*
U: *Yes, this would be great!*
K: *You certainly can still read the headings of the articles. Just tell me which one I shall read.*
... ...

2   Architecture of the KRISTINA Agent

Figure 1 shows the global design of KRISTINA, which is targeted to have the following characteristics embedded into linguistic, cultural, social and emotional contexts: (i) to be able to retrieve multimedia background content from the web in order to show itself informed and knowledgeable about themes relevant to the user; (ii) understand and interpret the concerns of the user expressed by a combination of facial, gestural and multilingual verbal signals; (iii) plan the dialogue using ontology-based reasoning techniques in order to be flexible enough and react appropriately to unexpected turns of the user; (iv) communicate with the user using verbal and non-verbal (facial and gestural) signals.[1]

The agent is composed of a collection of modules that ensure informed multimodal expressive conversation with a human user. The communication analysis modules are controlled by the *Social Signal Interpretation* (SSI) framework [34].

---

[1] Due to the lack of space, we cannot present a complete run of an interaction turn. Therefore, we merely introduce in what follows the individual modules and sketch how they interact.

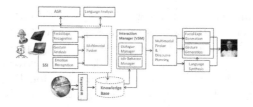

Fig. 1. Architecture of the KRISTINA agent

SSI supports audio and video signal streaming and realtime recognition, synchronization, analysis and high level fusion of the different modality signals within these streams: emotional speech, mimics, and head and body gestures. In KRISTINA, SSI is the central instance for the analysis and synchronization of video and audio signals with respect to displayed emotions. For this purpose, targeted machine learning modules for paralinguistic, facial and gesture analysis have been implemented as SSI components–which also ensures seamless interaction with the rest of the framework. For the linguistic analysis of the audio, the transcribed material is piped through SSI to the language analysis module.

The semantic structures obtained from the analysis modules are handed over by the dialogue manager (DM) to the knowledge integration (KI) module in order to be projected onto genuine ontological (OWL) structures, fused and stored in the knowledge base (KB). The dialogue-oriented modules are embedded in the *Visual Scene Maker* (VSM) framework [12]. While the original purpose of VSM has been to support the definition of the interactive behavior of virtual characters, we use it, on the one hand, as a communication shell between the DM module and the modules it interacts with, and, on the other hand, for modeling the idle behavior of the agent.

The DM chooses the best system reaction (in terms of ontological structures), in accordance with the analyzed user move, the user's emotion and culture and the recent dialogue history. For this purpose, it solicits first from the KI module possible reactions that are reasoned over the KB. In other words, in contrast to most of the state-of-the-art DM models, the determination of the turn of the system is distributed between a high level control DM and a reasoning KB module.

The ontological structures of the best system reaction are passed by the DM to the fission (or modality selection) and discourse planning module, which shall ensure an adequate assignment of the content elements chosen for communication to the individual modalities (voice, face, and body gesture) and their coherent and coordinated presentation. The three modality generation modules determine the form of their respective content elements. The language generation module feeds its intermediate and final outcome also to the facial expression and gesture generation modules in order to ensure, e.g., accurate lip synchronization and beat gestures of the virtual character.

A dedicated search engine acquires background multimodal information from the web and relevant curated information sources. The engine extracts content from web resources (including social media) to enhance the background knowledge of KRISTINA that is stored in the KB in terms of ontologies, which facilitates the realization of flexible reasoning-based dialogue strategies.

3   The Knowledge Model of the KRISTINA Agent

To ensure that the agent is "knowledgeable" about the topic of the conversation and thus able to interpret the multimodal input (question, comment, request, etc.) of the user and come up with the appropriate reaction, the knowledge representation in the agent must be theoretically sound and scalable. The knowledge repositories must separate the representation of the state of an ongoing conversation from the high level typology of the conversation (or dialogue) acts and be dynamically extendable, i.e., the agent must be able "to learn" from both the input of the user and the external world.

3.1   Knowledge Representation, Integration and Interpretation

KRISTINA's multimodal knowledge representation framework includes ontologies designed to support the dialogue with the user and to represent the relevant basic care and healthcare background information from the web. The ontologies cover: (i) models for the representation, integration and interpretation of verbal and non-verbal aspects of user communication piped in by the DM [27]; (ii) domain models that capture the various types of background knowledge, including user profile ontologies [15]; ontologies for modeling routines, habits and behavioural aspects [25], and healthcare and medical ontologies [28].

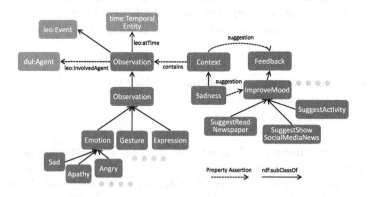

Fig. 2. Observation and context models

The knowledge integration and interpretation models define how the structures can be combined to derive high-level interpretations. To achieve this, a lightweight ontology pattern is provided for capturing contextual semantics, i.e., the types of the structures that are of interest and the way they should be interpreted by the ontology reasoning task. Figure 2 depicts the vocabulary used for the interpretation of the user's statement *I feel sad* and the complementary information from the visual channel 'low mood' detected via the corresponding valence/arousal values [27]. The ontology extends the `leo:Event` concept of LODE [32] to benefit from existing vocabularies for the description of events and observations. Property assertions about the temporal extension of the observations and the agent (actor) are allowed, reusing core properties of LODE. The figure also depicts the relationship between observation types and context models in terms of the `Context` class, which allows one or more `contains` property assertions referring to observations.

In our example, the fact that the user is sad constitutes contextual information that is modeled as an instance of `Context`, which is further associated with an instance of `Sad`.

```
:sad1 a :Sad ;
  leo:atTime :t1 ;
  leo:involvedAgent [a dul:Agent].
:t1 a time:TemporalEntity ;
  time:hasBeginning [a time:Instant ;
    time:inXSDDateTime"2017-01-02T18:06:46"];
  time:hasEnd [a time:Instant ;
    time:inXSDDateTime"2017-01-02T18:06:51"].
:ctx1 a :Context;
  :contains :sad1 .
```

Figure 2 also displays an excerpt of the domain ontology used to infer feedback and suggestions based on the emotional state of the user. For each context, one or more `suggestion` property assertions can be defined to associate it with feedback instances that can improve user's mood. In our example, `Sadness` is a subclass of `Context`, defined in terms of the following equivalence axiom:

$$Sadness \equiv Context \sqcap \exists contains.Sad$$

It also defines a property restriction that specifies the type of feedback needed when this emotional context is detected:

$$Sadness \sqsubseteq \exists suggestion.ImproveMood$$

As such, the `ctx1` instance of the example is classified in the `Sadness` context class, which further inherits the restriction about the potential feedback that could be given to improve the mood of the user. All three subclasses of the `ImproveMood` concept are retrieved and sent back to the DM in order to finally select the one that should be returned to the user.

3.2 Dialogue Act Representation

As already mentioned in Sect. 2, the DM is responsible for choosing the best suited system action among the suggestions of the KI module. Different aspects, such as the user's emotion and culture as well as the recent dialogue history, are taken into account. The rule-based choice is grounded in the dedicated model of dialogue acts shown in Fig. 3.

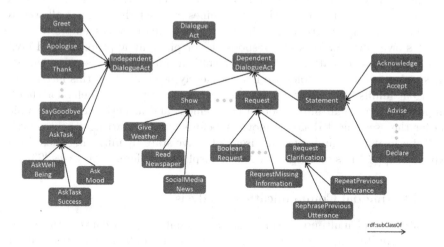

Fig. 3. Excerpt of the dialogue acts ontology

In order to avoid the predefinition of all user and system actions and be able to handle arbitrary input from both the language analysis and the KI modules, the rules are not defined for specific actions, but rather for general features such as the respective dialogue act and the topics, constituted by the classes associated with the possible system actions. For instance, in our example, three system actions are available. They share the dialogue act `Statement`. However, the topics differ. Thus, the first action has the topics `newspaper` and `read`, the second `socialmedia` and `read`, and the third `activity`. Individuals from a collectivistic culture tend to be more tightly integrated in their respective social groups, while individuals from an individualistic culture less so [16]. Therefore, the DM would propose to the user with a collectivistic culture background to read aloud news from social media, and select one of the other options if the user's culture is individualistic.

4 Multimodal Interaction

With the knowledge model as its core, the KRISTINA agent performs the entire multimodal interaction, which involves dialogue management and multimodal communication analysis and generation.

4.1 Dialogue Management

Besides the maintenance of the dialogue state and selection of the next system action sketchd in the previous section, dialogue management deals with the control of the agent's turn-taking behavior and the control of a variety of non-verbal idle behavior patterns [22]. To manage these two tasks, we use the *Visual Scene-Maker* (VSM) platform [12,21]; see also Sect. 2. VSM determines the agent's participant role changes during the dialogue, based on the observed user input and the agent's own actions selected by the DM. The turn-taking decisions are made on the basis of a policy that determines whether the agent is allowed to interrupt the user's utterance and how it reacts to the user's attempts to barge in in its own turn. VSM is also responsible for planning appropriate and vivid non-verbal behavior patterns while the agent is listening to the user or whenever the speaker and listener roles are not yet clearly negotiated. In this latter case, the agent fulfills the role of a bystander by displaying an idle behavior that is supposed to create an impression of engagement and attentiveness while waiting for the user's next dialogue move or before actively starting a contribution itself, for example, mimicking the user's affective state by mirroring their facial expressions, gestures or body postures or displaying different eye gazes [23].

4.2   Multimodal Communication Analysis

The objective of multimodal communication analysis is to convert the verbal and affective information captured from the user into abstract representations that are projected onto ontologies.

The analysis of verbal (spoken) communication consists of two major tasks: speech recognition and language analysis.[2] For speech recognition, we use the Vocapia ASR[3], which exploits statistical speech models for both acoustic and language modeling [19]. Language analysis captures the function of an utterance, i.e. speech act, which is mapped onto the dialogue act of the DM, and transforms the transcribed utterances into structured representations via deep dependency parsing [3], rule-based graph transduction [5], and ontology design patterns [11]. A frame semantics [10]-oriented knowledge extraction paradigm is followed in the course of which incrementally abstract representations are distilled: 1. *surface-syntactic* → 2. *deep-syntactic* → 3. *predicate-argument* → 4. conceptual, which are translated into OWL knowledge graphs that capture entities and their relations as OWL *n*-ary relation patterns, and, in particular, as instantiations of DOLCE Ultralite's (DUL) Description and Situation (DnS) patterns. Cf. Figure 4 for the representations 1–4 of the transcription '*I feel sad*'. Its knowledge graph representation is a declarative statement containing an instantiation of the `dul:Situation` class, which interprets the instances of `:CareRecipient` and `:Sad` classes as the experiencer and experienced emotion respectively of the event class `:Feel` instance:

```
:declare a da:Declare ;
   da:containsSemantics :feelCtx1 .
:feelCtx1 a dul:Situation ;
   dul:includes :user1 ;
```

---

[2] Essential is also the recognition of prosody as a means to detect the thematic and emphatic patterns in the move of the user [6,7].

[3] http://www.vocapia.com/.

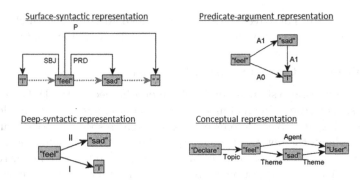

Fig. 4. Example semantic language analysis representations

```
dul:includes :sad1 ;
dul:includesEvent :feel1 ;
dul:satisfies :feelDesc1 [a dul:Description] .
:feel1 a :Feel [rdfs:SubClassOf dul:Event] ;
dul:classifiedBy :Context [rdfs:SubClassOf dul:Concept] .
:sad1 a :Sad [rdfs:subClassOf :Emotion] ;
    dul:classifiedBy :Theme [a dul:Concept] .
:user1 a :CareRecipient [rdfs:SubClassOf dul:Person] ;
    dul:classifiedBy :Experiencer [rdfs:SubClassOf dul:Concept] .
```

Multimodal cues that reflect certain affective states are measured and recognized through the application of sensor technologies, signal processing and recognition techniques. Facial and paralinguistic cues are the most prominent cues. Traditionally, affective face analysis revolved around the recognition of static facial expressions [8,30]. Nowadays there is a consensus on the need for a dynamic analysis. Commonly, *Action Units* (AUs) from the *Facial Action Coding System* [9] are used as a standard representation [31]. In order to determine facial AUs in a fully automatic manner, we first extract SIFT-based features from sets of automatically detected facial landmarks and then apply a set of independent linear classifiers to associate a probability to each of the targeted AUs. The classifiers are trained following [29], which allows training AU classifiers using datasets with a reduced amount of ground truth (only prototypical facial expressions are needed). Extraction of paralinguistic affective cues is done following [33]. Extracted facial and paralinguistic cues are combined through fusion strategies in order to generate a final prediction. Our work on fusion draws on Lingenfelser's [20] "event-driven" fusion, which is based on [13]. The algorithm does not force decisions throughout considered modalities for each time frame, but instead asynchronously fuses time-sensitive events from any given number of modi. This has the advantage of incorporating temporal alignments between modi and being very flexible with respect to the type and mode of used events. In [20], this algorithm was used to combine the recognition of short-timed laugh (audio) and smile (video) events for a continuous assessment of a user's level of positive valence. For KRISTINA, it is extended to cover the whole valence arousal space, spanned by positive and negative valence and arousal axes.

4.3 Multimodal Communication Generation

Once the appropriate system action has been determined by the DM, the fission module assigns to the individual mode generation modules the content elements from the OWL graph that are to be expressed by the respective mode. Language generation follows the inverse cascade of processing stages depicted for analysis; see Fig. 5 for the successive representations of the system reaction in our running example, namely the suggestion to present to the user news harvested from social media. As generation framework, we use multilingual rule-based [35] and statistical [2] graph transduction modules, which are further adapted to the idiosyncrasies of spoken language. The surface sentence is then spoken by the agent using the CereProc TTS.[4]

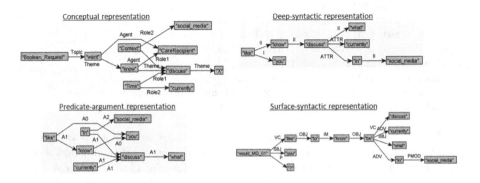

Fig. 5. Example language generation representations

For its non-verbal appearance, KRISTINA is realized as an embodied conversational agent (ECA). The embodiment is realized through a credible virtual character. Credibility (as opposed to realism) implies the believability of the rendering of the agent, avoidance of the trap of the uncanny valley [24], and animation through facial expressions and gestures, when appropriate. Gestures and facial expressions are generated according to the semantics of the message that is to be communicated. Since the generation of facial expressions using tags (smile, surprise, etc.) would limit the possible facial expressions and require a manual design of all possible expressions for each character, we use the valence-arousal representation of emotions [14]; cf., also [17,18]. Our model can generate and animate facial expressions in the continuous 2D and 3D valence-arousal space by linearly interpolating only five extreme facial poses. Because of its parametric nature, the valence-arousal space can be easily applied to a variety of faces. Using the semantics and other features, gestures are generated, keeping in mind the cultural context of the conversation.

---

[4] https://www.cereproc.com/.

5 Conclusions

We presented the first prototype of a knowledge-centred ECA, which is aimed to conduct socially competent emotive multilingual conversations with individuals in need of advice and support in the context of basic care and healthcare. So far, the agent's conversation skills are restricted to German, Polish, and Spanish; Arabic and Turkish are about to be added. Three different use cases have been setup to validate the progressively increasing functionality of the agent. In the first, it acts as a social companion of elderly with German respectively Turkish background, in the second as an assistant of Polish carers, and in the third as an healthcare adviser of migrants with North African background. Evaluation trials of the 1st prototype have been carried out with users from Germany and Spain with respect to trustworthiness, competence, naturalness of the avatar, friendliness, speech and language understanding and production quality, etc. Cf. the outcome of the questionnaire (on a Likert scale from '1' ("disagree") to '5' ("compeletely agree") on the competence of KRISTINA in Table 1.

Table 1. Outcome of the evaluation of the competence of the 1st prototype

Evaluation statement	Likert scale value (SD)
It is clear what KRISTINA wants to communicate	3.23 ($\pm$1.42)
KRISTINA does not provide the right amount of information	2.73 ($\pm$1.10)
The conversation with KRISTINA is confusing	2.84 ($\pm$1.27)
KRISTINA behaved as expected	3.0 ($\pm$1.21)
KRISTINA acted on own initiative	3.25 ($\pm$1.29)

Acknowledgments. The presented work is funded by the European Commission as part of the H2020 Programme, under the contract number 645012–RIA. Many thanks to our colleagues from the University of Tübingen, German Red Cross and semFYC for the definition of the use cases, constant feedback, and evaluation!

References

1. Anderson, K., et al.: The TARDIS framework: intelligent virtual agents for social coaching in job interviews. In: Reidsma, D., Katayose, H., Nijholt, A. (eds.) ACE 2013. LNCS, vol. 8253, pp. 476–491. Springer, Cham (2013). doi:10.1007/978-3-319-03161-3_35
2. Ballesteros, M., Bohnet, B., Mille, S., Wanner, L.: Data-driven sentence generation with non-isomorphic trees. In: Proceedings of the 2015 Conference of the NAACL: Human Language Technologies, pp. 387–397. ACL, Denver, Colorado, May–June 2015. http://www.aclweb.org/anthology/N15-1042
3. Ballesteros, M., Bohnet, B., Mille, S., Wanner, L.: Data-driven deep-syntactic dependency parsing. Natural Lang. Eng. **22**(6), 939–974 (2016)
4. Baur, T., Mehlmann, G., Damian, I., Gebhard, P., Lingenfelser, F., Wagner, J., Lugrin, B., André, E.: Context-aware automated analysis and annotation of social human-agent interactions. ACM Trans. Interact. Intell. Syst. **5**(2) (2015)

5. Bohnet, B., Wanner, L.: Open soucre graph transducer interpreter and grammar development environment. In: Proceedings of the International Conference on Language Resources and Evaluation, LREC 2010, 17–23 May, Valletta, Malta (2010)
6. Domínguez, M., Farrús, M., Burga, A., Wanner, L.: Using hierarchical information structure for prosody prediction in content-to-speech application. In: Proceedings of the 8th International Conference on Speech Prosody (SP 2016), Boston, MA (2016)
7. Domínguez, M., Farrús, M., Wanner., L.: Combining acoustic and linguistic features in phrase-oriented prosody prediction. In: Proceedings of the 8th International Conference on Speech Prosody (SP 2016), Boston, MA (2016)
8. Du, S., Tao, Y., Martinez, A.M.: Compound facial expressions of emotion. Proc. Nat. Acad. Sci. **111**(15), E1454–E1462 (2014)
9. Ekman, P., Rosenberg, E.L.: What the Face Reveals: Basic and Applied Studies of Spontaneous Expression Using the Facial Action Coding System (FACS). Oxford University Press, Oxford (1997)
10. Fillmore, C.J.: Frame Semantics, pp. 111–137. Hanshin Publishing Co., Seoul (1982)
11. Gangemi, A.: Ontology design patterns for semantic web content. In: Gil, Y., Motta, E., Benjamins, V.R., Musen, M.A. (eds.) ISWC 2005. LNCS, vol. 3729, pp. 262–276. Springer, Heidelberg (2005). doi:10.1007/11574620_21
12. Gebhard, P., Mehlmann, G.U., Kipp, M.: Visual SceneMaker: a tool for authoring interactive virtual characters. J. Multimodal User Interfaces **6**(1–2), 3–11 (2012). Interacting with Embodied Conversational Agents. Springer-Verlag
13. Gilroy, S.W., Cavazza, M., Niranen, M., André, E., Vogt, T., Urbain, J., Benayoun, M., Seichter, H., Billinghurst, M.: PAD-based multimodal affective fusion. In: Affective Computing and Intelligent Interaction and Workshops (2009)
14. Gunes, H., Schuller, B.: Categorical and dimensional affect analysis in continuous input: current trends and future directions. Image Vis. Comput. **31**(2), 120–136 (2013)
15. Heckmann, D., Schwartz, T., Brandherm, B., Schmitz, M., Wilamowitz-Moellendorff, M.: GUMO – the general user model ontology. In: Ardissono, L., Brna, P., Mitrovic, A. (eds.) UM 2005. LNCS, vol. 3538, pp. 428–432. Springer, Heidelberg (2005). doi:10.1007/11527886_58
16. Hofstede, G.H., Hofstede, G.: Culture's Consequences: Comparing Values, Behaviors, Institutions and Organizations Across Nations. Sage, Thousand Oaks (2001)
17. Hyde, J., Carter, E.J., Kiesler, S., Hodgins, J.K.: Assessing naturalness and emotional intensity: a perceptual study of animated facial motion. In: Proceedings of the ACM Symposium on Applied Perception, pp. 15–22. ACM (2014)
18. Hyde, J., Carter, E.J., Kiesler, S., Hodgins, J.K.: Using an interactive avatar's facial expressiveness to increase persuasiveness and socialness. In: Proceedings of the 33rd Annual ACM Conference on Human Factors in Computing Systems, pp. 1719–1728. ACM (2015)
19. Lamel, L., Gauvain, J.: Speech recognition. In: Mitkov, R. (ed.) OUP Handbook on Computational Linguistics, pp. 305–322. Oxford University Press, Oxford (2003)
20. Lingenfelser, F., Wagner, J., André, E., McKeown, G., Curran, W.: An event driven fusion approach for enjoyment recognition in real-time. In: MM, pp. 377–386 (2014)
21. Mehlmann, G., André, E.: Modeling multimodal integration with event logic charts. In: Proceedings of the 14th International Conference on Multimodal Interaction, pp. 125–132. ACM, New York (2012)

22. Mehlmann, G., Janowski, K., André, E.: Modeling grounding for interactive social companions. J. Artif. Intell. **30**(1), 45–52 (2016). Social Companion Technologies. Springer-Verlag

23. Mehlmann, G., Janowski, K., Baur, T., Häring, M., André, E., Gebhard, P.: Exploring a model of gaze for grounding in HRI. In: Proceedings of the 16th International Conference on Multimodal Interaction, pp. 247–254. ACM, New York (2014)

24. Mori, M., MacDorman, K.F., Kageki, N.: The uncanny valley [from the field]. IEEE Robot. Autom. Mag. **19**(2), 98–100 (2012)

25. Motik, B., Cuenca Grau, B., Sattler, U.: Structured objects in OWL: representation and reasoning. In: Proceedings of the 17th International Conference on World Wide Web, pp. 555–564. ACM (2008)

26. Ochs, M., Pelachaud, C.: Socially aware virtual characters: the social signal of smiles. IEEE Signal Process. Mag. **30**(2), 128–132 (2013)

27. Posner, J., Russell, J., Peterson, B.: The circumplex model of affect: an integrative approach to affective neuroscience, cognitive development and psychopathology. Dev. Psychopathol. **17**(3), 715–734 (2005)

28. Riaño, D., Real, F., Campana, F., Ercolani, S., Annicchiarico, R.: An ontology for the care of the elder at home. In: Combi, C., Shahar, Y., Abu-Hanna, A. (eds.) AIME 2009. LNCS (LNAI), vol. 5651, pp. 235–239. Springer, Heidelberg (2009). doi:10.1007/978-3-642-02976-9_33

29. Ruiz, A., Van de Weijer, J., Binefa, X.: From emotions to action units with hidden and semi-hidden-task learning. In: Proceedings of the IEEE International Conference on Computer Vision, pp. 3703–3711 (2015)

30. Sandbach, G., Zafeiriou, S., Pantic, M., Yin, L.: Static and dynamic 3D facial expression recognition: a comprehensive survey. Image Vis. Comput. **30**(10), 683–697 (2012)

31. Savran, A., Sankur, B., Bilge, M.T.: Regression- based intensity estimation of facial action units. Image Vis. Comput. **30**(10), 774–784 (2012)

32. Shaw, R., Troncy, R., Hardman, L.: LODE: linking open descriptions of events. In: 4th Asian Conference on The Semantic Web, Shanghai, China, pp. 153–167 (2009)

33. Wagner, J., Lingenfelser, F., André, E.: Building a Robust System for Multimodal Emotion Recognition, pp. 379–419. Wiley, Hoboken (2015)

34. Wagner, J., Lingenfelser, F., Baur, T., Damian, I., Kistler, F., André, E.: The social signal interpretation (SSI) framework-multimodal signal processing and recognition in real-time. In: Proceedings of ACM International Conference on Multimedia (2013)

35. Wanner, L., Bohnet, B., Bouayad-Agha, N., Lareau, F., Nicklaß, D.: MARQUIS: generation of user-tailored multilingual air quality bulletins. Appl. Artif. Intell. **24**(10), 914–952 (2010)

36. Yasavur, U., Lisetti, C., Rishe, N.: Let's talk! speaking virtual counselor offers you a brief intervention. J. Multimodal User Interfaces **8**(4), 381–398 (2014)

37. Zeng, Z., Pantic, M., Roisman, G., Huang, T.: A survey of affect recognition methods: audio, visual, and spontaneous expressions. IEEE Trans. Pattern Anal. Mach. Intell. **31**(1), 39–58 (2009)

Demo Papers

Demonstration of MAGPIE: An Agent Platform for Monitoring Chronic Diseases on Android

Albert Brugués[1(✉)], Stefano Bromuri[2], and Michael Schumacher[1]

[1] Applied Intelligent Systems Laboratory,
University of Applied Sciences Western Switzerland, Sierre, Switzerland
{albert.brugues,michael.schumacher}@hevs.ch
[2] Management Science and Technology,
Open University of the Netherlands, Heerlen, The Netherlands
stefano.bromuri@ou.nl

Abstract. In this demonstration, we show how the MAGPIE agent platform works. The aim of this platform is to help on the development of Personal Health Systems (PHSs) for monitoring chronic diseases. The agents of the platform use a symbolic reasoning approach to formalize the events happening to the patient. We developed an Android application based on MAGPIE where we formalized the reasoning for monitoring patients affected by diabetes mellitus.

1 Introduction

Personal Health Systems (PHSs) consist on the decentralization of healthcare services by approaching sampling technologies into the hands of the patients, with the aim of involving them in the management of their illnesses and in their own well being. This way of providing healthcare services removes time and physical barriers and enables the paradigm of *healthcare to anyone, anytime and anywhere* [4]. The use of PHSs has been reported as a prominent way to face the healthcare expenditures due to the increase of life expectancy and its assosiated prevalence of chronic diseases [3].

As shown in Fig. 1, the typical architecture of a PHS consists on three tiers, namely: Tier 1 Body Area Network (BAN), Tier 2 Personal Server and Tier 3 Remote Server. The BAN consists in a set of sensors deployed in the body to collect physiological parameters of the patient, which are transmitted to the Personal Server. The Personal Server is usually a mobile device (smartphone or tablet) with network connectivity that aggregates the data and transmits them to the Remote Server. This last component provides assistance to patients and medical doctors for the management of the disease.

The application of agent technology in PHSs simplifies the modeling of medical knowledge, as agents are autonomous software entities that pursue a set of goals in an intelligent way by applying artificial intelligence reasoning techniques such as deduction, and act proactively, without necessarily receiving a stimulus from the user. This set of properties can benefit the current definition of PHSs by having monitoring tools that are capable of reasoning in a complex and proactive way on the patients' physiological parameters.

© Springer International Publishing AG 2017
Y. Demazeau et al. (Eds.): PAAMS 2017, LNAI 10349, pp. 299–302, 2017.
DOI: 10.1007/978-3-319-59930-4_24

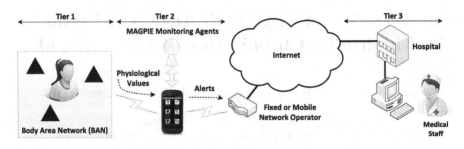

Fig. 1. Architecture of a PHS developed with the MAGPIE agent platform

2   Main Purpose

In the context of PHS, we developed the MAGPIE agent platform [1] as an Android framework for the development of the Tier 2 of PHSs. MAGPIE links the concept of an agent environment in multi-agent systems (MAS), with the patient's environment in PHSs in the sense that monitoring sensors become a source of health information that can be exploited by agents to track the health status of the patient, and perform an action when a potentially dangerous situation is detected. The source code of the platform is available in GitHub[1].

MAGPIE models three different components that can be mapped to the elements of a publish/subscribe system. These are: (i) *agents*, as subscriber entities to events happening into the environment, which are responsible to monitor the health status of the patient; (ii) *context entities*, as abstractions that encapsulate a source of information from the real world, such as a sensor, and publish into the environment patient-related events like physiological measurements; and the (iii) *environment*, which is an entity that act as an event service by mediating the interactions taking place between context entities and agents. This design strategy, based on the publish/subscribe pattern, shields agents and context entities from knowing the implementation details about each other.

More in details, agents are composed by two main parts: a body and a mind. The agent body situates the agent mind in the environment; while the agent mind is the cognitive part of the agent, and is responsible to produce actions according to the perceived events and how the medical knowledge is modeled in the mind. Such medical knowledge is based on temporal reasoning. In particular, the mind models temporal patterns that combine different types of events by exploiting the properties of Event Calculus (EC) [2]. EC is a logic formalism for representing actions and their effects in time. Therefore, it is suitable for modeling expert systems representing the evolution in time of an entity by means of the production of events. EC is based on many-sorted first-order logic predicate calculus, known as domain independent axioms, which can be represented as normal logic programs executable in Prolog.

The medical knowledge is modeled as EC domain dependent axioms that define combinations of events within a time window, which trigger an alert to

---

[1] https://github.com/aislab-hevs/magpie.

be notified; and an event is the measurement of a physiological parameter. We consider two different kinds of rules: (i) *complex*, where the order of the events is not considered; and (ii) *sequential* where the order of the events matters.

3   Demonstration

To demonstrate MAGPIE, we developed an application that tracks the health status of a diabetic patient. In such application, the patient can introduce values of glycemia, weight and blood pressure measurements, as well as the time when the measurements where taken. An agent keeps track of monitoring the patient by reporting alerts related to these three physiological values.

We track glucose rebounds, where blood glucose levels go from low to high in a short period of time, with the following sequential rule,

$$
\begin{aligned}
\text{initiatesAt}(alert(p1) &= \text{`brittle diabetes'}, T) \leftarrow \\
& \text{happensAt}(\text{glucose}(V_1), T_1), \text{happensAt}(\text{glucose}(V_2), T_2), \\
& V_1 \leq 3.8, V_2 \geq 8.0, T_2 > T_1, \\
& \text{last\_six\_hours}(T_1, T_2), \\
& \text{not happensAt}(alert(p1), Ta), \\
& \text{last\_six\_hours}(Ta, T).
\end{aligned} \tag{1}
$$

The rule above states that a brittle diabetes alert is triggered if two different glucose measurements go from less than or equal to 3.8 mmol/L to more than or equal to 8.0 mmol/L, and three different temporal conditions apply. First, $T_2 > T_1$ specifies the order in which the specified events must happen. Second, the predicate last_six_hours/2 specifies the temporal window in which the events apply. In that case, the predicate checks that the fist event happens no more than six hours before the second event. Third, the last two lines specify the "no alert" condition, which checks that the same alert has not been triggered during the temporal window. This condition avoids possible overwhelming of alerts due to events that make the temporal pattern to hold within the temporal window.

Another sequential rule following the same structure is used to control when the patient is gaining weight, which may indicate that the treatment is not effective and should be revised.

Diabetic patients can also present high blood pressure values, which we track with the following complex rule,

$$
\begin{aligned}
\text{initiatesAt}(alert(p3) &= \text{`pre-hypertension'}, T) \leftarrow \\
& \text{not happensAt}(alert(p3), Ta), \\
& \text{last\_week}(Ta, T), \\
& \text{more\_or\_equals\_to}(2, (\\
& \quad \text{happensAt}(\text{blood\_pressure}(Sys, Dias), Tev), \\
& \quad (120 \leq Sys \leq 139, 80 \leq Dias \leq 89), \\
& \quad \text{last\_week}(Tev, T))).
\end{aligned} \tag{2}
$$

This rule states that a pre-hypertension alert is triggered if within the last week, there are two blood pressure readings whose systolic component is within 120 and 139 mmHg and its diastolic component is within 80 and 89 mmHg. The first two lines of the rule specify the "no alert" condition as in the sequential rules. However, for the complex rules it is not feasible to define the other two temporal conditions in the same way that are defined for the sequential rules. The reason is that complex rules do not take into account the ordering of the events. Therefore, a single rule per each temporal permutation of the events should be defined. To deal with that, we define the predicate more_or_equals_to/2 as follows,

$$
\begin{aligned}
\text{more\_or\_equals\_to}(Number, Expr) &\leftarrow \\
\text{findall}(\_, Expr, List), & \\
\text{length}(List, Val), & \\
Val &\geq Number.
\end{aligned}
\tag{3}
$$

This predicate counts the number of events in the agent mind that satisfy the conditions defined in its second argument (Expr), and it is evaluated as true if the number of such events is at least equals to the number specified in its first argument.

4   Conclusions

In this demonstration, we show through an Android app how we apply the MAGPIE agent platform to track the health status of a patient affected by diabetes mellitus. Such task is done with temporal rule-based agents that process events related to physiological values of the diabetic patient. Future work in MAGPIE involves its integration with eHealth standards such as FHIR to send the alerts produced by the agents to Tier 3 of the PHS in an interoperable way.

References

1. Brugués, A., Bromuri, S., Pegueroles-Valles, J., Schumacher, M.I.: MAGPIE: an agent platform for the development of mobile applications for pervasive healthcare. In: Proceedings of the 3rd International Workshop on Artificial Intelligence and Assistive Medicine, pp. 6–10 (2014)
2. Shanahan, M.: The event calculus explained. In: Wooldridge, M.J., Veloso, M. (eds.) Artificial Intelligence Today. LNCS, vol. 1600, pp. 409–430. Springer, Heidelberg (1999). doi:10.1007/3-540-48317-9_17
3. Touati, F., Tabish, R.: U-healthcare system: state-of-the-art review and challenges. J. Med. Syst. **37**(3), 9949 (2013)
4. Varshney, U.: Pervasive healthcare and wireless health monitoring. Mobile Netw. Appl. **12**(2), 113–127 (2007)

Message Analysis Between Agents for Detection of Emerging Behaviors in Open Environments

Rodolfo Castello and Carlos Ventura(✉)

Instituto Tecnológico y de Estudios Superiores de Monterrey, Monterrey, Mexico
{rodolfo.castello,cventura}@itesm.mx

1 Introduction

Emerging multi-agent behaviors are explained as conducts that appear during run-time in multi agent software applications [1]. These categories of actions are not detected at the validation and verification stages. Proposals such as architectures, patterns for their detection and metrics have been presented and so far, more research is required in this area [2, 3]. The demonstration in this document proposes to visually find the patterns exhibited by agent communication in a visually analyzable and traceable format.

This demonstration is centered in the premise that as multi agent systems (MAS) grow in scope and complexity and additional task are attached, unexpected behaviors start to arise within the system and messages between agents could be analyzed with new techniques.

The application developed for this demonstration is for agents in platforms that allow mobility in open spaces, such as drones or terrestrial reconnaissance vehicles.

This demonstration, although the main research is agent messages using a visualization algorithm, is the framework developed for testing proposes. 3DvistEB showed in Fig. 1, can be used to find strange objects in the real world using a virtual world using automated vehicles.

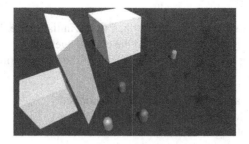

Fig. 1. Main screen of 3DVistEB

Y. Demazeau et al. (Eds.): PAAMS 2017, LNAI 10349, pp. 303–306, 2017.
DOI: 10.1007/978-3-319-59930-4_25

2   Main Purpose

3DVistEB was developed to validate the research being done on the analysis of messages. 3DvistEB is a visual tool that allows to see in a synchronous approach the position of terrestrial reconnaissance vehicles, and how these interact to meet the established goals.

For demonstration, a basic surveillance model is proposed in a controlled two-dimensional area, where software agents are programed as sentinels. These agents are in an idle state until an agent called Master Control informs them to perform a task of recognition. A restriction by the current working environment is that a foreign object is exterminated when a robot vehicle makes contact for a time t defined as a parameter s as the size of the foreign object.

The task of master control agent is to scan zones and detect foreign objects, and for purposes of this simulation is done only in the virtual world using the algorithm of Ray Casting [4], which works for positions and distances of foreign objects. The master control is delimited by a pyramidal frostrum[1] as showed on Fig. 2 with the far plane at floor level. This limitation allows the master control not no invade territories that may be controlled by another Master Control.

Fig. 2.   Frostrum

3   Demonstration

The presented algorithm scans an area defined in the initial phase. If there is an intersection with an agent it makes a request to the closest agent.

The messages that are handled, for simplicity of the visualization of the algorithm by the agents are:

- RequestSupport. - agents in a radio r only are notified
- FalseAlarm. - the foreign object is not a threat
- Panic. - all available agents should report (mandatory)
- Returning idle. - returns to its original position
- TakeMeToX. - Used for the Control agent to Guide agent X to specific coordinates
- Ignore. - agent ignores request
- Confirm. - agent confirms attending to the request
- MissionComplete. – Task has been completed

---

[1] http://mathworld.wolfram.com/PyramidalFrustum.html.

For this research JADE[2] is used as the container, communication to the physical world is performed via local network. The reconnaissance vehicles are implemented using Raspberry pi[3].

For the accurate detection of robot positioning the software Tracker[4] is used with a motion detection laboratory that gives the vehicles a margin of error of less of one inch.

The demonstration will consist of the interaction with 3DVistEB defining spots with foreign objects. The master agent will detect them in the virtual environment. An architecture is defined that includes the messages that are presented in the hardware devices in the virtual environment. This visually shows the interrelation of message (yellow edge) relations between agents (cyan/blue vertices) and physical devices as Fig. 3 shows.

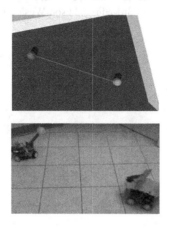

Fig. 3. 3DVistEB and recon vehicles showing visual communication (Color figure online)

4 Conclusions

3DvistEB is a visual tool that allows to observe the communication between agents in a synchronous approach. The nature of autonomous vehicles allows the testing of 3Dvisteb and find alternate forms to analyze messages that arise with agents coordinating in open spaces.

---

[2] http://jade.tilab.com/.

[3] https://www.raspberrypi.org/.

[4] https://www.vicon.com/products/software/tracker.

References

1. Hendijani, F., Far, B.L.: Detection and verification of a new type of emergent behavior in multiagents systems. In: IEEE 17th International Conference on Intelligent Engineering Systems
2. Birsey, L., Szabo, C.: An architecture for identifying emergent behavior in multi-agent systems. In: Proceedings of the 13th International Conference on Autonomous Agents and MultiAgents Systems (2014)
3. Khan, T., Wang, J.: On formalization of emergent behaviors. In: MultiAgent Systems with Limited Interactions. IEEE Press (2016)
4. Hughes, J., Van Dam, A., McGuire, M., Skalar, D., Foley, J., Feiner, S., Akely, K.: Computer Graphics, Principles and Practice, 3rd edn. Addison-Wesley (403–411). ISBN 978-0-321-39952-6

Managing Disruptions with a Multi-Agent System for Airline Operations Control

António J.M. Castro[1]([✉]) and Ana Paula Rocha[2]

[1] MASDIMA Lda. LIACC, University of Porto, Porto, Portugal
acastro@masdima.com
[2] LIACC, DEI, Faculty of Engineering, University of Porto, Porto, Portugal
arocha@fe.up.pt

Abstract. Airline companies face a difficult task in controlling their daily operations, in particular managing irregular operations that result from unexpected disruptions affecting scheduled plans. This demo presents MASDIMA, a Multi-Agent System that manages disruptions in airline operational plans producing intelligent solutions, in the sense that its outcomes are the result of autonomous and collaborative decision making. MASDIMA is able to learn both implicitly, from interactions that happen between their internal agents, and explicitly, from interaction with users.

1 Introduction

Operational plans are the result of a complex optimization process, seeking to maximize company revenues while making an efficient use of its resources. In Airline Operations Control, this process is even more crucial because resources are limited and expensive. However, these optimized plans are frequently affected by unexpected events that can cause a disruption, implying a fast and efficient repair of it, requirement especially important here, not only in solving the disrupted plan but also in minimizing the effects in subsequent plans [2].

A disruption in an airline operational plan affects three main dimensions: aircraft, crew and passengers. Its resolution is typically performed by the Airline Operations Control Center (AOCC), in a sequential way by specialists in each of these dimensions, being first solved the aircraft problem, then the crew problem and finally the passengers problem. The need for a sequential resolution is justified by the existence of dependencies between dimensions, and the order in which dimensions are solved is justified by the scarcity and value of the involved resources. However, this sequential approach leads to unbalanced solutions and miss the global view of the problem. A Multi-Agent System (MAS) possesses inherent coordination between multiples problem solvers (agents), promoting the efficiency in solving complex problems and enabling to deal with interdependency issues. The adoption of a MAS in the disruption management allows an integrate solution, contrary to the traditional sequential one, eliminating the drawbacks enumerated above. Also, the use of learning enhances the system with the capacity of reasoning about given feedback in current or new resolutions.

© Springer International Publishing AG 2017
Y. Demazeau et al. (Eds.): PAAMS 2017, LNAI 10349, pp. 307–310, 2017.
DOI: 10.1007/978-3-319-59930-4_26

2 Multi-Agent System for Disruption Management

MASDIMA is a Multi-Agent System responsible for solving disruptions in air-line operational plans [1]. Its architecture comprises three main decision levels: *bottom level*, composed of multiple **specialists** for each of the three dimensions (aircraft, crew, passenger); *middle level*, composed of three **managers**, one for each dimension, that selects the best solution proposal of its own dimension and cooperates with others to complete the global solution; *top level*, includes the **supervisor** responsible for presenting the final solution to the user. Each manager uses an utility function to evaluate a specific solution proposal, that takes into account two variables: cost and delay (for passengers manager, cost comprises direct and quality costs).

The cooperation process that occurs between managers allows an integrated solution. The multi-round negotiation and learning process that occurs between managers and supervisor allows better proposals over time. The purpose of the learning mechanism is to endow managers with the capability of learning what is better from the supervisor point of view and, at the same time, to maximize its own utility. We use a reinforcement learning mechanism, Q-learning, where feedback is sent by supervisor to managers related to each solution proposal received. Learning is also presented in the supervisor agent, and emerges with the interaction with human AOCC operators (Human Supervisor), that gives feedback to the solution proposed by MASDIMA.

3 Demo

The application example corresponds to the use of MASDIMA with real data and connected to live production systems of an European Airline in real-time. The main goal is to show a complete end-to-end disruption management process, from operation monitoring to final acceptance from the Human Supervisor.

Step 1 - Operation Monitoring and Situational Awareness: Figure 1 shows the main GUI. It allows real-time situational awareness for a specific operational time window. The world map (with 2D and 3D features) shows airborne flights with color notifications: green for on-time, yellow for delayed flight and red for a delayed flight with passengers that will miss connections. Clicking an aircraft, information about the flight times (schedule, estimated and actual) is presented as well as information about the crew.

On the left-hand side a list of airborne and not yet departed flights is also shown, using the same color alarmist. Real-time KPI's for the operational time window are also available, for example, number of delayed flights and number of passengers with missed connections, crew-members with missed connections, costs of the disruptions and cost savings (direct and goodwill). All this allows the AOCC user to always be aware of the operation status and easily spot operational problems.

Step 2 - Automatic Event Detection and Impact Assessment: MAS-DIMA detects automatically events that might disrupt the operation. These can

Fig. 1. Operation control center monitoring (Color figure online)

be SLOT, Maintenance, Weather, ETD or ETA messages, among others. After detecting the event MASDIMA starts to perform the impact assessment on the three dimensions of the problem: the schedule of the aircraft, the schedule of each crew member assigned to each flight performed by the aircraft and the passenger connections for each passenger on each flight performed by the same aircraft. At the same time, the costs related with the aircraft/flight, crew and passengers, including goodwill, are also calculated.

By double clicking on the event a graph with the impact appears (Fig. 2). As it is possible to see, an ETA (Estimated Time of Arrival) event was detected that disrupts flight 551 from MUC (Munique) to LIS (Lisbon) by arriving 17 min after the STA (Schedule Time of Arrival) and two subsequent flights. A passenger will miss flight 1685 from LIS-FNC by 16 min. Costs and the cause and reason that triggered the disruption are also shown.

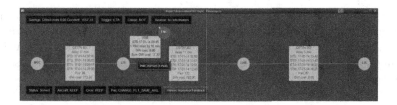

Fig. 2. Impact assessment graph

Step 3 - Integrated Problem Solving and Human-in-the-loop: After the impact assessment, the system starts solving the problem in an integrated way and using the approach mention in Sect. 2. From the graph in Fig. 2, it is possible to see that the problem is solved and that the best solution actually was to keep the flight delay (keeping aircraft and crew) and to re-accommodate the passenger. Passing the mouse over the recovery action the proposed solution appears. Left side of Fig. 3 shows an example for the aircraft solution. From the same graph the Human Supervisor (HIL) can accept or reject the solution and provide feedback (right side Fig. 3). If accepted, the system asks for a classification of the solution, so that it can be used by the learning capabilities of the system and commits the changes on the operational plan. If not accepted a qualitative feedback can be provided regarding the importance of each dimension and MASDIMA will try to find another solution according the feedback received.

Fig. 3. Left: Example of an aircraft solution. Right: Acceptability GUI for the HIL

Step 4 - What-if scenarios: MASDIMA also allows the human user to make what-if scenarios, to see the impact, costs and solution for specific situations. Through a specific GUI the user can manually insert events, e.g., an airport closure, and MASDIMA will perform the same tasks as if it was a detected event. It is up to the user to accept or not the proposed solution and commit the changes.

4   Conclusions

A prototype of a multi-agent system for disruption management in airlines operations was presented. It includes an automated negotiation algorithm that allows to achieve deals, even when there are different points of view at stake. A demo following a typical use case, from event detection to integrated problem solving and human-in-the-loop participation was also presented.

References

1. Castro, A.J.M., Rocha, A.P., Oliveira, E.: A New Approach for Disruption Management in Airline Operations Control. Springer, Heidelberg (2014)
2. Kohl, N., Larsen, A., Larsen, J., Ross, A., Tiourine, S.: Airline disruption management-perspectives, experiences and outlook. J. Air Transp. Manage. **13**(3), 149–162 (2007)

ESL: An Actor-Based Platform for Developing Emergent Behaviour Organisation Simulations

Tony Clark[1]([✉]), Vinay Kulkarni[2], Souvik Barat[2], and Balbir Barn[3]

[1] Sheffield Hallam University, Sheffield, UK
t.clark@shu.ac.uk
[2] Tata Consultancy Services Research, Pune, India
[3] Middlesex University, London, UK

1 Introduction

Specification and analysis of complex systems can be approached top-down or bottom-up [11]. A top-down approach conceptualises a system using a global state and the behaviour represented using an aggregated macro-behaviour of the system elements. For example, the System Dynamics (SD) model [8] uses the concepts of stocks, flows, feedback loops and time delays. A top-down approach considers a reductionist view [10] to understand system using the mathematical rigour from operational research, optimization theory, and sophisticated AI algorithms. A bottom-up approach, in contrast, considers the micro-behaviour of individual elements and their interactions. Conceptually, the bottom-up approach relies on emergentism [9] as advocated in actor model of computation [1], and agent-based systems [6].

Top-down approaches are a popular choice for analysing and understanding complex systems in the context of critical business needs such as decision making activities. Existing modelling and analysis tools that support top-down approaches are extremely efficient for describing and simulating the aggregated system behaviour. However, we propose that they are not appropriate for precise understanding of complex and dynamic systems that can only be understood in terms of emergent behaviour, for example systems that contain large numbers of socio-technical [7] elements having adaptive, autonomous and dynamic behaviours.

Our recent work in this area [2–5] has performed a domain analysis of organisations with socio-technical characteristics with a view to simulation and analysis leading to improved decision-making. This work has led us to choose a bottom-up approach for simulating emergent behaviour based on concepts represented using an actor-based model of computation. Our project has developed a conceptual model for simulation based on goals, measures, levers and adaptation and we are working on an actor-based simulation platform called ESL that supports these concepts. This tool demonstration will show features of ESL in terms of a real-world simulation.

© Springer International Publishing AG 2017
Y. Demazeau et al. (Eds.): PAAMS 2017, LNAI 10349, pp. 311–315, 2017.
DOI: 10.1007/978-3-319-59930-4_27

2 Main Purpose

The purpose of this demonstration is to: (1) Introduce the ESL actor-based
language and associated development environment. (2) Demonstrate a conceptual approach to the analysis of emergent behaviour. (3) Show how ESL can be
applied to a real-world case study.

3 Demonstration

3.1 ESL

ESL[1] is an text-based language that supports the actor model of computation
extended with the following features: pattern-matching over structured data,
higher-order functions that can be used to implement complex actor interaction
patterns, probabilistic behaviour as required by simulations, and data-locks. ESL
execution produces a history that contains a description of actor behaviour.
Histories can be visualised using a range of graphical libraries or interrogated
using a logic-based query language that is provided by the ESL platform. ESL
is written in Java using a virtual-machine and ESL simulation development is
supported by an environment called EDB, shown in Fig. 1(a), that supports
real-time syntax and type checking. for ESL applications.

ESL generates output during execution that and also supports an iterative
approach based on histories: (1) identify the actors in the system; (2) model their
behaviours; (3) run and capture the history; (4) formulate a theory about the
system; (5) list particular theorems that should hold; (6) express each theorem
as a query; (7) test that the theorem holds by running the query against the
history.

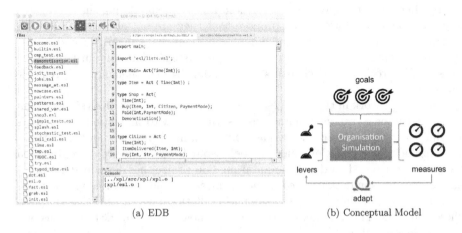

(a) EDB   (b) Conceptual Model

Fig. 1. ESL development Environment and method

---

[1] https://github.com/TonyClark/ESL.

3.2   Conceptual Approach

Figure 1(b) shows the proposed conceptual model for constructing ESL-based simulations. The goals for decision-making guide the construction of levers that parameterise the simulation which in turn produces measures which are defined by functions over the simulation histories. Adaptation is performed in terms of the histories and the levers.

3.3   Case Study

This demo will use a real-world case study to show the features of ESL and EDB for emergent simulation behaviour. The study is taken from the recent Demonetisation initiative in India. The cash in circulation in Indian economy has increased significantly over the years[2] and the cash in circulation was 15.4 trillion rupee notes in November 2016. This led to an undesirable shadow economy and funds used for illegal activities. As a corrective action, the Indian government announced the demonetisation of large denomination notes on November 8 2016 wherein the 87% cash in circulation were pulled out from Indian economy with a plan to replenish the cash in a controlled manner[3]. Limitations were imposed on the exchange of old notes, ATM withdrawal, and daily bank withdrawals to control the negative impacts of the demonetisation.

However, the sudden nature of the demonetisation event, the incomplete knowledge about possible consequences, and unforeseen behaviours of the citizens that emerged due to demonetisation made an impact on the economy in the weeks that followed. The citizens were inconvenienced and often economically threatened due to the prolonged cash shortages. The government tried to minimise the impacts of the demonetisation by monitoring the situation in real-time and adopting new courses of action on the fly.

We believe that a simulation based on ESL can help in analysing the efficacy of actions arising from demonetisation. We use an ESL based simulation

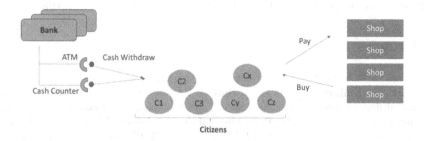

Fig. 2. Overview of demonetisation actors

---

[2] https://data.gov.in/resources/statistics-notes-circulation-india-2001-2015/download.

[3] http://finmin.nic.in/press_room/2016/press_cancellation_high_denomination_notes.pdf.

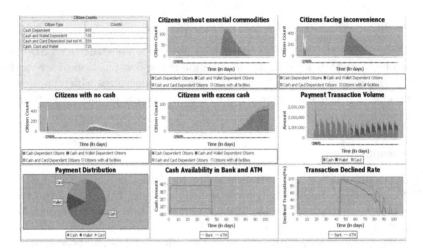

Fig. 3. Simulation results

to understand the impact of demonetisation on a synthetic but near real world Indian society and perform various what-if experiments to explore the implication of various actions. In particular, we use ESL to specify Bank, Citizens, Shops and their interactions as depicted in Fig. 2 to perform what-if analyses. Figure 3 shows a dashboard snapshot that is produced by ESL from the demonetisation case study.

4   Conclusion

ESL and EDB are actively being developed. Current plans are to add reasoning to actors in the form of logic programming over local histories, and to develop a monitor language. The former will be used to add intelligence and planning abilities to actors, and the latter will be used to encode adaptation rules.

References

1. Agha, G.: An overview of actor languages, vol. 21. ACM (1986)
2. Barat, S., Kulkarni, V., Clark, T., Barn, B.: A simulation-based aid for organisational decision-making. In: Maciaszek, L.A., Cardoso, J.S., Ludwig, A., van Sinderen, M., Cabello, E. (eds.) Proceedings of the 11th International Joint Conference on Software Technologies (ICSOFT 2016), ICSOFT-PT, Lisbon, Portugal, 24–26 July 2016, vol. 2, pp. 109–116. SciTePress (2016)
3. Barn, B.S., Clark, T., Kulkarni, V.: Next generation enterprise modelling - the role of organizational theory and multi-agent systems. In: Holzinger, A., Libourel, T., Maciaszek, L.A., Mellor, S.J. (eds.) Proceedings of the 9th International Conference on Software Engineering and Applications, ICSOFT-EA 2014, Vienna, Austria, 29–31 August 2014, pp. 482–487. SciTePress (2014)

4. Clark, T., Kulkarni, V., Barat, S., Barn, B.: Actor monitors for adaptive behaviour. In: Gorthi, R.P., Sarkar, S., Medvidovic, N., Kulkarni, V., Kumar, A., Joshi, P., Inverardi, P., Sureka, A., Sharma, R. (eds.) Proceedings of the 10th Innovations in Software Engineering Conference, ISEC 2017, Jaipur, India, 5–7 February 2017, pp. 85–95. ACM (2017)
5. Kulkarni, V., Barat, S., Clark, T., Barn, B.S.: Toward overcoming accidental complexity in organisational decision-making. In: 18th ACM/IEEE International Conference on Model Driven Engineering Languages and Systems, MoDELS 2015, Ottawa, ON, Canada, 30 September–2 October 2015, pp. 368–377 (2015)
6. Macal, C.M., North, M.J.: Tutorial on agent-based modelling and simulation. J. Simul. 4(3), 151–162 (2010)
7. McDermott, T., Rouse, W., Goodman, S., Loper, M.: Multi-level modeling of complex socio-technical systems. Procedia Comput. Sci. 16, 1132–1141 (2013)
8. Meadows, D.H., Wright, D.: Thinking in Systems: A primer. Chelsea Green Publishing, White River Junction, Vermont (2008)
9. O'Connor, T., Wong, H.Y.: Emergent properties (2002)
10. Stoecker, R.: Emergence or reduction? Essays on the prospects of nonreductive physicalism. Philos. Phenomenological Res. 55(3), 701–706 (1995)
11. Thomas, M., McGarry, F.: Top-down vs. bottom-up process improvement. IEEE Softw. 11(4), 12–13 (1994)

Heráclito: Learning Environment to Teach Logic

Fabiane Flores Penteado Galafassi[1(✉)], Cristiano Galafassi[2], João Carlos Gluz[3],
Rosa Maria Vicari[1], and Rafael Koch Peres[1]

[1] Instituto de Informática, Universidade Federal do Rio Grande do Sul,
Porto Alegre, RS 91501-970, Brazil
fabiane.penteado@gmail.com, rosa@inf.ufrgs.br,
rafaelkperes@gmail.com
[2] Universidade Federal do Pampa (UNIPAMPA), Campus Itaqui, Itaqui, RS 97650-000, Brazil
cristianogalafassi@gmail.com
[3] Programa Interdisciplinar de Pós Graduação em Computação Aplicada (PIPCA),
Universidade do Vale do Rio dos Sinos (UNISINOS), Caixa Postal 275, São Leopoldo,
RS 93022-000, Brazil
jcgluz@unisinos.br

Abstract. The present paper aims to present the Heráclito environment. The Heráclito is an Intelligent Tutoring System focused on teaching Logic and assists students in solving exercises that ask them to calculate the logical value of a formula, going through truth table exercises, and even doing argument-proof exercises through rules of Natural Deduction. In order to do so, it provides the Electronic Logic Exercise Notebook - LOGOS (Free to use at http://obaa.unisinos.br/heraclito/.) [1] (with two different test editors) that allows creating and editing formulas, truth tables and proofs of Natural Deduction to Propositional Logic.

1 Introduction

The subject of Logic [6], addressed in higher education, is a basic and compulsory subject for all courses covering computer science and informatics [2]. Fundamental to the training of undergraduates, the Logic discipline enables the development of the skills of logical analysis, formalization and problem solving. These skills, in turn, are necessary for the understanding of the several contents and activities found in the curricular components of computer science and informatics. A statistical survey [5] conducted in the last ten years pointed to very high rates of fail and dropout, leading to higher retention of students. These dropouts, in particular, tend to occur at the beginning of the subject, especially when the contents of Natural Deduction began to be addressed in the context of Propositional Logic. In practice, the difficulties begin when concepts such as formula, rule of deduction and formal proof begin to be presented. In order to improve the presented indexes, a dialectical teaching method was used, associated to a sociohistorical approach, and a model of computer mediation, modeled in an Intelligent Tutor System (ITS), which was called Heráclito Environment.

Y. Demazeau et al. (Eds.): PAAMS 2017, LNAI 10349, pp. 316–320, 2017.
DOI: 10.1007/978-3-319-59930-4_28

The Heráclito environment is an ITS and can be termed as a learning object that aims to support the teaching of Logic. Its test editors have the main functionality of assisting the elaboration of exercises and to calculate the logical value of a formula, truth table exercises and proofs of formal arguments through the rules of Natural Deduction in Propositional logic. Its focus is associated with the use of agent technologies with pedagogical characteristics that make use of teaching-learning strategies, seeking to help the student in his reasoning process in solving a problem in the form of exercise [4].

The current version has the support of a tutor (online) in the process of resolution of exercises and its access is via Web Browser, which has made the tool adaptive. Associated with this responsive characteristic, its recent reprogramming, using the Prolog language, standardized the set of pedagogical agents (students profile, mediator and specialist) that work together with the specialist system, also developed in Prolog.

The Heráclito environment is part of the OBAAMILOS project [7], and its software architecture is compatible with the MILOS[1] agent infrastructure. To facilitate interoperability between devices and the reusability of the Heráclito environment, it is encapsulated in the form of a Learning Object (LO) and is part of the OBAA Educational Content Repository, at Federal University of Rio Grande do Sul.

2 Main Purpose

Developed in 2011 and updated since then, the Heráclito environment [5] has gone through versions for Desktop and Mobiles until arriving at a graphical interface that uses Web Browsers for access with responsive characteristics, combining technologies that comprise HTML 5, CSS 3, Java and also JavaScript.

The environment can be used in two ways: offline, as a visiting user, but without tutoring services; and online, with the support of the tutoring service, being necessary to log in to access the resources. The procedure for log in and access to the system in online mode is through a simple registration, where it requires minimum user information such as: email, name and a password. After registration, to log in the environment requires email and the password that were previously registered.

The Heráclito environment was developed through the use of agent technology for pedagogical purposes, responsible for student interaction with the system and also access to the intelligent tutor that assists in the development of the resolution of the exercises indicating correct, incorrect and not recommended paths during the course of the proof. This tutorial service aims to help the student in the step by step of solving the exercises, playing the teachers role. As a student interacts with the environment, the agents are monitoring their actions, ready to assist in case of need. If the student is unable to advance in a test, the student can also ask the tutor for tips or suggestions through the Help button (which can also be activated at any time during the exercise). This tutorial service uses a set of learning strategies, developed specifically for Logic, based on classroom experiences that help the student perform, for example, a Natural Deduction test.

---

[1] More information at: http://www.portalobaa.org/padrao-obaa/relatorios-tecnicos/copy_of_1o-relatorio-parcial-obaa-milos-comunidade-finep/AnexoA-EspecArqMILOSV10.pdf/view.

When developing the Web interface of the Heráclito environment, we choose for the client-server architecture. This choice was made due to the security and performance that this methodology, coupled with adequate programming languages, can offer to the system. It should be noted that this interface was also developed with the purpose of portability, *i.e.*, to be portable for different devices with different capacities, screen sizes and different performances as well. With the use of the client-server architecture, it is possible to exchange messages between the interface and the system, leaving all the logical and the agents' part being processed entirely inside the server, which makes the system extremely light and portable for any device that has a web browser.

Aiming at increasing security, robustness, compatibility with various systems and screen sizes, was used to develop the Bootstrap framework. This framework provides a range of ready-made elements in HTML 5, CSS 3 and JavaScript that help in adapting the site to different screen sizes and several systems making them responsive, which means that the LO can be distributed, with only one version, to several different platforms reaching a greater number of users.

3   Demonstration

As mentioned before, the Heráclito environment uses the technology of pedagogical agents and is composed of a set of agents named: Students Profile, Mediator and Specialist. These agents are responsible for the interaction of the student with the environment and the specialist system, as well as the form of communication between these agents and the editor of formulas and proofs of the Heráclito environment. These agents are responsible for one or more scenarios and can be demonstrated at: http://obaa.unisinos.br/heraclito/index.jsp. Its organization is structured as follows:

- **Student Profile Agent:** This agent represents the student model, which in the Heráclito environment is based on the exercise resolution process;
- **Mediator Agent:** This agent represents the role of the teacher in his didactic-pedagogical function;
- **Specialist Agent:** This agent also represents the role of the teacher, but in his role of specialist in the field of teaching logic.

All agents of the Heráclito environment were developed in the Prolog language and have an interface in Java with JADE platform support for communication between them. This communication between agents in JADE is based on asynchronous messages, that is, an agent that wants to communicate must only transmit a message to an identified destination (or set of destinations), and there being no type of temporal dependence between the transmitter and the receiver.

The messages exchanged between these three agents must pass through the mediating agent, who mediates this communication between the student profile agent and the specialist agent. It is responsible for incorporating the role of the teacher or tutor within the Heráclito environment, the mediator agent provides pedagogical support to the student in its learning process. The main situations in which the Mediator agent will interfere through the application of some mediation strategy are:

1. When an incorrect insertion of hypotheses occurs;
2. When an incorrect deduction rule application occurs;
3. When a correct rule-based application occurs: in this case, even if the application is correct at the operational level, this rule can still be problematic at the behavioral level and can be categorized as useful, redundant, and harmful. The application of a useful rule assumes that the rule is correct (operationally) and contributes to the resolution of the exercise. The application of a redundant rule may be correct at the operational level, but it does not contribute to the resolution of the exercise, and the student only increases the number of lines and rules applied without obtaining the expected result. The harmful rule, when applied, ends up leading the student to a path with no return, that is, with its application, the exercise can not be solved;
4. When the student is idle or does not advance in the resolution of the exercise;
5. When a significant percentage of the test is reached the student is informed and receives an incentive to continue;
6. When there is one step left to complete the resolution, the student is informed in the form of an incentive to finish;
7. When the student asks for help. The answers to the help requests can be three types: a tip, where the system provides the next step to be taken to continue in the resolution process; an example of an appropriate demonstration for the current situation of the student; and how much is missing, This option tells you the number of steps remaining for the end of the exercise.

4   Conclusions

The development and upgrade of the Heráclito environment, it is hoped that it will contribute, not only to a better understanding of the contents covered in the discipline of Logic, but also to reduce the number of dropouts and fails in this context. In relation to future work, the Heráclito environment has been developed in parallel with its current version, in order to identify the level of knowledge of a student within a specific context of logic, expressing mainly what occurs during the interactions with the environment between the student and the teacher (tutor). Using specific teaching-learning strategies for each student profile found.

References

1. Heráclito Environment. http://obaa.unisinos.br/heraclito/. Accessed 01 Feb 2017
2. Portal MEC: Diretrizes Curriculares - Cursos de Graduação. Computação. http://portal.mec.gov.br/component/docman/?task=doc_download&gid=11205&Itemid=. Accessed 01 Feb 2017
3. PortalTAOS3: Sistema de Ensino de Lógica. http://obaa.unisinos.br/drupal7/?q=node/33. Accessed 01 Feb 2017
4. Galafassi, F.F.P., Santos, A.V., Peres, R.K., Vicari, R.M., Gluz, J.C.: Multi-plataform interface to an ITS of proposicional logic teaching. In: Bajo, J., Hallenborg, K., Pawlewski, P., Botti, V., Sánchez-Pi, N., Duque Méndez, N.D., Lopes, F., Julian, V. (eds.) PAAMS 2015. CCIS, vol. 524, pp. 309–319. Springer, Cham (2015). doi:10.1007/978-3-319-19033-4_26

5. Galafassi, F.F.P.: Agente Pedagógico para Mediação do Processo de Ensino-Aprendizagem da Dedução Natural na Lógica Proposicional. Dissertação de Mestrado. UNISINOS (2012). http://biblioteca.asav.org.br/vinculos/000003/00000335.pdf. Accessed 01 Feb 2017
6. Gluz, J.C., Py, M.: Lógica para Computação. Coleção EAD. Editora Unisinos (2010)
7. Viccari, R., Gluz, J., Passerino, L., et al.: The OBAA proposal for learning objects supported by agents. In: Proceedings of MASEIE Workshop – AAMAS 2010, Toronto, Canada (2010)

Computational Platform for Household Simulation and Emulation to Test and Validate Energy Management Methodologies

Luis Gomes[✉] and Zita Vale

GECAD – Research Group on Intelligent Engineering and Computing for Advanced Innovation
and Development, Institute of Engineering – Polytechnic of Porto (ISEP/IPP),
Rua Dr. António Bernardino de Almeida, 431, 4200-072 Porto, Portugal
{lufog,zav}@isep.ipp.pt

Abstract. The integration of microgrids brings advantages for the end-prosumers as well for the grid energy management. Small and medium players became able to actively participate in microgrids. However, is needed a study and the appearance of methodologies that can efficiently integrate these players. The use of load optimization inside households is common in scientific researches. This paper proposes a Java library that can simulate a household using a combination between real and simulated loads. The library also enables the execution of optimization algorithms, to be tested and validated. The paper will present a small demonstration of the library capabilities.

Keywords: Households simulation · Load optimization · Smart homes

1 Introduction

The application of microgrids brings significant advantages to power systems [1], such as, reduce the energy losses, improve the energy quality for the end-prosumers, and bring the small and medium players to active rules [2].

The application of Demand Response (DR) programs in top of microgrids enables an efficient way for small and medium players to interact and actively participate in microgrid and smart grid [3]. These programs depend on the players' response, for this reason, the end-prosumers must have response mechanisms to successfully participate in these programs.

The concept of Smart Homes brings intelligent to our households. This concept has a clear fit with the DR participation, as can be seen in [4, 5]. A Smart Home enables the energy management in our houses while providing intelligence to our lives. The aggregation of IoT devices and energy intelligent management methodologies can be integrated in Smart Homes to provide autonomous and intelligence responses to DR programs.

This paper proposes a Java library capable of simulate a Smart Home using simulate and/or real devices (sensors and energy devices). The library was developed in Java and

© Springer International Publishing AG 2017
Y. Demazeau et al. (Eds.): PAAMS 2017, LNAI 10349, pp. 321–324, 2017.
DOI: 10.1007/978-3-319-59930-4_29

provides the ability to create and manage loads, create living scenarios, and execute load optimization algorithms.

For the demonstration, the library will be applied in a Multi-Agent System (MAS) that simulates a microgrid. Their agents will use the Smart House Library (SHL) to simulate loads and integrate real loads available in our laboratory. For testing the optimization capabilities, a continuous optimization algorithm will be executed. The algorithm, presented in [6], allows a real-time load optimization during a given period. The optimization complies with user preferences and house context, using environmental variables to identify the house context.

After this introduction section, the paper will describe the library main purpose in Sect. 2. A demonstration scenario will be presented and analyzed in Sect. 3, using a load optimization algorithm. And in Sect. 4 is presented the main conclusions.

2   Main Purpose

The main purpose of this work was to build a Java library with house simulation capabilities, using simulated energy devices and real energy devices. This library enables the testing and validation of load optimization algorithm to be applied in households. A previous version was presented in [7].

The proposed library can represent environmental aspects of the house, such as, the number and location of the people inside the house, the outside and inside temperature, and the inside clarity. Regarding energy loads, the library is able to work with simulated loads (simulated locally or externally) and real loads. The combination of simulated and real devices powered the library to a more complete solution.

The library powers up Multi-Agent Systems (MAS), such as, MASGriP [8], enabling the presence of simulated houses in the MAS. This brings highly advantages if the MAS focus is, or depends on, the household energy optimization and management.

3   Demonstration

For this demonstration, it will be shown the advantages of the proposed library when integrated with MASGriP. It will be used a continuous optimization algorithm for load optimization [6]. The optimization will react to the users' action.

Figure 1 shows the android interface used as a library external interface. Using this interface is possible to see general parameters of the house, as well as, monitor and control all the loads and execute optimization algorithms. The demonstrated house has the following set of loads available for optimization:

- 1 set of lamps, in the living room (390 W) – this is a real variable load that can range their consumption between 0 W to 390 W;
- 1 refrigerator, in the kitchen (120 W) – this is a simulated discrete load;
- 2 heaters, one in the living room and other in the room, (2.0 kW) – these are simulated discrete loads;
- 1 water heater, in the attic (1.5 kW) – this is a simulated discrete load.

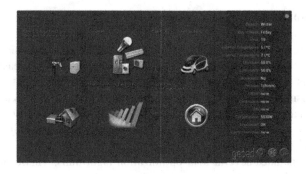

Fig. 1. Android interface for tablet

The house in configured in the library were is possible to add multiple loads, such as, real loads controlled using Modbus/TCP (directly or through a Programmable Logic Controller), simulated loads (discrete or variable) and continuous loads (simulated loads that follow real load profiles).

The continuous optimization, available in SHL, is used for this demonstration scenario. This optimization runs through a given period of time and reacts to the users actions, maintaining a limit consumption (offset) in the house overall consumption. The optimization offset can be stablish for the user or received by the microgrid as part of a DR program. For this demonstration the offset is: ***3500 W***. The actions of the user during the algorithm execution are:

- *Action 0* - in this action the optimization starts having a person in the bedroom. The loads that are turned on are: Heater 1 and 2, the Lights and the Water Heater;
- *Action 1* - the user enters the living room and turns on Heater 2 and the Lights;
- *Action 2* - in the last action, the user turns off Heater 2.

Table 1 shows the results of the algorithm using the previous actions.

Table 1. Demonstration scenario

Rooms	Loads	Act. 0	Res	Act. 1	Res	Act. 2	Res
Bedroom	Heater 1	2000	2000	2000	-	-	
Living	Lights	333	355	360	365	375	370
Room	Heater 2	2000	-	2000	2000	-	
Kitchen	Refrigerator	-	-	-	-	-	
Attic	Water Heater	1500	-	-	-	-	1500
		5833	2355	4360	2365	375	1870

At the starting point, where the user is at the bedroom, the algorithm turns off Heater 2 and the Water Heater. When the user moves to the living room the algorithm opts to turn off Heater 1. In action 3, the user turns off Heater 2 and the algorithm takes the reaction of turn on the Water Heater that previously was turned off.

4 Conclusions

The Smart House Library is a versatile and complete solution for house simulation using a combination between real and simulated loads. Being a library, it is easy to integrate with multi-agent systems that operate in smart grids and microgrids fields.

The dynamism of the library enables the creation of multiple houses using the same library. The scenario, loads and environment can be determined by the user. The Android interface enables the users to go 'inside' the house in real-time. The ability to integrate real loads brings the reality to the simulation world.

The library includes several load optimization algorithms. This enables the load optimization for demand response participation and energy management. The algorithms take into account the users preferences according to the house environment. Each house, can choose a different algorithm to run, seeing the different results.

References

1. Fu, Q., Montoya, L.F., Solanki, A., Nasiri, A., Bhavaraju, V., Abdallah, T., Yu, D.C.: Microgrid generation capacity design with renewables and energy storage addressing power quality and surety. IEEE Trans. Smart Grid 3(4), 2019–2027 (2012)
2. Gomes, L., Faria, P., Morais, H., Vale, Z., Ramos, C.: Distributed, agent-based intelligent system for demand response program simulation in smart grids. IEEE Intell. Syst. 29, 56–65 (2014)
3. Siano, P.: Demand response and smart grids - A survey. Renew. Sustain. Energy Rev. 30, 461–478 (2014)
4. Tsui, K.M., Chan, S.C.: Demand response optimization for smart home scheduling under real-time pricing. IEEE Trans. Smart Grid 3, 1812–1821 (2012)
5. Fernandes, F., Carreiro, A., Morais, H., Vale, Z., Gastaldello, D.S., Amaral, H.L.M., Souza, A.N.: Management of heating, ventilation and air conditioning system for SHIM platform. In: IEEE PES Innovative Smart Grid Technologies Latin America (ISGT LATAM), Montevideo, pp. 275–280 (2015)
6. Gomes, L., Faria, P., Fernandes, F., Vale, Z., Ramos, C.: Domestic consumption simulation and management using a continuous consumption management and optimization algorithm. In: IEEE PES T&D Conference and Exposition, Chicago, IL, USA, pp. 1–5 (2014)
7. Gomes, L., Amaral, H.L.M., Fernandes, F., Faria, P., Vale, Z., Ramos, C.: Dynamic approach and testbed for small and medium players simulation in smart grid environments. IFAC Proc. Volumes 47(3), 31–36 (2014)
8. Morais, H., Vale, Z., Pinto, T., Gomes, L., Fernandes, F., Oliveira, P., Ramos, C.: Multi-agent based smart grid management and simulation: Situation awareness and learning in a test bed with simulated and real installations and players. In: 2013 IEEE Power and Energy Society General Meeting, Vancouver, BC, pp. 1–5 (2013)

Learning Styles Multi-agents Simulation

Emilcy Juliana Hernandez[1]([✉]), Luis Felipe Londoño[1], Mauricio Giraldo[2],
Valentina Tabares[1], and Néstor Darío Duque[1]

[1] Universidad Nacional de Colombia Sede Manizales, Manizales, Colombia
{ejhernandezl,lflondonor,vtabaresm,ndduqueme}@unal.edu.co
[2] Universidad Nacional de Colombia Sede Medellín, Medellín, Colombia
maugiraldooca@unal.edu.co

Abstract. This article aims to give an approach of a simulation of students with their learning styles which going to receive a learning resources or learning objects (LO) from the teacher and the students simulated it going to change their behavior according to the LO received. The multi-agent system is basing in some rules in order to calculate the best behavior of the student's group. To obtain the behavior it use a set of rules that was develop and previously developed works.

1 Introduction

Learning styles progress has generated new academic spaces that can improve the performance and the acquisition of knowledge of students in classes. The development of different works where analyze the impact and de effects of the learning styles for diverse purposes [1–3]. This works shows changed results, for that reason in this work it going to do a simulation of students with their learning styles which going to receive a learning resources or learning objects (LO) from the teacher and the students simulated it going to change their behavior according to the LO received. When the simulation is over the user it going to have a list with the learning objects and the students that accept them.

2 Main Purpose

The main purpose of this work is do a simulation where it can shows how the behaviors of the agents changed according to the resource that receive. To do the change of the behaviors of the agents, was defined some rules in based to the rules of the RAIM project [4].

The learning style model that was adopt in this work was the hybrid model purpose for Rodríguez, Duque y Ovalle in the work [5]. This hybrid model is a combination between Felder y Silverman model and the VARK model.

In the Fig. 1, it shows the model that was purpose for this multi-agent simulation of learning styles and a chart with the acceptance rules. This model shows that the simulation had four modules; the first module is the user interaction with the interface and upload the file with the agents that it going to be create. The second module is the

© Springer International Publishing AG 2017
Y. Demazeau et al. (Eds.): PAAMS 2017, LNAI 10349, pp. 325–328, 2017.
DOI: 10.1007/978-3-319-59930-4_30

communication between the interface and de controller agent, the third module is where the controller agent send the behaviors of the agents that the simulation going to create. The fourth module is when the agents created receive the resources and change their behaviors according to the resources, for this module is used, the acceptance rules which has three rules for each of the eight learning styles and it can shows near to the model and the last module is when the user obtain the results of the simulation.

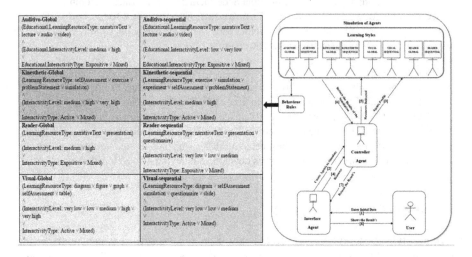

Fig. 1. Learning styles simulation model

3 Demonstration

In the Fig. 2, it can see how the simulation works. First of all the user upload a file to the system with the users to simulate. After that, the user enter the search string of the thematic of the class. Then the system search the learning object that exist in the repository of learning objects roapRAIM and list the results where the user select a learning objects who is going to enter the simulation. Subsequently the simulation start to work and when is over, it shows the result to the user with the learning objects and a list with the user to may be accept the contents of the thematic with the LO. In addition, it is presented through a visual aid which students react to the presented learning object. At the start of the simulation all the boxes of students appear in gray, then when making the LO the boxes of the students that react to the LO change to blue color.

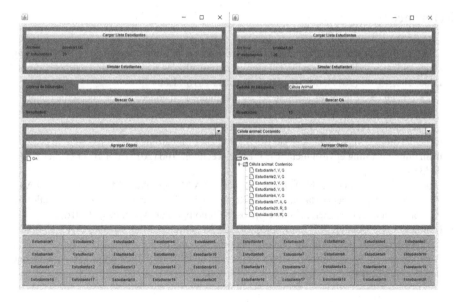

Fig. 2. Learning styles multi-agent simulation. (Color figure online)

4   Conclusions and Future Work

The developed of the simulation shows potential for the multi-agent system in issues of educational informatics and especially in problems of allocation of educational resources for a group of students with diverse styles of learning. The paper introduces a demo about how to allocate the educational resources into a simulate environment through agents that representing students.

The system can be used for the teacher to manage the allocation of educational resources to a group of students, since it allows:

- Verify how many students properly receive the assigned educational resource
- Determine whether an educational resource designed for a particular learning style really fits for the students
- The simulation allows reducing times that the teacher would take in verifying if the educational resources are adapted according to the learning styles of its students

As future work, it going to do real simulation of persons with their learning styles which going to evaluate the learning objects and we going to compare the results with the results of the multi-agent simulation and validate if the multi-agent simulation that was done is similar to the real simulation.

References

1. Buckley, P., Doyle, E.: Individualising gamification: an investigation of the impact of learning styles and personality traits on the efficacy of gamification using a prediction market. Comput. Educ. **106**, 43–55 (2017). doi:10.1016/j.compedu.2016.11.009
2. Li, X., Yang, X.: Effects of learning styles and interest on concentration and achievement of students in mobile learning. J. Educ. Comput. Res. **54**, 922–945 (2016). doi: 10.1177/0735633116639953. 0735633116639953
3. Cela, K., Sicilia, M.Á., Sanchez-Alonso, S.: Influence of learning styles on cognitive presence in an online learning environment. Br. J. Educ. Technol., 100 (2015). doi:10.1111/bjet.12267. 3433707
4. Morales, V.T., Méndez, N.D.D., Rodríguez, P.A.M., Giraldo, M.O., Ovalle, D.A.C.: Plataforma Adaptativa para la Búsqueda y Recuperación de Recursos Educativos Digitales. In: XI Conferencia Latinoamericana de Objetos y Tecnologías de Aprendizaje (2016)
5. Morales, V.T., Méndez, N.D.D., Rodríguez, P.A.M., Giraldo, M.O., Ovalle, D.A.C.: Análisis de Características del Perfil de Usuario para un Sistema de Recomendación de Objetos de Aprendizaje. In: IX Conferencia Latinoamericana de Objetos y Tecnologías de Aprendizaje, pp. 487–493 (2014)

Hardware Integration and Real-Time Control in an Agent-Based Distribution Grid Simulation

Nils Loose[1(✉)], Sebastian Törsleff[2], Christian Derksen[1], Rainer Unland[1], and Alexander Fay[2]

[1] DAWIS, ICB, University of Duisburg-Essen, Essen, Germany
{nils.loose,christian.derksen,rainer.unland}@icb.uni-due.de
[2] IfA, Helmut Schmidt University, Hamburg, Germany
{sebastian.toersleff,alexander.fay}@hsu-hh.de

1 Introduction

In recent years, several developments in the energy sector have been imposing major challenges on our energy supply infrastructure. Due to the liberalization of the energy markets that started in the 1990s, longstanding monopolies are being broken up and new actors enter the stage. An increasing awareness regarding the environmental impacts of fossil fuel-based electricity generation put renewable energy sources like wind and solar on a lasting growth path. The volatility inherent to these sources and the shift from centralized to decentralized generation necessitate new approaches as to how energy is marketed, distributed and consumed. The smart grid, i.e. equipping the energy infrastructure with modern information and communication technology, is widely considered essential in addressing the challenges outlined.

The research project Agent.HyGrid[1] aims to contribute to the future smart grid by developing an agent-based control solution for low voltage distribution grids. Following initial simulations of our control solution and serving as a precursor to the field test, we are currently in the stage of evaluating elements of the control solution in a testbed environment. The following section summarizes the theoretical foundations of our approach. In Sect. 3 we present the testbed environment. The paper closes with conclusions and a brief outlook.

2 Theoretical Foundations

Several coordination mechanisms for smart grids that employ multi-agent systems have been proposed [1–3]. While these concepts share a focus on energy markets, we aim to elaborate on the modeling and control of technical systems and thus establish a more robust foundation for determining flexibilities in terms of energy production, consumption and storage. The foundations of our approach are unified Energy Agents [4] and the Energy Option Model (EOM) framework [5].

---

[1] www.agent-hygrid.net.

© Springer International Publishing AG 2017
Y. Demazeau et al. (Eds.): PAAMS 2017, LNAI 10349, pp. 329–332, 2017.
DOI: 10.1007/978-3-319-59930-4_31

An Energy Agent is a software entity that controls an arbitrary technical system in a smart grid. To do so, the agent is equipped with a model of the technical system that is based on the EOM framework and serves as the internal knowledge model, making the Energy Agent a deliberative agent in the sense of the BDI concept [6]. The model comprises the operating states of the system, state durations and transitions, and control and state variables. Hence, the Energy Agent is enabled to determine the system's flexibility with respect to consumption, conversion, and/or storage of energy. Being based on the fundamentals of thermodynamics, the EOM framework is not limited to electricity. Instead it allows to model arbitrary energy carriers as well as conversion processes between them.

The EOM-based model facilitates the implementation of evaluation and control strategies, which can be used within agent behaviors for schedule generation and real-time control of the underlying technical system.

The engineering process applied in Agent.HyGrid is based on [4]. Following requirements engineering, design and initial implementation, the resulting Energy Agents are tested in a simulation environment. In the next stage, we proceed to a testbed environment, where the Energy Agents are deployed on distributed hardware whilst the electricity grid they are interacting with is still simulated. The final stage is a field test in which the Energy Agents control real-world systems.

3   Demonstration

Our demonstration illustrates the deployment of an Energy Agent in a testbed environment. In this execution mode, the Energy Agent runs on dedicated hardware and interacts with a technical system, while being connected to a simulated electricity grid. The technical system controlled by the agent can either be a simulated one or real hardware. A detailed discussion on deploying Energy Agents in testbed scenarios is given in [7]. In our demonstration, we focus on three aspects:

1. The interaction of testbed agents with the simulation
2. The integration of real hardware into the simulation
3. The real-time control of energy conversion systems

The simulation runs on Agent.GUI [8], a simulation environment that is based on the well-known JADE framework[2]. Agent.GUI provides various tools to support the development and execution of agent-based simulations, e.g. the definition of network-based environment models.

In our demonstration, we use the model of an electric distribution grid. The model mainly comprises generic prosumer agents, who are following fixed energy consumption or production schedules. Two specialized agents with detailed system models and dynamic behavior are involved: A wind turbine and an electrolyzer agent. The network model is shown in Fig. 1.

---

[2] http://jade.tilab.com/.

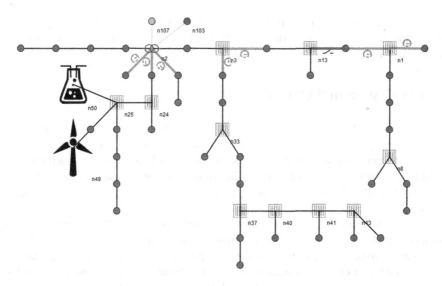

Fig. 1. The network model (Color figure online)

In Agent.HyGrid, a power flow calculation algorithm has been implemented that determines the grid state based on the information provided by the involved systems. The runtime visualization of the grid state is aligned with the Smart Grid Traffic Light Concept defined by the German Association of Energy and Water Industries [9]:

– Green: No critical network situation exists
– Amber: Potential or actual network shortage
– Red: Direct risk to the security of supply

The testbed agent in the demonstration scenario represents a wind turbine. The agent is deployed from the simulation environment and executed on an industrial PC that will be used in the planned field test as well. Unlike the prosumer agents, electricity production of the wind turbine is determined using a dynamic EOM-based model that takes the wind speed as input. To demonstrate the integration of a real technical system, a toy wind turbine is used to provide real-time data for the wind velocity. The turbine is attached to an Arduino Nano that has been programmed to digitize analogue input data. Via an interface the data measured by the Arduino Nano is scaled up and mapped to the wind turbine model, which in turn calculates the generated power. This value is then passed over to the power flow calculation algorithm for the simulated distribution grid. By blowing at the wind turbine, the user can control its power generation, and observe how it influences the state of the simulated distribution grid.

As can be seen from the demonstration, a high feed-in from the wind turbine can easily cause upper voltage limit violations. Therefore, in the second stage of the demonstration, we introduce an electrolyzer model to the simulation that is dynamically controlled by a second Energy Agent. An electrolyzer produces hydrogen from electric power. The hydrogen can be fed into the gas network. Through observation of the voltage at its grid connection point, the Energy Agent controlling the electrolyzer determines when to increase hydrogen production and thereby positively influences voltage levels, i.e. it helps reduce voltage limit violations. The violations henceforth only occur for very brief moments.

4 Conclusions and Outlook

We have demonstrated a testbed agent that is operating in a simulated environment while also interacting with a real energy conversion system. By blowing at a toy wind turbine, one can influence the power fed into a simulated distribution grid. Furthermore, the capability of the EOM to implement real-time control strategies has been demonstrated. When the voltage reaches a critical level, an Energy Agents ramps up a simulated electrolyzer to decrease the voltage.

The next step will be to control a real technical system. For that purpose, we will implement an Energy Agent for a photovoltaic inverter that is connected to a small scale solar plant. Furthermore, the capability of the EOM to handle different energy carriers has not been fully exploited in our demonstration. In future simulations, we will integrate a gas grid in which the hydrogen can be fed into, and impose additional restrictions, e.g. time-variant feed-in constraints.

References

1. Lehnhoff, S.: Dezentrales vernetztes Energiemanagement. Vieweg+Teubner, Wiesbaden (2010)
2. Linnenberg, T., Wior, I., Schreiber, S., Fay, A.: A market-based multi-agent-system for decentralized power and grid control. In: ETFA2011, pp. 1–8 (2011)
3. Kok, K.: The PowerMatcher: smart coordination for the smart electricity grid. Amsterdam (2013)
4. Derksen, C., Linnenberg, T., Unland, R., Fay, A.: Unified energy agents as a base for the systematic development of future energy grids. In: Klusch, M., Thimm, M., Paprzycki, M. (eds.) MATES 2013. LNCS, vol. 8076, pp. 236–249. Springer, Heidelberg (2013). doi: 10.1007/978-3-642-40776-5_21
5. Derksen, C., Linnenberg, T., Unland, R., Fay, A.: Structure and classification of unified energy agents as a base for the systematic development of future energy grids. Eng. Appl. Artif. Intell. **41**, 310–324 (2015)
6. Rao, A.S., Georgeff, M.P., et al.: BDI agents: from theory to practice. In: ICMAS 1995, pp. 312–319 (1995)
7. Loose, N., Derksen, C., Unland, R.: Testbed application of energy agents. In: SmartER Europe 2017 Conference Proceedings (2017, accepted for publication)
8. Derksen, C., Branki, C., Unland, R.: Agent.GUI: a multi-agent based simulation framework. In: 2011 Federated Conference on Computer Science and Information Systems (FedCSIS), pp. 623–630 (2011)
9. German Association of Energy and Water Industries: Smart Grid Traffic Light Concept – Discussion Paper (2015)

Electric Vehicle Urban Exploration by Anti-pheromone Swarm Based Algorithms

Rubén Martín García[1]([✉]), Francisco Prieto-Castrillo[1,2],
Gabriel Villarrubia González[1], and Javier Bajo[1]

[1] BISITE Research Group, University of Salamanca, Edificio I+D+i, 37008 Salamanca, Spain
{rubenmg,franciscop,gvg}@usal.es, jbajo@fi.upm.es
[2] MediaLab, Massachusetts Institute of Technology, 20 Amherst Street, Cambridge, MA, USA
fprieto@mit.edu

Abstract. In this work we show how a simple anti-pheromone ant foraging based algorithm can be effective in urban navigation by reducing exploration times. We use a distributed multi agent architecture to test this algorithm. Swarm collaboration is analysed for a synthetic scenario. The maps were generated with a random-walk type process. We validate our approach by monitoring the dynamics of three real prototypes built at the laboratory, we check both the feasibility of our approach and the robustness of the algorithm.

Keywords: Smart Cities · Route optimization · Swarm intelligence · Robots

1 Introduction

A major challenge in Smart Cities (SC) [1] is the dynamic optimization of routes under different criteria. The objective is to manage a flood of electrical vehicles efficiently and in a sustainable way. The problem can be solved with different strategies, one of the most common found in literature is the use of a bio-inspired algorithms [2].

In this work we provide an implementation of a well-known bio-inspired meta-heuristic to analyze the collaborative routing of electric vehicles in cities. Moreover, we investigate the behavior of a swarm of robots in real environments.

The main difficulty in coordinating a robot swarm lies in the communication among units. In this regard, previous works can be split into implicit/indirect and explicit/direct communication. Implicit communication –also known as *stigmergy*– is based on the context and some of its most typical uses can be found in [3–5]. In this regard, the Pioneer work of Pierre-Paul Grasse in termite colonies revealed the communication mechanisms of these insects by means of chemical signalling and in particular by pheromones [6]. These observations resulted in an ant-based exploration algorithm [7]. Here, each ant leaves a pheromone trail in its foraging activity. This trail persists for some time and it is followed by other ants in the search of food resources.

Also, the pheromone approach has been widely adapted to several artificial intelligence problems in its converse flavour (i.e. anti-pheromones) [8, 9]. In particular, some researchers have used anti-pheromone (APH) proxies to optimize robot exploration [10].

© Springer International Publishing AG 2017
Y. Demazeau et al. (Eds.): PAAMS 2017, LNAI 10349, pp. 333–336, 2017.
DOI: 10.1007/978-3-319-59930-4_32

The main advantage is that each unit accesses a different region fostering the diversity of the solutions by means of indirect and decentralized communication.

On the other hand, the efficient exploration and target localization in urban environments is gaining more and more attention [11, 12]. However, bio-inspired algorithms tailored to optimize robot exploration and dynamic route generation in SC are somewhat separate research fields.

2   Aim

In this work we propose an APH-based robot swarm exploration strategy to optimize routes in Smart Cities. In particular, we combine knowledge from robotics with the SC paradigm to analyse intelligent routing of cooperating electric vehicles. We describe how a simple APH-based algorithm can be effective in locating targets in a city.

For the distributed execution of the Anti-pheromone swarm algorithm we have used the multi-agent architecture PANGEA [13], previously developed in the BISITE research group. This Multi-Agent System (MAS) allows the implementation of embedded agents in computationally limited devices, allowing a simple communication among the different elements.

To this end, we have also built real robot prototypes in order to test the APH navigation strategy in the laboratory.

3   Demonstration

3.1   Robot Swarm City Exploration

The reason for using real robots in our experiments is that, as electric vehicles, they are subjected to events which are similar to those commonly found in real EV scenarios. In particular, the measurement errors of position in a real environment map to our prototype setting. Moreover, the lab tests allow us to explore the robustness of our approach, which is the major concern in real implementations.

The laboratory tests have been implemented with the MAS design mentioned above. The map has been constructed by printing connected segments of black lines on a white surface according to the general patterns in our simulations.

Each robot moves forward through the lines until it reaches an intersection. Then it sends an MQTT message to the Conflicts and Monitor VOs to determine the next move. This is done by counting the current APH level of the possible paths at the cross and by selecting that with the minimum APH amount. Once the path is selected the APH level is updated.

3.2   Anti-pheromone Algorithm

The navigation algorithm we present in this work (pseudocode in Fig. 1) is an adaptation of the classical two-dimensional APH gradient [4] to a 1D gridded world. This world consists of a set of parallel and perpendicular lines arranged in a way that mimics urban topologies.

```
while current location ≠ target do
    if current location = intersection then
        [paths] ← get all paths with the lowest and same level of
            anti-pheromones;
        if size (paths) > 1 then
            | angle ← angle of random path in [paths];
        else
            | angle ← angle of the path in [paths];
        end
        turn ( angle );
        go on;
    else if current location = dead end then
        | turn ( 180° );
    else
        | drop anti-pheromone;
        | go on;
    end
end
```

Fig. 1. Anti-pheromone navigation algorithm. Each time a robot reaches an intersection which is neither a target nor a dead end, a negative APH gradient based route is followed.

4 Conclusions

In this work the classical anti-pheromone ant foraging algorithm has been adapted to the problem of optimal routing in Smart Cities. We have validated our approach by real laboratory tests with robots. The maps were generated with a random-walk type process. Swarm collaboration results in a significant reduction of the arrival times.

We have validated the possibilities for a real implementation of our strategy in the laboratory facilities of the BISITE research group at the University of Salamanca. To this end, three prototypes have been constructed to check the proposed MAS architecture and the robustness of the APH based strategy in real conditions.

From the statistical analysis of the experiments the collaboration among robots has been quantified in terms of the elapsed times to reach a target. We have shown how an increase in the number of units and in map complexity results in higher exploration times. The swarm collaboration mechanisms of our design has shown to be effective both in simulations and laboratory and can be implemented in real Smart City scenarios.

Regardless of the topology of the city, the proposed decentralized collaborative navigation strategy can be valuable to the design of new routing patterns without compromising efficiency. At its current stage the navigability improvement is only shown when compared with the non-swarm limit.

References

1. Degbelo, A., Granell, C., Trilles, S., Bhattacharya, D., Casteleyn, S., Kray, C.: Opening up Smart Cities: citizen-centric challenges and opportunities from GIScience. ISPRS Int. J. Geo-Inf. **5**(2), 16 (2016)
2. Zambonelli, F.: Engineering self-organizing urban superorganisms. Eng. Appl. Artif. Intell. **41**, 325–332 (2015)
3. Payton, D., Estkowski, R., Howard, M.: Compound behaviors in pheromone robotics. Robot. Auton. Syst. **44**(3–4), 229–240 (2003)
4. Kramer, R.: Animal & Machine Intelligence Essay Stigmergic Communication: Achieving so much without saying a word (2005)
5. Mir, I., Amavasai, B.P.: A fully decentralized approach for incremental perception. In: Proceedings of the 1st International Conference on Robot Communication and Coordination, Piscataway, NJ, USA, pp. 10:1–10:7 (2007)
6. Grassé, P.-P.: La reconstruction du nid et les coordinations interindividuelles chezBellicositermes natalensis etCubitermes sp. la théorie de la stigmergie: Essai d'interprétation du comportement des termites constructeurs. Insectes Soc. **6**(1), 41–80 (1959)
7. Dorigo, M., Birattari, M., Stutzle, T.: Ant colony optimization. IEEE Comput. Intell. Mag. **1**(4), 28–39 (2006)
8. Fossum, F., Montanier, J.M., Haddow, P.C.: Repellent pheromones for effective swarm robot search in unknown environments. In: 2014 IEEE Symposium on Swarm Intelligence, pp. 1–8 (2014)
9. Oliveira, J.R., Calvo, R., Romero, R.A.F.: Integration of virtual pheromones for mapping/exploration of environments by using multiple robots. In: 5th IEEE RAS/EMBS International Conference on Biomedical Robotics and Biomechatronics, pp. 835–840 (2014)
10. Ravankar, A., Ravankar, A.A., Kobayashi, Y., Emaru, T.: On a bio-inspired hybrid pheromone signalling for efficient map exploration of multiple mobile service robots. Artif. Life Robot. **21**(2), 221–231 (2016)
11. Billhardt, H., Lujak, M., Sánchez-Brunete, V., Fernández, A., Ossowski, S.: Dynamic coordination of ambulances for emergency medical assistance services. Knowl.-Based Syst. **70**, 268–280 (2014)
12. Lujak, M., Giordani, S., Ossowski, S.: Route guidance: bridging system and user optimization in traffic assignment. Neurocomputing **151**, part 1, 449–460 (2015)
13. Villarrubia, G., De Paz, J.F., Bajo, J., Corchado, J.M.: Ambient agents: embedded agents for remote control and monitoring using the PANGEA platform. Sensors **14**(8), 13955–13979 (2014)

Modeling Social Influence in Social Networks with SOIL, a Python Agent-Based Social Simulator

Eduardo Merino, Jesús M. Sánchez, David García,
J. Fernando Sánchez-Rada, and Carlos A. Iglesias[(✉)]

Intelligent Systems Group, DIT, E.T.S. de Ingenieros de Telecomunicación,
Universidad Politécnica de Madrid, 28040 Madrid, Spain
{eduardo.merinom,jesusmanuel.sanchez.martinez,
david.garcia.martin}@alumnos.upm.es, {jfernando,cif}@dit.upm.es
http://www.gsi.dit.upm.es

Abstract. The application of Agent-based Social Simulation (ABSS) for modeling social networks requires specific facilities for modeling, simulation and visualization of network structures. Moreover, ABSS can benefit from interactive shell facilities that can assist the model development process. We have addressed these problems through the development of a tool called SOIL, which provides a Python ABSS specifically designed for social networks. In this paper we present how this tool is applied to simulate viral marketing processes in a social network, and to evaluate the model with real data.

Keywords: Social network · SOIL · Python · Viral marketing · Brand reputation · Rumor propagation

1 Introduction

Social networks have become relevant in our professional and personal relationships. Thus, social network analysis and simulation can be effective for understanding and exploiting homophily and social influence processes in social networks. Marketing techniques are usually applied to exploit social influence in social networks, in applications such as viral or word-of-mouth marketing, rumor spreading and online reputation management. This paper complements the demo presented at PAAMS 2017 on the use of the Python-based ABSS SOIL tool for social network modeling and analysis, which is illustrated with a number of developed models.

2 Main Purpose

SOIL aims at providing a research environment for ABSS in Python, with a strong focus on interoperability with existing libraries. It integrates with the

© Springer International Publishing AG 2017
Y. Demazeau et al. (Eds.): PAAMS 2017, LNAI 10349, pp. 337–341, 2017.
DOI: 10.1007/978-3-319-59930-4_33

popular network processing library NetworkX[1] and with network visualization tools such as Gephi[2].

3   Demonstration

In this paper we present a case study that models the social influence of users in the social network Twitter. In particular, we study the role of social influence in rumor propagation and brand monitoring. In both applications, a diffusion message (rumor or brand advertisement) is propagated in the social network with the aim of infecting users. Users are considered infected when they accept or embrace the content of the message. The model presented is $M_{2.2}$ [4]. Twitter users are modeled as agents which can be in three states: *neutral*, if they are not affected by the message; *infected*, if they accept the message; *vaccinated*, if they have not been infected yet and believe in the antirumor or are infected by a message from a different brand; and *cured*, if they have been infected, but now believe the antirumor or are infected by a different brand. Additionally, the model includes a specific kind of users, called beacons, which detect the propagation of the message and try to combat it. Beacons are modeled after authorities that prevent rumor diffusion and competing influencers in social media. Agents include two additional states, beacon-off and beacon-on to represent beacons before and after detecting a rumor in a close node (neighbor).

The spread model starts with an initial number of infected users. In every simulation step, the state of each user may change though a series of interactions, each of which happens with a different probability. Infected users try to infect their neutral neighbors. Neutral agents may also become vaccinated with a given probability based on external factors (i.e. news). Vaccinated users attempt to cure or vaccinate their neighbors. Lastly, beacon agents spread anti-rumors to their neighbors, and follow these neighbors' contacts.

Table 1. Datasets of Twitter rumors and brand monitoring

Dataset	Number of tweets	Purpose	Period	Reference
Ford	348	Brand monitoring	13 months	[1]
Toyota	582	Brand monitoring	14 months	[1]
Obama	4975	Rumor propagation	8 days	[3]
Palin	4423	Rumor propagation	10 days	[3]

We have validated this diffusion model on four datasets (Table 1). The first two datasets (Ford and Toyota) are subsets of the Replab dataset [1], which focuses on monitoring the reputation of companies and individuals in Twitter.

---

[1] https://networkx.github.io/.
[2] https://gephi.org/.

Each tweet is classified as related (or unrelated) to an entity, the polarity for the entity's reputation (positive, negative or neutral), and the priority of the topic cluster the tweet belongs to (alert, midly important, unimportant). We have filtered the dataset and selected two automotive brands, Ford and Toyota, which can simulate how two brands advertise themselves on social media. In this case, the advertisement message is propagated and succeeds if the brand gets a good reputation. The last two datasets (Obama and Palin) are rumor datasets [3] that deal with identifying the spread of misinformation in social networks, such as Obama being a muslin or Palin's divorce. The dataset is labeled as endorses (propagate the rumor), denies (deny the rumor), questions (doubt about rumor credibility) or unrelated (not related to the rumor).

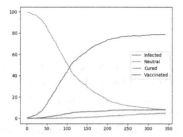

Fig. 1. Agent evolution

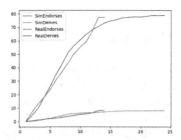

Fig. 2. Realism evaluation

The demonstration may be run in an IPython interactive shell, where simulation parameters can be defined. After running the simulation, the results are stored as Python objects, which can be inspected and visualized. For example, Fig. 1 shows the temporal evolution of agent states. The x axis represents the days and the y axis the number of simulated agents. In addition, the platform includes facilities for evaluating the realism of the simulation. For this purpose, we compare the daily number of endorsers and deniers in the dataset and the simulation. Figure 2 shows a comparison for the dataset of Toyota as a monthly evolution of the ratio of users that accept the diffusion message (endorsers) or reject it (deniers).

In addition, the platform generates a Graph Exchange XML Format (GEXF) file that can be used for analyzing the simulation with network analysis tools such as Gehpi. In particular, the visualization can be animated to show the temporal evolution of the spread model. Figure 3 shows a screenshot of the animation, where the colors denote infected (red), vaccinated (blue), cured (green) and beacon-off (yellow). Another interesting experiment is validating the realism of the simulation. An alternate view of the network is shown in Fig. 4.

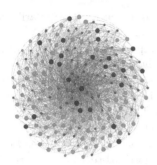
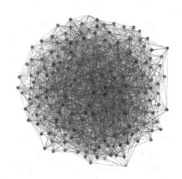

Fig. 3. Network visualization in Gephi (Color figure online)

Fig. 4. Alternate network visualization

4   Conclusions

This demonstration shows the application of a Python ABSS specifically designed for social network modeling and its application to information diffusion in social networks. The models in this paper had an existing implementation written in Java [4], combining MASON [2] and the graph library GraphStream[3]. Porting them to SOIL was straightforward and resulted in much simpler comprehensible code. The main benefits from using SOIL derive from using a simple yet extensible interface and the Python programming language. As a result, it is very easy to extend agent behavior while leveraging the existing ecosystem to integrate machine learning algorithms or semantic interfaces, to name a few. Moreover, the use of an interactive shell such as IPython[4].

Acknowledgements. This work is supported by the Spanish Ministry of Economy and Competitiveness under the R&D projects SEMOLA (TEC2015-68284-R) and Emo-Spaces (RTC-2016–5053-7), by the Regional Government of Madrid through the project MOSI-AGIL-CM (grant P2013/ICE-3019, co-funded by EU Structural Funds FSE and FEDER), and by the European Union through the project MixedEmotions (Grant Agreement no: 141111). The authors want to thank Vahed Qazvinian for making available the rumor datasets for our research.

References

1. Amigó, E., Carrillo de Albornoz, J., Chugur, I., Corujo, A., Gonzalo, J., Martín, T., Meij, E., Rijke, M., Spina, D.: Overview of RepLab 2013: Evaluating online reputation monitoring systems. In: Forner, P., Müller, H., Paredes, R., Rosso, P., Stein, B. (eds.) CLEF 2013. LNCS, vol. 8138, pp. 333–352. Springer, Heidelberg (2013). doi:10.1007/978-3-642-40802-1_31
2. Luke, S.: MASON: A multiagent simulation environment. Simulation **81**, 517–527 (2005)

---

[3] http://graphstream-project.org/.
[4] https://ipython.org/.

3. Qazvinian, V., Rosengren, E., Radev, D.R., Mei, Q.: Rumor has it: Identifying misinformation in microblogs. In: Proceedings of the Conference on Empirical Methods in Natural Language Processing, pp. 1589–1599. Association for Computational Linguistics (2011)
4. Serrano, E., Iglesias, C.A.: Validating viral marketing strategies in twitter via agent-based social simulation. Expert Syst. Appl. **50**(1), 140–150 (2016)

Prototyping Ubiquitous Multi-Agent Systems: A Generic Domain Approach with Jason

Carlos Eduardo Pantoja[1,2(✉)] and José Viterbo[2]

[1] Centro Federal de Educação Tecnológica (CEFET/RJ),
Av. Maracanã 229, Tijuca, RJ, Brazil
pantoja@cefet-rj.br
[2] Universidade Federal Fluminense (UFF),
Av. Gal. Milton Tavares de Souza, São Domingos, Niterói, RJ, Brazil
viterbo@ic.uff.br

Abstract. This work presents a generic domain approach for programming ubiquitous Multi-Agent Systems using Jason framework and ARGO in electronic prototypes. The approach aims to provide a ready-to-use platform that is heterogeneous and independent from the hardware selected to be used in several domains. In order to validate the approach, two examples in distinct domains and based on case studies were implemented, prototyped and discussed. The results show that the approach is adequate to develop such kind of systems.

1 Introduction

Agents are intelligent and autonomous entities that can be implemented in both hardware and software. They are proactive and able to communicate to each other in organizations. A Multi-Agent Systems (MAS) is a system composed of agents acting upon an environment to achieve mutual or conflicting goals [7]. Ubiquitous Systems and Ambient Intelligence (AmI) are electronic ambient that aids humans in common or complex situations in a pervasive way aided by intelligent systems. Accordingly to [2], the characteristics of the MAS approach can be exploited for the development of such kind of systems.

Applying the MAS approach in prototyping is not a simple issue since several limitations can occur when integrating hardware devices and the software responsible for the reasoning. One of these limitations provides tied solutions integrating MAS platforms and prototypes where the software is tied to the hardware technology employed, such as [3]. When it happens, the software is coupled to the hardware and it is not possible to change it for another one from a different type without rework. Besides, in most of the cases, it is only possible to use one kind of controller. Another limitation is that several works, such as [5], provide solutions where the software is strictly developed to one specific domain, do not offering generic constructions for programming robotic agents.

ARGO[1] [4] is a Jason's customized architecture that tries to facilitate the development of MAS for robotic platforms by allowing agents to control

---

[1] http://argo-for-jason.sourceforge.net.

© Springer International Publishing AG 2017
Y. Demazeau et al. (Eds.): PAAMS 2017, LNAI 10349, pp. 342–345, 2017.
DOI: 10.1007/978-3-319-59930-4_34

heterogeneous microcontrollers. Jason [1] is a well-known agent-oriented programming language. We assert that Jason and ARGO agents can be employed in the development of ubiquitous Multi-Agent Systems (uMAS) in a generic domain approach, uncoupled and independent from the type of controllers used.

2   Main Purpose

The main objective of this work is to provide an easy way of prototyping uMAS using BDI agents in a generic domain approach without concerning with the hardware technology employed in the prototype. The approach aims to be used in ubiquitous prototyping using Jason and ARGO independently of the domain chosen for the development of uMAS. In other words, in combining Jason and ARGO agents, it is possible to create agents capable of controlling hardware devices by means of microcontrollers. The designer of the prototype just has to concern with the agents' programming and the functionalities of the devices. All infrastructure (e.g. middleware) for transferring the perceptions from hardware to agent's knowledge base is inserted into the reasoning cycle of ARGO agents.

ARGO counts with a mechanism capable of processing sensorial information as perceptions directly into the belief base of specific kind of agent and it allows hardware controlling without concerning with the technology. Several internal actions are available to program some specific behaviors of an ARGO agent, which is able to decide: whether or not perceive the environment using its sensors; to act upon the environment using its actuators; the time interval between each environment sensing; if it is necessary to filter information for the sake of performance and; select which device to control in a specific moment. All of these characteristics can be exploited at runtime, offering a dynamic solution for programming and prototyping ubiquitous systems based on the agent approach.

In order to clarify the proposed approach, two examples in complete distinct domains are shown: in the first example it will be used a smart home prototype controlled by several ATMEGA controllers in a situation with a hearing impaired person living at a house and the second example will present an autonomous vehicle capable of identifying a wall and stop based on its sensors. Complementing the approach, the controllers from the first example will be changed for a different type and the example will be executed again.

3   Demonstration

This section shows the examples[2] using the generic domain approach employing Jason along with ARGO in two practical examples in distinct domains. The first example, based on [6], presents a smart home where a hearing impaired person is living in. In this smart home, if someone presses the door bell in front of the main door, the hearing impaired is not able to hear it and the smart home warns the person blinking the lights of the house. A prototype represents the smart

---

[2] https://youtu.be/9osZIMKvftA and https://youtu.be/0QzXHwzLSj8.

home using two ATMEGA328 (Arduino): one for controlling the bell and another one responsible for the lights of the house. The MAS responsible for controlling the prototype has an ARGO agent, which is responsible for identifying if exists somebody at the front door and another one responsible for blinking the lights of the house. For instance, agent Kate is responsible for the bell and agent Bob is responsible for the lights. Figure 1 depicts the prototype, Kate and Bob.

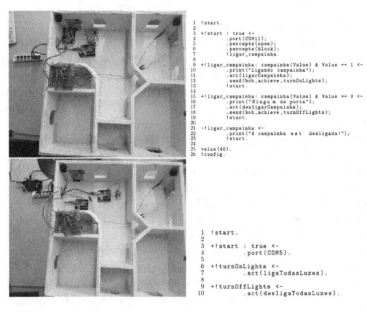

Fig. 1. The prototype employing Arduino (top left); agent Kate (top right); the prototype employing Galileo (bottom left) and; agent Bob (bottom right).

The second example is an autonomous unmanned vehicle, which is able to stop before it crashes into a wall. The vehicle is a 4WD platform with 4 distance sensors on each side of the prototype plugged in an Arduino board and an

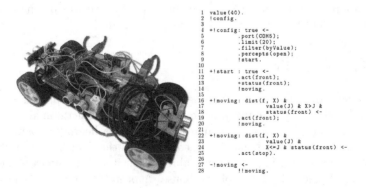

Fig. 2. The autonomous vehicle (left) and the agent code (right).

intelligent agent is responsible for perceiving the environment and to move until it perceives the wall. Figure 2 depicts the vehicle and the agent code. Finally, the first example was repeated using an Intel Galileo board instead of the Arduino board for agent Kate (Fig. 1) without modifying the agent's code. Bob still controls the other Arduino board. It is possible to see that the demonstration combines two different controllers in the same prototype in a heterogeneous approach. The result shows no difference in both executions.

4   Conclusions

This paper presented a generic domain approach using Jason and ARGO for prototyping uMAS and two practical examples in different domains were presented. The proposed approach is generic since it is possible to program agents for different domains without being aware or bonded to the type of controller employed. Because the software layer is independent of the controller employed it is allowed to use different types of controllers (even together or separated). Besides, they can be replaced without changing the MAS. For adding new controllers, they must comply with the protocol used in ARGO which uses serial ports as the communication channel between low-level layers and the software. For instance ARGO accepts ATMEGA and PIC controllers. These characteristics of the approach can be exploited to develop ubiquitous systems, where heterogeneous hardware are employed and intelligent agents can be used for providing an autonomous behavior of the system.

References

1. Bordini, R.H., Hübner, J.F., Wooldridge, M.: Programming Multi-Agent Systems in AgentSpeak using Jason. Wiley, Chichester (2007)
2. Chaouche, A.C., Seghrouchni, A.E.F., Ilié, J.M., Saïdouni, D.E.: A higher-order agent model with contextual planning management for ambient systems. In: Kowalczyk, R., Nguyen, N. (eds.) Transactions on Computational Collective Intelligence XVI. LNCS, vol. 8780, pp. 146–169. Springer, Heidelberg (2014). doi:10.1007/978-3-662-44871-7_6
3. Cook, D.J., Youngblood, G.M., Heierman, E.O., Gopalratnam, K., Rao, S., Litvin, A., Khawaja, F.: Mavhome: an agent-based smart home. PerCom. 3, 521–524 (2003)
4. Pantoja, C.E., Stabile, M.F., Lazarin, N.M., Sichman, J.S.: ARGO: an extended jason architecture that facilitates embedded robotic agents programming. In: Baldoni, M., Müller, J.P., Nunes, I., Zalila-Wenkstern, R. (eds.) EMAS 2016. LNCS (LNAI), vol. 10093, pp. 136–155. Springer, Cham (2016). doi:10.1007/978-3-319-50983-9_8
5. Sun, Q., Yu, W., Kochurov, N., Hao, Q., Hu, F.: A multi-agent-based intelligent sensor and actuator network design for smart house and home automation. J. Sens. Actuator Netw. 2(3), 557–588 (2013)
6. Villarrubia, G., De Paz, J.F., Bajo, J., Corchado, J.M.: Ambient agents: embedded agents for remote control and monitoring using the pangea platform. Sensors 14(8), 13955–13979 (2014)
7. Wooldridge, M.: An Introduction to MultiAgent Systems. Wiley, New York (2009)

Training Emotional Robots Using EJaCalIVE

Jaime Andres Rincon[1], Agelo Costa[2], Paulo Novais[2], Vicente Julian[1(✉)],
and Carlos Carrascosa[1]

[1] Universitat Politècnica de València. D. Sistemas Informáticos y Computación,
Valencia, Spain
{jrincon,vinglada,carrasco}@dsic.upv.es
[2] Centro ALGORITMI, Escola de Engenharia,
Universidade do Minho, Guimarães, Portugal
{acosta,pjon}@di.uminho.pt

Abstract. This article presents EJaCalIVE as a possible tool for the design of Emotional Intelligent Virtual Environments (EIVE). This article presents a practical case, in which real robots are integrated with virtual entities. In order to train an assistance robot. In the simulation, each one of the virtual entities communicates emotions to the robot, which reacts according to the emotions received.

1 Introduction

The first robot was created by *Westinghouse Electric Corporation* between 1937 and 1938. This robot measured two meters in height and weighed 265 pounds. In turn, the robot had a humanoid appearance, it could say 700 words and it responded to voice commands. To this Whileday, robots have evolved in size, intelligence, and applicability. To date, it is possible to find robots in the industry (this being the main idea of application), medicine and in our homes. These robots incorporate new elements of interaction through different channels of communication, such as voice recognition, artificial vision, pattern recognition, etc. From this interaction robots learn from our tastes, they recognize our emotional states and could help if necessary. All these features make robots a useful tool, to help the elderly. However, working with older people is not easy, because some of these people have some health problems associated with age. *EJaCalIVE* was designed as a tool for the design and simulation of *Emotional Intelligent Virtual Environments (EIVE)*. *EJaCalIVE* incorporates emotional models like PAD [1] and Circumplex Model [2], as well as personality models like the OCEAN [3]. This allows the developer to perform simulations with emotional agents. In turn, *EJaCalIVE*, also allows the developer to access with different hardware elements that allow agents to interact with the real world. *EJaCalIVE* allows you to communicate with commercial robots and not commercial. This paper presents *EJaCalIVE* as an approach to solving this problem. *EJaCalIVE* is a tool based on multi-agent systems, which allows you to design and simulate *Emotional Intelligent Virtual Environments (EIVE)*. As well as the incorporation of elements of perception and action (algorithms of machine learning, artificial vision, speech recognition and

© Springer International Publishing AG 2017
Y. Demazeau et al. (Eds.): PAAMS 2017, LNAI 10349, pp. 346–349, 2017.
DOI: 10.1007/978-3-319-59930-4_35

communication with social robots and wearable devices), allowing to design and to construct *EIVE* capable of interacting integrally with human beings.

2   EJaCalIVE (Emotional Jason Cartago Implemented Intelligent Virtual Environment)

This section focuses on the presentation of the *EJaCalIVE* framework. This framework allows the design and programming of intelligent virtual environments, as well as the simulation and detection of human emotions for the creation of *Internet of Things (IoT)*, *Ubiquitous Computing (UC)* and robot applications. *EJaCalIVE* is divided into two parts, the first focuses on the design and programming of the *Intelligent Virtual Environment (IVE)* and the second on the detection and simulation of emotional states. *EJaCalIVE* incorporates emotions and is an evolution of the *JaCalIVE* presented in [4]. *EJaCalIVE* is supported by four engines: cognitive, artifacts, physical and emotional. Each of these engines allows the developer to design and program an *Emotional Intelligent Virtual Environment (EIVE)*. The *Cognitive Engine* is supported in turn by Jason who is the agent platform. Jason allows scheduling of each of the behaviors of the agents. The *Artifact Engine* is supported with *CArtAgo* which allows you to create the various objects that are inside the *EIVE*. *EJaCalIVE* has a *Physical Engine*, which is supported by Jbullet. Jbullet allows to introduce physical restrictions (gravity, IVE-Artifact position, speed, acceleration, among others) which will govern the IVE workspace. The emotional engine is responsible for simulating and classifying human emotions as well as for the calculation of social emotion and the emotional dynamics of human-agent society. Each of the engines is defined by the developer through an XML file, which will later be interpreted by *EJaCalIVE* creating the different templates. Within these templates are all the characteristics defined within the XML.

3   Emotional Robot Simulation

In this section, we present the case study to use *EJaCalIVE*. In this simulation we want to train an emotional robot for the assistance of older people. Due to the complexity of working with older people, a simulation was designed using *EJaCalIVE*. This is a platform based on multi-agent systems where each agent simulates an older person. Each of these agents is capable of expressing emotional states, which are perceived by the robot. The Fig. 1 shows the design of the simulation with the different entities that compose it. In which we can highlight the emotional agents, which simulate the elderly and the human caregiver is simulated by the *Emotional Human Immersed Agent*. This simulation allow to the robot learn and take a decision based on emotions. If the robot perceives a negative emotion (bored or angry) it can execute preprogrammed actions in order to modify the emotion. In case the robot can not modify the emotion the caregiver takes the corresponding action.

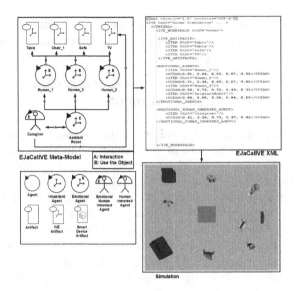

Fig. 1. Design environment.

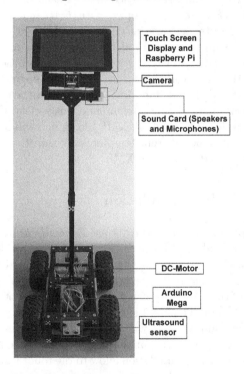

Fig. 2. Prototype of assistant robot.

Robot training is improved by the simulation and the developer checks that decisions taken were correct. In this way, when the robot is properly trained, it can be introduced into the real elderly residence.

The robot is programmed using a *SPADE* agent[1]. Agents representing elderly people communicate their emotions to the robot by messages. The Fig. 2 shows The figure shows complete structure of the proposed robot. The robot is compoused by four ultrasound sensors, to detect obstacles, and one magnetometer, for detecting the relative orientation to the Earth's magnetic north. There is also a touch screen, to enhanced the user interaction, and a camera, to detect human emotions using image processing.

4   Conclusions and Future Work

A new framework called *EJaCalIVE* for the simulation of *Emotional Intelligent Virtual Environment*is proposed. This framework differs from other works in the sense that it integrates concepts of personality, emotion simulation and emotion detection. This framework allows to simulate emotional intelligent entities. The proposed framework is used to train an emotional robot able to detect the emotional state of elderly people. elderly individuals were simulated by an artificial intelligent entity due the complexity of training the robot with real people. *EJaCalIVE* allows to create a bridge between the robot and agents in order to determine robot behaviours. As a future work we are working in introduce more robots in our simulation and in implement these robots in a real elderly residence.

Acknowledgements. This work is partially supported by the MINECO project TIN2015-65515-C4-1-R and the FPI grant AP2013-01276 awarded to Jaime-Andres Rincon.

References

1. Mehrabian, A.: Framework for a comprehensive description and measurement of emotional states. Genet. Soc. Gen. Psychol. Monogr. **121**(3), 339–361 (1995)
2. Russell, J.A.: A circumplex model of affect. J. Pers. Soc. Psychol. **39**, 1161–1178 (1980)
3. Kelly, W.E.: The "OCEAN" and the night-sky: relations between the five-factor model of personality and noctcaelador. Coll. Stud. J. **38**(3), 406 (2004)
4. Rincon, J.A., Poza-Lujan, J.-L., Julian, V., Posadas-Yagüe, J.-L., Carrascosa, C.: Extending MAM5 meta-model and JaCalIVE E framework to integrate smart devices from real environments. PLOS ONE **11**(2), 1–27 (2016)

---

[1] https://github.com/javipalanca/spade.

Towards a Self-healing Multi-agent Platform for Distributed Data Management

Arles Rodríguez[1,2]([✉]), Jonatan Gómez[2], and Ada Diaconescu[3]

[1] Fundación Universitaria Konrad Lorenz, Bogotá, Colombia
arlese.rodriguezp@konradlorenz.edu.co
[2] ALIFE Research Group, Universidad Nacional de Colombia, Bogotá, Colombia
jgomezpe@unal.edu.co
[3] Telecom ParisTech, IMT, Paris-Saclay University, Paris, France
ada.diaconescu@telecom-paristech.fr

Abstract. We demonstrate a self-healing multi-agent simulation platform for distributed data-management tasks, including data collection and synchronisation. Collective tasks can be simulated within two types of environments: uncharted terrains with various obstacles, and computing networks with different complex topologies. Agents explore their environment, collect and update local data, and exchange data with agents that they encounter, until the collective task is completed. We have previously implemented several agent exploration algorithms and evaluated their performance in terms of completion speed (essential when agents may fail) and resource overheads (essential in constrained environments). Here, we focus on the agents' ability to self-heal, via local replication, so as to ensure task completion. We focus on computing network environment, where software replication is more feasible. Envisaged applications include data management in computing clouds, distributed databases, sensor networks, robot swarms and the Internet of Things.

Keywords: Multi-agent · Simulation · Self-healing · Data-management tasks

1 Introduction

Data centres, server farms and clouds are distributed systems consisting of a myriad of computing resources interconnected via a network, and coordinating their actions, transparently to users, in order to accomplish various tasks [1]. Such systems are difficult to manage – e.g. software updates, failed component replacements – and downtimes can cost companies in the order of thousands of dollars per minute [2]. Autonomic Computing [2,3] drew inspiration from nature and proposed to enable computing systems to self-manage, minimising expensive and error-prone human intervention. Notably, self-healing allows systems to recover and pursue their tasks despite failures [4,5].

The proposed demonstration presents a multi-agent simulator for exploring decentralised self-healing functions and evaluating robustness in distributed systems. Within this simulator, we model and experiment with failure-prone agents

© Springer International Publishing AG 2017
Y. Demazeau et al. (Eds.): PAAMS 2017, LNAI 10349, pp. 350–354, 2017.
DOI: 10.1007/978-3-319-59930-4_36

which cooperate to achieve collective data-management tasks, such as data collection from uncharted terrains [6] and data synchronisation across complex networks [7]. We evaluated different agent exploration algorithms, e.g. based on random movement, swarm intelligence and Lévy walks. In uncharted terrain environments, results show that a pheromone-based exploration approach ensures the fastest task completion and hence better robustness in case of agent failures. In complex network environments, the same pheromone-based algorithm performs best for most network topologies (e.g. Random, Community, or Small World), yet random exploration is better in topologies with large hubs – i.e. with large values for the standard deviation of the betweenness centrality of their nodes (e.g. some Scale Free or Hub & Spoke topologies).

The present work proposes a self-healing function based on local agent replication. In short, each distributed node keeps track of agents departing for neighbouring nodes. Upon arrival at a new node agents send a confirmation message back to their departing node, which consequently stops tracking them. When a node does not receive a confirmation message from a departed agent within a *time-out* interval, it creates a new agent and injects its local state (i.e. local data) into it. If a confirmation message arrives late (i.e. after the time-out and after a replica has already been created) the node removes the next agent that arrives at the node (after copying its data) and updates its local time-out (i.e. learning). Details and results are available from the accompanying paper[1].

The simulator provides results on task success rates, completion speed and replication overheads (e.g. extra memory and communication). We believe that these findings and platform can help to experiment with various multi-agent solutions for a wide variety of data-intensive distributed systems.

2   Platform Purpose and Implementation

The presented simulation platform[2] allows developing various multi-agent data-management solutions, with self-healing capabilities, and evaluating their performance and robustness in different distributed environments. The simulator is implemented in Java, based on the multi-agent platform in [8] – with agents implemented via a family of classes, and running in separate Threads. In demonstrated scenarios the agents are specified as in [7] in terms of exploration algorithms, data management and inter-agent exchanges. The environment is defined as another extensible family of classes that allows agents to interact (e.g. a bi-dimensional terrain or a complex network).

Simulation metrics are defined using the Observer design pattern, which separates simulations from generated metric reports. These reports allow obtaining various statistics (e.g. box-plots and histograms), including the number of steps required for task completion, the number of message exchanges, task success

---

[1] "Replication-based Self-healing of Mobile Agents Exploring Complex Networks" – submitted to PAAMS 2017.
[2] http://www.alife.unal.edu.co/%7Eaerodriguezp/networksim/.

rates, or the evolution of agent numbers over time. The simulator's statistics module can also be extended and modified to develop custom metrics.

3   Demonstration

The demonstration shows different types of simulations that were developed using the proposed platform. Firstly, as in Fig. 1a, we provide a simulation of failure-prone agents with different strategies for exploring a bi-dimensional terrain [6]. In Fig. 1a, the upper part shows the agents' terrain coverage (purple traces), the middle part shows the terrain information collected (yellow marks), and the bottom part shows graphs plotting the live agents (failing with a certain probability) against the simulation round number. This simulation allowed us to determine which exploration strategies are more robust in case of agent failures, faster in terms of simulation rounds, and lighter in terms of resource overheads.

Secondly, as in Fig. 1b, we present a simulation of agents (in yellow) collecting and synchronising data within various complex networks [7]. Locations explored by agents are in blue and locations not explored in red. Implemented topologies include Small World, Scale Free and Community (using JUNG [9]), as well as simpler ones such as Hub & Spoke, Lattice, Line and Circle (for testing extreme conditions). This allows us to profile the performance and dependability of different agent exploration strategies against each network topology, for different agent failure rates. Results show a correlation between these evaluation metrics and the standard deviation of the node betweenness centrality – intuitively, pheromone-based exploration techniques are hindered by topologies featuring large hubs and few alternative routes, since hubs get pheromone-marked and become temporarily inaccessible for further passing.

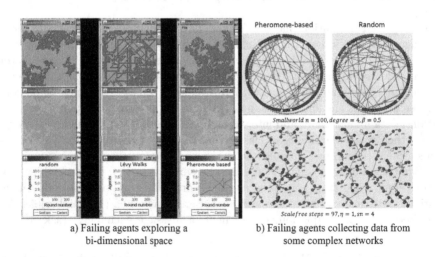

a) Failing agents exploring a
bi-dimensional space

b) Failing agents collecting data from
some complex networks

Fig. 1. Different simulations generated

Thirdly, we extend the previous simulation by endowing agents with self-healing capabilities. In this case, results show that agents can successfully complete the collective task even in the presence of high-failure rates (which was not the case without self-healing), while inducing limited local overheads.

4   Conclusions and Future Work

This demonstration shows an agent-based simulator for modelling distributed tasks. Agents are modelled to carry internal states, to explore their environments (either continuous surfaces or complex networks), to perform local data-management tasks, and to communicate with each other when they meet.

The main contribution of this simulator is to help design and evaluate different decentralised data-management solutions, applicable to various distributed environments, with different characteristics (e.g. diverse tasks, resource constraints, performance requirements, or agent failure rates).

The simulator collects metrics that enable statistic analysis, which are critical for profiling new agent designs. So far, this allowed us to determine the best agent exploration strategy for performing a distributed task in different types of terrains and network topologies, with different agent failure rates.

Future work will model and simulate new strategies for recovering from node failures and corrupt data collection. Our objective is to provide a theoretical and experimental base for developing real applications for different distributed environments – e.g. data collection and replication in clouds, clusters and the Internet of Things. The source code and results obtained are available at http://www.alife.unal.edu.co/%7Eaerodriguezp/networksim/.

References

1. Tanenbaum, A., Steen, M.V.: Distributed Systems: Principles and Paradigms. Prentice-Hall, Upper Saddle River (2006)
2. Lalanda, P., Mccann, J.A., Diaconescu, A.: Autonomic Computing: Principles, Design and Implementation. Springer, Heidelberg (2013)
3. Kephart, J.O., Chess, D.M., Jeffrey, O., David, M.: The vision of autonomic computing. Computer **36**, 41–50 (2003)
4. Hu, J., Gao, J.I., Liao, B.S., Chen, J.J., Jun, W.: Multi-agent system based autonomic computing environment. In: Proceedings of 2004 International Conference on Machine Learning and Cybernetics, vol. 1, pp. 105–110 (2004)
5. Bisadi, M., Sharifi, M.: A biologically-inspired preventive mechanism for self-healing of distributed software components. In: The Second International Conference on Advanced Engineering Computing and Applications in Sciences, ADVCOMP 2008, pp. 152–157 (2008)
6. Rodriguez, A., Gomez, J., Diaconescu, A.: Foraging-inspired self-organisation for terrain exploration with failure-prone agents. In: 2015 IEEE 9th International Conference on Self-Adaptive and Self-Organizing Systems, pp. 121–130. IEEE, October 2015

7. Rodriguez, A., Gomez, J., Diaconescu, A.: Exploring complex networks with failure-prone agents. In: Verlag, S. (ed.) 15th Mexican International Conference on Artificial Intelligence, MICAI 2016. LNCS (2016)
8. Gomez, J.: Unalcol agents (2016). https://github.com/jgomezpe/unalcol/tree/master/agents/src/unalcol/agents
9. White, S.: Analysis and visualization of network data using JUNG. J. Stat. Softw. **VV**, 1–35 (2005)

AGADE-TRAFFIC
Multi-agent Simulations in Geographical Networks

Serge Rotärmel[1], Michael Guckert[1], Thomas Farrenkopf[1(✉)],
and Neil Urquhart[2]

[1] KITE - Kompetenzzentrum für Informationstechnologie,
Technische Hochschule Mittelhessen, Giessen, Germany
Serge.Rotaermel@iem.thm.de,
{michael.guckert,thomas.farrenkopf}@mnd.thm.de
[2] School of Computing, Edinburgh Napier University, Edinburgh, Scotland
n.urquhart@napier.ac.uk

Abstract. AGADE-TRAFFIC is a tool for simulating traffic flow in networks. Traffic participants are modelled as NetLogo agents and are visualised in a graphical user interface. Geographic information is stored in a graph database and AGADE-TRAFFIC communicates with that database through a NetLogo extension. Routing capabilities of the database are used while respecting the current traffic situation that is continuously reflected into the database. Different models of congestion effects are available and can be investigated in flexible traffic assignment models. Real world networks can be imported from Open Street Map. The tool allows the definition of specific cost and pricing schemes so that effects of selfish routing and social optimisation can be compared.

Keywords: Multi-agent simulation routing · Traffic assignment · Graph databases · Traffic simulation · Congestion effect

1 Introduction

AGADE-TRAFFIC is a tool for simulations of traffic flow in traffic networks with individuals travelling from origins to destinations that can freely be defined. Its main purpose is the examination of the overall traffic behaviour and effects on objective functions defined globally, typically mean or average travel times. With an easy to use Netlogo front-end it allows an intuitive approach for interactively setting up simulations. AGADE-TRAFFIC has an integrated interface to the Neo4J graph database via a two-way service layer implemented as a NetLogo extension. The graph database contains geographic information imported from Open Street Map (OSM). Other than comparable tools like TrafficGen (see [1]) AGADE-TRAFFIC aims at simulating large scale scenarios to model the overall traffic flow rather than the individual behaviour in more detailed traffic situations e.g. overtaking. For this purpose AGADE-TRAFFIC reflects traffic to the graph database so that the routing algorithms always consider the current traffic distribution. The architecture can run in a distributed environment using the distribution mechanisms of the database.

© Springer International Publishing AG 2017
Y. Demazeau et al. (Eds.): PAAMS 2017, LNAI 10349, pp. 355–358, 2017.
DOI: 10.1007/978-3-319-59930-4_37

2   Main Purpose

AGADE-TRAFFIC allows elaborate experiments with congested traffic assignment (see [5]). The tool can be used to simulate congestion effects in traffic networks through appropriately calibrated functions that describe congestion dependant travel times which are defined on the route segments i.e. the edges of the graph that represents the network. Individuals always choose optimal routes according to cost functions that considers travel times and possible additional external costs. The interface to the routing algorithm of the graph database can be adapted so that different congestion functions and pricing schemes can be used and those already pre-defined can easily be adapted for changing scenarios. The tool can therefore be used to model different concepts of traffic control i.e. different pricing schemes for tolling or centrally controlled route assignment to find equilibria in the traffic system and to fine tune the process of mechanism design to create optimal traffic assignments.

3   Demonstration

AGADE-TRAFFIC uses NetLogo agents to model the flow of traffic in a network of roads. Start and end of journeys can be set through the interface as well as the amount of individual traffic participants on each origin destination relation can be defined there. The agents travel on shortest routes which are calculated by the graph database using an integrated implementation of the A*-algorithm. The position of each agent is immediately reflected to the database so that the calculations respect the amount of traffic on each segment. Speed and travel time can either be determined by a simple linear function or by a parameterised BPR function (see for example [3]) (Fig. 1).

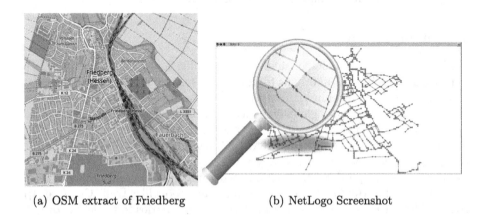

(a) OSM extract of Friedberg   (b) NetLogo Screenshot

Fig. 1. Real world map integrated in Netlogo.

AGADE-TRAFFIC uses a NetLogo extension to establish a bidirectional communication with the database to retrieve geographic information to draw a map in which traffic is visualised, for initialising and retrieving results from routing calculations and for perpetually updating the positions of the agents in the database (Fig. 2).

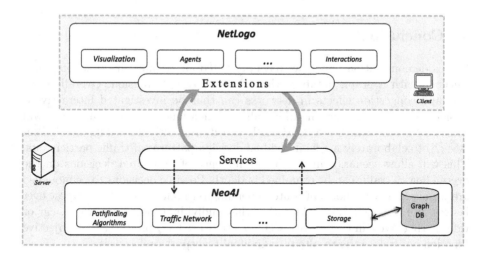

Fig. 2. Architecture.

AGADE-TRAFFIC uses geographic information imported and transformed from OSM by means of OSMSOSIS (see [6]) and the OSMToNeo4JConverter which is built by that project on top of the Neo4J Spatial extension (see [4]). During this conversion necessary information taken from OSM is transferred into properties of the components of the graph structure in Neo4J (Fig. 3).

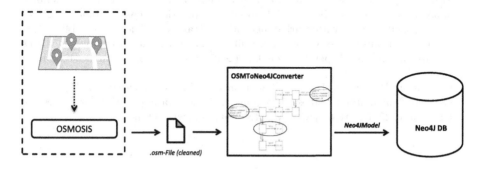

Fig. 3. Import process OSM to Neo4J.

The advantage of using the graph database lies in its natural representation of links and nodes which can well be used for a basic representation of the geographical network and beyond that in its ease to model additional abstract information about the network e.g. maximum speed and derived capacities of route segments. Upon that it offers routing mechanisms that are efficiently implemented in the database. However, a more systematic benchmarking of the integration is still a task to be carried out and is part of the future work of this project.

4   Conclusion

In this demonstration paper, we have presented an architecture that integrates NetLogo with a graph database through a NetLogo extension. Overall traffic flow and congestion effects in networks can thus be investigated interactively. Besides the necessary benchmarking already mentioned before future work will consist of a full integration of AGADE and its semantic modelling capabilities (see [2]) to elaborately model individual decision patterns of traffic participants. This will allow scenarios in which the influence of individual decisions on the overall flow of traffic can be examined in depth. Possible decisions to be modelled are for example the choice of route depending on preferences like cheapest over fastest, use of public transport rather than individual motor car traffic, car or ride sharing. We can then create scenarios that use CO_2 production as objective function and relate the results to individual transport preferences.

References

1. Bonhomme, A., Mathieu, P., Sébastien, P.: A versatile multi-agent traffic simulator framework based on real data. Int. J. Artif. Intell. Tools **25**(01), 1660006 (2016)
2. Farrenkopf, T., Guckert, M., Urquhart, N.: AGADE using personal preferences and world knowledge to model agent behaviour. In: Demazeau, Y., Decker, K.S., Bajo Pérez, J., de la Prieta, F. (eds.) PAAMS 2015. LNCS (LNAI), vol. 9086, pp. 93–106. Springer, Cham (2015). doi:10.1007/978-3-319-18944-4_8
3. Mtoi, E.T., Moses, R.: Calibration and evaluation of link congestion functions: applying intrinsic sensitivity of link speed as a practical consideration to heterogeneous facility types within urban network. J. Transp. Technol. **4**, 141–149 (2014)
4. Neo4J-Contributors: Neo4j spatial is a library of utilities for neo4j that faciliates the enabling of spatial operations on data (2017). https://github.com/neo4j/spatial. Accessed
5. Ortuzar, J., Willumsen, L.: Modelling Transport. Wiley, Chichester (2011)
6. Osmosis-Contributors: Osmosis is a command line java application for processing OSM data (2017). https://wiki.openstreetmap.org/wiki/Osmosis

Automated MMORPG Testing – An Agent-Based Approach

Markus Schatten[(✉)], Bogdan Okreaša Đurić, Igor Tomičič, and Nikola Ivkovič

Artificial Intelligence Laboratory, Faculty of Organization and Informatics,
University of Zagreb, Zagreb, Croatia
{markus.schatten,dokresa,igor.tomicic,nikola.ivkovic}@foi.hr,
http://ai.foi.hr/modelmmorpg

Abstract. A work-in-progress agent-based framework for automated testing of an open-source massively multi-player on-line role playing game (MMORPG) called *The Mana World* is presented. The implemented system, in its current state, allows for model-driven development of tests using a graphical user interface (GUI), implementation of automated artificial players (bots) and their use in testing the quests (player tasks) of the game. The system is implemented using Python, SPADE, SWI Prolog and AToM[3].

Keywords: MMORPG · Automated testing · Agents · Bots · Artificial players

1 Introduction

Automated testing of computer games is a complex task, especially in the context of multi-player games since, apart from testing the game logic, the interaction between players has to be tested as well. In massively multi-player on-line (MMO) games where thousands of players may play simultaneously, the task of automated testing becomes even more challenging. Role playing games (RPGs) on the other hand, require testing procedures that are able to solve complex tasks and puzzles (quests) that might include numerous actions like collecting items, fighting monsters, talking to non-playing characters (NPCs) etc. All of these challenges are combined in massively multi-player on-line role playing games (MMORPGs). Herein we will present a work-in-progress agent-based and model-driven approach to testing an open-source MMORPG called "The Mana World" (TMW)[1].

The presented approach is agent-based in terms of artificial players or bots being modelled as agents within a TMW environment. The agents are implemented using SPADE (Smart Python Agent Development Environment) [2] with an implemented belief-desire-intention (BDI) architecture using an SWI Prolog knowledge base for reasoning. The approach is model-driven since a graphical

---

[1] See https://www.themanaworld.org/ for details.

© Springer International Publishing AG 2017
Y. Demazeau et al. (Eds.): PAAMS 2017, LNAI 10349, pp. 359–363, 2017.
DOI: 10.1007/978-3-319-59930-4_38

modelling language is used to model the tests to be implemented and used for experiments. The graphical modelling tool was implemented using the AToM³ meta-modelling toolkit [1].

2 Main Purpose

The demonstration is focused on automated solving of an initial tutorial quest of TMW in order to show some of the most significant elements of the presented framework. The process of testing a part of the game using the framework consists of a number of steps. Firstly, the test is modelled using a graphical modelling language already presented in [3,4]. Besides of modelling structure, processes, roles, objectives, and other organizational features, the language also allows modeling organizational dynamics through temporal logic and graph grammars as the example shows on Fig. 1.

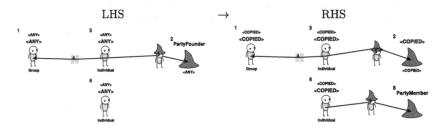

Fig. 1. Example graph grammar rule related to joining a party inside TMW

The modeling tool can be used for generating an application template to be connected with a special game plug-in developed for the purpose of this framework. The plug-in consists of a low-level interface (dealing with the actual network level protocol establishing a connection to the game servers), and a high-level interface (a SPADE agent template connecting the low-level interface to a knowledge base [KB] and planning system). The high-level interface is basically a BDI agent having various behaviours including updating of its KB (beliefs) based on actual percepts provided by the low-level interface, updating of objectives and quests to be solved (desires), as well as obtaining plans on how to solve a given quest (intentions). For example, the method that selects the next objective (quest) to be solved is shown in Listing 1.

```
def selectObjective( self , objectives ):
    ''' Select most relevant objective (quest) to be solved next '''
    query = "sort_quests('%s '),quest_no(_NPC,'%s ',_Name,_No_)." % ( self .
        avatar_name , self . avatar_name )
    quests = self . askBelieve ( query )
    if quests:
        next = sorted ( quests , key=lambda x: x[ 'No' ] )[ 0 ][ 'Name' ]
        self . say ( 'My next objective is quest: ' + next )
    return next
```

Listing 1. Example method – selecting the next objective

Additionally, the agent has the ability to act on the TMW environment (again through the low-level interface) and check if its actions were successful. The last step, after connecting the application template and the plug-in is to start the tests and analyze them.

3 Demonstration

The model of the initial TMW quest, given by an NPC called Sorfina is presented in Fig. 2. The player has to move slightly within the confines of the first gaming area, have a conversation with two NPCs, equip some items, and leave the area. Using the modeling tool, this quest can be broken into several tasks.

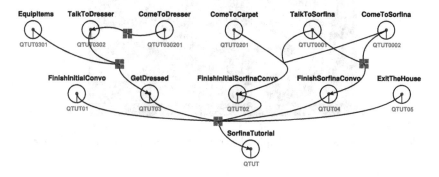

Fig. 2. Tutorial quest breakdown into tasks

In the current version of the framework, these tasks are reflected as actions inside plans for solving the given quest or part of the game. Actions have their preconditions (for example, some other quests have to be solved in order to attain the current one) and postconditions (for example and action `goToLocation( Map, X, Y )` has the postcondition `location( Map, X, Y )`).

For the sake of this demonstration we have implemented a plan for Sorfina's tutorial quest.[2] The algorithm of the planner is quite simple in this case: firstly the planner sorts all given quests by priority of solving. In case the agent hasn't got any current quest, a default random walk quest is assigned to it, in order to find an NPC or other means to acquire a quest. Then, the quest with the highest priority for which all preconditions are met, is selected for solving. The planner starts the quest and derives one action after another to be enacted by the agent. The agent then fulfils the action and checks if the action's postconditions have been achieved by updating its KB. If an action fails, the planner returns the quest into the list of waiting quests and starts over. If all actions have been

---

[2] The source code of the testing framework and modelling tool are available on GitHub at https://github.com/tomicic/ModelMMORPG and https://github.com/Balannen/LSMASOMM respectively.

achieved successfully (e.g. all envisioned postconditions have been met) the quest
is marked as achieved and the planner starts over.

We have tested the implemented quest on a dedicated TMW server with
multiple parallel agents trying to solve Sorfina's quest. Figure 3 shows an example
session in which 8 agents are solving the quest. While the times for solving the
quest have differed (mostly due to random walks of players) all agents were able
to solve the quest.

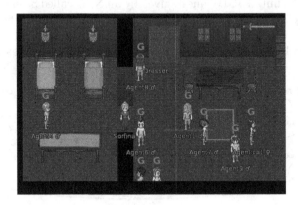

Fig. 3. A screenshot of multiple player agents trying to solve Sorfina's quest

4   Conclusions

In this demonstration we have shown some of the features of a work-in-progress
automated testing framework for MMORPGs. The presented framework has
the advantage to be able to visually model the expected behaviour of artificial
players (agents) and generate an application template. To be usable on a concrete
MMORPG a plug-in for each game has to be developed as we have done for
TMW.

Our future work is aimed towards enriching the framework with more complex and social elements to be able to solve even more demanding tasks.

Acknowledgment. This work has been supported in full by the Croatian Science
Foundation under the project number 8537. We would also like to acknowledge TMW
development team which often helped us with various implementation specific details.
Additionally, we would like to thank our students Marin Rukavina, Dario Belinic and
Lovro Predovan and prof. Marko Malikovic who helped in developing parts of the
knowledge base, planning system and server components respectively.

References

1. De Lara, J., Vangheluwe, H.: AToM^3: A tool for multi-formalism and meta-modelling. In: Kutsche, R.-D., Weber, H. (eds.) FASE 2002. LNCS, vol. 2306, pp. 174–188. Springer, Heidelberg (2002). doi:10.1007/3-540-45923-5_12
2. Gregori, M.E., Cámara, J.P., Bada, G.A.: A jabber-based multi-agent system platform. In: Proceedings of the Fifth International Joint Conference on Autonomous Agents and Multiagent Systems, pp. 1282–1284. ACM (2006)
3. Đurić, B.O.: A novel approach to modelling distributed systems: Using large-scale multi-agent systems. In: Mahmood, Z. (ed.) Software Project Management for Distributed Computing. CCN, pp. 229–254. Springer, Cham (2017). doi:10.1007/978-3-319-54325-3_10
4. Đurić, B.O.: Organizational metamodel for large-scale multi-agent systems. In: de la Prieta, F., et al. (eds.) Trends in Practical Applications of Scalable Multi-Agent Systems, the PAAMS Collection, vol. 473, pp. 387–390. Springer, Cham (2016)

Demonstration: Multi-agent System for Distributed Cache Maintenance

Santhilata Kuppili Venkata[1(✉)], Katarzyna Musial[2], Samhar Mahmoud[1], and Jeroen Keppens[1]

[1] Department of Informatics, King's College London, London, UK
santhilata.kuppili_venkata@kcl.ac.uk
[2] Faculty of Science and Technology, Bournemouth University, Poole, UK

Abstract. Innovations in science and technology is increasing the demand on huge data transfers and hence number of data caches. In this paper, we consider the community caching solution, CommCache, where many groups of users are working together on related projects distributed all over the world. We demonstrate the use of proactive caches for data placement problem with the help of multi-agent coordination.

Keywords: Distributed cache · Agent based modelling · Coordination strategies

1 Introduction

Construction of models and simulations using multi-agent systems (MAS) is not new. Architectures using MAS enable to create applications such as distributed situation assessment, coordination etc. help researchers to develop new insights [2]. We utilise this property to represent distributed data caching. When groups of users working on similar projects access data from multiple databases, often they need the same data at different locations at different times. Also, their queries to the databases overlap significantly. Distributed caching is a complex system consists of components such as data servers, communication networks, middleware cache storage units, cache server (processing resources), and users. Traditionally, cache storage units are small in size. Hence during the cache maintenance process, a decision has to be made about storing in cache units the most relevant data and removing the obsolete data. This means that we have to identify **'what data'** to store, **'where'** a given data segment should be stored, and for **'how long'**. With the goal to reduce the response time and overall data transfers, multiple cache units need to coordinate together to cache each unit of data segment at an appropriate cache unit. Typical diagnostics used for decision making in placing data segments are: *frequency* of each data segment queried, *time* when a data segment was used, *location* preference where the data segment was requested, *association* among data segments at a given location, *number of joins* in a query, storage *capacity* of the cache unit, and *workload characteristics* depicting the pattern of query requests. We have designed **CommCache**,

Y. Demazeau et al. (Eds.): PAAMS 2017, LNAI 10349, pp. 364–368, 2017.
DOI: 10.1007/978-3-319-59930-4_39

an agent based community cache framework to represent the distributed cache environment. In this paper, we examine five coordination strategies to represent centralised and peer-to-peer architectures.

2   Coordination Strategies Among Multiple Agents

The multi-agent model is shown in Fig. 1. User agents (UA) are modelled as the software representation of humans that query databases. Query response time is measured as the time elapsed from the query sent from UA to the reply received by a user (Fig. 1). Query analysis agent (QAA) assumes coordinator role in the distributed caching. It has combined responsibilities for analysis and management. Cache agents are designed to take active part in cache maintenance. They are cooperative agents. Cache agents handle local data during active phase and prepare meta data to be used during maintenance phase. Placement agent is an executor agent in the cache maintenance phase. It revises and recreates data placement plans and supports QAA. Database agents are resource (passive) agents. Other supporting agents are not discussed as they are not part of the demo. We choose the most common strategies used in distributed computing [1].

In **Master/slave coordination** strategy, query analysis agent (QAA) (usually a proxy server) acts as the master coordinating agent. With the help of a planning agent, master follows greedy strategy and ensures to place each data segment at a first available best position. **Voting strategy** enables cache agents to vote for the QAA's (coordinator) decisions. Cache agents participate pro-actively to vote based on the local knowledge (bias) such as affinity among all data stored within a cache unit. A plan is accepted when it is accepted by majority of voters.

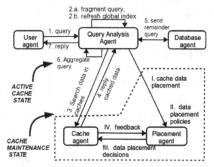

Fig. 1. Multi-agent architecture for distributed cache

In **Multi-agent planning** strategy, cache agents develop individual plans keeping local benefits as heuristics. The Placement Agent acts as coordinator and resolves conflicts and develops a new global plan. All the above three are examples of centralised architecture. **Negotiation** allows peer to peer communication with other cache agents to discuss plans. Agents negotiate with each other till they reach to a mutually agreed solution. **Feedback strategy** employs a negotiation agent to provide feedback after every iteration to cache agents. When negotiations are not contributing to the improvement in the performance, negotiation agent may provide negative feedback refraining concerned agents from further negotiations.

3 Demonstration

Description of the Scenario: To evaluate the proposed multi-agent system for distributed cache maintenance, we narrate a fictitious scenario of television watching patterns. Many television viewers residing within nearby student accommodation blocks watch television programmes using the Internet streaming catchup television services. The catchup services allow to download television shows and watch up to a predefined number of days. In order to reduce the volume of data transfers and hence the costs of Internet downloading, it was decided to install a cache storage unit at each of the accommodation block. Cache units are inter-connected with each other. For this scenario, we consider each user request to download programme(s) is considered as a query. A user can request a single programme (or shows) or multiple programmes within a single query. For the centralised architecture, a query analysis agent examines each request and generates sub-queries (partial queries) by each of the show requested in the query. This agent finds an appropriate place for the storage of each of the shows. In peer-to-peer architecture, cache storage units decide among themselves where to place the show. Patterns are obtained from the requests containing more than one show. The patterns thus obtained are used for the relocation of a show from one cache unit to another. Relocation clears the cache from storing shows that are locally not popular. A least frequently watched show is evicted as the cache refresh policy.

Experiment: We have generated workloads (list of 30,000 requests to watch shows over a period of seven days) using various statistical distributions for the evaluation (workload generation is not part of the demo). Viewers are given with a choice of 100 unique shows to choose from.

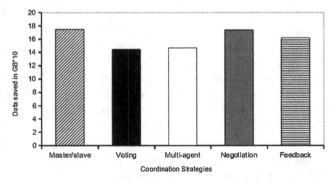

Fig. 2. Comparison of volume of data transfers saved

About 35 shows are repeatedly requested according to a poisson distribution. Each show requires from 0.75 GB to 2 GB of memory space. All requests are made to watch minimum two shows or at the most three shows in a row only. Each request is identified by a unique identification number to determine the frequency (the popularity) of a particular show/ sequence of shows. We have set up a cache network with five cache storage units. There are 5 cache units set up for the execution of this experiment. We have developed a Java based simulator to test and evaluate the coordination strategies.

For the evaluation we need multiple metrics to be calculated based on the type of application. For example, in the above scenario, we need to compare the volume of data transfers saved as the result of coordination. The performance of different strategies for data placement for viewing requests is shown in the Fig. 2. Voting and Multi-agent planning show considerable advantage over others in this case. A screen shot of the demo is shown in Fig. 3. It accepts a configuration file to setup the distributed environment and the query input workload file in a predefined XML format[1]. System calculates the performance with respect to each of the metrics across strategies. The best strategy for the given input conditions will be implemented during maintenance. This demo demonstrates the decision making with the help of two bar charts: one (on the left), displays a comparison of strategies for the chosen performance metric. The second chart (on the right) displays a comparison of the performance metric (volume of data transfers in this case) with the chosen coordination strategy (master-slave here) and no coordination among agents at all.

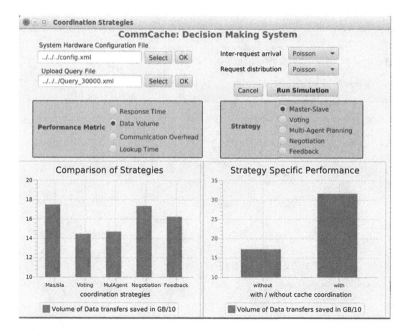

Fig. 3. A demonstration for volume of data transfers saved with Master-slave strategy

4   Conclusion

In this paper, we have described the applicability of multi-agent system for distributed data caching with the help of an example scenario. Implementation of coordination strategies are tested on the simulator for given query workloads.

---

[1] Generation of XML files is not part of this demo.

A demonstration is given with the help of five most suitable coordination strategies in the distributed environment. We would like to demonstrate comparison of more metrics in future.

References

1. Coulouris, G., Dollimore, J., Kindberg, T., Blair, G.: Distributed Systems - Concepts and Design, 5th edn. Addison Wesley Publishing Company, Reading (2011)
2. Kravari, K., Bassiliades, N.: A survey of agent platforms. J. Artif. Soc. Soc. Simul. **18**, 11 (2015)

Using Geo-Tagged Sentiment to Better Understand Social Interactions

Elizabeth Vivanco[(⊠)], Javier Palanca, Elena del Val, Miguel Rebollo, and Vicent Botti

Universitat Politècnica de València, Camino de Vera s/n, 46021 Valencia, Spain
elvisan1@inf.upv.es, {jpalanca,edelval,mrebollo,vbotti}@dsic.upv.es

Keywords: Social network analysis · Sentiment analysis · Geo-located data

1 Introduction

Social media have played a relevant role in facilitating communication and coordination among people. Digital traces generated by users in social media sites provides a promising source of data for use in different contexts. The avast amount of data contains information not only about the content of the message but also about who generated the information and to whom it was directed, the instant of time it was published, or the location of the user at the time of publication. Thanks to all this meta-information, the study of users' actions can be analyzed at different levels of detail and taking into account different perspectives.

This data availability has increased the interest among the research community in analyzing users' behavior from a specific perspective such as communication patterns or mobility patterns [1–4]. In some cases, it is interesting to analyze the interplay between different perspectives. Currently, there is a lack of studies coupling several aspects in the same analysis. For instance, there are a few proposals that consider the integration of physical locations and social relationships obtained from online social networks [5]. A few studies investigate the feasibility of combining social interactions and sentiment analysis and social structure [6,7]. Other approaches integrate sentiment analysis and locations to obtain an holistic view of the general mood and the situation "on the ground" [8].

2 Main Purpose

A comprehensive analysis of human behavior requires to bring together three perspectives: geospatial dimensions of social data, sentiment analysis, and structural analysis of the users' interaction social network. The aim of this work is to develop a model that integrates these three dimensions. We describe the implementation of the architecture and the main outputs of the analysis and the available visualizations. In this work, we seek to obtain a whole picture of users' interactions in online social networks from different perspectives.

© Springer International Publishing AG 2017
Y. Demazeau et al. (Eds.): PAAMS 2017, LNAI 10349, pp. 369–372, 2017.
DOI: 10.1007/978-3-319-59930-4_40

3 Demonstration

We describe a tool that facilitates the data collection from Twitter to perform an analysis of the behavior of users during an event taking into account where the activity is, the emotions associated with that activity and what relationships exist between the users who have participated in the event. The tool is composed of two main modules that deal with the previous described tasks: the *Geo-located Sentiment Analysis* and *Structural Social Network Analysis*

3.1 Geo-Located Sentiment Analysis

This module receives a set of tweets associated to an event during a time interval specified by the user and a map that contains the Points of Interest (PoIs) specified by the user. The module is responsible for filtering geo-located tweets associated to an event during a period of time.

Geo-located tweets are those tweets that have a value in the attribute 'coordinates' (i.e., the geographic location of the tweet as reported by the user or client application). There are tweets that have this attribute empty. For those tweets, the module infers a location using attributes from the profile of the user that wrote the tweet or from the tweet itself. The user's profile associated to the tweet has the following attributes that provide information about the location of the tweet: 'location' and 'time_zone'. 'Location' attribute represents the user-defined location for the user's profile account. 'Time_zone' describes the time zone the user declares himself within. In both cases, the value of the attribute should be translated into coordinates. The tweet also provides other attributes related to the location. This is the case of the attribute 'place' that indicates if the tweet is associated (but not necessarily originated from) a place. A place in Twitter refers to a specific, named location with corresponding geo coordinates.

Considering the total geo-located tweets, the module calculates the sentiment analysis of each tweet. The value associated to the sentiment ranges in the interval $[-1, 1]$, where values close to -1 are negative, values around 0 are neutral, and values around 1 are positive. Then, the user can upload a GeoJSON file with the polygons around the PoIs that he is interested in (districts, countries, states, neighborhoods,...), to analyze their sentiment. For each polygon, the module calculates the aggregated sentiment as the average of the sentiment of the tweets located in that area (see Fig. 1). Based on the sentiment, the module assigns a color: red for negative, grey for neutral, and green for positive sentiment. A darker or lighter color implies a higher/lower value of positive/negative sentiment respectively.

3.2 Structural Social Network

The Structural Social Network module provides a vision of the evolution over time of users' communication in Twitter. This module is responsible for building temporally annotated networks based on tweets (geo-located or not) associated to an event. A node of the network represents a user that participated in the

Fig. 1. Geo-located sentiment analysis user interface.

event by writing a global or individual messages (i.e., retweet, mention or reply to user) with the hashtag associated to the event or when another user references him in an individual message. Links of the network are established when a user writes an individual message to an existing or new user. Therefore, the network is directed.

Once the social interaction network is created, the module offers the possibility of visualizing the interaction network of the event and performing structural analysis during a specific time interval. The granularity of the time interval is a day (see Fig. 2). The visualization and analysis can be performed following two approximations: (i) considering the network generated by the interactions that occur in each single day of the time interval; (ii) or considering the network generated by the aggregated interactions from the start date until the end date of the time interval.

The structural analysis performed considers the giant component of the interaction network. The analysis consists on two levels: *global* and *individual*. The *global level* consists on the analysis of the evolution of structural properties of the network such as: diameter, clustering, modularity, density, average path length, symmetric links, assortativity, and degree distribution. The analysis of the evolution provides a more accurate view of the interactions during a period of time

The *individual level* calculates the relevance of each user in the network based on different criteria. The metrics used to evaluate the relevance are structural centrality metrics such as betweenness, closeness, in-degree, out-degree, pagerank, and eigenvector. The module creates a set of rankings of most relevant users according to each criteria of centrality.

This module provides the required functionality to analyze the social behavior of users in different types of events in order to characterize each event and determine similarities and differences in the resultant social structures that emerge from social interactions.

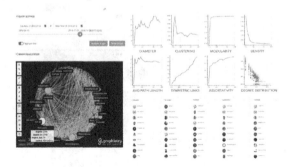

Fig. 2. Structural social network user interface.

4   Conclusions

The presented tool integrates two views of the users' activity in Twitter. The Geo-located Sentiment Analysis view provides information about the opinion of users in an specific location about certain event. The Structural Social Network view shows the evolution of the communication structure of an event. Both perspectives provide a more comprehensive analysis of human behavior.

References

1. Del Val, E., Rebollo, M., Botti, V.: Does the type of event influence how user interactions evolve on Twitter? PLOS ONE **10**(5), 1–32 (2015)
2. Del Val, E., Palanca, J., Rebollo, M.: U-Tool: A urban-toolkit for enhancing city maps through citizens activity. In: 14th PAAMS, pp. 243–246 (2016)
3. Del Val, E., Martínez, C., Botti, V.: Analyzing users activity in online social networks over time through a multi-agent framework. Soft Comput. **20**, 4331–4345 (2016)
4. Del Val, E., Martínez, C., Botti, V.: A multi-agent framework for the analysis of users behavior over time in on-line social networks. In: Proceedings of SOCO, pp. 191–201 (2015)
5. Grabowicz, P.A., Ramasco, J.J., Gonçalves, B., Eguíluz, V.M.: Entangling mobility and interactions in social media. PloS ONE **9**(3), e92196 (2014)
6. Gryc, W., Moilanen, K.: Leveraging textual sentiment analysis with social network modelling. In: From Text to Political Positions: Text Analysis Across Disciplines, vol. 55, p. 47 (2014)
7. West, R., Paskov, H.S., Leskovec, J., Potts, C.: Exploiting social network structure for person-to-person sentiment analysis. arXiv preprint arXiv:1409.2450
8. Caragea, C., Squicciarini, A., Stehle, S., Neppalli, K., Tapia, A.: Mapping moods: Geo-mapped sentiment analysis during hurricane sandy. In: Proceedings of ISCRAM

Author Index

Printed in the United States
By Bookmasters